Toward a New American Literary History

Toward a New American Literary History

Essays in Honor of Arlin Turner

Edited by
Louis J. Budd
Edwin H. Cady
Carl L. Anderson

Duke University Press · Durham, N.C. · 1980

Printed in the United States of America
by Heritage Printers, Inc.

Contents

Introduction

Though probably a tradition dying as our distance, after more than a century, increases from the day of our direct use of the old German university as a model, the *Festschrift* remains a signal honor. In Arlin Turner's case, his life's work, especially with the *American Literature* journal, makes the honor signally fit. His friends in the profession, together with his former students, could easily fill several volumes. So the editors had to decide, reluctantly, to limit it to some of those scholars who had served—after election by their colleagues in the American Literature Section of the Modern Language Association—on the Board of Editors of *American Literature*. Of the two exceptions, one has served with Arlin Turner in the same department for many years and has achieved eminence as a scholar-critic; the other is not only a long-time friend and neighbor, he is also, among many other distinctions, a great expert in southern literature, thus representing another of the many fields of Arlin Turner's strong interest.

The title springs from a conviction, perhaps partly intuitive on the editors' part, that the day is dawning for a new and major American literary history—representing for our times what *The Cambridge History of American Literature*, the first edition of *The Literary History of the United States*, and then *The Literature of the American People* did for their generations. We do not pretend that this is or was meant to be that history. We did suggest to the contributors that, if they felt so moved, they write to prophesy by example what a new synthesis might in part become. It is evident that some were so moved more directly than others.

But that result was to be expected. One dare not so much as wish to put such contributors as these upon any Procrustean frame. The strength, sometimes the novelty, always the authority of these essays by these authors more than justify the book and fulfill its aim. Though Arlin Turner's scholarship and writings have ranged widely, he has returned regularly to the varieties of literary history. While the reader may explore to see where and whether this may be an initiating volume toward a new history of American literature for the 1980's, the editors need assert no more than that its contents encourage the judgment that scholars everywhere have learned and divined enough to warrant the more major enterprise and stimulate the faith that its time is upon us.

With its long list of distinguished contributors, honoring so eminent a scholar-critic, Arlin Turner's *Festschrift* becomes in itself a substantial item of literary history. In ways that must elude our ability to look ahead, future scholar-critics in their successive drive toward understanding their forbears will find that it registers the thought and standards of the 1970's. It is safe to predict that our heirs will find continuing intrinsic value in these essays. The current reader, we hope, will find them worthy of the scholar they honor and will, like the three editors, be grateful to Arlin Turner for serving as the motive for bringing them together.

L. B.
E. C.

Toward a New American Literary History

The Cycle and the Roots: National Identity in American Literature

ROBERT E. SPILLER

I

The recent celebration of the bicentennial of the birth of this country as an independent nation, with parades, pageants, speeches, exhibits, tours, and parties, has made all of us more aware of our formative years and their relationship to what we are today. The seventeenth and eighteenth centuries furnished the wellsprings of our national identity, yet often there seems to be little connection between what we were then and what we are today. I hope to help bridge this gap in our self-understanding by drawing from our colonial and early national literature some general principles of cultural development and then, by applying them to later stages and phases in our evolution, to move toward a better understanding of our complex but nonetheless distinctive national character.

An American national character began to take shape about the time of the American Revolution—that is, between 1763 and 1789.[1] After the fighting was over, the Founding Fathers set to work to create a new nation and to give it voice in a new and self-confident literature.

Why then do we have so many doubts about our national identity today? The authors of the Declaration of Independence seemed to have no such doubts when they stated that the colonies were about to "assume among the Powers of Earth the separate and equal station to which the Laws of Nature and Nature's God entitled them," based on the "unalienable rights of Life, Liberty, and the Pursuit of Happiness."

Yet the author of an article on "Recent Interpretations of the American Character" introduces his discussion of some sixty or more books on the subject published since 1960 with the remark: "It is a commonplace that Americans are more concerned with their national identity and spend more time trying to explain themselves to themselves than people of other

This essay was an address read at the Bicentennial Conference of the Early American Literature Section of the Modern Language Association of America at the College of William and Mary, Williamsburg, Virginia, December 9, 1976.

1. Kenneth Silverman, *A Cultural History of the American Revolution* (New York, 1976), pp. 3–69.

nations." [2] Why are we thus haunted by our sense of insecurity and inadequacy? Why do we write such books as *The Challenge of Diversity, The Search for Identity, The American Way of Violence,* and *The End of the American Era*? I am not asking what the American identity is because I do not believe that it ever has been just one thing; I am asking you rather to join me in a rapid look back over our literature and its history in the hope that we may find in it a clue to the complex and changing mystery of our national identity today. For, even if we cannot finally reduce the American character to a single definition, perhaps we can discover a way of understanding its unique vitality and virtues.

This may not be as easy as it sounds, for, as recently as a half a century ago, it was generally assumed that there was no such thing as an *American* literature. At that time there were no departments and few courses in American literature as such in our colleges and universities; there were no scholarly societies or journals devoted to its study; the specialists in American literary research could be counted on one hand, and to so announce oneself was virtually to commit professional suicide; and histories of the subject were generally deprecatory and apologetic. Typical is the statement in an elementary school text of 1897: "American literature is an offshoot of English Literature, and shares the life of the parent stock. It uses the same language. . . . The culture of this country is distinctively English in origin and character; the differences are but modifications growing out of the new environment." [3]

Contrast this statement with that of Henry Canby in his introduction to *Literary History of the United States*: "The literary history of this nation began when the first settler from abroad of sensitive mind paused in his adventure long enough to feel that he was under a different sky, breathing new air, and that a New World was all before him with only his strength and Providence for guides." [4] Consider for a moment the fundamental difference between those two statements. The first is mechanical; it assumes that American literature is a part of English literature merely because it is usually written in the English language. The second is organic; it assumes that American literature in any language is American because it expresses the experience and culture of the American people. "It is hard to believe today," comments the psychohistorian Erik Erikson, "—if you believe we started it in our time—how conscious these early Americans were of the job of developing an American character out of the regional and generational polarities and contradictions of a nation

---

2. Thomas L. Hartshorne, "Recent Interpretations of the American Character," *American Studies International,* XIV (Winter, 1975), 10.

3. F. V. N. Painter, *Introduction to American Literature* (Boston, 1897), p. 5.

4. Robert E. Spiller, Willard Thorp, Thomas H. Johnson, and Henry S. Canby, *Literary History of the United States* (New York, 1948), I, xiii.

of immigrants and migrants."[5] Because the evolutionary process of creating a national character and then giving it expression in literature is organic, it is deeply rooted in the ever-moving, ever-changing experience of a transplanted and multiethnic people. Throughout our history, the horizontal movements of migration have tended to come in waves or cycles of uprooting and rerooting of cultures, and the vertical growth of new cultures in a new land in each case reenacts the life cycle of growth from birth, through maturity, into decline.

In this essay I shall not attempt to offer a definition of American identity as the fixed and final shape of American experience, but rather to suggest a method of approach to an understanding of any specific organic movement at every stage of its growth and change. This method is based on the principle of rooting and cyclic growth which varies only in application to time and place. It is the task of the anthropologist and the demographer to study as many as he can of the forces of migration and immigration which have created the American identity; it is the task of the literary historian to understand and to explain the expressions of the resulting American people in the arts of writing.

I use the term *culture* in the sociological rather than the aesthetic sense. Culture, in this sense, is the way that people in any time and place have agreed to live together. Toynbee quotes Bagby's definition as being "regularities in the behaviour, internal and external, of the members of a society, excluding those regularities which are clearly hereditary in origin."[6] But again, because they are organic rather than static, such cultural configurations remain fluent and shape and reshape themselves with the movements and growth of experience.

French, German, Italian, Spanish, Scandinavian, British culture had each, by the seventeenth century, gone through a similar process of evolution and achieved a degree of stability based on language, social structures, and relatively static geographical limits, in spite of political uncertainty and change. The new culture of America, on the other hand, had—with the possible exception of that of the Indian—no such stability. Its chief distinguishing characteristics were its heterogeneous and multiethnic components and its constant immigration and migration for almost three centuries. Mobility and diversity are and always have been the controlling factors in forming the American cultural identity—factors which were not shared to anything like the same extent by the European cultures in the parallel developments in South America, Australia, and New Zealand. The recurring impact of mature cultures on relatively primitive environments and the mingling of one with another provide the keys to

---

5. Erik H. Erikson, *Dimensions of a New Identity* (New York, 1974), p. 59.
6. Arnold Toynbee, *A Study of History*, new ed. rev. and abr. (London, 1972), p. 43.

the making of a new national identity and are therefore basic to an understanding of the literature of the new nation up to at least 1801 and even well thereafter.

Of course, such cultural conflicts and mergings are basic to all human history and are commonplaces of the ancient world. Why then the sudden explosion of exploration and settlement of the Western hemisphere by the peoples of the Eastern in the thirteenth to the sixteenth centuries? Lewis Mumford has put it in a sentence: "The settlement of America had its origins in the unsettlement of Europe."[7] In other words, the westward movement of European man was but a part of the breakdown of medieval Europe and the explosive forces of the new science, humanism, the Renaissance, and the Reformation. Whether the motivation was scientific curiosity about what lay beyond the horizon and beyond the stars, the search for new trade routes to the rich Orient, the desire for religious and political freedom, or merely the greed for wealth, these were centuries of sudden and powerful mental and physical expansion. We should bear in mind that the thrust of all European peoples was almost as much to the East and South as to the West, but only in the West, on a relatively unexplored and unexploited continent, did the Dutch, Spanish, British, Swedes, and French find open sea and open land ahead. In America at least, the frontier movement of the multiethnic cultures of Europe followed the path of the rising and setting sun for many centuries.

We must also remember that this horizontal westward thrust of the culture, wave on wave, was a continuing and oft-repeated process and not a single historical event. It did not happen in any one period in American literary history nor in only one part of the American continent. Once the impact of a mature culture on a new environment has been made, does the vertical process of evolving a new culture in any one area follow a predictable series of stages, like a growing plant from root to flower? Is the cultural history of colonial Philadelphia parallel in the stages of its organic growth to, say, the nineteenth-century history of Louisville, Kentucky, or modern San Diego, California? When I was lecturing some years ago on colonial American literary history to a graduate class, a brilliant young journalist from New Zealand came up after class and said to me in some astonishment, "Now I understand my country; we have just reached the year 1830!"

We seem to be approaching a cultural model which could be useful in all phases and stages of our effort to understand not only the early but perhaps even the far more complex later American identity in literature. At least there are some questions we can now ask: (1) From our general knowledge of the history of American literature, particularly that of the

---

7. Lewis Mumford, *The Golden Day* (New York, 1926), p. 11.

original colonies as they grew into a unified nation, can we derive a theoretical model of this evolutionary process? (2) Can we next apply this model in detail to the literature of the eastern seaboard from 1492 to about 1800 or 1820 to see how our theory works? (3) Can we then test these results by applying the same model to the settlement and development of the continental nation? And finally (4), is there a possibility that this same model may apply to the complex and multiethnic culture and literature of the later years and today? Thus we can perhaps move from a reasonable certainty through increasing complexity toward a definition of American national identity in literature without doing much more than clarify a series of problems for future study and provide a useful tool for their solution.

II

Two basic factors in the making of a distinctive American culture and its expression in literature may be assumed: first, the constant movement of European cultures westward over a continent new to them; and second, the multiethnic character of this migration. Although each of these factors is repeated an infinite number of times in the course of our history, it is possible to detect in each of them an organic process which remains constant throughout.

The process of westward movement, however, did not result from a single impulse or develop a continuous flow. As I have already suggested, it was varied in kind and time and moved more like the waves on a beach than the current of a river. Each wave was a cycle of its own, with an origin in alien soil, a period of time and a new locale of its own to shape the process of transfer, a crisis of adjustment and new growth, and finally a merging into the composite culture of the New World. Like all human experience, the frontier process consisted of a series of varied and overlapping cycles of growth and change. Each phase of history can be likened to one form of the life of a single organism, and all such life has beginning, middle, and end, even the horizontal movement of people and groups of people across land and sea.

But there is a vertical as well as a horizontal aspect of this cultural evolution, namely the rooting of the new culture in the New World and its growth from the seed planted, through the stages of maturing, to a new form of life, a new flowering. It is a sort of Johnny Appleseed procedure—first the spreading of the seed across the field, and then the nurturing and cultivation of each seed where it has fallen, from sprout to fruit. Does each seed pass through a similar series of stages, and, if we observe one throughout its life, do we understand at least the process of growth of the others even though the details and mutations may vary?

These two images—the cycle and the roots—have been basic to my thinking throughout my whole career as a literary historian, and all that I have written about the evolution of culture and literature is related in some way to organic nature and the life cycle. I first used the analogy of the plant from roots to flowering as the title of my anthology of early American literature, *The Roots of National Culture*, in 1933, and I first developed what later came to be spoken of as "the two-cycle theory of American literature" in a 1941 address at Fordham University.[8]

The Cycle of American Literature (1955) was an outgrowth of the years of planning and producing *Literary History of the United States*. As a literary history of an evolving culture rather than a history of a national literature, the editors adopted at the start a balanced plan of organization based on the theory of American literature as the expression of two major waves of European culture which moved, first across the Atlantic to settle the eastern seaboard from Maine to Georgia between 1607 and about 1835; and second, across the continent to the Pacific, with the breakthrough of the Allegheny Mountains beginning about 1775 and, in successive waves and counterwaves completing the frontier movement west to the Pacific, north to the Canadian border, and south to Mexico about—to adopt Turner's date—1890.

So much for the westward movement of American culture. The problem of the stages of organic growth in any one place is more complicated, but again, in order to make clear a fundamental theory of American cultural history, I oversimplified the American story in *The Roots of National Culture*. I am now standing still in one place and watching the seed that has been planted grow from first sprout to the final flowering. Experience teaches that each new culture must take its own time in growing and must go through a series of recognizable stages of maturing before it can bear fruit. Therefore, when there is an impact of an alien culture on a new environment, there must be a more or less predictable kind of preparatory expression before a major writer can appear.

I suggest that these stages can be accurately defined and that each new culture passes through them in the same succession. In 1933, I proposed four and I still find these four to be reasonably accurate, with allowable variations of time, place, and circumstance.[9] Of course, however, it is a continuous process, and someone else might break it down into three, or five, or like the melancholy Jaques of Shakespeare, seven stages.

The first stage is a period of exploration and settlement which produces narrative and descriptive journals and letters. In the second stage the new

---

8. "Blueprint for American Literary History," *The Third Dimension* (New York, 1965), pp. 26–36.

9. "The First Frontier," Introduction to *The Roots of National Culture* (1933). Reprinted in *The Third Dimension*, pp. 52–65.

settlement creates its own society with instruments of culture such as schools, printing presses, town halls, transportation, and shops, which in turn produce newspapers, broadsides, and magazines, lectures and sermons, book-stores and libraries, and other embryonic means of cultural communication. All of these lead to intellectual activity and even controversy on all subjects, but mainly on politics and religion, as the new community discovers the shape and power of its own mind. This second stage, taken as a whole, can therefore be described as one of Instruments and Ideas. When the time is ripe—and that may be very early in the evolutionary process—all of this leads to a third stage, in which there is a demand for the "leisure arts," especially literature. Even in the sixteenth century, the North American Spanish made a few attempts at producing drama, epic poetry, and fiction—the last a natural outgrowth of their dreams of far inland cities of unbelievable luxury and wealth. But the new society was still too crude to produce its own forms of literary expression for the exciting new experience of conquering and settling a continent. At this point, eyes are turned eastward and, with the importation of books and journals from the homeland, comes imitation of the familiar forms, as the new material is twisted and turned to fit into them, like a farmer's broad-toed foot being pressed into a ballroom slipper; and all this is part of the learning process. Finally, in the fourth stage, new literature steps out with its new experience wrapped about it in natural folds. Only then can the major writer find within him a mature creative power and outside of him an educated and receptive audience.

III

Coming back to our use of the Atlantic seaboard as a model for this evolutionary process, we find the first stage of exploration extended from the Columbus letter of 1493 reporting the "discovered islands" to the King and Queen of Spain, down to Harriot's *New Found Land of Virginia* in 1588 and beyond.[10] The next century was studded with narratives, journals, and even histories of settlement by John Smith, William Bradford, William Penn, William Byrd, and many others.

The second stage, Instruments and Ideas, began in the mid-eighteenth century as the seaboard towns developed into cultural centers with their printing presses, magazines, libraries, and colleges. Benjamin Franklin, with his many inventions and discoveries, is the epitome of this era, while the mind of the new nation was being shaped by the theological wars which culminated in Jonathan Edwards, followed by the political wars between Tories and Rebels and the debates in the Continental Congresses

---

10. Evelyn Page, *American Genesis: Pre-Colonial Writings in the North* (Boston, 1973), pp. 108–110, 208–210.

as the Founding Fathers created not only a new nation, but a new kind of nation.

It seems to be a general assumption that the Enlightenment period which followed the Revolution was a time when an organized body of political and social ideas were absorbed by these philosopher-statesmen from the rationalistic thinkers of France and England and written into the Declaration of Independence and the Constitution as a firm platform for a government and an idealistic way of life—a new deal for the Old World. Recent scholarship has questioned this conclusion and has tended to attribute the success of the American democratic system to its ability to absorb and reconcile opposites. As Joseph Ellis puts it: "The dominant metaphors of the age constantly invoked the ideal of balance: the equilibrium achieved by political juxtaposition of opposing interests; the judicious blending of monarchic, aristocratic, and democratic tendencies in a 'mixed government'; the educated man's control over conflicting 'faculties,' with the passions subordinated to the rational faculty and all governed by the moral sense."[11] It was our good fortune, therefore, that the first shaping of the distinctive American character came at a time— the third quarter of the eighteenth century—when at last Western man had learned to live in a flexible intellectual world governed by a reconciliation of contrasts. The contradictions between an absolute moral idealism and a practical common sense are polarized and made flexible and useful in the minds of American literary and intellectual leaders from Franklin to Emerson to William James and down to the present.

Thus this second stage in our paradigm seems to have come to an end in a period of political storm and chaos. When the cloud lifted, Americans were at once ready to enter the third stage of building a new national literature. "The people of the United States," wrote our first professional novelist Charles Brockden Brown in 1802, "are, perhaps, more distinguished than those of Europe as a people of business. . . . When, now that our population is increased, our national independence secured, and our government established, and we are relieved from the necessities of colonists and emigrants, there is reason to expect more attention to polite literature and science."[12]

"Polite literature," to Brown, meant novels in the forms of Gothic horror, psychological perversion, and social problems, but lack of castles and dungeons and our classless society hampered his style, and he turned to the wilderness, to sleep-walking, and to spontaneous combustion for his

---

11. Joseph Ellis, "Habits of Mind and an American Enlightenment," *American Quarterly*, XXVIII (Summer, 1976), 164.

12. *The American Review and Literary Journal* (New York), January 1802. Quoted in Spiller, *The American Literary Revolution, 1783–1837* (New York, 1967), pp. 32–33.

excitement. An earlier Poe in many ways, Brown was far ahead of his times, but his novels creak in the joints and are just barely readable, although hardly more primitive than much that we see on TV today.

Our early drama did somewhat better, for, in a torrent of imitations, adaptations, and productions of foreign plays in the theaters which soon sprang up in the coastal cities, we produced at least one good social comedy, Royall Tyler's *The Contrast*. In form and style confessedly modelled on the plays of Sheridan and Goldsmith, it had a central American theme—the contrast between the pseudosophistication of provincial society and the crude honesty of the native American Jonathan.

> Exult each patriot heart! [speaks the Prologue]—this night is shewn
> A piece which we may fairly call our own;
> Where the proud titles of "My Lord! Your Grace!"
> To humble Mr. and plain Sir give place.
> Our Author pictures not from foreign climes
> The fashions, or the follies of the times;
> But has confin'd the subject of his work
> To the gay scenes—the circles of New-York.[13]

But it is at least interesting that the muse again displays her powers by treating the new theme of the contrast between opposite ways of life and the comic balance of tension attained by this very polarity. It is indeed the first truly American play.

The poetry that was written after 1783 exhibits the same balanced dualism. Torn between the desire to put the tremendous American experience into immortal verse and the need to turn to foreign models for form and style, poets like Freneau and the Connecticut Wits met the romantic violence of Blake and Byron on the one hand and the neoclassical rules of Pope and Dryden on the other. Freneau wrote everything from a melancholy dirge on the death of Death to sharp political satire in ironic rhymed couplets. And Joel Barlow, when he decided that the one thing the new nation needed most was an epic great enough to fit its grandeur, turned to Columbus as his hero and found so little to celebrate in the past that his lumbering verse became vague rantings about the future glories of America. "The author rejected," says Barlow, "the idea of the regular Epic form, and has confined his plan to the train of events which might be represented to the hero in vision."[14]

As Lewis Leary has so conclusively proved, this apprentice period in American literature not only did not, but it could not produce a major

---

13. Quoted in Spiller, *The American Literary Revolution*, p. 27.
14. Ibid., p. 15.

literary artist.[15] What it did produce as typical of the times were such successful mediocrities as John Blair Linn and Thomas Branagan. Great minds like Franklin, Edwards, and Jefferson did not produce great literature, probably for much the same reasons. When the time had come—after 1820—for a Poe, a Cooper, or an Irving, the wilderness of the American literary mind was almost ready for the literature of major tensions and rich balance which produced *The Scarlet Letter, Moby Dick, Leaves of Grass*, and the moving addresses and journals of Thoreau and Emerson. American literature of the Romantic period was born of inner conflicts and achieved its first maturity by the taming of violence which took form in a balanced polarity of conflicting forces. The fourth stage of our paradigm did not appear before 1850–55, on the eve of our greatest national crisis, the Civil War.

IV

And now for the question that I raised earlier: Is this series of four stages in the development of the early American literature of the eastern seaboard merely the record of a single period in American cultural history, or does it provide a model by which to test the development of all American literary history, a process repeated again and again as the frontier moved west and the immigrant groups of other cultural backgrounds came over to settle new parts of the continent?

The subject is far too complicated for detailed study here. All that can be safely said is that as long as the frontier moved westward across the continent at a reasonable pace, the formula seemed to work, but as the land spread out flat ahead, it moved more swiftly and erratically, and as immigration turned into migration in all directions, the process became more and more complicated and variable. Yet I am convinced that in all the phases and stages of American growth toward a national identity, the principle of the overlay of one culture on another or on an alien environment is basic.

The obvious next place to try out our theory is the Middle West, or the area between the Appalachian Mountains and the Mississippi River, in the period from about 1775 when Daniel Boone, as agent of the Transylvania Company, led a band of colonists through the Cumberland Gap and founded Boonesborough, Kentucky. The process of evolution lasted through the nineteenth century and may be said to have come to a climax with the Columbian Exposition in Chicago in 1893.

As in the story of the eastern seaboard, the first stage began with a century of exploration and discovery, this time by French missionary

15. Lewis Leary, *Soundings: Some Early American Writers.* (Athens, Georgia, 1975).

monks, hunters, and traders who, while the British were busy settling the
Atlantic coast, explored the region of the Great Lakes and the Mississippi
Valley without, in the long run, leaving "a perceptible influence on the
growth of European culture in the west."[16]

The period of letters and journals describing the new adventure was
comparatively brief because the migrants wrote more to their friends and
families in the East than to their more distant relatives in Europe. Boone
himself left no record, but the legend of the coonskin cap and the westward trek was preserved in John Filson's biography of him in 1784.[17]
Among other narrative accounts are the early records of exploration, like
the journals of Lewis and Clark, and the later ones, more strictly limited
to the middle western frontier, like those of Timothy Flint (1826) and
James Hall (1828).

The second stage—that of Instruments and Ideas—again followed more
swiftly and, as in the eastern towns of Boston, New York, Philadelphia,
and Charleston, middle western culture began with the permanent settlement of Lexington, Kentucky, in 1799, followed by Louisville, Cincinnati,
New Harmony, St. Louis, and ultimately Chicago. Also, this period was
characterized by debate in religion, politics, and education, mainly by
Methodists and Baptists rather than Calvinists and Quakers. The founding of Transylvania University in 1787 was followed by many other colleges and universities, mostly sectarian, and by 1840 they were the rule in
most major towns.

Printing presses and newspapers followed, and, by the thirties, the middle western culture was ready for the third stage, with magazines and an-
nuals ready to issue the novels and tales of Flint, Hall, Frederick Thomas,
and many others of even less originality and skill, with the ghosts of Irving
and Cooper hovering over many of them. Poetry began with reprinting
from eastern journals and homely ballads by local bards long lost in history, such as "The Michigan Emigrants' Song":

> My Eastern friends who wish to find
> A country that will suit your mind,
> Where comforts all are near at hand,
> Had better come to Michigan.[18]

There were the more vigorous cowboy adaptations of traditional ballads
to tell of their lonely and adventurous lives. Louisville was a center for
drama in the early days, but it was not until the 1870's that the Middle

---

16. Ralph L. Rusk, *The Literature of the Middle Western Frontier* (New York, 1926),
I, 16ff.

17. John Filson, *The Discovery, Settlement, and Present State of Kentucke* (Wilming-
ton, Del., 1784).

18. Rusk, I, 307.

West developed a mode of its own in the mild realism of John Hay, Edward Eggleston, and finally William Dean Howells.

By that time, however, the frontier had already swept across the prairies, leapt the Rockies, and met the Oriental and other cultures of the Pacific slope and the Spanish-Mexican culture of the Southwest. The final phase of fully mature achievement in middle western literature was but a part of the new literature of the Continental nation with its centers in Chicago, St. Louis, and San Francisco and its dominant mode the naturalism of Crane, Norris, London, and Dreiser at the end of the century. The second cycle of the frontier impact therefore did not pause anywhere long enough, as the eastern seaboard had, to mature a regional culture. There was a continual making and breaking of cultural patterns until Chicago emerged, at the end of the century, as the commercial and cultural center of the Continental nation as a whole.

That story is fraught with violence and conflict, which had never really surfaced in the Old Middle West, but had to surface and then be absorbed in some way before a new national identity could develop. After the Mexican War of 1845–48, the annexation of huge tracts of new land from Mexico and in Oregon opened, with the earlier Louisiana Purchase, more than twice the area of the pre–Civil War United States to exploration and exploitation. We do not need to be reminded of the bloody Indian wars, the cowboy battles between the cattle and sheep ranchers, the Gold Rush of 1849, the ruthless mining of the Rockies, the slaughter of the buffaloes, the vast prairie fires, the blazing of overland trails and later of the railroads for thousands of hapless immigrants, all of which were parts of the final rise of the industrial empire of the time of the Robber Barons to complete the commercial triumph of Chicago, Detroit, and St. Louis. Out of such anarchy came the careful accounts, first of Lewis and Clark, and then of John Wesley Powell, Clarence King, and the naturalist John Muir, as well as the regionalism and local color of the Californian Bret Harte and the Mississippian Mark Twain. It was Mark Twain finally who forced the opposites of the genteel East and the raw barbarism of the open West into a still somewhat crude new American mould in which humor triumphed over violence and the comic spirit (mixed with tragedy) again created a major literature. Thus, if we are thinking organically rather than chronologically, the humor of Irving is contemporary in cause and kind with that of Mark Twain because they both were aroused by the incongruities in the frontier situation. By the end of the nineteenth century, however, the polarity of opposites was beginning to reach a precarious balance so that by about 1920 Wolfe, Hemingway, Steinbeck, Faulkner, Frost, Eliot, and O'Neill could join in a second renaissance of American literature between the two world wars.

V

Perhaps my story should end there if we are willing to restrict our theory of the making of an American cultural identity in literature to the westward movement of Old World culture across a new continent. If we are, the basic evolutionary development of literature in any one place in four stages would seem to work if applied with a degree of flexibility. But American culture as we see it and live it today is too complex to be so limited. So far we have only touched on the problem of multiethnicity, as the movement of migration lost its westward direction but remained nonetheless active, and the evolutionary process became more and more the overlay of one culture on another, rather than the movement of a mature culture into a primitive environment as it had been in the days of steady frontier movement. Early examples of this kind of overlay are the blending of the basically English westward migration with the Mexican-Spanish culture of the Southwest and with the French cultures of New Orleans and Quebec.

I realize that, apart from noting the ethnic diversity of the early explorers and settlers, I have paid little attention to the hordes of immigrants that poured into the United States from the non-British nations of Europe during the nineteenth century and up to 1914 when immigration began to be restricted by law. Yet multiethnicity is and always has been one of the principal determinants of the flexibility and strength of our democratic society.

The problem is a complicated one and cannot, of course, be treated adequately in such a brief discussion. We can, however, as a start, distinguish three kinds of ethnic groups which were not parts of the main frontier movement. These are the immigrant groups which came to this country comparatively late; the blacks who were brought to this country under special circumstances; and the Jews who in all their history have mingled with, but rarely become totally absorbed into, any alien culture. All three are of great importance to the American identity today as expressed in its ever-changing literature, but only immigrations from European countries other than Great Britain followed a course close enough to our model to suggest inclusion here, even though the remarkable achievements of the Jews and the blacks in contemporary American literature suggest that—given a slightly different model—their contributions to our culture would lend themselves to similar analyses.

I will conclude, therefore, with a note on the immigrations from European countries other than England. However multiethnic the original settlers of the North American continent may have been, historians agree that by the end of the eighteenth century, British culture and its language were overwhelmingly dominant in that part of it which formed the original thirteen colonies and later became the United States. Other strains like the German, the Scotch-Irish, and the Irish tended to become absorbed quickly into the main cultural stream as the frontier pushed westward; but by the time of the Civil War, the impact of other European ethnic groups had begun to be felt, and it became customary to think of them as "aliens" or "immigrants." Even in the 1820's and 30's the Scotch-Irish and others began to move out of the eastern cities and to take over the lands evacuated by the earlier pioneers in New York, Pennsylvania, North Carolina, and Ohio, and thus were absorbed into the general frontier movement. Concentrated German settlements grew up in Wisconsin and Minnesota where later they were followed by Norwegians and Swedes, who moved quickly westward to Minnesota and then to Oregon. But the main flood of Europeans peaked in the last decades of the century and came from central and southern Europe—Italians, Czechs, Poles, and others who supplied the labor for the rapidly developing industrial revolution.

During the greater part of the nineteenth century, the "melting pot" theory held. It was based on the assumption that the leveling and mixing processes of American society were so great that ethnic cultural differences would wear down in two or three generations at most and all immigrants would merge into one composite American Democratic Man. This theory may have applied when foreign-born immigrants had no permanent settlements of their own to come to, but later the process became more and more one of the coexistence of "cultural islands" within or beside each other, with each preserving a degree of integrity of its own and evolving through our four stages independently and in parallel. Many of the later immigrants tended to concentrate in cities where they set up islands of their own culture and resisted the tendency to merge with the mainstream.[19] Thus there were German, Scandinavian, Italian, Czech, Greek, and many other settlements or urban islands in which the culture retained the language, customs, and inheritance of the homeland, and literature developed from journals and letters through educational, religious, and political institutions and ideas, to fiction, poetry, and drama imitative of a special ethnic tradition. In his pioneering study of the literature of these American-ethnic cultures in 1948, Henry A. Pochmann concluded a rapid survey of such writing with the statement, "The early desire to cast the Old World into a mythical melting pot has given place to a conviction that the immigrant serves his adopted country best when he is steeped in the traditions of his fatherland; that various and lively regional cultures increase the vitality of the culture of the United States."[20] The

19. Marcus Lee Hansen, *The Immigrant in American History* (Cambridge, Mass., 1940), pp. 150–151.
20. *Literary History of the United States*, II, 693.

study of these literatures in parallel with the mainstream and against the background of their own cultures was brought to a focus with the founding in 1974 of the Society for the Study of Multiethnic Literature in the United States (popularly called "Melus") and with the publication of special studies such as Rose B. Green's work on the Italian-American novel, but our knowledge of many of them is still scant.[21] In his introduction to Rose Green's book, Mario Pei asserts that "there is no question that an Italian-American literature, in English, exists. It has its own distinctive traits and bears its own peculiar imprint." The author then identifies five stages in the evolution of an indigenous literature: (1) explanatory narratives, (2) analysis of this impact as a coculture, (3) attempts at identification with the native American strain, (4) return to a distinctive ethnic heritage, and (5) the rooting of Italian culture in American soil with the production of a mature literature which is ethnically Italian yet culturally American.[22]

This process has often been accompanied by various kinds of violence, and such violence has been much deeper than the mere physical, as Richard Slotkin has pointed out when he defined American mythology as "regeneration through violence." Starting with the confrontation of the European settler with the dark wilderness and its dark inhabitants, the American myth emerges through various kinds and degrees of conflict and violence into that of the hunter as archetypal American and mediator between civilization and the wilderness.[23] I have tried to trace the evolution of the national identity in much the same terms, but with emphasis on the resolution of violence itself—the violence of cultural conflict—into great literature without so full and specific an analysis of mythology. Behind the comic detachment of an Irving, a Mark Twain, or a Faulkner and the tragic confrontations of a Melville, a Dreiser, or an O'Neill there lie the peculiarly American forms of conflict and growth—the constant movement and mixing of a nation in the making

Why, then, do we celebrate our nation's founding if the national identity seems today to have so little of the single-minded moral idealism, individual freedom, and political stability that we are taught to associate with the names of the Founding Fathers? The answer is that this image is itself a myth. Those honorable gentlemen were far more wise, flexible, and fallible than we give them credit for. They did not found the perfect state in which the laws and institutions were so strong that they could resist change and growth under all circumstances and to the end of time. Instead they had the courage to found an open state and society fortified

---

21. Rose Basile Green, *The Italian-American Novel* (Rutherford, N.J., 1974).

22. Ibid., pp. 10, 23–24.

23. Richard Slotkin, *Regeneration Through Violence: The Mythology of the American Frontier, 1600–1860* (Middletown, Conn., 1973), p. 23.

with many internal checks and balances so that conflict, idealism, growth, and decay had a chance to work themselves out to solutions based on human nature and human experience.

In addition to the usual conflicts and tensions that, according to American habits, create violence which may or may not resolve itself into the creative balance of polarity, these multiethnic groups suffer the additional conflicts that are created by the interaction of an imported culture with one already entrenched. The problem is complicated and we are not yet far enough into it fully to appreciate its ramifications, but there is no reason to believe that, when cultural equilibrium is achieved by any one group in any one place and time, major literary work might not result. So far that has happened rarely, but at least we can study the early stages.

Through trial and error we learned in our first century, as we opened up and developed the culture of the continent, that the vital mobility and ethnic diversity of our first frontier—the eastern seaboard—had given us a process of cultural evolution which could be carried forward from one experience to the next. As our culture became more complex in the second century we learned to adjust to and absorb new cultures by developing equilibrium rather than resolution of conflicts, without hampering the strength and fluidity of an open and still growing society. This, it seems to me, is the key to our unique national identity as expressed best in our literature.

The Southern Literary Vocation

LEWIS P. SIMPSON

The history of civilization is nearly, if not absolutely, the same as the Philosophy of History, or the Education of Mankind.—The Southern Review, I (January, 1867).

I use the term *literary vocation* with the understanding that it properly implies a career to which the man of letters in the American South has been summoned by a force greater than mundane need. Although I would not suggest that southern writers have been called by God to fulfill history, I would suggest that they have been summoned to the literary life by the psychic force of history as the modern symbol of human existence. A struggle to reveal the nature (the purpose, the message, the truth) of the South's historical experience—this has been the common career of its writers. Like the prophets in the Bible who were recalcitrant to the call of God, southern writers, or some of them, may have resisted the call by history. But for two hundred years and more, like the biblical prophets responding to the Hebraic historicism, they have in their very resistance always been obedient to their summons. In fact, their response has been so consistent that it has particularized the character of the literary vocation in the South. We assume not simply that the literary vocation exists here; we assume the existence of a specific vocation to letters—of the southern literary vocation.

Yet we know little about the basis of such an assumption—that is to say, about the history of the southern literary commitment to history. The most convincing theory concerning this subject is still that proposed over forty years ago by Allen Tate in his classic essay entitled "The Profession of Letters in the South."[1] Essentially, Tate postulates an analogy between two renascent literary situations: that in Elizabethan England and that in the American South of the 1920's and 1930's. Like the England of Shakespeare's day, Tate says, the South has arrived at a historical crossing of the ways, when a traditional order is being destroyed and a new order is simultaneously coming into existence. In this circumstance the southern writer has been invested with a "peculiarly historical consciousness," and is creating a literature informed by the experience of cultural change and the reaction to this experience—a literature conscious of the past in the present.

---

1. *Essays of Four Decades* (Chicago, 1968), pp. 517–534.

Like any theory bearing a strong intuition of truth, Tate's hypothesis has tended to become dogma and thus has not only been insulated from suspicion of error but has lost the capacity to insinuate further truths. It is important to realize, I believe, that Tate's analogy between the literary flowering in Elizabethan England and that in the modern South intimates more than a comparison of two historical epochs. It suggests their historical continuity. It opens the possibility that Faulkner's sense of vocation is continuous with Shakespeare's; that with (not merely like) Shakespeare, Faulkner experienced the present not as a static, integral moment but as a volatile, ironic expression of the displacement of the past by novel conditions; that, in sum, the southern writer's experience of the relationship between the modern historical consciousness and the modern literary consciousness is not only comparable to the Elizabethan writer's but is part of it. Indeed Tate's conception of the profession of letters in the South implies that the rationale of the southern writer's sensibility of vocation is truly expansive. It is nothing less than the historical continuum of the modern literary consciousness: its movement out of the society of myth and tradition (the medieval society) into the society of mind (the Renaissance and Enlightenment society) and finally into the fully developed society of history and science (the present society).

Lacking both the space and the learning requisite for an adequate description of the continuum of the literary consciousness, I will leave its skeletal frame hanging before the reader, hoping it will serve as a general reference for a tentative analysis of the origins and development of the southern literary vocation.

The origins lie in the time when the medieval community of thought and emotion began to be displaced by mind; that is by rationality or intellect.

In his distinguished essay *Mind in the Modern World*, the late Lionel Trilling remarks on a strange phenomenon in the English life of the sixteenth century. The aristocrats and the gentry began to send their sons to Winchester and Eton and thence to Oxford and Cambridge. These institutions had heretofore been largely for boys from the lower classes who were destined for ecclesiastical careers. Now instead of seeking to impart to their boys only the manners and graces, the upper classes became interested in instilling in them the quality of intellectual energy.

> Apparently the upper classes [Trilling says] had somehow got hold of the idea that mind, not in one or another of its specific formal disciplines but in what any one discipline might imply of the essence of mind, was of consequence in statecraft and in the carrying on of the national life. What they would seem suddenly to have identified and wanted to capture for themselves was what nowadays we might call

the *mystique* of mind—its energy, its intentionality, its impulse toward inclusiveness and completeness, its search for coherence with due regard for the integrity of the elements which it brings into relation with each other, its power of looking before and after. In some inchoate way these ambitious upper-class parents of the sixteenth century sought the characteristic traits of mind which they might incorporate into the activities of government; and in so doing, in pursuing their inarticulate intuition that mind made the model of the practical activity of society, they proposed the ideal nature of the modern nation-state.[2]

In effect—and I may somewhat extend Trilling's thesis—the sixteenth-century aristocrats, without understanding what they were doing, responded to an incipient rise of mind as the model of social existence.

This revolutionary phenomenon was forecast when the rational mind began to project its own operations as the model of nature; and not only this, but to conceive the mechanical instruments, notably the spring clock and the telescope, which would demonstrate that nature is modelled on cognitive processes. The internalization of time and space effected by the clock and the telescope reversed the notion that mind is modelled on nature as it appears to basic sensory perception; and, as the most immediate and drastic effect on mankind, destroyed the society joined in blood and cosmic mystery. The right model of man the social creature became not the experience of society but mind's organizational faculty. As the vision of society in relation to an unchanging myth of the cosmic continuum gave way to the idea of society as an imitation of the capacities of rational, secular mind, the imitation of mind as orderly process became the means of discovering not only the right order of the universe but the right order of society. As the reversal of the traditional relation of mind and society became more evident, the expense of it began to emerge— namely, the radical displacement of the old hierarchical, corporate, prescriptive community of Christendom as the model of consciousness. The greatness of this expense was most evident to those most sensitive monitors of change, the poets, who had always assumed a community structured by myth and tradition as the model of consciousness. The poetic registration of the trauma attending the displacement of this model was not only immediate but was to continue for several centuries after the first shock waves of displacement were felt.

By the beginning of the seventeenth century a deeply meditated reaction appears in Marlowe's *Faustus*, a still more profound one in *Hamlet*. *Hamlet* undoubtedly is the central expression of the dismay attendant upon the discovery of the new relation between literary consciousness and his-

---

2. *Mind in the Modern World* (New York, 1972), pp. 38–39.

tory. Courtier and soldier, Prince Hamlet is also poet and scholar; and it is as poet and scholar—as man of letters—that he enters into the inner depths of the drama in which he is involved. He is the first man of letters to experience the peculiar literary burden of modern history: its internalization in the consciousness of the individual. Only when we grasp this do we grasp the impossibility of Hamlet's task in the restoration of order to his world and feel the full impact of his tormented cry: "The time is out of joint: O cursed spite That ever I was born to set it right!" Unable to refer his need for action to the ancient community of blood and mystery, Hamlet not only is exposed to the disorders of history, he absorbs them, drives them into the self, and in his desperate subjectification of history is forced to the point of trying to decide for himself whether he should exist or not—whether or not he should be. A pre-Cartesian prince, creation of a poet before body and mind were wholly sundered, he does not, however, have to decide whether or not he does in fact exist.

My interpretation of the most interpreted character in dramatic literature, I hasten to say, may please no student of the play. I seek to elucidate an undercurrent of meaning more than to explicate the pattern of action in *Hamlet*. What Shakespeare articulates obliquely John Donne exposits directly in "Anatomy of the World" (1611):

> And new philosophy calls all in doubt,
> The element of fire is quite put out;
> The sun is lost, and th' earth, and no man's wit
> Can well direct him where to look for it.
> And freely men confess that this world's spent,
> When in the planets, and the firmament
> They seek so many new; then see that this
> Is crumbled out again to his atomies.
> 'Tis all in pieces, all coherence gone;
> All just supply, and all relation:
> Prince, subject, father, son, are things forgot,
> For every man alone thinks he hath got
> To be a phoenix, and that then can be
> None of that kind, of which he is, but he.

In Donne's vision the replacement of the medieval cosmology by the dissected—the anatomized—world of the New Science, and the accompanying elevation of rational mind, as exemplified by Copernicus, Kepler, and Galileo, as the model of universal order, has resulted in the disintegration of man's societal structure as his model of order. Yet Donne does not in "Anatomy of the World" say a farewell to poetry. Envisioning the loss of the image of everyman as the symbol of man, Donne sees each individual determined to rise in the image of the phoenix, the magical bird who is his own father. It is now every man, and every poet, for himself. But, Donne intimates, in his new condition of being as an isolated entity in history, the poet will find new force of being. In the very act of writing "An Anatomy of the World" (and against his implied opposition to his own vision), Donne assumes a power unknown to ancient or medieval bards, a power hardly figured forth in the Faust legend, though implicit in it: the poet's capacity to liberate poetry—the whole imagination of existence—from the community of myth and tradition and to relocate it in the dominion of the individual consciousness. In this novel presumption of the poetic power, the poet associates himself with what he opposes: the transference by the "new philosophy" of man, world, and universe into mind.

Yet in making this association and so becoming alienated from the bardic world, it is to be observed, Donne has not become detached from the literary continuum. The self-conscious critic of the process of internalization marks himself as having become, whether he wants to be or not, a modern man of letters and as such a member of an emergent realm of cosmopolitan mind. Differentiating itself from the realms of church and state, this community of secular mind—commonly called the Republic of Letters—constituted a Third Realm in the Western orders of civilizational existence. The Third Realm, Carlyle said, is the modern church.[3] Established in its ecumenic dominion, it has defied alike the loss of Latinity and the rise of the modern vernacularism. All literary nationalisms, including those promoted by the most censorious dictatorships, have proven sensitive to the continuing incorporation of mind in the Third Realm. Not only this, but all forms of self-willed alienation have proven to be relative to its existence. Nothing finally may be more significant in modern history than the world polity of mind. Whether this polity is considered under the aspect of a literary or a scientific cosmopolitanism, its origins lie in the age when the realm of "letters and learning"—which comprehends literature and knowledge as synonymous—asserted the primacy of mind in modern history; when the man of letters like Francis Bacon envisioning mind as the model of the historical society and the man of letters as the primary agent of history, said in prophetic summary of the future: "Knowledge is power."

While I may seem to digress, it is in the interest of providing a background for the following observation: the literary vocation in the American South has its beginnings in the Virginian experience of a historically fortuitous displacement of the society of myth and tradition—the society embodied in church and state—by the modern society modelled on secular

---

3. See Lewis P. Simpson, "Foreword," *The Literary Correspondence of Donald Davidson and Allen Tate*, ed. John Tyree Fain and Thomas Daniel Young (Athens, Ga., 1974), pp. vii–xix.

rationality, the society embodied in the Third Realm. The intention in the settlement of Virginia, Perry Miller has aptly argued, was the transplantation of a society which would preserve and extend an order sanctioned by God and King.4 But the purpose became a casualty of history. Seizing on the coincidence of climate and soil and the new market for tobacco, the Virginia colonists made a life based on time and chance. The adventitious quality of the Virginia enterprise was heightened when the colonists embraced the historical contingency of African chattel slavery to solve their labor problem. Losing the aura of a mission launched by crown and ecclesia, Virginia, the colony destined to be the intellectual center of the South in the later colonial and early national periods, became more open to the developing autonomy of mind than theocratic Massachusetts. In New England, where the vocation of the man of letters was intimately identified with the Puritan ministry, the secularization of the mind was a long and complicated drama. It reached its last phase not until Henry Adams, in fear of the civilizational apocalypse he saw as implicit in the scientific bent of modern mind, got down on his knees before the Virgin. Adams knew the Virgin represented the spent energy of the community of faith, but he sought somehow to experience the image of belief in which St. Michel and Chartres had been built. Not until this lonely, ironic moment was the expense of living in a world in which the hierarchical community had been displaced by mind truly realized in the New England literary consciousness. The vocation of the New England mind to modern history and the awareness of New England as a displaced society may be traced from Adams (and William Dean Howells, whose displacement from Ohio into New England gave him special insights into New England's lapse into secular history), through Robinson and Frost, into (one supposes) its final expression in Robert Lowell.

But in Virginia the awareness of displacement reached the stage of literary articulation as early as 1705, when Robert Beverley published *The History and Present State of Virginia*. Beverley reaches for an image of Virginia as a rational and happy society rooted in the land, knowing in his poetic awareness that the grasping is a resistance to actuality. Tracing the destruction of the native inhabitants of Virginia and sketching the perfidies of the colonial government, he more nearly writes a record of two worlds lost—the world of the Indians and the world the European settlers brought with them—than an account of a new world of promise. Beverley's Virginia, in short, is a place where history has happened. It is the place of a beginning, yet it is a place haunted by the feeling that it is already too late to begin.

---

4. See Miller, *Errand into the Wilderness* (New York, 1964), pp. 99–140.

The divided perspective in *The History and Present State of Virginia* suggests the drama of ambivalent attitudes found toward the development of Virginia in its men of letters during the eighteenth century. Reaching its culmination in Jefferson, this drama may be characterized as a struggle between the tendency to look on Virginia as the historical triumph of a society conceived as a paradigm of rationality and the countertendency to view it as a world that will never escape its origination in the unmaking of an old world community.

Consider Jefferson's crucial representation of the world historical man of letters: how the vocation to mind underlying his massive career is qualified by, or haunted by, the opposition of historical exigency to mind's imperatives to order and harmony. Consider the Declaration of Independence. This manifesto of mind places the man of letters at the center not simply of the historical situation existing between the American colonies and the British Crown but at the center of the world historical movement of man out of the old society into mind. Where had stood king, bishop, and the hierarchical order to lords and servants (to use Hegelian terms, of masters and slaves) now stands the man of letters and the Third Realm. Mind is realized as the model of government. But while it conclusively implied the great political and sociological alteration announced by the Puritan Rebellion and ratified by the Glorious Revolution—the vanquishing of the monarchical sociality of blood by the rationale of society and government discovered under the aegis of mind (whether this be mind as represented by John Locke, the Scottish Common Sense philosophers, or "intellectual middlemen" like John Trenchard and Thomas Gordon)—the Declaration is almost devoid of any suggestion as to mind's relation to the actual American society it presumed to declare independent of British rule. The actual society was the disparate one of the Atlantic seaboard settlement in which chattel slavery, evolving from historical fortuity into a primary institution in the southern colonies, had become crucial to the future of whatever order the thirteen colonial entities might attain after they achieved independence. The Declaration refers to slavery only once: in the charge, somewhat obliquely stated, accusing the King of committing an atrocity of war by "exciting domestic insurrection amongst us." The specific historical event behind the accusation was the appeal in 1775 by Lord Dunmore, governor of Virginia, for slaves to rise against their masters. Jefferson's struggle to generalize the horror of Lord Dunmore's act resulted in a lengthy, convoluted denunciation of the King for having "waged cruel war against human nature itself" by enslaving unoffending Africans, trafficking in them, and then encouraging them to turn on their masters; "thus paying off former crimes committed against the LIBERTIES of one people, with crimes which he urges them to commit against the LIVES of another."[5] Setting up an un-resolvable tension between the values of liberty and life, Jefferson points to the irrationality of the King who would loose slaves upon their masters, yet in so doing suggests the more fundamental irrationality of slavery it-self. Reducing Jefferson's involved, ambivalent rehearsal of the King's fomentation of a slave uprising, the congressional version of the Declara-tion implies not only the general sanction of slavery by the revolting colonies (which the southern members of the Congress wished to affirm) but an accommodation of mind (the model of the Declaration) to the in-stitution of slavery. The document thereby associates the perpetuation of the order of masters and slaves with the man of letters and the literary order. The fatefulness of this association was revealed in the 1830's, when the American man of letters appeared on the scene in the guise of abo-litionist. The American man of letters as abolitionist and the American man of letters as slavery advocate became world historical literary figures. The American slave master and man of letters like Jefferson, who could question and even oppose slavery while he assented to its peculiar appro-priateness under certain conditions—the Jefferson who penned the Decla-ration of Independence—disappeared. Keeping to a course on the slavery issue which, although directed toward emancipation through colonization, held in view slavery's regional distinctiveness in the American Republic, Jefferson tacitly accepted the institution as necessary to the South, and to him personally. He attempted to avoid the dire underlying meaning of his position: to wit, that the slave society demanded the conformance of mind to society.

The threat of slavery to mind remained nonetheless a constant tensional element in Jefferson's thought. In the *Notes on the State of Virginia* it is evident in the part stressing the mental inferiority of Africans. It is more evident in the fierce outcry against slavery in Query XVIII. Jefferson depicts the institution as such a destruction of the morals and industry of the masters and such a desecration of the humanity of the slaves that God in His wrath may decree the overturning of the social order by the slaves. This unexpected denunciation of slavery was provoked, we surmise, neither by Jefferson's simple moral aversion to slavery nor by his fear of slave insurrection. The outcry measures the degree to which the historical dilemma of African chattel slavery had become subjectified in the con-sciousness of Jefferson. In the midst of a book intended to present Vir-

---

5. *The Writings of Thomas Jefferson*, ed. Andrew A. Lipscomb and Albert Ellery Bergh (Washington, D.C., 1905), I, 34–35. On the interpretation of the Declaration of Independence, see not only Carl Becker's classic *The Declaration of Independence: A Study in the History of Political Ideas* (New York, 1922) but the strongly revisionist inquiry by Garry Wills, *Inventing America: Jefferson's Declaration of Independence* (New York, 1978). Also, see Bernard Bailyn, *The Ideological Origins of the American Revolution* (Cambridge, Mass., 1967).

ginia as a promising instance of a society developing on the model of
mind, the author (the Virginia philosophe, Jefferson, addressing answers
to the queries propounded by a fellow French philosophe) acknowledges
that slavery may hold—almost surely does hold—dominion over mind in
Virginia. In his "peculiarly historical consciousness"—in his singular
awareness of the historical particularity of his world—Jefferson is the first
American man of letters to assume southern history as a psychic burden.
Our appreciation of the character of this burden is enhanced by the argu-
ment in Edmund S. Morgan's *American Slavery | American Freedom: The
Ordeal of Colonial Virginia*. Morgan describes how the Virginian lords
in the later seventeenth and early eighteenth centuries, fearing the increase in the poor resulting from the use of indentured white laborers and
being unable in a postfeudal (or prebourgeois) historical situation to enslave the poor of their own color, turned to African slavery. This expediency averted the problem of an insurgency on the part of the landless
white poor by replacing them with laborers whose status as human beings
was considered to be so inferior that their enslavement required no justifi-
cation. By means of this expediency, and with no deliberate intent, the
Virginians created a society in which large and small landowners, freed
of the fear of potential mob violence, could unite in the Enlightenment
idealism of liberty and equality—or, to use the metaphor I have been employing, in a society modelled on mind. Without acknowledging it, without even knowing it in any overt way, the Virginians stood on African
slavery as the pragmatic historical condition of American independence
from King and Church.[6]

We can imagine that Jefferson might have relieved himself from the
burden of history by admitting, in the private recesses of his understanding, that the commitment of a Virginia man of letters to freedom ironically demanded his support of slavery. Or we can conceive that Jefferson
might have lifted the burden of history entirely by quietly making an
even more devastating admission: the contingencies of history constitute
the inescapable shaping force of both mind and society. But Jefferson
himself hardly entertained either notion. He balanced the burden of
history with his conviction, reasserted to the end, that the Revolution was
an act of mind freed from traditionalism and transcendent over the ac-
cidents of history. The revolutionary situation "presented to us an album
on which we were free to write what we pleased," he said in 1824. "We had
no occasion to search into musty records, to hunt up royal parchments, or
to investigate the laws and institutions of a semi-barbarous ancestry." In
the last letter from his pen, a response to the fiftieth anniversary of American independence and written less than a month before his death, Jeffer-

---

6. See Morgan, *American Slavery/American Freedom: The Ordeal of Colonial Virginia* (New York, 1975), especially pp. 363–387.

son conceives the origin of the American Republic to lie in the "unbounded exercise of reason and freedom of opinion."[7]

It is ironic but not strange that the proslavery argument is dominantly concerned with presenting the southern slave society not as a harking back to reactionary traditionalist order but as the fulfillment of a rational theory of civilizational order. The tone the argument assumed among post-Jeffersonian men of letters is represented by Chancellor Harper's essay "Slavery in the Light of Social Ethics." Harper points to Thomas Dew's opinion that "the institution of slavery is a principal cause of civilization."

> Perhaps nothing can be more evident [Harper declares] than that it is the sole cause. If anything can be predicated as universally true of uncultivated man, it is that he will not labor beyond what is absolutely necessary to maintain his existence. Labor is pain to those who are unaccustomed to it, and the nature of man is averse to pain. Even with all the training, the helps, and motives of civilization, we find that this aversion cannot be overcome in many individuals of the most cultivated societies. The coercion of slavery alone is adequate to form man to habits of labor. Without it, there can be no accumulation of property, no providence for the future, no tastes for comforts or elegancies, which are the characteristics and essentials of civilization. He who has obtained the command of another's labor, first begins to accumulate and provide for the future, and the foundations of civilization are laid. We find confirmed by experience that which is so evident in theory. Since the existence of man upon the earth, with no exception whatever, either of ancient or modern times, every society which has attained civilization has advanced to it through this process.[8]

Abstracting the development of African chattel slavery from the complex actualities of history and holding it up as an agency of civilization which experience has confirmed, Harper invests the institution of slavery as it is known to the South with the quality of rational historical process. The value of slavery is a truth self-evident to the lettered mind. The predominance of the southern clerisy—which included besides Harper and Dew such figures as James H. Hammond, George Frederick Holmes, John C. Calhoun, Albert Taylor Bledsoe, and William Gilmore Simms—supported the southern society as representing a patriarchical yet rational, moral, beneficent modern order. They saw it too as an order with a world destiny ordained by a rational God. The Hebraic God of shattering wrath,

---

7. *The Portable Thomas Jefferson*, ed. Merrill D. Peterson (New York, 1975), pp. 578, 584–585.
8. *Cotton Is King*, ed. E. N. Elliott (Augusta, Ga., 1860), pp. 551–552.

momentarily glimpsed by Jefferson, was more nearly of use to the abolitionists than ever He was to the proslavery advocates. Truly only one well-known member of the proslavery clerisy saw the illogic of establishing the southern society on the model of mind. But no more than any nineteenth-century American man of letters could George Fitzhugh escape from the reversal of the roles of society and mind in the founding of the Republic. The southern society, he says in *Cannibals All! Or, Slaves Without Masters* (1856) must renounce the attribution of its origins to the Lockean contractual hypothesis and view itself as being continuous with the order rooted in nature: "Men, and all other social and gregarious animals, have a community of thought, of motions, instincts, and intuitions. The social body is of itself a thinking, acting, sentient being." The history of the social body, Fitzhugh asserts, is not to be differentiated by intellectual analysis from its organic functioning: "Wise men know that there is too much of complexity in the tangled web of human affairs to justify the attempt at once to practice and philosophise, to act and to reason. Fools and philosophers too often mar the good works of such men, by pretending to see clearly, and to define accurately, the principles of action which have led to those works."[9] And yet even as he declares the organic integration of society and history, Fitzhugh, the self-conscious man of letters, essays to differentiate the principles of action underlying the works of wise men like George Washington. Endeavoring to formulate a prescriptive doctrine of social order, Fitzhugh—employing insights that are anthropological, sociological, and psychological—arrives at an anticapitalist theory of the relationship between the southern society and modern history that bears the distinct influence of Karl Marx. No less than the Jefferson he so severely condemns as "the architect of ruin" and "inaugurator of anarchy," Fitzhugh was the slave owner as world historical intellectual.[10] Although he was impelled to the notion that the South must somehow repudiate the elevation of mind by the American Revolution, he comprehended as well as any post-Cartesian intellectual that when intellect had discovered the principle of reality in the separation of body and mind, society and the individual had been sundered; and that, moreover, the breach could never be repaired, save through a recovery, in the deepest levels of consciousness, of the reality of a cosmos closed in unquestioning faith. Such a recovery was not a possibility for Fitzhugh, in his own way a Carlylean (even a Nietzschean or Spenglerian) man of letters, whose austere and driving interpretation of southern society superficially envisions it as a natural and permanent order but which in its

---

9. *Cannibals All! Or, Slaves Without Masters*, ed. C. Vann Woodward (Cambridge, Mass., 1968), pp. 132, 130.

10. Ibid., p. 135. On Fitzhugh's relation to socialism see especially Eugene D. Genovese, *The World the Slaveholders Made: Two Essays in Interpretation* (New York, 1969).

inner meaning sees it as a society that can survive only by conforming to an abstract ideology of modern history. Nothing in *Cannibals All!* is more significant than Fitzhugh's appeal to the common ideological motivation of the southern and northern "physicians" to society.

> As we are a Brother Socialist, we have a right to prescribe for the patient; and our Consulting Brethren, Messrs. Garrison, Greeley, and others, should duly consider the value of our opinion. Extremes meet —and we and the leading Abolitionists differ but a hairbreadth. We, like Carlyle, prescribe more of government; they insist on No-Government. Yet their social institutions would make excellently conducted Southern sugar and cotton farms, with a head to govern them. Add a Virginia overseer to Mr. Greeley's phalansteries, and Mr. Greeley and we would have little to quarrel about.[11]

The Jeffersonian vision of free, enlightened mind as the model of society implied the displacement of the society of myth and tradition; the proslavery ideology of slavery (although ironically set forth in the name of its recovery) implied the total destruction of the society of myth and tradition. The interiorizing of this implication in the consciousness of the southern clerisy—resulting in their intimate awareness not only of the multiple dilemmas and involved ironies of history but in their increasing sensitivity to modern history as a psychic deprivation—would seem to help to explain the tendency of the proslavery argument to become at times a nostalgic evocation of a lost world, a dream of a South that had been a land of pastoral peace and idyllic community. In fact, David Donald has argued cogently that the chief meaning of the proslavery literature is to be discerned not in its defense of "slavery-as-it-was" but in its dream vision of "the South-as-it-might-have-been." It celebrated a "bygone age in which southern life had had—or was supposed to have had—cohesion, unity, and grace." Its chief motive finally was to counter, as George Frederick Holmes said, "those feelings of dark uncertainty, of skepticism and of despair, produced in apprehensive minds by the whirl and confusion of tottering creeds and crumbling institutions." It pleaded for "the restoration of community."[12]

Whether or not the nostalgic element in the proslavery writings is to be given as much weight as Donald assigns to it is a problem that may be passed over here. In terms of the discussion I have been trying to develop, it is clear, I trust, that both the rationalistic and the nostalgic motives in the proslavery argument were formed by fundamental historical imperatives: the transference of history into the southern mind; the internaliza-

---

11. Ibid., pp. 260–261.
12. Donald, "The Proslavery Argument Reconsidered," *Journal of Southern History,* XXXVII (Feb., 1971), 17.

tion of history—its contingencies, demands, and anxieties—in the consciousness of the southern man of letters; and the pressure on the southern clerisy to conform the South to the ideological character of the emergent society of history and science in the West.

Observing the dramatic and inescapable commitment to history by the southern man of letters as ideologue, we are no doubt better able to understand why the southern man of letters as storyteller has for 150 years found his subject and his vocation in an apprehension—emotional and intellectual—of history as consciousness and consciousness as history. In short, in a historicism of consciousness. Concluding these remarks on the southern literary vocation, I may perhaps illustrate this phenomenon by referring to several fictive representations of the southern man of letters as storyteller-historian. Let me move rapidly from Poe's Roderick Usher (1839) to Walker Percy's Lancelot Lamar (1977).

Related by a narrator whose identity is never clearly established and who could actually be telling a tale that he is convinced of but which may have occurred in his mind, the history of Roderick has all the more force of reality because we know that it is probably not empirically true. Standing before the ancient, decaying mansion of the Ushers, the narrator experiences the state of the opium eater who is returning from the drugged condition to actuality: "the hideous dropping off of the veil." This reversal of what we would in fact expect—that the traveller from the sane outside world into the dominion of Usher would experience an entry into an unreal world—prepares us for finding in Usher's history a reality ordinarily masked by sanity. It is this reality that the narrator carries back with him to the world of presumed normalcy when at the tale's conclusion he flees, aghast, the House of Usher collapsing after him into the dark waters of the tarn. The narrator is not only witness to, but cannot help being participant in, a situation that might be generalized as follows: the destruction of the society of myth and tradition by intellect and the subsequent destruction of mind by a "hideous throng" of avenging demons, which—in "The Haunted Place," the poem Usher has composed about his fate and which he sings in the middle of the story—appear inexplicably in the triumphant monarch Thought's dominion. Last of his line, living in a state of psychic incest with his twin sister Madeleine, Usher suffers from an agonizing, demonic awareness of his own consciousness. The totality of his absorption in himself is confirmed by his identity with the house in which he dwells. A house divided, it is doomed to fall with the expansion of the fissure which the narrator detects in its walls as he first approaches the house (shall we call it the Cartesian split?). To use Hegelian terms, the situation in Poe's story suggests that the dialectical conflict of traditionalism and historicism seeks a terrifying synthesis in the consciousness of the poet. When the narrator escapes, he carries back with him into what has become for him the unreality of the normal world the poet's—the story-teller's—knowledge of reality: the permanent isolation of the modern individual in the subjectivity of modern history. All this is made still more suggestive by the implication that the author-narrator is a figure of the man of letters, who tells about the fate of another man of letters, the poet and scholar, Roderick Usher—who could be the double of the narrator. Aware that his attachment to the old community of myth and tradition is the measure of his alienation from the modern society of history and intellect, the scholar and poet is, in his Poesque image, a self imprisoned in the consciousness of its immutable historicity. In a still deeper sense, in its Poesque image the poet's essential self is the very creature of history.

As unlikely as it may seem, an image of the southern author as the historical self—one rivalling that of Poe's Usher in evocative power—is found in the literature of mid-nineteenth-century southern humor. I have in mind George Washington Harris's portrayal of Sut Lovingood. A parody figure of the man of letters, Sut is, as he says, the "orthur" of the tales he tells; for the collected edition of them (1868) he composed both a preface and a "Dedicatory." The precise extent to which Harris merged his identity with Sut is indeterminable. But Harris's biography, especially its record of his obsessed concern with contemporary American history, indicates that in Sut he created a character on whom to unload some of the burden of history he himself experienced. The ultimate significance of Sut may be that he is locked in the historical consciousness of his society. Flouting society but in no wise able to escape it, he is in his aggressive ignorance a symbol of the ruthless historicism of the literary consciousness once it is sufficiently freed from the directing reference either of traditionalist society or enlightened mind. Harris's transference of the role of the man of letters to Sut bears the imputation of a despairing surrender to history.

Twenty years after the Civil War, Mark Twain climaxed the symbolic assignment of the role of the southern man of letters to the historical self when he gave this role to the narrator of *Adventures of Huckleberry Finn*. One of the truly bone-chilling scenes in American literature occurs, I think, when, in the later part of his tale, Huck tells about sitting alone on the raft and engaging in an awesome inner struggle to resolve his relationship with Jim. Will he do the right thing in the historical society of which he is a member and see that the runaway slave is returned to his owner? Even though he figures it means his damnation, he decides to stick to Jim. But in spite of Huck's magnificent declaration, "All right then I'll go to hell!" the impact of his decision to tear up the letter to Miss Watson revealing Jim's whereabouts is strangely undercut by his immediate rationalization of it. Does Huck really make any decision at all? Does he not actually do just what his role in the historical society tells him to do? Does he not continue being what he is comfortable being, an outcast "brung up to wickedness" and who "may as well go the whole hog" in his wickedness? Huck has no suprahistorical model of behavior to guide him. Incapable either of affirming or denying his subjection to his society, he flees from it to no purpose save to become more entangled in history. While in one moment he seems to exemplify the Enlightenment concept of natural virtue—to have, as Mark Twain said of Huck, "a sound heart and a deformed conscience"—in the next moment he accepts the image of his action held up to him by the slave society. The literary consciousness is submerged in the modern historical society: this is the crucial realization—is it not?—that breaks through in the book that Huck has made. It is appropriate for Huck to end his book as he begins it by affirming his identity as a figure of the author, yet at the same time relinquishing it. "If I'd 'a' knowed what a trouble it was to make a book I wouldn't 'a' tackled it," he says, "and ain't going to no more." Storytelling as a transcendent act of the imagination, Huck seems to sense, has been closed down by modern history. The last episode of Huck's book, it is hardly incidental to remark, is an ironic comment on such a possibility. Huck relates the tale of the "splendid," mixed-up rescue of Jim—a story dominated by Tom Sawyer, the historical romancer, and another parody figure of the man of letters. Tom is determined at whatever cost to anyone to rescue Jim according to the code of Alexandre Dumas. He keeps history open to the imagination by falsifying history and degrading the imagination.

Mark Twain died in 1910. His later years were spent in growing bitterness as he tried—with his great intuitive powers, and an abundant fund of reading, but without an adequate comprehension of the high culture of Western civilization—to fathom the nature of modern man, the creature of history. Elsewhere the subject was pursued by men of letters like Mann, Proust, Kafka, and Joyce; and, too, by a lonely young man who came from a Mississippi River community well known to Mark Twain, T. S. Eliot of St. Louis, Missouri. After the First World War and the South's fuller reentry into national and world letters, southern men of letters, carrying in their cultural genes the long southern vocation to history, came into vivid contact with these and numerous other writers who represented a continuing affirmation of the world historical Third Realm. For fifty years now southern authors have participated fully in the complex dialectic of traditionalism and historicism which has been the substance of Western literature since the age of Shakespeare.

On the whole this participation has shown an increased complexity of response to the vocation to history but little tendency to find the calling to history salvational. Among fictive representations of historian-storytellers none is more convincing than Faulkner's Quentin Compson III (of all his characters the one most identifiable with Faulkner himself). Existing profoundly in the historicism of his consciousness, Quentin has a sense of being unknown to Roderick Usher, Sut Lovingood, or Huckleberry Finn (even, we might say, to Hamlet): he knows himself to be a creature of history. But Quentin's self-knowledge is his doom. Only in one twentieth-century fictional representative of the southern literary vocation does the awareness of the historical identity of the self assume a genuinely hopeful character. This is in the case of Jack Burden, the "student of history" who serves as the narrator of *All the King's Men*. Going out of the house of his father "into the convulsions of the world, out of history into history, and the awful responsibility of Time," Jack has, or thinks he has, become morally responsible for history. But Jack Burden is exceptional. Warren has not imagined another figure of the southern moralist-historian who conceives with any assurance that he is capable of taking up the burden of history. Other Warren heroes, possibly all more complicated than Jack, perceive their solitude in history without being able to do much about it. I think notably of Jeremiah Beaumont in *World Enough and Time*, Brad Tolliver in *Flood*, and Jed Tewksbury in Warren's latest novel, *A Place to Come To*. Jack Burdens do not exist in the works of Warren's southern contemporaries either. In her figures of the storyteller Eudora Welty presents none who are self-aware questers for their historical identity. Flannery O'Connor is unique among southern fictionists in that she exhibits the influence of the vocation to history by flaunting it and transforming southern settings into landscapes of eternity. Walker Percy, another southern Catholic novelist, might do likewise, save that he cannot escape the conviction that the soul is so intricately imprisoned in modern history that theology cannot free it. His novels all deal with the historicism of the soul and the soul's struggle to break out of the body of its death, the consciousness of the historical creature. In the recently published *Lancelot*, the destruction of the House of Lamar is, like the destruction of the House of Usher, an apocalypse of the historical self. Louisiana aristocrat, member of the bar, amateur historian of the Civil War, in his earlier years a football star and a Rhodes Scholar, Lancelot Andrewes Lamar tells his lurid tale in a dialogue (largely implied) with his priest-psychiatrist friend, Percival. Whether Lancelot's is a tale told by a madman or by the only sane person left in the world is up to the reader to decide. But Lancelot succeeds in presenting in an overwhelming way the issue hidden in the transference of man and nature into mind and thence into the historicism of consciousness: either, Lancelot says, the Sodom and Gomorrah the American nation has become in pursuit of its historical destiny will rediscover the transcendent classical-Christian ethos; or it will yield to the iron discipline of a new prophet—that is, to

Lancelot himself, who declares "I am my own instrument." The closure of history in the self has left no way open for the ego save its own deification. Nietzsche perceived this and proclaimed the superman. Walker Percy perceives it and suggests the investment of all authority in the ego of a crazed southern lawyer and surrogate figure of the man of letters. The suggestion is ludicrous: Lancelot is a parody of the Nietzschean self. But so was Hitler. The hopeful thing about Lancelot is that he has not yet entirely closed history in himself. He has not yet made his mind the model of history, which is to say, he has not yet responded to the ultimate summons of modern history: to identify self-consciousness as God.

The Literary Climate of Jamestown Under the Virginia Company, 1607-1624

RICHARD BEALE DAVIS

The earliest permanent English settlement in continental North America is usually remembered literarily and historically for two accounts of its inhabitants and their red neighbors by Captain John Smith, one the tale of the lazy and dissolute "gentlemen" who were blasphemous and snobbish, and the other the tale of Smith and Pocahontas and her English husband, John Rolfe. Some may remember the accounts of the Indian massacre of the 1620's which set back expansion for decades and educational development for more than a half century. But no one seems to have paid much attention to the remarkable number of well-educated individuals in Smith's time, in the period of De la Warr and Dale and Gates and Argall and Harvey, and especially in the last five years under the Company. Nor does anyone seem to have studied the genuine interest in writing shown by these men, and by others whose personal, cultural, and intellectual backgrounds are unknown, writing which related from many different angles and in several forms the history of this stirring period, writing which included verses on varied subjects and in varied forms, meditative and religious and commendatory and propagandistic, from crude news ballads to the polished couplets of a major Renaissance translation from the classics. Nor has it been emphasized that a number of men in the colony had published before they came to America, continued to write while they were here, and in the instances when they returned to Britain for their latter years wrote yet more, in several cases with distinction.

"Gentlemen," or those so classified by Captain John Smith in *A Relation* (1608), *A Map* (1612), and *The Generall Historie* (1624) and in the surviving records including those of the Virginia Company of London itself, were indeed in too great proportion for the effective building of a colony, too great especially in the earliest years. But if one checks the list of these allegedly idle parasites against the known lists of writings about the colony, he may be startled to find how many of them recorded the colonists' actions with perspicacity, an eye for the colorful and marvelous, and a desire to promote the undertaking by stressing the rosier aspects of the situation. And in addition to these gentlemen there were individuals designated as soldiers or sailors or physicians or yeomen who expressed themselves on paper with vehemence, enthusiasm, gusto, or occasionally even despair.

Both historically and literarily the years in Virginia under the London joint-stock Company fall rather naturally into three segments: the age of Captain John Smith, 1607–1612, in which his published expression was the major but by no means only writing; the age of Dale and Gates and Rolfe and Hamor, 1613–1619, a period in which written discourses were primarily from "amateurs," albeit significant and varied; and finally the Yeardley-Wyatt years, 1619–1624, marked by the number of resident university-educated men and poets and translators and by remarkable documents such as the John Pory account of the first representative British legislative proceedings in the New World and the trenchant prose pamphlets and letters and reports attending the controversy over the Company's management of affairs. A few individuals lived and wrote through the whole era and beyond, as did Captain John Martin and probably Raleigh Crashaw. A greater number lived through two of the three subperiods. But most lived—and many died in the colony—within only one of the three roughly clustered periods of the Company's eighteen-year administration.

In the whole of the Virginia Company's time there were a number of books in the colony. Many of these are known by title, as William S. Powell has shown. By implication it is evident that almost every colonist had a Bible and perhaps a Book of Common Prayer. The clergy quite clearly had relatively extensive libraries, naturally primarily theological; but if one may judge by a surviving inventory of one parson a few years after the Crown took over, their books included many of literary or belletristic and utilitarian interest. Historians, contemporary and recent, have marvelled that the first Anglican minister, the Reverend Robert Hunt, M.A., made no complaint when the whole of his fine library was lost in a fire. A little later an impecunious young clergyman just arriving was told that he could furnish himself with a splendid library from those of the several ministers who had died in the colony. At least one parson, the Reverend Thomas Bargrave, brother of the Dean of Canterbury, when dying in Virginia in 1621 left his books to the infant College of Henrico. The Reverend J. Stockham, one of Captain Smith's "sources," wrote in the same year that he was "no statesman nor love[d] to meddle with any thing but [his] Bookes." And among laymen, William Strachey and John Pory, while composing their letters and journals and even histories in Virginia, had printed volumes beside them, as Pory acknowledges in a letter quoted below. Governors such as Lord De la Warr, Sir Thomas Dale, and Sir Francis Wyatt had books about them, the last probably including in his library the work of Machiavelli. And the French scholar and writer Pierre Erondelle (Arundel) and the English poets Christopher Davison and George Sandys must have had at least modest collections with them. George Percy, brother of the Earl of Northumberland, narrating his version of the first planting, used the pens and ink and paper and books his relative the peer sent him probably for recreation as well as reference.[1]

Undoubtedly the reading matter in the colony from first planting to the dissolution of the Company was primarily religious, including theological. But the first freshly composed "literary cargo" dispatched to Britain was entirely secular, as most Virginia writing throughout the seventeen years and ever afterwards was to continue to be, though the sermon-letter of Alexander Whitaker of 1612 (published 1613) is a notable exception, and even the official reports are pious in tone and frame of reference.

Philip L. Barbour's edition of *The Jamestown Voyages under the First Charter* includes the texts or the contemporary references to the items no longer extant sent back to England in 1607. The letter from the resident Council in Virginia of June 22 of that year, probably written by the soldier and first president, Edward Maria Wingfield, was addressed to the Council of the Company in London. It is brief yet glowingly descriptive of the new land. Also on this first return voyage went three narrative-descriptive accounts probably by Gabriel Archer, first secretary of the colony, a man trained in law and manners at Gray's Inn. "A relatyon . . . written . . . by a gent of ye colony" is roughly in journal form and touches on the discoveries of an expedition into the interior (probably as far as the fall

---

1. William S. Powell, "Books in the Virginia Colony before 1624," *William and Mary Quarterly*, 3rd ser., V (1948), 177–184; Edward Maria Wingfield, "Discourse," *The Jamestown Voyages under the First Charter 1606–1609*, ed. Philip L. Barbour (Cambridge, Mass., 1969), pp. 226, 229, 230 (Wingfield's books), 393 (Hunt's books); Howard M. Jones, *The Literature of Virginia in the Seventeenth Century*, 2nd ed. (Charlottesville, Va., 1968), passim; Richard B. Davis, "Volumes from George Sandys's Library Now in America," *Virginia Magazine of History and Biography*, LXV (1957), 450–457, and *George Sandys, Poet-Adventurer* (London and New York, 1955), passim; M. A. Rogers, "More Books from the Library of George Sandys," *VMHB*, LXXXIV (1976), 362–364; "A Virginia Minister's Library, 1635," ed. R. G. Marsden, *American Historical Review*, XI (1905/6), 328–332; Susan M. Kingsbury, ed., *Records of the Virginia Company of London* (Washington, D.C., 1905–1935), III, 643 (Bargrave's library valued at 100 marks); William S. Powell, *John Pory, 1572–1636: The Life and Letters of a Man of Many Parts* (Chapel Hill, N.C., 1977), p. 109 (ltr. 1609 to Sir Dudley Carleton). For Wyatt, see Davis, *Sandys*, passim, and "A Letter of Advice to the Governor of Virginia, 1624," eds. J. Frederick Fausz and Jon Kukla, *William and Mary Quarterly*, 3rd ser., XXXIV (1977), 104–129. See also John W. Shirley, "George Percy at Jamestown, 1607–1612," *VMHB*, LVII (1949), 235, etc. Erondelle and Davison appear in Davis, *Sandys*, passim, and Kingsbury, ed., *Records Va. Co.*, passim, and Strachey's life and work are discussed in S. G. Gulliford, *William Strachey 1572–1621* (Charlottesville, Va., 1965), Jones, *Lit. Va. Seven. Cent.*, and Philip L. Barbour, *The Three Worlds of Captain John Smith* (Boston, 1964).

line). It contains some colorful depictions of Indians, including the Queen of Appomattox. "A Description of the River and Country" is an elaboration beyond the official letter noted above as to the delightful aspects of the country. And the third essay probably by Archer, "A Brief discription of the People," gives picturesque details of chiefs' or kings' costumes and physiques, the social position of women, and some comment on the desirability of converting all these natives to Christianity. Perhaps the first personal letter in a long tradition of colonial epistles is that of Robert Tindall, Gunner, to his patron Prince Henry, an epistle originally accompanied by a journal and a map of the river region (only a contemporary copy of the latter survives) by a seaman who later rose to the rank of captain in the Royal Navy, a terse and competently written note which makes us yearn to discover his journal enclosure. A fragment of a letter in good rhetorical prose by a William Brewster who died later in 1607 remains, but known-to-have-been-written letters from a Dutchman (in Latin) to John Pory and from George Percy to a Master Warner have not been discovered.

In the next few years all sorts of people wrote to relatives or friends or officials at home. Their letters, usually composed with the rhetorical rules of the Renaissance in mind, were from these earliest years frequent in the cargos of ships returning to Britain.[2] Peter Wynne, Councilor, writing on the Welsh ancestry of the red men in 1608, was so impressed by the country that "I am now willing here to end my days" (and so he did). Francis Perkins, gent., in the same year addressed a rather long descriptive and analytical letter to a friend in England. He announced that he was shipping home some natural products of the new land. Gabriel Archer and John Ratcliffe in 1609 and George Percy in 1611 composed epistles worth considering as literature. Perhaps the most significant letter of these early years is a 1608 communication addressed by Captain John Smith himself to the Treasurer (Director) and Council of the Virginia Company in London, a devastating reply to uninformed criticism from home, in itself the inauguration of a colonial literary-political tradition of refusal to accept unjust regulation or disparagement.[3]

The epistolarians and others of 1607–1612 were the authors of more ambitious and more lengthy writings. Some of the one-time students at Oxford and Cambridge and the Inns of Court, the clergy and physicians and officials such as Dr. Lawrence Bohun, the parsons Glover and Hunt

2. Richard B. Davis, "The Gentlest Art in Seventeenth-Century Virginia," in *Literature and Society in Early Virginia 1608–1840* (Baton Rouge, La., 1973), pp. 43–62, and Jones, *Lit. Va. Seven. Cent.*, pp. 4, 72–85.

3. For these letters and comment upon them, see Barbour, ed., *The Jamestown Voyages*, passim; Jones, *Lit. Va. Seven Cent.*, passim; and Shirley, "George Percy at Jamestown," pp. 227–243.

and Bucke, and governor Sir Thomas Gates have survived in little extant written expression. But the obscure "R. Rich" in *Newes from Virginia. The lost Flocke Triumphant . . .* (London, 1610) gives us in news-ballad rhyme the story of the wreck in the Bermudas and the subsequent voyage on to Virginia, including the well-known lines:

> Wee hope to plant a Nation
>   where none before hath stood
>
> To glorifie the Lord tis done,
>   and to no other end:

And in his preface to the reader Rich acknowledges his hurry to get back to Virginia again. Among other known versifiers of these years are William Strachey, John Smith, and Raleigh Crashaw, as well as a few others who are better known as the authors of prose accounts incorporated into Smith's *A Map* or his *Generall Historie*. Strachey's verses in his *Historie of Travell into Virginia Britania* are more than competent. Crashaw's complimentary lines included in Smith's 1616 *A Description of New England* referring to their years together in Virginia are not at all bad occasional rhyme. Crashaw was still living in the Virginia of 1623/4, as George Sandys notes in a letter. Smith's abilities as a poet are evident in several examples scattered through his prose work. That the moving "The Sea Marke" is his seems to be supported by the quality and form of two recently discovered printed commendatory poems by the Captain.[4] Three of the authors of narratives incorporated into Smith's *A Map* (1612) showed that they also could indite verses in a joint complimentary piece published, like Crashaw's, in the 1616 *Description of New England*. These were Michael and William Phettiplace (Fettiplace) and Richard Wiffin, gentlemen and soldiers.

Other prose writers indicate that they were often enthusiastic and perceptive and at least fairly learned. The Reverend Alexander Whitaker, whose epistle-sermon published in London in 1613 as *Good Newes from Virginia* shows him as the Cambridge-educated scholar he was, also is represented by letters of 1611–1614 to friends in England. He was enormously interested in Indian customs, compares the red man's gyrations to those of "our Morris dances," cites biblical and classical analogies for the

---

4. "Two 'Unknown' Poems by Captain John Smith," ed. Philip L. Barbour, *VMHB* LXXV (1967), 157–158, and Everett Emerson, *Captain John Smith* (New York, 1971), pp. 91–93. For the verses of Crashaw and his fellow-"collaborators" see *The Travels and Works of Captain John Smith*, eds. Edward Arber and A. G. Bradley (Edinburgh, 1910), I, 184–186. For Strachey's verse, Culliford, *Strachey*, passim, and Strachey's *Historie of Travell into Virginia Britania*, eds. L. B. Wright and Virginia Freund (London, 1953), passim.

natives' behavior, and sees their priests as practitioners of the black arts. This good puritan Anglican was drowned at the age of thirty-three in 1617 in the James River.5

George Percy, the man of the highest social standing among the first planters and probably a sometime student at Oxford and certainly at the Middle Temple, apparently drove the quill all during his years at Jamestown, though he was also busy in voyages of discovery, as commandant at Jamestown, and twice as acting governor. The writing materials and books his brother the Earl of Northumberland sent to him he put to good use, keeping a daily journal and writing several letters. From his diary he composed the earliest known account of the voyage and first settlement by a participant, "Observations gathered out of a Discourse of the Plantation of the Southerne Colonie in Virginia by the English, 1606," incorporated by Samuel Purchas in his *Hakluytus Posthumous, or Purchas His Pilgrims* (London, 1625). Arrogant, alert, opinionated, Percy had an eye for colorful detail and a capacity for wonder at what he saw. His word-picture of the flute-playing, red-tufted chieftain is as effective as a John White drawing from the earlier Roanoke colony. Again almost surely based on his Jamestown notes is "A Trewe Relacyon of the Procedings and Occurants of Moment w*ch* hapned in Virginia from the Tyme S*r* Thomas Gates was shipwreckte upon the Bermudes an*o* 1609 until . . . 1612," not published until this century, a grim narrative defending his American career against aspersions of an unnamed author, perhaps Smith. In a letter to his brother from Jamestown, Percy mentions that he is obliged to keep a table for gentlemen who drop in, a group which certainly included a number of other educated people who wrote of the colony, as Lord De la Warr and William Strachey, Sir Thomas Dale, and Sir Thomas Gates, all of whom appeared after Captain Smith had left the Virginia scene but before Percy himself departed in 1612.

William Strachey, educated at Cambridge and at Gray's Inn, was the compiler of *For the Colony in Virginea Britannia: Lawes Divine, Morall and Martiall, etc.* (London, 1612), though its authors include Dale (hence the pejorative designation "Dale's Laws"), Gates, and whoever designed English military laws at home. A recent edition of these *Lawes* includes a perceptive defense and explanation of them by a distinguished legal historian. All together these regulations are a literary expression of legally

---

5. *Good Newes from Virginia* (London, 1613) contains Whitaker's letter to Sir Thomas Smith of July 28, 1612; a letter to the Reverend William Crashawe, August 9, 1611, is in Alexander Brown, *Genesis of the United States* (Boston, 1890), I, 497–500; and a third epistle to his cousin the Reverend "M. G." [William Gouge], June 18, 1614, is an appendix in Ralph Hamor's *A True Discourse of the Present State [Estate] of Virginia* (London, 1615, rpt. Richmond, 1957). Whitaker refers to other earlier letters to England now lost.

and militarily trained individuals who wrote with vigor and clarity.[6] But Strachey's more original contributions to literature, written in and / or about Virginia, are much more impressive than this compilation. As recorder or secretary of the colony, he had the opportunity to see much, and he jotted down a great deal he later revised and dispatched to persons in England. "A True Reportory of the Wreck and Redemption of Sir Thomas Gates, Knight . . . ," including description of storms and the wreck of ships in the Bermudas, has long been associated with the name of Shakespeare, who probably employed it for theme and local color in *The Tempest*. First printed in *Purchas His Pilgrims*, it is also a major contribution to the early history of colonization in America. Written in the form of a letter to a noble lady at home, the account is as colorful in its depiction of Jamestown in 1609 as of the Bermudas. It is accurate in its detail, delightful in its depiction of the pageantry during De la Warr's administration, erudite in its allusions yet intimate in its tone. Equally significant is the perhaps fragmentary *Historie of Travell into Virginia Britania*, surviving in three manuscripts of a preface and two books. One version was printed in the mid-nineteenth and another in the mid-twentieth century. In rhetorical style and historical and classical allusion and analogy it is an immensely learned work. Though Strachey employs Smith's *A Map*, his own "True Reportory," and earlier accounts of discovery for much of his narrative, he adds a good deal of literary and historical and ethnological significance from his own observation of Indians and their language, by appropriate introductory verses, and by a most valuable Algonkian "Dictionarie." Strachey's biographer gives us a number of other poems from his pen which, though they may have little or nothing to do directly with America, indicate the quality and intellectual character of this man of letters.[7]

Like Alexander Whitaker's *Good Newes fom Virginia* and Rich's *Newes from Virginia* and many another later piece, *The Relation* (London, 1611) of Strachey's superior, the first full-fledged governor Thomas West, Lord De la Warr, was a promotion piece. A strong defense of the character of the Virginia colonists is implicit in this narrative of natural catastrophes and the means taken to combat them. It also suggests the author as a man of firm mind and enfeebled body. Eventually he was to meet his death in the cause of English colonization.[8]

---

6. *For the Colony in Virginea Britannia: Lawes . . . compiled by William Strachey*, ed. David H. Flaherty (Charlottesville, Va., 1969).

7. Jones, *Lit. Va. Seven. Cent.*, passim; Culliford, *Strachey*, passim; Strachey, *Historie*, eds. Wright and Freund, passim. Another manuscript than that of Wright and Freund was edited by R. H. Major for the Hakluyt Society, 1849. "A True Reportory" has been conveniently reprinted in *A Voyage to Virginia in 1609. Two Narratives . . .* , ed. L. B. Wright (Charlottesville, Va., 1964).

8. *The Relation* is reprinted in Lyon G. Tyler, ed., *Narratives of Early Virginia*

In part an intellectual (sometimes despite himself) Captain John Smith remains the major literary figure of the period of the first planting. Employing the narratives of his friends and companions in Virginia, Thomas Abbay, Raleigh Crashaw, Dr. Walter Russell, Thomas Momford, Dr. Anthony Bagnall, Geoffrey Abbot, W. Tankard, William Box, William Cantrill, Richard Pot(t)s, Thomas Hope, Nathaniel Powell, Michael and William Phettiplace, Thomas Studley, and Richard Wiffin, among others, he appears to have imposed upon all their accounts the stamp of his character and personality. Most of Smith's "collaborators" are listed as gentlemen, and surely a number of them, perhaps all, were as well educated as Smith himself: that is, in a classically oriented grammar school. And surely several of them had attended one of the universities or the Inns of Court. After due allowance for editorial changes by Smith or other "supervisors" in Britain, it is clear that these collaborators were highly literate men, aware of history and geography and of Renaissance belles-lettres.

In the middle years under the Virginia Company, 1613–1619, there were fewer conscious composers of essays or verses than in the periods just before and after, but there continued to be numbers of well-written official reports and promotional accounts of the new land. The surviving records of the Company are in the main for the last years, though there are a few, together with semi-official or official letters, from Dale and Argall. Two of the several colonial Bargrave brothers (in turn brothers of Isaac, the Dean of Canterbury) and a third at home wrote about Virginia, though little of their expression is extant. The Reverend Thomas, already noted, and sea captain George lived in Virginia, and Captain John a few years later wrote a treatise on the colony of some significance in determining the Company's fate.9 Among the highly literate clergy was the Reverend Richard Bucke, an Oxford graduate who married John Rolfe and Pocahontas and gave the opening prayer at the first meeting of the General Assembly in 1619, of which more below. Rolfe in 1616 called Bucke a very good preacher. The parson and his wife died in 1624, leaving several children and 750 acres planted. Dale was in Virginia in much of this period and some of his letters from thence, as one of June 18, 1614, show piety, a sense of politics and government, and an eye for the picturesque.10

The two most significant writings in Virginia in this period were the

---

1606–1625 (New York, 1952), pp. 205–214, and in *Purchas His Pilgrims*. See also Jones, *Lit. Va. Seven. Cent.*, pp. 30–31.

9. Kingsbury, ed., *Records Va. Co.*, III and IV; Brown, *Genesis*, II, 823–824; and Davis, *Sandys*, passim.

10. For more of Bucke, see Kingsbury, ed., *Records Va. Co.*, passim; Dale's letter to "Mr. D. M." is included in Ralph Hamor's *A True Relation* (of which more below), pp. 51–59. Brown, *Genesis, II,* 869–874, includes other communications from Dale.

work of men also important for other reasons. One was Ralph Hamor, son of a leading merchant tailor, who had attended the famous Merchant Taylors School and seems to have matriculated at Brasenose College, Oxford, in 1606 at the age of seventeen. He landed with Gates in Virginia after the wreck in Bermuda. In 1614 he visited Britain and while there published *A True Discourse of the Present Estate of Virginia . . . till the 18 of June. 1614 . . . with [letters]*, by Raphe Hamor, late Secretarie in that Colony (London, 1615). He was a captain in Virginia during the 1622 massacre, and in 1623 George Sandys wrote querulously that he was miserably poor and thus obliged "to shiftes." In composing his *Discourse* Hamor was in the tradition of at least two of his predecessors in the secretaryship, Gabriel Archer and William Strachey. Howard Jones admits the historical value of this firsthand observation of American life, with fresh insights and a New World point of view, but feels that it is badly written and organized. A. L. Rowse, in his preface to a recent edition of the work, is more favorable, praising the account and the writer for "scholarly standards, . . . pious devotion to truth, . . . [and justice of mind]," regretting that Hamor did not give us a more extensive history of Virginia to set beside John Smith's. In the dedication to Sir Thomas Smith and the address to the reader, however, the author shows himself a conscious stylist and a master of the periodic sentence, and his penchant for colorful detail makes his work entertaining reading.[11]

At all odds the most intriguing personally among the writers of the middle period is John Rolfe, who married Pocahontas as the second of his three wives and who is usually acknowledged as the father of the tobacco industry in British North America. He and his first wife sailed for Virginia in the *Sea Venture* in 1609, were wrecked in Bermuda, and arrived at Jamestown in the spring of 1610. Before 1612, probably after the death of his first wife, Rolfe introduced the cultivation of a West Indian tobacco, much superior to what Virginia Indians smoked, and the great staple of the colonial Chesapeake colonies was established. By 1614 Hamor in his *Discourse* showed some understanding of the economic significance of this importation, and in the appendix to his book included an oft-quoted 1614 letter by Rolfe to Sir Thomas Dale concerning the reasons for wishing to marry Pocahontas.

This introspective, rationalizing, Calvinist, and pious letter is one of the indications of the kinship between the Virginia colonial mind and the Pilgrim or Puritan mind. The epistle suggests, as any reader will realize, the consciousness of these first Virginians that they were paralleling, as later were the Saints of New England, the experience of the Israelites in the land of Canaan. Keeping in mind that God was displeased with His Chosen People who married strange wives, Rolfe tells of the worthy love he bore the Indian maiden, the Christian obligation to convert the heathen, and the political expediency of what he wished to do. He may have had a larger reading group in mind than Governor Dale. Altogether, it is perhaps the most rhetorical, reasoned, and meditative letter remaining from this period of the colony.[12]

In 1951 was first printed in a facsimile-plus-letterpress edition an equally significant document by Rolfe, "A True Relation of the State of Virginia Lefte by Sir Thomas Dale Knight in May Last 1616" (1617), basically a promotion piece as an invitation to adventure and a "sober description" of the New World which was Virginia. Interesting etymological spelling, and the tradition-forming mingled yarn of agriculture, business, and politics are qualities of an essay which shows again the introspective and pious and zealous mind of the author. A succession of well-turned sentences suggest possibly that, as many of his descendants believe, this gentleman attended one of the universities. At least he was sufficiently literate and learned to be, like several others already noted, secretary of the colony 1614–1618/19, and after that until his death about 1622 he was a member of the Council resident in the colony. And one should remember that he was coauthor of two long sections of Smith's *Generall Historie*.[13]

In the twilight period under the Company, 1619–1624, Virginia held an astonishing number of educated and articulate men, including four or five well known in London as men of letters who continued to write in America. Along with them were John Martin, Ralph Hamor, John Rolfe, Raleigh Crashaw, the Reverend Richard Bucke, and some others educated in the law, including former members of the Inns of Court, and some trained at the English universities. The lesser "literary" figures wrote letters significant in content and well-turned phrases, or journals, or polemical-descriptive pamphlets, or even occasionally verses. Major or minor

---

12. The letter, appended to Hamor's *Discourse* (pp. 61–68), also is printed in Tyler, ed., *Narratives*, pp. 238–244; *VMHB*, XXII (1914), 152–157; and from the original manuscript in Philip L. Barbour, *Pocahontas and Her World* (Boston, 1969), 247–252. Other Rolfe letters are in Kingsbury, ed., *Records Va. Co.*, III, 70–73, 241–248, and *VMHB*, X (1902/3), 134–138.

13. *Smith, Works*, eds. Arber-Bradley, passim. For Rolfe's "A True Relation" see the 212-copy edition of 1951 (privately printed, New Haven, Conn.), with pertinent preliminary essays by John C. Wyllie, John M. Jennings, and Francis L. Berkeley, Jr., of the Pembroke-Taylor copy. This text with the same editorial introductory material was reprinted without the facsimile reproduction by the University Press of Virginia (Charlottesville, 1971). Barbour in *Pocahontas and Her World* gives us about all that is known about John Rolfe. Berkeley in the 1951 and 1971 editions describes all three known manuscripts of "A True Relation."

writers, or as far as we know merely professional men, were former students of the universities or Inns of Court: clergy such as Hawte Wyatt and Richard Bucke and Samuel Maycock attended Oxford or Cambridge, and Wyatt in addition studied at Gray's Inn. Doctor John Pott, onetime acting governor, and probably college administrator George Thorpe attended Cambridge. Councilors such as Roger Smith and Michael Lapworth and the veteran Ralph Hamor were all of Oxford.[14] Some written expression survives from most of these.

The Reverend Jonas Stockham (Stockton), Oxford-trained minister of two Virginia parishes from his arrival in 1621 to 1627, wrote a letter advocating extermination of "priests and ancients" among the Indians, and composed an account of Virginia incorporated into Smith's *Generall Historie*.[15] Governor Sir Francis Wyatt, who arrived in 1621 and remained until 1626 and then returned as governor many years later, through his brother the clergyman Hawte Wyatt left descendants in Virginia surviving to this day. Almost surely university educated (we know he attended Gray's Inn) as was his brother Hawte, Sir Francis composed several biting, at times ironic letters defending his own and the Company's administration of the colony, including one epistle aimed at Captain Nathaniel Butler for his slanders. Wyatt was not a bad poet, as his complimentary verses in his uncle-in-law George Sandys' *Paraphrase upon the Divine Poems* (1638) and his manuscript occasional and elegiac pieces extant in the Romney Papers testify. The recently published letter received in Virginia from his father George Wyatt indicates that both father and son were political philosophers.[16]

The Captain Nathaniel Butler who was the object of Wyatt's withering sarcasm was, like so many other of these early colonists, a controversial figure. A much traveled seaman who had probably been George Sandys' companion in the Holy Land and for a time governor of Bermuda, Butler was a resident of Virginia in 1622/3 and fought against the Indians. He is now believed to have been the author of *The History of the Bermudaes or Summer Islands* (c. 1621?) and of *Six Dialogues about Sea Services between a High Admiral and a Captain at Sea* (published in 1685 long after his death) and was certainly the author of "The Unmasked Face of or

14. Davis, *Sandys*, p. 190n, and passim.

15. *Smith, Works*, eds. Arber-Bradley, II, 564–565.

16. The Wyatt MSS., Earl of Romney Papers, formerly on deposit at the London Public Records Office and then at the British Library, are now available on microfilm at the University of Virginia Library. "A Letter of Advice to the Governor of Virginia, 1624," eds. J. Frederick Fausz and John Kukla, by George Wyatt, is among these papers. Sir Francis' letter concerning Butler was published in the *William and Mary Quarterly*, 2nd ser., VI (1926), 114–121. There are other Wyatt items in Kingsbury, ed., *Records Va. Co.*, IV, passim. The Virginia Historical Society possesses several photostats from the Romney Papers made about 1925.

Colony in Virginia as it was in the Winter of ye year 1622" (read in London April 23, 1623), one of the major literary weapons of the anti-Sandys-Southampton faction in their attack which led to the dissolution of the Virginia Company. When Butler arrived in Jamestown under a cloud after three years as governor of Bermuda, he was cordially received by Governor Wyatt and George Sandys. But as Wyatt wrote, he and all his Council were soon agreed "in distaste of him, though his usage was in every way fair and courteous." Their devastating, and indeed picturesque, answers to Butler's charges, "A Declaration made by the Counsell for Virginia" and "A true answer to . . ." were probably written in part, or at least based in part on his reports, by George Sandys, who had acted as secretary for Davison while the latter was in England in the winter Butler was in the colony. One of Butler's motivations in attacking the government resident in Virginia was that it had not elected or admitted him to its Council. The General Assembly (probably acting secretary George Sandys), noting that Butler accused them of ignorance, replied that "they held him to be no competent Judge of those, who so far transcended him in Point of Learning and Ability. For he had never been bred to the Law (as was not unknown to some of them) nor yet in other of the liberal sciences . . . ," some indication of the colonists' own consciousness of the level of education of their leaders.[17]

Among those not already mentioned as bred to the law and the liberal sciences was Christopher Davison (arrived 1621, died in Virginia January? 1623/4 after one trip back to Britain), son of one of Queen Elizabeth's secretaries of state. He had as a youth in 1597 attended one of the four resident law colleges in London (that mentioned now several times, Gray's Inn) in which Virginians down to the Revolution were trained in legal matters and (as also intimated above) in polite letters and manners. Brother of two other poets, Francis and Walter, Christopher wrote verses, including paraphrases of the Psalms, which survive in manuscript volumes along with some of theirs. Christopher's renditions of Psalms XV and CXXV, one in couplets and the other in more involved stanzaic rhymes, are among the better attempts to "English" Old Testament poetry. Pro-

---

17. For Butler, see *D.N.B.* under Nathaniel Boteler (fl. 1625–1627) concerning a captain in the Royal Navy whose "Six Dialogues" was published by Moses Pitt in 1685; Brown, *Genesis*, II, 836–837; the Hakluyt Society's edition of *The History of the Bermudaes* (ed. J. H. Lefroy, London, 1882); Davis, *Sandys*, passim, including the quotations from the Council and Assembly; Kingsbury, ed., *Records Va. Co.*, II, passim, for the "Unmasking" and the replies; E. G. Swem, et al., *A Selected Bibliography of Virginia 1607–1699*, Williamsburg, Va., 1957; and a MS volume of Nathaniel Butler's which contains the Dialogical Discourse Concerninge Marine Affairs" (printed as *Six Dialogues*) and a diary beginning 1639 (evidently of the governor of a British colony). One Virginian, Miles Kendall, refers to "that machiavell butler" and another to his forgeries (Kingsbury, ed., IV, 119, 536–537).

fessor Harold Jantz is inclined to believe that brother Francis Davison may also have come to Virginia and composed verse there. At any rate, Christopher came to the colony as secretary of state. With his good friend George Sandys, who assumed his duties when he made his brief journey back to London, Davison shared an interest in poetic composition and the court circle in Great Britain. Though at this time Sandys was writing on nonscriptural themes, a decade later he too was to compose metrical paraphrases of the Psalms of David.[18]

One man of letters who lived several years in Virginia and died there had his residence at Buckroe and only occasionally visited Jamestown. This was Peter Arundel, actually Pierre Erondelle, born in Normandy but residing in London from at least 1586. In that year he published in English *A Declaration and Catholick Exhortation to succour the Church of God and Realme of France*, in 1605 *The French Garden: for English Ladyes and Gentlewomen to Walke in . . .* , and in 1612 *The French Schoole-Maister*. He had also composed in 1609 a translation of and a preface for Champlain's *History of New France* as *Nova Francia, or the description of that part of New France which is one Continent with Virginia*, published by Hakluyt, who had asked Erondelle to do the work. A popular teacher of French in London, Erondelle went to Virginia in 1621 and in 1623/4 was living in Elizabeth City county at Buckroe with John, Elizabeth, and Margaret Erondelle. He built a silkhouse at his own charge and mentions it in several letters to such people as Sir Nathaniel Rich, "Mr. Cañing," and John Smith of Nibley.[19] His epistles indicate that he saw a good deal of his neighbors, and that Governor Wyatt and Treasurer Sandys visited his home to see his silkworm house.

The legislative record of the Assembly of the first colony from 1619 represents the beginning of American-English prose style for public purposes which continued to develop down through the Revolution. The excellence of the first entries is due to the literary ability of John Pory (1572–1636), "a Man of Many Parts," as his quite recent biographer William S. Powell calls him. Secretary of the colony in 1619, he was chosen Speaker of the legislature which met in that year. Master of Arts of both Cambridge and Oxford, onetime member of the British Embassy staff in Constantinople, and frequently a minor diplomatic agent in the Netherlands, France, and Italy, Member of Parliament 1605–1611, he was a friend

---

18. See *D.N.B.* under "Francis Davison"; an essay in the *New England Historical and Genealogical Register*, XXXI (April, 1877), 152–153; Francis Davison's *Poetical Rapsody* (orig. ed., London, 1602; rpt. Sir Egerton Brydges, Kent, 1814); the MS Psalms of three brothers in Harleian, MSS., British Library 6930; Davis, *Sandys*, passim; and Kingsbury, ed., *Records Va. Co.*, II, passim.

19. George B. Parks, *Richard Hakluyt and the English Voyages*, 2nd ed. (New York, 1961), p. 221; Brown, *Genesis*, II, 887; Kingsbury, ed., *Records Va. Co.*, III, 60, 463, 534, 589; IV, 89–90, 92, 230–231, 558.

and professional news correspondent of a number of the prominent men of his time. In 1600 he had published his embellished edition of John Leo's *Historie of Africa*, a "Geographicall Historie" which remains one of the major Elizabethan translations, a work encouraged by the famed Richard Hakluyt. The book was a manual for African explorers well into the nineteenth century. And before Queen Elizabeth's death in 1603, John Norton the London printer brought out Pory's *An Epitome of Ortelius His Theatre of the World, Wherein the principal regions of the earth are described in smalle Mappes*, designed to be useful to the reading public which had not mastered Latin.

All this and much more, including alcoholism, lay in John Pory's background when he was chosen in 1618 Secretary of Virginia for a three-year term. From Jamestown he explored rivers in Maryland, Virginia, and North Carolina and the Chesapeake Bay, composed the official reports of the resident Council to the Company administration at home, and wrote some graceful and picturesque personal letters. His most extensive extant writing from this period of his life is his account of "The proceedings of the first assembly of Virginia. July 1619," frequently printed (most recently in facsimile and letterpress), and written in what has been called "the grand historical manner," certainly with some consciousness of the political and symbolic significance of the acts of the first representative legislature in British America. Pory had the sort of eye for color that his predecessor in office, Strachey, had shown in "The True Reportory," and in addition much more of an understanding of the process of legal enactment and legislative procedure.

Pory had made at least part of his living earlier by writing his news letters to interested English gentlemen or noblemen abroad or in the country outside London who wanted to keep abreast of what was going on. In Virginia he wrote ingratiating letters home to Sir Edwin Sandys and other Company leaders, though it is evident that in this period there was some suspicion that he was secretly an ally of the anti-Sandys faction, a suspicion confirmed for the Sandys group when later in London in 1624 he was made one of the commission to investigate the affairs of the Company and the colony. In 1624 he bribed the clerk of the resident Council and Assembly into betraying their secrets. George Sandys, evidently Pory's friend in the former's first year in the colony (1621–1622), was probably as disappointed as Wyatt and the rest of the Council in this underhand dealing. Pory was clearly an opportunist impelled by his poverty and perhaps his alcoholism.

Pory's earlier letters were masterpieces of the gentle art. The author displays his considerable erudition in Greek and Roman literature, a penchant for the antiquarian and mythological, and a love of gossip per se. One epistle to Sir Dudley Carleton of October 31, 1618, describing the sombre and yet dramatic scene at the death of Sir Walter Raleigh, is certainly one of the best sources extant for that tragic moment. In Virginia he wrote glowing letters not only to Sir Edwin Sandys but to his old friend Sir Dudley Carleton, perhaps the most famous of which describes the fair New World and the opportunities at Jamestown, opportunities made the most of by "our Cowe-keeper" at Jamestown whose wife appears at church in beaver hat and flaming silks, and the whilom penniless soldier Governor Sir George Yeardley as now a man of impressive wealth. This was written on September 30, 1619. Its best-known passage is probably the declaration that ". . . I am resolved wholly to mind my business here, and nexte after my penne, to have some good book always in store, being in solitude the best and choicest company. Besides among these Christall rivers, and odoriferous woods I doe escape muche expense, envye, contempte, and vexation of minde."

Pory lived on to 1636, residing principally in London, composing a stream of letters to his "clients," working "at Court" for the Earl of Warwick, and publishing at least one more book. In the 1624 period as commissioner he apparently was not entirely unfavorable to the Company, as a 1625 letter suggests, and in subsequent years he served (until the death of James I) on a committee for managing the affairs of the colony. A new commission established under Charles I in 1631 included Pory's old fellow-colonist George Sandys, who appears to have become its secretary. Pory and Sandys were two of Britain's first colonial experts, chosen in part for their experience but also for their ability to write about it.[20]

George Sandys (1568–1644), son of an Archbishop of York and brother of knights Sir Edwin and Sir Samuel and baronet Sir Myles Sandys, still holds the priority of writing the first genuine poetry in British North America and at the same time producing the first scholarly book composed (largely) on the American shores. Before he came to Jamestown with his nephew by marriage Sir Francis Wyatt he had attended Oxford and the Middle Temple and had traveled extensively in the Mediterranean countries. His account of Turkey, Egypt, Palestine, and Italy, *A Relation of a Journey begun . . . A. D. 1610* (London, 1615), went through nine editions before 1700 and was the most popular travel account of the seventeenth century. Captain John Smith's principal biographer, Philip L. Barbour, thinks that it was used as a model for the *Generall Historie* in 1624 in prose style, poetic-translations as embellishment, and elaborate engravings. *A Relation*, like all Sandys' later writings, was dedicated to Prince and then King Charles. A member of the court circle, the poet was prob-

---

20. For Pory, including many of his letters in the text or in the microfiche appendix, see William S. Powell, *John Pory 1572–1636*, passim; Davis, *Sandys*, passim; Kingsbury, ed., *Records Va. Co.*, III and IV, passim; Jones, *Lit. Va. Seven. Cent.*, pp. 8–9, 65–72.

ably already before 1621 a Gentleman of the Privy Chamber as he was after his return from America in 1625.

Sandys had been a candidate for the governorship of Bermuda which Nathaniel Butler had received in 1618, and he was sent to Virginia as treasurer and director of industry. Though he was severely critical of the management of Virginia affairs by his brother Sir Edwin and the latter's deputy John Ferrar, when the fight between the factions in the Company broke into the open he showed that his had been meant as constructive criticism, and that he had no use at all for the Sir Thomas Smith–Earl of Warwick group which finally wrecked the Company.

In Virginia the poet-traveler was a busy man, reestablishing a glass works, setting up an iron furnace, superintending the building of a shipyard, collecting the unpopular rents or taxes due the Company from "tenants" on its land, after the massacre leading a retaliatory expedition against neighboring Indians, and while Davison was away and later after his death composing the official reports sent back to London. He corresponded with the great naturalists and collectors the Tradescants about the fauna and flora of the New World. His confidential letters severely critical of the Sandys-Ferrar management unfortunately fell into the hands of its enemies. These surviving epistles show him to have been a hard realist who wrote in grim and ironic tones and terms, including more than a touch of dark humor, of the Virginia situation, including character analyses of many of his fellow colonists of the resident Council.

Before he came to America, Sandys had published in 1621 his translation of the first five books of Ovid's *Metamorphoses*. So well was the little book received that Michael Drayton in lines addressed "To Master George Sandys" urged him to continue the work and thus establish the Muses in Virginia. Sandys wrote another friend that he translated two more books amidst the roaring of the seas and the rattling of the shrouds on the way over. At Jamestown, in the house of Captain William Pierce, the commandant of the little fort, in the hours snatched from night and repose, he completed his version of this Ovid in pentameter couplets. Immediately on his return to England he published (actually in 1626) the complete *Metamorphosis* [sic], a translation in which the first five books are considerably altered from their 1621 form. In 1632, in a more elaborate illustrated edition which is another reworking of the entire fifteen books, Sandys included many references to the New World and especially Virginia in the prose "Philosophical Commentaries" on each book. In the 1630's and early 1640's he continued to publish verse, including *Paraphrases upon the Divine Poems* and a translation of Grotius' play *Christ's Passion*. Never did he forget Virginia. He served as agent for the colony in 1639–1640, and in his meditative farewell poem, "Deo. Opt. Max.," he thanks his God for saving him in many perilous situations. Among the dangers,

> Thou sav'dst me from the bloudy Massacres
> Of faithless Indians, from their treacherous Wars;
> From raging Feavers, from the sultry breath
> Of tainted Aire; which cloy'd the jawes of Death.
> Preserv'd from swallowing Seas; when towring Waves
> Mixt with the Clouds, and opened their deepe Graves.

He must have regaled the Great Tew circle in Oxfordshire, which in the 1630's included Ben Jonson and Lucius Cary, Viscount Falkland, with tales of what he had seen in Virginia, for members of that literary group who contributed commendatory verses to Sandys' later volumes frequently refer to his New World experiences.

In his dedication to the King in the 1626 Ovid, Sandys mentions that though his work was "Sprung from the Stocke of the ancient Romanes," it was "bred in the New-World, of the rudenesse whereof it cannot but participate; especially having Warres and Tumults to bring it to light instead of the Muses." In its various forms his *Metamorphosis* had a great deal to do with the development of the heroic couplet in English. Among others, Dryden and Pope acknowledged their indebtedness to him.[21]

Thus belles-lettres as well as political prose (legislative and administrative) was produced at Jamestown by a remarkable group of educated men. Probably no English town of comparable size included within brief five-to-seven-year periods as many articulate and even erudite writers. Almost all that survives is secular, but Sandys inaugurated a classical tradition which has survived in the South into the twentieth century, Smith and Percy showed often inadvertently a consciousness of the epic quality of their American experience, and governors and secretaries and burgesses established a pattern of distinguished political and forensic prose. The river and forest were without order and therefore crude or rude, and the dwellings were austere in their simplicity. But the land was magnificent, and all these writers at one time or another attempted to express their appreciation of its grandeur or its potential as a pastoral Eden. From 1607 through 1624 there were always persons of intellectual interests who expressed themselves in the written word. Whether they wrote in private or read their expressions to others before shipping them to Britain, they knew that there were fellow colonists who were writing. Percy and Archer and a dozen keepers of journals used by Captain John Smith certainly knew

---

21. All the letters written by Sandys may be seen in Davis, *Sandys*, passim, and in Kingsbury, ed., *Records Va. Co.*, III and IV, passim.

that others were employing their pens, and some surely discussed what they wrote. Perhaps at no other place in America during the seventeenth century were there gathered together so many genuinely literary men as were at Jamestown from 1619 to 1624. Jamestown under the Virginia Company of London, despite its storm and stress, was not a place to stifle the Muses.

Rhetoric and History in Early New England: The Puritan Errand Reassessed

SACVAN BERCOVITCH

Perry Miller's "Errand into the Wilderness" may be the single most influential essay in early American studies. Written just after the completion of the second volume of *The New England Mind*, it offers an eloquent and impassioned summing-up of what remains the most impressive achievement in American intellectual history. To say that the essay is also deeply problematic in no way detracts from that achievement. What I suggest is that Miller's "Errand" has become influential in the wrong way—that it has shaped our view of Puritanism rather than engaging us in the Puritan writings themselves. My purpose is to reopen our inquiry into the meaning of the errand by comparing Miller's essay with its equally eloquent and impassioned precursor, Samuel Danforth's election-day address of 1670, *A Brief Recognition of New England's Errand into the Wilderness*.

Let me begin with the better known of the two addresses. Perry Miller centers his argument on what he terms a "figure of speech," the ambiguity inherent in the Puritan concept of errand. An errand, Miller observes, may be either a venture on another's behalf or a venture of one's own, and the tragedy of the New England Puritans was that their errand shifted from one meaning to another in the course of the seventeenth century. The first settlers saw themselves as an outpost of the Reformation, a detour (and hopefully a shortcut) on the road leading from the Anglican establishment to a renovated England. After 1660, however, with the collapse of Cromwell's revolution, the colonists found themselves isolated, abandoned. "Their errand having failed in the first sense of the term, they were left with the second." They turned inward, accordingly, to fill their venture "with meaning by themselves and out of themselves"—and discovered there, in what was meant to be utopia, "nothing but a sink of iniquity." Hence the vehemence of their "literature of self-condemnation": they had been twice betrayed. Not only had the world passed them by, but the colony itself, the city set on a hill as a beacon to mankind, had degenerated into another Sodom. They vented their outrage in an "unending monot-

---

Some of the ideas in this essay are more fully developed in The American Jeremiad *(Madison, Wis., 1978).*

onous wail," a long threnody over a lost cause, in which they came increasingly to acknowledge that New England was sick unto death. But the very vehemence of the lament, Miller tells us, implied something quite different. The latter-day New England jeremiad registers

> bewilderment, confusion, chagrin but there is no surrender. A task has been assigned upon which the populace are in fact intensely engaged . . . [Thus] while the social or economic historian may read this literature for its contents—and so construct from the expanding catalogue of denunciations a record of social progress—the cultural anthropologist will look slightly askance at these jeremiads. If you read them all through, the total effect, curiously enough, is not at all depressing: you come to the paradoxical realization that they do not bespeak a despairing frame of mind . . . whatever they may signify in the realm of theology, in that of psychology they are purgations of the soul; they do not discourage but actually encourage the community to persist in its heinous conduct. The exhortation to a reformation which never materializes serves as a token payment upon the obligation, and so liberates the debtors. Changes there had to be: adaptations to environment, expansion of the frontier, mansions constructed, commercial ventures undertaken. These activities were not specifically nominated in the bond Winthrop had framed. They were thrust upon the society by American experience. . . . Land speculation meant not only wealth but dispersion of the people, and what was to stop the march of settlements? . . . [The first emigrants] had been utterly oblivious of what the fact of the frontier would do. . . . Hence I suggest that under the guise of this mounting wail of sinfulness, this incessant and never successful cry for repentance, the Puritans launched themselves upon the process of Americanization.[1]

I have quoted this passage at length because it so clearly shows the grounds of Miller's analysis. What he meant by ambiguity was opposition: the errand is either for oneself or for someone else; the jeremiads either discourage or encourage. Clearly, this stems from a "paradoxical realization" that somehow the errand functioned both ways, and that the jeremiads included both threat and hope. But for Miller the realization is an ironic one—it lies in the reader's capacity to see conflicting elements at work in the same act. The Puritans' sense of a failed errand, he claims, led them to make the errand their own. Their "cry for repentance" furthered the community's "heinous conduct." And the reader's ironic awareness, in turn, builds upon a series of static oppositions: content versus

---

1. Perry Miller, "Errand into the Wilderness" (1952), in *Errand into the Wilderness* (Cambridge, Mass., 1956), pp. 2, 8–9, 15.

form, social progress versus catalogues of denunciations, psychology versus theology, the march of settlements versus the ideal of theocracy, and summarily the "American experience" (manifest in land speculation, growing wealth, population dispersion) versus the Puritan lament, a "mounting wail of sinfulness" that issues in a self-defeating ritual of purgation. Methodologically, this implies the dichotomy of fact and rhetoric. Historically, it posits an end to Puritanism with the collapse of the church-state. From either perspective, in what is surely a remarkable irony in its own right, Miller's analysis lends support to the dominant anti-Puritan view of national development—that the "American character" was shaped (in Miller's phrase) "by the fact of the frontier."

We need not discount the validity of this frontier thesis to see what it does not explain: the persistence of the rhetoric of "errand" throughout the eighteenth and nineteenth centuries, in all forms of the literature, including the literature of westward expansion. Indeed, what first attracted me to the study of Puritanism was my astonishment, as a Canadian immigrant, at learning about the prophetic errand of America. Not of North America, for the prophecies stopped short at the Canadian and Mexican borders, but of a country that despite its arbitrary territorial boundaries —despite its bewildering mixture of race and genealogy—could believe in something called America's mission, and could invest that patent fiction with all the emotional, spiritual, and intellectual appeal of a religious quest. I felt then like Sancho Panza in a land of Don Quixotes. Here was the anarchist Thoreau describing his "Westward walk" as an emblem of "America's errand into the future"; here, the solitary singer Walt Whitman, claiming to be the American Way; here, the civil rights leader Martin Luther King, descendant of slaves, denouncing segregation as a violation of "America's errand to freedom"; here, an endless debate about national directions, full of rage and faith, Jeffersonians claiming that they, and not the priggish heirs of Calvin, really represented the errand, conservative politicians defending the errand against its "un-American" critics, left-wing polemics recalling the nation to its divine origins, the Good Old Way of revolution and progress. The question in these latter-day jeremiads was never "Who are we?" but, as though deliberately evading that common-sense problem, "When is our errand to be fulfilled?"—"How long, O Lord, how long?" And the answers, again as in the seventeenth-century sermons, invariably joined lament and celebration in reaffirming American exceptionalism.[2]

This litany of hope, which seems to me a direct challenge to Miller's

2. See my essays on "How the Puritans Won the American Revolution," *Massachusetts Review*, XVII (1976), 597–630, and "The Image of America: From Hermeneutics to Symbolism," *Bucknell Review*, XX (1972), 3–12.

concept of ambiguity, leads back to Danforth's *Brief Recognition of New England's Errand into the Wilderness*. Danforth delivered the address exactly forty years after the *Arbella* fleet landed, and no one at that emotional gathering felt more keenly than he that the new promised land was far from won. Yet what he said then remains a great testament to the persistence of the founders' dream. Taking his text from Christ's "encomium of John the Baptist" (Matt. 11:7–9), Danforth praises the errand as a migration from a "soft" civilization to the purity of the "wilderness-condition." To forsake worldly vanities for Christ, he points out, is the mark of every believer, in any time or place, and accordingly he invests the errand with the general import of pilgrimage. "What went ye out into the wilderness to see?" becomes the Christian's ultimate challenge: "What must I do to be saved in the wilderness of this world?" "How shall I seek the spirit through the wilderness of my own hard heart and recalcitrant will?" The subject was wholly fitting to the occasion. Election-days in the Puritan church-state were a civic affair, but an affair nonetheless reserved for the regenerate and their children. Drawn by their spiritual calling, they had gathered together and shipped for America. They had built their theocracy to serve God. Like all saints, Danforth reminded them, they needed constantly to rededicate themselves to the *itinerarum mentis*, the errand within from self to Christ.[3]

The rhetorical effect here may be termed ambiguous, but emphatically not in the sense of contradiction. Danforth is not posing an alternative between pilgrimage and migration, but offering a synthesis; his terms are not *either/or* but *both/and*. They imply the union of saint and society, the spiritual and the historical errand; and in this context they lead him to still another ambiguity. The parallels that Danforth urges upon his listeners, between John the Baptist and Danforth the preacher, between the Arabian and the New England desert, develop into a sweeping prophetic comparison—of the errand then, at the birth of Christianity with the errand now, to bring history itself to an end. In this sense, errand means progress. It denotes the Church's gradual conquest of Satan's wilderness-world for Christ. Significantly, Danforth's exegesis devolves neither on "errand" nor on "wilderness," but as it were beyond these on the relative stature of John the Baptist. The question "What went ye out for to see?" is "determined and concluded," Danforth points out, when Christ describes John as "a prophet . . . and more than a prophet." The Baptist, that is, resembles and supersedes his predecessors; his role as exemplum is at once recapitulative and prospective.

---

3. Samuel Danforth, *A Brief Recognition of New England's Errand into the Wilderness*, in *The Wall and the Garden: Selected Massachusetts Election Sermons*, ed. A. William Plumstead (Minneapolis, 1968), p. 59.

John was the Christ's herald sent immediately before his face to proclaim his coming and kingdom and prepare the people for the reception of him. . . . John was greater than any of the prophets that
were before him, not in respect of his personal graces and virtues (for
who shall persuade us that he excelled Abraham in the grace of faith
. . . or Moses in meekness . . . or David in faithfulness . . . or Solomon
in wisdom . . . ?), but in respect of the manner of his dispensation. All
the prophets foretold Christ's coming, his sufferings and glory, but
the Baptist was the harbinger and forerunner. . . . All the prophets
saw Christ afar off, but the Baptist saw him present, baptized him,
and applied the types to him personally. . . . "But he that is least in
the kingdom of heaven is greater than John" (Matt. 11.11; Luke 7.28).
The least prophet in the kingdom of heaven, i.e., the least minister
of the Gospel since Christ's ascension, is greater than John; not in
respect of the measure of his personal gifts nor in respect of the manner of his calling, but in respect of the . . . degree of the revelation of
Christ, which is far more clear and full . . . than in the day when
John the Baptist arose like a bright and burning light . . . proclaiming
the coming and kingdom of the Messiah (which had oft been promised
and long expected).4

All the prophets saw Christ. Who could excel Abraham or Moses?—this
is history seen in the eye of eternity. All the faithful, Danforth is saying,
are one in Christ; our errand here in New England is that of any other
saint, or group of saints; our wilderness no different essentially from that
of Moses or John the Baptist. And yet the passage makes the difference
abundantly clear. Sacred history unfolds in a series of stages or *dispen-
sations*, each with its own (increasingly greater) degree of revelation.
Hence the insistent temporality of the rhetoric: *prepare, foretold, herald,
harbinger, forerunner,* and summarily *types*. Finally, Danforth insists,
there are crucial discriminations to be made. All of the Old Testament is
an errand to the New; and all of history after the Incarnation, an errand
to Christ's Second Coming. It leads from promise to fulfillment: from
Moses to John the Baptist to Samuel Danforth; from the Old World to
the New; from Israel in Canaan to New Israel in America; from Adam to
Christ to the Second Adam of the Apocalypse. The wilderness that Danforth invokes is "typical" of New England's situation above all in that it
reveals the dual nature of the errand as prophecy. In fulfilling the type,
New England becomes itself a harbinger of things to come. Like John the
Baptist, though with a brighter, fuller degree of revelation, the Puritan
colony is a light proclaiming the latter-day coming of the Messiah, a herald

---

4. Danforth, *Brief Recognition,* pp. 60, 62.

sent to prepare the world to receive His often-promised, long-expected Kingdom.

For Danforth, in short, *errand* has the ambiguity of the *figura*. It unites allegory and chronicle in the framework of the work of redemption. And in doing so, it redefines the meaning not only of *errand* but of every term in *New England's Errand into the Wilderness*. The new-ness of New England becomes both literal and eschatological, and (in what was surely the most far-reaching of these rhetorical effects) the American wilderness takes on the double significance of secular and sacred place. If for the individual believer it remained part of the wilderness of the world, for "God's peculiar people" it was a territory endowed with special symbolic import, like the wilderness through which the Israelites passed to the promised land. In one sense it was historical, in another sense prophetic; and as Nicholas Noyes explained, in a sermon on the errand more than three decades after Danforth's, "*Prophesie is Historie antedated*; and *Historie is Postdated Prophesie*: the same thing is told in both."[5] For these New England Jeremiahs, and all their second- and third-generation colleagues, the ambiguity confirmed the founders' design. They dwelt on it, dissected and elaborated upon it, because they believed it opened into a triumphant assertion of corporate destiny, migration and pilgrimage entwined in the progress of New England's holy commonwealth.

From that figural vantage point Danforth condemns the colonists' shortcomings and justifies their afflictions. And with that vision of the future before him, he assures them of success—not, he stresses, because of their efforts, but God's: "the great Physician of Israel hath undertaken the cure . . . he will provide . . . we have the promise."[6] Danforth's strategy is characteristic of the American jeremiad throughout the seventeenth century: first, a precedent from scripture that sets out the communal norms; then, a series of condemnations that detail the actual state of the community (while at the same time insinuating the covenantal promises that ensure success);[7] and finally, a prophetic vision that unveils the promises,

---

5. Nicholas Noyes, *New England's Duty* (Boston, 1698), p. 43.

6. Danforth, *Brief Recognition*, pp. 75–77.

7. One illustration must suffice (*Brief Recognition*, pp. 64–65). Speaking of how "we have . . . in a great measure forgotten our errand into the wilderness," Danforth calls to mind the precedent of the biblical exodus:

> The Lord foreseeing the defection of Israel after Moses his death, commands him to write that prophetical song recorded in Deuteronomy 32 as a testimony against them, wherein the chief remedy which he prescribes for the prevention and healing of their apostasy is their calling to remembrance God's great and signal love in manifesting himself to them in the wilderness, in conducting them safely and mercifully, and giving them possession of their promised inheritance (ver. 7–14). And when Israel was apostatized and fallen, the Lord, to convince them of their ingratitude and folly, brings to their remembrance his deliverance of them out of Egypt, his leading

announces the good things to come, and explains away the gap between fact and ideal. Perry Miller seems to have understood this form as a triptych, a static three-part configuration in which the center-piece—considered merely as lament—conveys the meaning of the whole. So interpreted, the New England sermons embody a cyclical view of history: the futile, recurrent rise and fall of nations that sustained the traditional European jeremiad. But the rhetoric itself suggests something different. It posits a movement from promise to experience—from the ideal of community to the facts of community life—and thence forward, with prophetic assurance, toward a resolution that incorporates both fact and ideal. The dynamic of the errand, that is, involves a use of ambiguity which is not divisive but progressive—or more accurately, which is progressive because it denies divisiveness, and which is therefore impervious to the reversals of history, since the very meaning of progress is inherent in the rhetoric itself.

This errand into ambiguity, if I may call it so, speaks directly to the contrast Miller posited between rhetoric and history. What Miller meant by history was the course of events—the "process of Americanization"— that led to the theocracy's decline; by rhetoric, he meant the lament— "unremitting and never successful"—over a failed enterprise. Thus while he stressed the affirmative "psychology" of the Puritan sermons, he interpreted the sermons themselves as certain psychologists interpret wish-fulfillment dreams. What counts is not the happy ending but the conflicts that prompted the need for fantasy in the first place. The conflicts are "real," the happy ending transparently a means to something else—avoidance, compensation, substitute gratification, or simply self-delusion. Now the fact of the theocracy's decline is incontrovertible. But we need not interpret it as Miller does. His "Errand into the Wilderness" is a hail and farewell to the Puritan vision. Danforth's *Errand into the Wilderness* attests to the orthodoxy's refusal to abandon the vision, and the fact is that the vision survived—from colony to province, and from province to

them through the wilderness for the space of forty years, and not only giving them possession of their enemies' land but also raising up even of their own sons, prophets . . . all which were great and obliging mercies.

As every member of Danforth's audience knew, Moses' "prophetical song" was traditionally interpreted as an address to the spiritual Israel, the true believers who were to have the "promised inheritance" of Christ—meaning not only the biblical Jesus, but also the Son of Righteousness who would literally transform the world's wilderness into the millennial kingdom. It is in this framework, both spiritual and historical, that Danforth recalls God's "great and obliging mercies" in the past. In this framework, too, he proceeds from Moses' "prophetical song" to discuss "our Savior's dialogism with his hearers" in the wilderness, and thence to the colonists' errand "over the vast ocean into this waste and howling wilderness." The story of all three errands is one of apostasy and backsliding, but the progression itself, from one errand to the next, attests to the process of fulfillment. Moses' rebuke is ultimately a "remedy" for "healing," Christ's "admonition" above all a "direction how to recover," and Danforth's lament, finally, an affirmation of what the emigrant fathers came into the American wilderness to see.

nation. The fact is, furthermore, that it survived through a mode of ambiguity which denied the contradiction between history and rhetoric—or rather translated this into a discrepancy between appearance and promise that nourished the imagination, and so continued to provide a source of social cohesion and continuity. In fact, that is, the New England orthodoxy succeeded, precisely through their commitment to the Puritan ideal, in transmitting a myth that remained central to the culture long after the theocracy had faded and New England itself had lost its national influence.

So perceived, the evidence presents us with a different perspective on the relation between rhetoric and history. Even if we grant that the jeremiads were a form of wish-fulfillment—even if we agree with Miller that their rhetoric served as a "guise" for "real" conflicts—we need not see them in opposition to the course of events. Suppose, for example, that the wish-fulfillment is profoundly relevant to those conflicts. What if it actually offers a resolution of sorts, a realistic way to deal with crisis and change, and so becomes a source of revitalization? Miller likened the second-generation Puritans to a husband who, while on an errand for his wife, discovers that his wife has forgotten all about her request—or worse still, denies she ever made a request at all. The analogy is accurate so far as it goes. But suppose the husband simply refuses to acknowledge that as fact. What if he persuades himself, in compensation for what everyone else sees as a mistake, that in fact his errand has nothing to do with his wife—and that in fact *he is correct?* What if, moreover, he does not harbor that "fantasy" in secret, like Walter Mitty, but proudly declares it to others, and for sound, pragmatic reasons—reasons that conform to the "real" course of events—*persuades them too?*

What I would suggest is that "the process of Americanization" began in Massachusetts not with the decline of Puritanism but with the Great Migration, and that the concept of errand, accordingly, as a prime expression of the Puritan venture, played a significant role in the development of what was to become modern middle-class American culture. I hope that in suggesting this I do not seem to be overstraining the worn links between Puritanism and the rise of capitalism. My point is simply that certain elements in Puritanism lent themselves powerfully to that conjunction, and precisely those elements came to the fore when the Bay emigrants severed their ties with the feudal forms of Old England and set up a relatively fluid society on the American strand—a society that devalued aristocracy, denounced beggary, and opened up political, educational, and commercial opportunities to a relatively broad spectrum of the population.

The argument has been demonstrated elsewhere so persuasively as hardly to need comment here. Tocqueville's well-known views on this matter are representative of a host of others, from Adam Smith through Engels and

Huizinga, down to a variety of social and economic historians in our own time:

> It was in the states of New England, that the two or three main principles now forming the basic social theory of the United States were combined. . . . [These] colonies as they came to birth seemed destined to let freedom grow, not the aristocratic freedom of their motherland, but a middle-class and democratic freedom of which the world's history had not previously provided a complete example. . . . In England the nucleus of the Puritan movement continued to be in the middle classes, and it was from those classes that most of the emigrants sprang. The population of New England grew fast, and while in their homeland men were despotically divided by class hierarchies, the colony came more and more to present the novel phenomenon of a society homogeneous in all its parts. . . . [Thus] the whole destiny of America [is] contained in the first Puritan who landed on these shores, as that of the whole human race in the first man.[8]

Tocqueville was making the point by hyperbole, but the point itself is valid enough to suggest a fundamental truth about our culture. The economists Douglass North and Robert Thomas have shown that "the colonization of [Anglo-]America was a direct outgrowth of . . . the decline of feudalism." The philosopher Ralph Barton Perry has argued the "affinity" of "Puritan individualism . . . with laissez-faire capitalism." The historian Robert Brown has pointed out that "property was [so] easily acquired" in New England that "the great majority of men could easily meet the requirements" for political franchise.[9]

These and many similar quantitative differences between old and New England are symptomatic, I believe, of a sweeping qualitative distinction between America and all other modern countries. In the Old World (and also in Latin America and Canada) capitalism was an economic system that developed dialectically, through conflict with earlier and persistent ways of life and belief. New England bypassed the conflict. It evolved from its own beginnings, as it were, into a middle-class culture. I should per-

---

8. Alexis de Tocqueville, *Democracy in America*, tr. George Lawrence, ed. J. P. Mayer (Garden City, N. Y., 1969), pp. 34–39, 56, 279.

9. Douglass C. North and Robert Paul Thomas, eds., *The Growth of the American Economy* (New York, 1968), p. 5; Ralph Barton Perry, *Puritanism and Democracy* (New York, 1944), p. 297; Robert E. Brown, *Middle-Class Democracy and the Revolution in Massachusetts, 1691–1780* (Ithaca, N.Y., 1955), p. 82. I do not, of course, mean to blur the stages of economic growth, from agrarian economy through urbanization, the "transportation revolution," credit economy, industrialization, corporate enterprise, and expansionist finance. My assumption is that every one of those stages (including the War of Independence) was more or less organic—that in effect the culture was committed from the start to what social scientists have termed the process of modernization.

haps place special emphasis here on the term *evolved*. The emigrant leaders did not give up their class prerogatives when they landed at Massachusetts Bay, but the forms they instituted tended to erode traditional forms of deference. They restricted opportunity in commerce and property ownership, but social power in the colony increasingly shifted to the commercial and property-owning classes. In all fundamental ideological aspects, New England was from the start a culture committed to the modern world—its emergent free enterprise economy buttressed by the decline of European feudalism, unhampered by lingering traditions of peasantry, aristocracy and crown, sustained by the prospects of personal advancement and the availability of land, and consecrated by a vision of divinely ordained progress.

I think it can be said without hyperbole that the process of consecration begins with the Great Migration of 1630. In his *Model of Christian Charity*, John Winthrop advocated a doctrine of vocational calling which (as Michael Walzer and others have shown) effectually undermined feudal hierarchy by its appeal to self-discipline and self-sufficiency. And several weeks before, as the *Arbella* passengers were about to embark from Southampton pier, John Cotton defended *God's Promise to His Plantations* through analogies to commerce for "gainesake":

> *Daily bread may be sought from farre.* Yea our Saviour approveth travaile for Merchants, when hee compareth a Christian to a Merchantman seeking pearles. . . . Nature teacheth Bees . . . when as the hive is too full . . . [to] seeke abroad for new dwellings: So when the hive of the Common wealth is so full, that Tradesmen cannot live one by another, but eate up one another, in this case it is lawfull to remove. . . . God alloweth a man to remove, when he may employ his Talents and gifts better elsewhere, especially when where he is, he is not bound by any speciall engagement. Thus God sent *Ioseph* before to preserve the Church: *Iosephs* wisdome and spirit was not fit for a shepheard, but for a Counsellour of State.[10]

Cotton's analogies, like Winthrop's concept of vocation, bespeak a moment of cultural transition: they reflect earlier ideals as well as foreshadowing later developments. But in both cases the direction is unmistakable. All of Cotton's examples, from nature and the Bible, are geared toward sanctifying an errand of entrepreneurs whose aim is re-

---

10. John Cotton, *God's Promise to His Plantations* (1630), in *Old South Leaflets* (Boston [1874–76]), vol. III, no, 53, p. 5 (see also p. 14). I mention this sermon and Winthrop's partly because they define the prophetic as well as theocratic aims of the *Arbella* migration; in an important sense, they may be said to be the first of a state-of-the-errand genre that extends past the seventeenth century through the Revolution and the Civil War.

ligion, or *mutatis mutandis* legalizing an errand of saints whose aim is entrepreneurial.

In this respect, as in others, a direct line may be traced from the first emigrants to the latter-day Jeremiahs. It runs from the *Arbella* sermons by Cotton and Winthrop to (say) Cotton Mather's *Magnalia Christi Americana*—where Joseph appears as a model for the rags-to-riches errand of several famous New Englanders—and it includes, at its center, *A Brief Recognition of New England's Errand into the Wilderness.* "John preached in the wilderness, which was no fit place for silken and soft raiment," Danforth observes, because the Baptist's "work was to prepare a people for the Lord." How could he do so amidst the "superfluous ornaments," the "delicate and costly apparel [of] . . . princes' courts"? This is neither a plea for the sanctity of poverty nor a summons to some ascetic retreat from the world. Nor is it merely a denunciation of the rich, in the manner of the Old Testament prophets. In effect, Danforth is urging upon New Israel the middle way of the Protestant ethic, reinforcing Cotton's analogies and Winthrop's model of vocation by reminding his audience that the prophecies they inherited, their promised future, entailed "the values of piety, frugality, and diligence in one's worldly calling." Economically as well as figurally, it was their mission to leave a "soft" Old World order, with its "courtly pomp and decay," for a "purer" kind of society, one that would provide them with the proper means for both "respectable competence in this world and eternal salvation in the world to come."[11]

Thanks largely to Perry Miller, Danforth's sermon has become a *locus classicus* for defining the American jeremiad. So it should be, I think, but not in the terms Miller suggests. As I have argued elsewhere, the American Puritan jeremiad was a mode of celebration rather than lament.[12] In deliberate opposition to the traditional mode, it set out to transform threat into promise, and the nature of the Puritan errand helps explain the transformation. The European jeremiad developed within a static hierarchical order; the lessons it taught, about historical recurrence and the vanity of human wishes, amounted to a massive ritual reinforcement of tradition. Its function was to make social practice conform to a completed and perfected social ideal. The American Puritan jeremiad was the ritual of a culture on an errand—which is to say, a culture based on a faith in process. Substituting teleology for hierarchy, it discarded the Old World ideal of stasis for a New World vision of the future. Its function was to create a climate of anxiety that helped release the restless "progressivist" energies required for the success of the venture. The European jeremiad also thrived

---

11. Danforth, *Brief Recognition*, pp. 59, 72; John G. Cawelti, *Apostles of the Self-Made Man* (Chicago, 1965), p. 4.
12. "Horologicals to Chronometricals: The Rhetoric of the Jeremiad," *Literary Monographs*, vol. III, ed. Eric Rothstein (Madison, Wis., 1970), p. 6, and passim.

on anxiety, of course. Like all "traditionalist" forms of ritual, it used fear and trembling to teach acceptance of fixed social norms. But the American Puritan jeremiad went much further. It made anxiety its end as well as its means. Crisis was the social norm it sought to inculcate. The very concept of errand, after all, implied a state of *un*fulfillment. The future, though divinely assured, was never quite there, and New England's Jeremiahs helped provide the sense of insecurity that would ensure the outcome. Denouncing or affirming, their vision fed on the distance between promise and fact.

I need hardly say that they were not revelling in crisis for its own sake. Anxiety was one result of the ritual, its day-by-day aspect. The other aspect, equally crucial to the concept of errand, was direction and purpose. Together, these two elements define the ritual import of the jeremiad: to sustain process by imposing control, and to justify control by presenting a certain form of process as the only road to the future kingdom. The emphasis on control is not difficult to explain. As Christopher Hill points out, in arguing the connection between Cromwell's revolution and the growth of the English middle class, one "important social function of Puritanism" was to harness "the turbulent force of individualism." That force was nowhere more turbulently manifest than in Puritan New England, a colony of radical dissenters—militant, apocalyptic, "irrepressibly particularistic and anti-authoritarian." In 1630, Edmund Morgan notes, "emigration offered a substitute for revolution."[13] But the hazards of settlement required the colonial leaders to seek a more permanent substitute. They found it, after a precarious beginning, in the New England Way of church-state, a sort of institutionalized migration, consciously modelled on the pattern of exodus. And they sought to enforce their Way through what proved to be perhaps their most durable creation, the jeremiadic ritual of the errand.

Danforth's sermon testifies eloquently to its distinctive qualities. In contrast to traditional tribal rituals, the American Puritan jeremiad evokes the mythic past not merely to elicit imitation but above all to demand progress. The fathers, says Danforth, were mighty men, as were Moses, Elijah, and John the Baptist—unexcelled in their piety and fervor—but the errand they began leads us toward a *higher, brighter dispensation*. Precisely because of their greatness, we have a sacred duty to go beyond them. To venerate and emulate is to supersede; in God's New Canaan all of life is a passage to something better. This outlook obviously derives from

---

13. Christopher Hill, *The Century of Revolution, 1603–1714* (Edinburgh, 1961), p. 97; Emery Battis, *Saints and Sectaries: Ann Hutchinson and the Antinomian Controversy in the Massachusetts Bay Colony* (Chapel Hill, N.C., 1962), p. 255; Edmund S. Morgan, "The Revolutionary Era as an Age of Politics," in *The Role of Ideology in the American Revolution*, ed. John R. Howe, Jr. (New York, 1970), p. 11.

Protestant ritual. One need only think of Bunyan's Pilgrim, whose life-long progress is shaped by a series of crises that point him forever forward toward a single preordained goal. But Pilgrim's crises, like those of every Reformed Christian, are personal and eschatological; they involve the con-flict between the "temptations" of society and the demands of faith, be-tween temporal commitments and "last things." More often than not, therefore, Pilgrim finds himself defying social authority. The society to which he conforms instead is the community of the elect, wherever they happen to be, journeying from a wicked world to their heavenly home. And the journey, moreover, is essentially retrospective—an *imitatio Christi*, patterned after the completed and perfected progress of the biblical Jesus. Pilgrim advances with his eyes fixed on the past. The New England Puri-tans fixed their gaze on the future. Christ's victory over Satan, they stressed, was itself a shadow or type of His greater victory to come, when He would usher in the millennium; and accordingly they grounded their covenant in prophecies still to be fulfilled. Even as they strove individually to imi-tate Christ, they absorbed the personal errand to Christ into a social errand toward the Second Coming. What for European Protestants was an ide-ational structure—the *New World* of regeneration, the *promised land* of heaven, the *wilderness* of temptation, the *garden* of the spirit—was for Danforth and his colleagues a political reality, the civic, religious, and economic structures of a covenanted New World society.

The contrast has far-reaching implications. Both Bunyan's Pilgrim and the New England saint are on an errand—constantly "betwixt and be-tween," forever at the brink of some momentous decision—but as rituals their errands tend in opposite directions. The ritual Bunyan adopts leads Pilgrim into what anthropologists call a "liminal state," a sort of cultural no-man's-land, where all social norms may be challenged.[14] And given the Calvinist tenet that salvation is a life-long enterprise, it is an errand fraught with all the religious and economic dangers of unfettered indi-vidualism: the excesses both of antinomianism and of self-interest. The American Puritan jeremiads seek (in effect) to prevent these excesses by turning liminality itself into a mode of socialization. Their errand en-tails a ritual that obviates the traditional distinction between preparation for salvation and social conformity—a carefully regulated process where the fear for one's soul is a function of historical progress, moral discipline a means to social success, and success a matter of constant anxiety about the future. And more than that. The ritual of errand enforces an identity that is at once transitional and representative; it identifies the community's "true fathers" not by their English background but by their exodus from Europe to the American strand; it establishes a mode of consensus by call-

14. Victor Turner, *The Forest of Symbols* (Ithaca, N.Y., 1967), pp. 93ff.

ing and enterprise rather than by (say) national tradition or genealogy; and it implies a form of community without geographical boundaries, since the wilderness is by definition unbounded, the *terra profana* "out there" yet to be conquered, step by inevitable step, by the advancing armies of Christ.

In all this, as it turned out, the Puritan concept of errand was well suited to the process of Americanization. I am speaking, of course, of implication and effect. According to Huizinga, "the factors that have dominated European history are almost absent from American history. . . . No stumps from a feudal forest remained, still rooted everywhere in the soil, as in Europe."[15] Again, as in Tocqueville's case, the formulation seems to me too strong. In one sense, the Massachusetts Bay theocracy was a stump transplanted from a feudal forest. In many of its specific attributes, the Puritan state was obviously transitional, the substance of a new social order encased in squirearchical and quasi-biblical forms. By 1670, when Danforth delivered his election-day address, the New England Jeremiahs were already on the defensive. The aspiring merchant class and the land-holding "lay brethren of the congregation" were challenging clerical control with increasing success—or better, increasingly assuming control in face of the inadequacy of theocratic forms. In 1669, a Third Church of Boston was formed by a group of tradesmen who dissented from the orthodox First Church. Shortly after this Richard Bellingham, the sternest of the Old Guard magistrates that followed John Winthrop to the post of governor, expressed his fear of "sudden tumult," and his council warned against "an invasion of the rights, liberties, and privileges of churches."[16] Only twenty of the fifty deputies in the General Court of 1669 were reelected in 1670. The issues of the half-way covenant threatened a widespread generational crisis. Whether or not all this indicated a decline in piety, as Danforth and his colleagues wailed, the colonists were forcing the institutions they lived under to comply openly with the political and economic realities of their New World society.

In this sense, there is some justice in Perry Miller's ironic image of the Old Guard "backing into modernity," at the end of the seventeenth century, in "crablike progress" from an "aristocratic" order to "a middle-class empirical enterprising society."[17] But his irony tends to obscure the fact that the New England Way was above all (to recall Huizinga's image) a plant of a modern new world. The halfway covenant which served to

15. Johan Huizinga, *America*, trans. Robert H. Rowen (New York, 1972), pp. 8–9. See also Michael Zuckerman, "The Fabrication of Identity in Early America," *William and Mary Quarterly*, XXIV (1977), 184–185, 194, 206, 210.

16. Larzer Ziff, *Puritanism in America: New Culture in a New World* (New York, 1973), p. 189.

17. Perry Miller, *The New England Mind: From Colony to Province* (Boston, 1961), p. 442.

secularize the colony was not a departure from but (as I have argued elsewhere)[18] an extension of theocratic ideals. The freemen who elected a new government in defiance of Governor Bellingham in 1670 were covenanted members of the visible churches of Massachusetts. The Third Church was built on land donated for that purpose by the widow of John Norton, a pillar of the first generation orthodoxy; among its first members was Sarah Cotton Mather, the widow of John Cotton and Richard Mather; and these widows were not betraying the "grand design" their husbands had sought to realize. Despite their allegiance to theocracy, the emigrant Puritans were part of the movement toward the future. Their rhetoric and vision facilitated the process of colonial growth. And in sustaining that rhetoric and vision, the latter-day Jeremiahs forged what was in effect a powerful vehicle of middle-class ideology: a ritual of progress through consensus, a system of sacred-secular symbols for a laissez-faire creed, a "civil" or "political" religion for a people chosen to spring fully formed into the modern world—America, the first-begotten daughter of democratic capitalism, the only country that developed, from the seventeenth through the nineteenth centuries, into a wholly middle-class culture.

---

18. "Horologicals to Chronometricals," pp. 27ff.

Apocalyptic History and the American Epic: Cotton Mather and Joel Barlow

WALTER SUTTON

Since the virtual disappearance of the verse epic as a distinct genre during the eighteenth century, the meaning of the word *epic* has become both broadened and confused. As early as 1742, in his preface to *Joseph Andrews*, Henry Fielding expanded the term to include extended narratives, both serious and comic, in verse or prose. Yet, over the intervening years there has been a continuing effort to write long poems and novels designed to match the traditional epic in scope and function. Though not so conventional or stylistically elevated as their precursors, these works are like them in their ambitiousness, their focus upon the life of a people or a society rather than merely of an individual, their concern for its aspirations and values, and their assumption of an encompassing historical process.[1] The writing of history itself can be and often is an expression of the same epic impulse. Such works—whether of verse, fiction, or history— have significant correspondences, intentional or not, with the purposes and the conventions of the traditional epic.

In America the earliest New England settlers brought with them a deep religious commitment and sense of epic mission. Their heroic purpose was later reinforced throughout the country by the revolutionary cause of nationhood, the challenges of expansion, and the struggle with nature on a vast scale in the process of peopling a continent. In American literature, the epic impulse has had from its beginnings a powerful deterministic strain deriving from both Puritan and Enlightenment conceptions of history as the working out, from one point of view, of God's providential design and, from the other, of an irresistible and inevitable progress toward a perfect democratic society. So compelling were these early teleological doctrines that they fostered apocalyptic ideas of history that have persisted—with reinforcements, qualifications, and reactions—into the twentieth century.

These contrasting Puritan and Enlightenment views are most fully

---

1. Ezra Pound's thumbnail definition of an epic as "a poem including history" is helpful though too limited; see *ABC of Reading* (1934; rpt. New York, 1960), p. 46.

represented in early American literature by the *Magnalia Christi Americana* (1702) of Cotton Mather and *The Columbiad* (1807), Joel Barlow's epic tribute to the new republic. Both are ambitious works in which the authors assume the dual social roles of historian and prophet. Though both are flawed in ways that present obstacles to the modern reader, they are important reflections of their authors' sense of history and are forerunners of more successful works in the American epic tradition.

The general outlook of the New England Puritans is familiar. Thinking of themselves as a tribe fleeing the corruption of the old world and, like the Israelites, chosen to establish a purified theocracy in the wilderness, they found evidence of God's support in His "providences" and from the beginning were eager to read symbolic expressions of the divine will in natural events. The cosmic plan also included, as its grand climax, the awful prospect of the end of the world at any time, at God's pleasure, the return of the Son of God, the resurrection of the dead, and the Last Judgment (as vividly pictured in Michael Wigglesworth's *Day of Doom* [1662]). For the millenarians among the Puritans, the return of Christ was to be accompanied by a world conflagration and the inauguration of His thousand-year reign on earth as prophesied in the book of Revelation.

God's providences could indicate displeasure as well as approval. Because His ways are beyond understanding, the Puritans harbored understandable doubts and misgivings about the divine will and about their own worthiness as chosen instruments. As the new settlements flourished and multiplied, the doubts grew deeper. Both William Bradford, who lamented the breaking off of new communities from the Plymouth colony as a result of prosperity, and Cotton Mather, who was obsessed by the general falling off into worldliness and sin, feared for the failure of the "errand into the wilderness." Could Boston (Lost-town) really be a type of the New Jerusalem? Such forebodings evidence an underlying strain of pessimism in the providential view of history.

Yet in more confident moods the Puritans took sinful pride in the magnitude of their New World venture. They had indeed weathered a fearful passage over the sea and endured the dangers of a savage land to found the city of God. Their wanderings and perils reminded them of such biblical and epic heroes as Moses, Odysseus, and Aeneas. Their strivings to defend and propagate the faith, their struggles with heretics and witches, and their wars with the Indians moved them to record the deeds of their religious and secular heroes.

Although the effort to write a truly national epic was to await the birth of the nation, it was anticipated on a regional scale by Cotton Mather's ambitious historical miscellany, *Magnalia Christi Americana: or the Ecclesiastical History of New-England from Its First Planting in the Year*

1620, Unto the Year of Our Lord 1698.[2] Its substantial mass of materials was parceled into seven books consisting of "Antiquities," including the discoveries of America and the history of New England; the lives of the governors; the lives of "many Divines"; the history of Harvard College and the lives of some of its graduates; "Acts and Monuments," an account of the organization and discipline of the churches, together with historical remarks on the synods; "Thaumaturgus," or "many Illustrious Discoveries and Demonstrations of the Divine Providence," concluding with the credulous account of witchcraft in the "Wonders of the Invisible World"; and the "Wars of the Lord" with adversaries including Antinomians, Quakers, impostors pretending to be ministers, and "Indian Salvages." Somewhat more than half of the bulk of the book (1,308 pages in the edition of 1852–1853) is given over to the biographies of the spiritual leaders, and of these pages a remarkable portion (about a seventh) is devoted to the lives of the author's grandfather, John Cotton, and of other Mathers, not including his father, Increase, of whom he was to write a separate biography.

In its general effect of discontinuity, except within the individual books, and in its multiplicity of "heroes" (the "saints"), the *Magnalia* might well seem closer to a fragmented modern epic than to classical models. But it does have an underlying mythos or plot in the form of the Christian cosmic drama of which the history of New England is regarded as a crucial part.

Introducing himself as a religious historian, Mather is impressed by the heroic nature of his subject, God's great works in New England, accomplished through the efforts of His servants. He repeatedly injects epic as well as other classical and biblical allusions and parallels, most conspicuously in the flourish with which he opens his general introduction, echoing Virgil while at the same time invoking the inspiration of his Puritan God: "I WRITE the *Wonders* of the CHRISTIAN RELIGION, flying from the Depravations of *Europe*, to the *American Strand*: and, assisted by the Holy Author of that *Religion*, I do, with all Conscience of Truth, required therein by Him, who is the *Truth* it self [*sic*], Report the *Wonderful Displays* of His Infinite Power, Wisdom, Goodness, and Faithfulness, wherewith His Divine Providence hath *Irradiated* an *Indian Wilderness*" (*Magnalia* [JHL], p. 89).

More directly, Mather evokes the opening of the *Aeneid* in the title

---

2. Ed. Thomas Robbins, 2 vols. (Hartford, Conn., 1853, 1855). Unless otherwise indicated, all further references by volume and page are to this edition. The recently published first volume of the John Harvard Library edition now makes the first two books of the *Magnalia* available in the first modern scholarly edition: *Magnalia Christi Americana. Books I and II*, ed. Kenneth B. Murdock, with Elizabeth W. Miller (Cambridge, Mass., 1977). Hereafter cited as *Magnalia* (JHL).

Arma Virosque Cano[3] of the sixth and final chapter of his seventh book ("of the Wars of the Lord"), which is devoted to an account of conflicts with the Indians. The special attraction of Virgil's work lies both in the poem as an epic of Rome's founding and destiny and in the filial piety of Aeneas, who carried his household gods with him through his wanderings from Troy to the new nation he was to found. So too the Puritans were concerned with the nurture of their fathers' faith, which they had brought to America in a hazardous journey and with the destiny of the theocracy (John Winthrop's "city on a hill") they hoped to establish in the new land.

Although such conventions reveal Mather's aspirations to epic, his most comfortable vehicle for the writing of history was the "life," or exemplary biography. Next to the lives, which occupy so much space in the *Magnalia*, the accounts of general history are skimpy and undeveloped. Except for the recurrent theme of "declension" from the heroic past of the first generation of settlers, there is little analysis of historical movement in the sequence of ideas and events. It is in the context of the biographies that Mather develops much of his most substantial historical information— and the most revealing of his personally interested treatment of his subjects.[4] For most of the lives, Mather's most important models were John Foxe's *Book of Martyrs* and the lives of the "Incomparable *Plutarch*" (*Magnalia* [JHL], pp. 96, 277). Mather drew upon the actual title of Foxe's work, *Actes and Monuments of these Latter Perilous Times Touching Matters of the Church*, for the title of his fifth book.

Mather's idealized portraits of the Puritan "saints" (like John Winthrop and John Eliot) illustrate their Christian virtues. Their lives are imitations of Christ's, just as the Puritan experience in the New World is a reenactment of biblical history, typologically interpreted. The lives also provide examples for emulation by a worldly and backslidden latter generation. Mather's method conforms most closely to the strategy of the jeremiad,[5] which holds up the model of an earlier age while castigating the sins of the present. Such castigation is a staple of the *Magnalia* in Mather's procla-

---

3. Mather's substitution of Virosque ("and of heroes") for Virgil's *virumque* is in keeping with his general effort to magnify his Puritan subjects.

4. Especially noteworthy is the previously published life of Sir William Phips, "*Pietas in Patriam*," appended to Book II, in which Mather gives an account of the witch trials and of his and his father's political involvement with Phips during his governorship, after the conclusion of which (upon Phips's death in England in 1695), the political fortunes of the Mather faction waned, and Cotton Mather's sense of declension intensified (*Magnalia* [JHL], pp. 272–359).

5. The form of the jeremiad and its use by Cotton and Increase Mather have been discussed, especially by Perry Miller, *The New England Mind: From Colony to Province* (Cambridge, Mass., 1953), pp. 27–39, 189–190; Peter Gay, *A Loss of Mastery: Puritan Historians in Colonial America* (Berkeley, 1966), pp. 67–81; and Robert Middlekauff, *The Mathers: Three Generations of Puritan Intellectuals, 1596–1728* (New York, 1971), pp. 113–116, 209–210, 267.

mations of the "decadence" of his time. In his 1698 lecture on the "state of Boston," brought into the history as an appendix to the first book, Mather sees the chief city of the theocracy, which should be "a special exemplar and depository of piety," [6] as a sink of sin, with its drinking and bawdy houses and profaning of the Sabbath. He mourns the passing of the almost forgotten *"Old Race* of our *First Planters,"* points to a great fire that destroyed seventy warehouses as a warning against the *"Vanity* of all *Worldly Possessions,"* and advises the young of impending destruction: "Ah, *my Young Folks,* there are few *First-fruits* paid unto the Lord Jesus Christ among you. From hence it comes to pass, that the consuming Wrath of God is every Day upon you. *New-England* has been like a *Tott'ring House,* the very *Foundations* of it have been shaking: But the house thus over-setting by the *Whirlwinds* of the Wrath of God, hath been like *Job's* House; *It falls upon the Young Men,* and *they are Dead!" (Magnalia* [JHL], pp. 195–196).

Opinions of Mather's achievement in the *Magnalia* embrace extremes of condemnation and praise. Most negatively, Mather has been judged to be a reactionary historian whose work reflects the collapse of the Puritan mission in America and whose style is disfigured by pedantry and obscurantism.[7] Most positively, the *Magnalia* has been lauded as a successful epic which, through the medium of appropriate symbolic imagery, achieves the status of a distinctively American myth and anticipates the romantic American vision of the imaginative realization of the self in the work of such later writers as Emerson and Whitman. In this view, the failure in history of the Puritans' hope for their mission is less important than their symbolic victory, captured by Mather in the *Magnalia*, of projecting the confident vision of a redemptive future, the culmination of God's design, through imagery which effectively serves, for Mather as for Emerson, a compensatory function.[8]

Although there are many strands of continuity between Puritanism and transcendentalism (including the idea of a divine will and the effort to

6. Mather introduces a Latin aphorism as an epigraph for his lecture-essay: *"Urbs Metropolis, ut sit maximae Auctoritatis, constituatur praecipuum pietatis Exemplum & Sacrarium"* ("A metropolitan city, in order to exercise the greatest authority, should become a special exemplar and depository of piety"). One of his several subtitles is "The History of BOSTON, Related and Improved" *(Magnalia* [JHL], p. 180).

7. Most incisively by Peter Gay, who sees the Puritan providential view as preventing Mather (together with Bradford and Edwards) from participating in the quickening of the secular spirit that brought in the age of modern history and learning generally. Gay also believes that Mather's glossing over of the evils of repression and vicious infighting among the saints shows a lack of candor if not outright dishonesty (pp. 25, 60, 73–76, and passim).

8. These points are all made by Sacvan Bercovitch in the course of the argument of *The Puritan Origins of the American Self* (New Haven, 1975), pp. ix, 124–135, 152–186, and passim.

see its symbolic expression in nature), the *Magnalia* presents difficulties for so optimistic an interpretation. It contains not only abundant praise of the spiritual triumphs of the saints but, to an equal degree, fear and doubts for the present and future. Mather is not, on the whole, confident of his redemptive vision, and his doubts cannot be canceled out by his protestations of faith. The prevailing tone of the book is not hopeful. Recurrently, and increasingly in the latter sections of the work, there is anxious concern for the obstacles to success and for evidences of God's displeasure. More important, as far as the overall effect of the *Magnalia* is concerned, the last paragraphs of the final chapter present not a prophecy of redemption but testimony to Mather's still unresolved struggle between confidence and fear: " 'Tis to our Lord Jesus Christ that we offer up our hallelujahs!—But it must, after all, be confessed, that we have had one enemy more pernicious to us than all the rest, and that is 'our own backsliding heart,' which has plunged the whole country into so wonderful a *degeneracy*, that I have sometimes been discouraged from writing the church-history . . ." (II, 579).

His parting words leave the impression not of faith but of an abiding, deep misgiving:

> And since this degeneracy has obtained so much among us, the wrath of Heaven has raised up against us a succession of other *adversaries* and *calamities*, which have cast the land into great confusions; to rescue us from which the jealous kindness of Heaven has not made such *quick descents* as in *former times*. . . .
>
> For which cause I now conclude our church-history, leaving to the churches of New-England, for their admonition, an observation which the renowned Commenius has made upon the famous churches of Bohemia, "that they were nearer to the sanctuary than other churches, by reason of a more pure discipline professed and embraced among them; and therefore, when they came to be depraved with apostasies, the Lord poured out his righteous displeasure upon them, and quickly made them sad examples to the other churches of the Reformation."
>
> God knows what will be the END. (II, 580)

This pessimism might be discounted if one could assume that for Mather the history of his degenerate time is less real than the vision of faith and salvation projected in his work as an imaginative reality. But such facile compensatory relief is not offered by Mather as it is later by Emerson. The author of *Nature* concludes his tract, more happily than Mather his history, with the assurance that the evils of the world, "the sordor and filths of Nature" (and the burdens of history), are "disagreeable appearances" which "the sun shall dry up and wind exhale" once one attains the wisdom and grace conferred by the higher Reason.

For the transcendentalist, both history and evil are phenomenal: they are maya, illusion. But for the Puritan the problem cannot be so easily got around. History cannot be dismissed, for it is the medium through which God works out his grand design. And fallen man, acting out his predestined role, is indeed depraved. As a seeker of salvation, he may reach a pitch of faith and confidence. But always aware of the dangers of sin and corruption within and without, he cannot be sure. Mather gives ample testimony, in the *Magnalia* and especially in his diaries, of his own sense of sin and unworthiness.9 And sin is real; it is an iron bar in the path of salvation. Moreover, God has already decided (but how?), and the destiny of the individual and his society stands indelible in the as yet undisclosed scroll.

Confidence in a redemptive future was held with more assurance, however, by American followers of a newer faith. Carl Becker has written memorably of the transformation of medieval European Christianity as the eighteenth-century *philosophes* "demolished the Heavenly City of St. Augustine only to rebuild it with more up-to-date materials"—and to find their promised land in a utopian future. Although Becker's lucid argument simplifies a complex subject, it accurately represents the historical shift from an otherworldly religious to a secular emphasis in social and historical thought.10 The Enlightenment faith in a perfected democratic society under the sway of reason rather than superstition, unshadowed by the Puritan sense of sin, was shared by many American revolutionaries and deists in the late eighteenth century. It is best represented in the early national period by *The Columbiad* (1807) of Joel Barlow, a revision of his earlier poem *The Vision of Columbus* (1787).

9. Mather's rapid oscillations between despairing self-abasement in the dust of his study floor and lofty assurance of God's special favor are one of the most conspicuous and revealing features of the *Diary of Cotton Mather*, 2 vols. (New York, 1957?). Bercovitch observes that "private anxiety underlies the [mythic] affirmation of national identity." Acknowledging Emerson's and Whitman's indications of their doubts, Bercovitch states that his own primary concern is with the expression of the "mythic self" (pp. 178–184). Yet the transcendentalist views of Emerson and Whitman are basically optimistic, in contrast to Mather's Calvinism; and in consequence the "mythic self" achieves a full expression in their work, as it cannot in Mather's *Magnalia*, where expressions of faith are persistently undercut by doubt.

10. Becker, *The Heavenly City of the Eighteenth-Century Philosophers* (New Haven, 1932), pp. 31, 118. In his lecture-essays, Becker does not take account of the extent to which seventeenth- and eighteenth-century English religious thought contributed to progressive utopianism or to which popular medieval European heresies anticipated Enlightenment ideas of natural law. These subjects have been treated by, respectively, Ernest L. Tuveson, *Millennium and Utopia: A Study in the Background of the Idea of Progress* (New York, 1964), and Norman Cohn, *The Pursuit of the Millennium*, rev. ed. (New York, 1970). Tuveson also discusses the relation of millennial thought to the idea of a redemptive American destiny in *Redeemer Nation: The Idea of America's Millennial Role* (Chicago, 1968). Also, since the completion of this essay, Sacvan Bercovitch has discussed the relation of Edwardsean revivalism to civil millennialism in "The Typology of America's Mission," *American Quarterly*, XXX (1978), 135–155.

Although often dismissed as a pretentious, unsuccessful poem, *The Columbiad* is significant as an ambitious attempt to write the first American national epic. In his efforts to magnify his subject, to provide views of America's past, present, and future, and at the same time to inculcate "republican" (that is, democratic) virtues, Barlow's purpose is like that of Mather, who worked to perform comparable offices for New England Puritan history and morality.

Also like Mather, Barlow echoes the *Aeneid* in his opening lines ("I sing the Mariner who first unfurl'd / An eastern banner o'er the western world"), but he invokes the spirit of freedom as his only muse, rather than the support of God or any supernatural force.[11]

In his preface, Barlow calls his work "a patriotic poem; the subject is national and historical." Without false modesty he observes that his "subject indeed is vast; far superior to any of those on which the celebrated poems of this description have been constructed" (II, 375). Looking back at earlier epics, he condemns the *Iliad* for inspiring young readers with an enthusiasm for military fame, teaching the "pernicious doctrine of the divine right of kings," and approving "military plunder" as an honorable way of acquiring property. The morality of the *Aeneid* is almost as harmful because its real design is to encourage leader worship and give sanction to "military depredation" (II, 378–380).[12]

In contrast, the "real object" of *The Columbiad* (underlying its fictive object of soothing and enlightening the mind of Columbus) is "to inculcate the love of rational liberty, and to discountenance the deleterious passion for violence and war; to show that on the basis of the republican principle all good morals, as well as good government and hopes of permanent peace, must be founded; and to convince the student in political science that the theoretical question of the future advancement of human society, till states as well as individuals arrive at universal civilization, is held in dispute and still unsettled only because we have had too little experience of organised liberty in the government of nations to have well considered its effects" (II, 382).

---

11. The passage reads

Almighty Freedom! Give my venturous song
The force, the charm that to thy voice belong;
Tis thine to shape my course, to light my way,
To nerve my country with the patriot lay,
To teach all men where all their interest lies,
How rulers may be just and nations wise:
Strong in thy strength I bend no suppliant knee,
Invoke no miracle, no Muse but thee.

The Works of Joel Barlow, 2 vols. (Gainesville, Fla., 1970), II, 414. Subsequent references in the text are to this edition.

12. Barlow does not refer to *Paradise Lost*, which, in its didacticism and its device of Adam's instruction by Michael, is the most obvious and direct model for *The Columbiad*.

If one allows for the didacticism, a common feature of epic, Barlow's aim is praiseworthy. His execution is not. Written in ten books, in relentless heroic couplets, the poem portrays the tutelage of Columbus, found despondent in a Spanish prison, oppressed by thoughts of the failure of his voyages, by Hesper, the "guardian genius" of the western continent. Hesper leads Columbus to the "mount of vision, which rises from the western coast of Spain," and summons up a view of the American continents.

Through a series of dioramic scenes, with commentary by Hesper, Columbus is shown first the early exploration and settlement of the Americas, with the cruelty of the Spanish conquistadors, the establishment of the English settlements, the struggle for independence, and then the progress of the arts, science, trade, and government, culminating in a glowing vision of the harmony of mankind under one democratic congress of all nations. Although there is action in the scenes depicted, especially in the descriptions of Revolutionary battles which occupy Books V–VII, it all is distanced and flattened in the unrolling panorama. Apparently because of Barlow's concern for the "unities,"[13] the dramatic conflict of the poem is centered not in the historical events displayed, but in the reactions of Columbus, the father of the New World, as he is moved from melancholy withdrawal to interest, to doubt and questionings, and finally to exaltation as he comprehends the human progress toward perfection in which he has been a prime mover.

The theme of progress is the shaping conception of the poem. Barlow sees the rise of science, democracy, and free institutions as speeding the process, and society as capable of improving its condition. Without the misgivings of a Mather, Barlow sees and Hesper projects a now steady march into a utopian future. The march involves not only mankind's conscious purpose but also (as later for Whitman) evolution, optimistically regarded as nature labors through eons to produce man, "the favorite child of earth" (II, 720), who undergoes growth and development through the advance of his civilizations.[14]

Barlow anticipates a predictable objection to his view of history. Citing the cyclical courses of earlier civilizations, Columbus in Book IX asks Hesper why, since Greece and Rome flourished and fell, America will not

---

13. In his preface, Barlow makes the point that "in no poem are the unities of time, place and action more rigidly observed: the action, in the technical sense of the word, consisting only of what takes place between Columbus and Hesper; which must be supposed to occupy but few hours, and is confined to the prison and the mount of vision" (II, 376). Also, in his earlier introduction to *The Vision of Columbus*, Barlow indicates that he has rejected the idea of "a regular Epic form" in favor of "the single poetical design constantly kept in view" which is effected by the use of the device of the vision (II, 121).

14. The idea of man as a "child of earth," the product of evolution, is in keeping with Barlow's effort to secularize his subject.

also reach a height and then decline. His answer is that modern man, freed of the clogs of king and priests and benefiting from the rise of science and the arts and the dissemination of knowledge and culture through education and the press, can now look forward to a limitless individual and social development (II, 737–747).

Barlow was not able, however, to cope satisfactorily with another problem: the present evil of slavery in a society officially dedicated to the proposition that all men are equal under the universal law of nature.[15] In Book VIII, Atlas, the guardian genius of Africa, protests to Hesper the crimes of the slaveholders against his people, listing, with a repeated "Enslave my tribes!" the contrasts between American principle and practice:

Enslave my tribes! what, half mankind imban,
Then read, expound, enforce the rights of man!
Prove plain and clear how nature's hand of old
Cast all men equal in her human mold!   (II, 691)

Rather than have Hesper, who must remain above the struggle, grapple with this problem in direct response, the author steps into the poem to "address his countrymen on that subject and on the principles of their government" (II, 680). Acknowledging the difficulty of his task, he urges that they "be not masters," since slavery cannot exist without the tyrannical impulse to be a master (II, 696–697).

In the face of the established evil of slavery, which he (unlike Cotton Mather[16]) opposed, Barlow takes recourse finally in rationalization and preachment. Insisting, in keeping with his belief that "Equality of Right is nature's plan," Barlow rationalizes that its presence is the heritage of imported European tyranny and feudalism. He concludes by assuring his countrymen that their "empire" is based on a "rock of right" and that if the "holy Triad" of equality, free election, and the "federal band" is taught to the rising generation, men will come to wonder" (in these codes inured) / How wars were made, how tyrants were endured" (II, 697–699).[17]

Though Barlow's final prescription seems both a pious hope and an evasion, it does reflect his own necessitarian belief that men's characters and motives are determined, not by divine decree, but by their environment and education.[18] The scene then shifts, and Hesper is again edifying

15. In his chapters 10–13, Cohn cites classical and medieval Christian antecedents for this Enlightenment conception.

16. In his diary entry for December 13, 1706–1707, Mather expresses his sense of gratification at the gift of a "very likely *Slave*" from some of the gentlemen of his congregation (*Diary*, I, 579).

17. Barlow's inclusion of "free election" in the triad that displaces the Christian trinity is in deliberate contrast with the Calvinist idea of God's arbitrary election of his saints. Barlow's characteristic animus against tyrants and tyranny is not unlike the millennialist Christian's feeling toward the Antichrist.

18. For a helpful brief discussion of Barlow's necessitarianism, see Leon Howard, *The*

his appreciative pupil with a display of American progress, from its primitive beginnings, in trade, industry, science, education, morality, and the arts.

In Book X, the vision of progress is extended to encompass "the whole earth" (II, 750) as Hesper reveals how human society, like a child, learns to curb its passions. With the growth of reason and enlightened self-interest, war gives way to peaceful commerce, and, in anticipation of Whitman's "Passage to India," internal improvements (for Barlow, canals) bind together the parts of the nation, and internal trade routes unify the world.

New energies animate "epic song" as the Bard need no longer "load his numbers with a tyrant's name" but turns to "nobler objects" suggested by progress in knowledge and virtue (II, 763). Under the broadening influence of reason and universal benevolence, nationalism gives way to brotherhood, and the babel of separate tongues to "one pure language" (unspecified) that facilitates a harmonious international union of states.

Eager to behold the "famed Apocalypse its years unfold," Columbus anticipates a Christian millennial return of the "Prince of Peace, the King of Salem" ("On clouds of fire, with angels at his side") and begs that the visions may rise again. But Hesper takes pains to explain that such spiritual revelation would destroy his senses and that it is enough that his

> delighted mind
> Should trace the temporal actions of thy kind . . .
>
> . . . .
>
> Till all the paths in nature's sapient plan
> Fair in thy presence lead the steps of man,
> And form at last, on earth's extended ball,
> Union of parts and happiness of all.   (II, 774–775)

Book X recapitulates the accomplishment of world progress and closes with the secular apocalypse which is the reward of Columbus's labors. Even though mankind has discarded, with other emblems of fraud and error, the crescent and the cross, the edifice in which the "long rows of reverend sires are seated" is a "sacred mansion," and their convening is imaged in a Miltonic simile which describes the coming together of angels in a divinely ordered council at the "mount of God" (II, 777–779).

It is clear that Barlow is trying, in *The Columbiad* more than in *The Vision*, to secularize his work by calling man a "child of earth," distinguishing between secular and spiritual revelation, and rejecting the

---

Connecticut Wits (Chicago, 1943), pp. 277–285. Other useful sources for Barlow and *The Columbiad* include James Woodress, *A Yankee's Odyssey: The Life of Joel Barlow* (1958: rpt. New York, 1968); R. H. Pearce, *The Continuity of American Poetry* (Princeton, N.J., 1961), pp. 63–69; and A. L. Ford, *Joel Barlow* (New York, 1971).

familiar symbols of religious faiths. Yet such details cannot offset the supernaturalistic effect of the conventions he established in the earlier poem and carried over into *The Columbiad*, most notably the device of an angelic character who functions as the poem's center of consciousness and the author's mouthpiece. To this personage Barlow ascribes, as he must, supernaturalistic powers (II, 751).

The euphoric vision of the future projected in *The Columbiad* also has affinities with the blissful view of salvation expressed by Cotton Mather in his more confident moods. But Barlow gives no hint of Mather's doubt and fear of failure. For Barlow these and like evils belong to the dead past of superstition and error.

As aspirants to epic scope, Mather and Barlow treat ambitious subjects from contrasting apocalyptic viewpoints. Mather believed literally in the second coming of Christ as an impending cataclysmic event.[19] Barlow believed, though less literally than *The Columbiad* indicates, in progress leading toward a more perfect society. The last two of his fifty notes to the poem are devoted to a discussion of the nature and function of history and to a denunciation of the classical idea of the Golden Age as pernicious because it discourages belief in social improvement. In contrast to it, "one of the most operative means of bringing forward our improvements and of making mankind wiser and better than they are, is to convince them that they are capable of becoming so. Without this conviction they may indeed improve slowly, unsteadily and almost imperceptibly, as they have done within the period in which our histories are able to trace them. But this conviction, impressed on the minds of the chiefs and teachers of nations, and inculcated in their schools, would greatly expedite our advancement in public happiness and virtue. Perhaps it would in a great measure insure the world against any future shocks and retrograde steps, such as heretofore it has often experienced" (II, 852).

This more moderate view of progress indicates that Barlow's millennialism is not to be taken literally and that his utopian vision was probably intended, at least in part, as a useful way of "educating" (that is, indoctrinating) his readers. Both his deeply held belief in the influence of environment and training and his disillusionment with the French Revolution after the Reign of Terror began are consistent with the idea of progress toward a perfect society as possible rather than inevitable.[20]

The political history of the past, in Barlow's view, has been largely a

---

19. For discussions of the Chiliasm of Cotton and Increase Mather, see Miller, pp. 185–90, 408, and passim; Middlekauf, pp. 179–187, 332–349.

20. In *The Enlightenment in America* (New York, 1976), Henry F. May comments on millennial deists among the American radicals but does not identify Barlow with them. Rather, he sees Barlow as tending toward an "uncompromising naturalistic determinism" like that of more modern radicals (pp. 231–233, 239–243). In *Redeemer Nation*, Tuveson also distinguishes between Barlow and the millennialists (pp. 66–67).

"history of human errors," as in assuming the existence of a Roman "republic." Moreover, it is not enough that the historian accurately narrate the events of the past. He should also "develop the political and moral tendency of the transactions he details." The historian, no less than the poet, has a social responsibility: "And why should we write at all, if not to benefit mankind? The public mind, as well as the individual mind, receives its propensities; it is equally the creature of habit. Nations are educated, like a single child. They only require a longer time and a greater number of teachers" (II, 848–850).

Thus, like Mather, Barlow emphasizes the moral and pedagogic responsibilities of the historian. Unlike Mather, however, who thinks of New England's Golden Age as coterminous with the experience of the first generation of settlers, Barlow is a progressivist and, for his time, a not uncritical one.

Neither Barlow nor Mather presents a single active hero. Mather's heroes, the saints, have lives that often involve adversity and struggle comparable to those of Odysseus or Aeneas. But unlike these, their "lives" are cut, as Peter Gay has noted,[21] to a standard exemplary pattern, and they observe, as a condition of their sainthood, humility and submission to God's will. Columbus is the designated hero of *The Columbiad*, but his heroic actions belong to a past that is not specifically evoked except in his own melancholy reminiscence at the opening of the poem (I, 415–418). His role is that of a passive observer who reflects and comments on the experiences brought to him through the scenes projected by Hesper. As a reflecting consciousness he may anticipate somewhat the central consciousness that has replaced the active hero in most modern epic poems,[22] but he lacks the creative imagination and awareness of complexity which they reflect.

Also, Barlow and Mather both seem more concerned in their works with the destinies of the societies with which they identify themselves than with individual consciousness (this despite Mather's well-known obsession with the state of his soul). Here Barlow has greater scope than Mather. Although theoretically the Puritan view of history was universal, since God's creation, the expression of His will, was all-embracing, practically it was limited by the extent of the communion of the true church.[23] Because their "nation" was confined to the New England of the faithful, orthodox American Puritans were increasingly in the position of a beleaguered minority, surrounded by red savages and white heretics. In con-

---

21. Gay, p. 64.

22. For a discussion of the problem of the hero in relation to the identity of the poet, see Pearce, pp. 59–136, passim.

23. And limited it was, regardless of whether the church was that of the entire "nation" of New England Puritans or only of the "visible saints." For a discussion of the "Church of the Pure," see Middlekauff, pp. 113–138.

sequence, despite (or because of) their ideological rigor, both their actual and their envisioned culture reflect not only regional but parochial limitation. And this sense of limitation is acknowledged in the pessimistic "God knows" with which Mather concludes the *Magnalia*.

But Barlow, as a revolutionary nationalist, sees the continent as the stage of the unfolding drama of expansion. Unburdened by the Calvinist sense of sin and unworthiness, the prophet of the religion of democracy speaks for an evergrowing "communion" to which the franchise is the only requirement for full acceptance. Neither religious nor political orthodoxy can restrict membership since what the Puritans called "heresies" must be accounted "differences of opinion," necessary grist for the mill of a working representative government.[24] *The Columbiad*, which went to press about the time of the return of the Lewis and Clark expedition in the fall of 1806, introduces the nationalistic theme of manifest destiny that was to capture the popular imagination during the middle years of the century. It also anticipates later literary and political expressions of the one-world theme.[25]

Yet as a "historian," Barlow, like Mather, is limited by a compulsion to bend the facts of experience to fit his preconceptions. Just as Mather, through his selection of details, distorts his "history of Boston," Barlow ignores the practical difficulties of social change. In both men the sense of history is damaged by a natural inclination toward propaganda and preachment.

Although such tendencies run against the grain of most modern historical writing, they have enjoyed an uninterrupted vogue in literature. In poetry, religious and epic prophecy, whether of salvation or of doom, is a long established convention persisting into the nineteenth and twentieth centuries in various forms in the work of Walt Whitman, T. S. Eliot, Hart Crane, Robinson Jeffers, and Ezra Pound. So too the apocalyptic spirit of earlier religious and revolutionary enthusiasts, though alien to the skeptical spirit of science, can be seen as a continuing force in literature as in society. The obsolete machinery of the jeremiad, associated with the gone past of Puritan hellfire and brimstone, still creaks away in the castigations of social decadence by writers of modern epics committed to the values of earlier religious or political or aesthetic golden ages.[26]

24. Theoretically true, although Barlow was subjected to bitter attacks in the press of his native New England for his political and religious radicalism.

25. Whitman was almost certainly influenced by Barlow in such poems as "The Prayer of Columbus," in which Columbus speculates doubtfully on the value of his striving, and "Passage to India," in which the spanning of the continent and the cultural unification of the world are treated as a fulfillment of Columbus's mission ("Ah Genoese, thy dream! thy dream!"). And Hart Crane, after Whitman, introduces the figure of Columbus alone, as a visionary seer in the "Ave Maria" section of *The Bridge*.

26. Also the influential idea that modern man is the victim of a "dissociated' sensi-

Even the utopian vision of the Enlightenment, darkened by twentieth-century catastrophes, can be seen, not only through inverted forms, but more positively in modern fiction and poetry, as in the image of the ideal city maintained by Pound throughout *The Cantos.*

In short, these conventions, intellectually suspect though they may be, have provided literary means of expression of the aspirations and values of every period in which they have been used. Although the explicit moralizing and exhortation of the *Magnalia* and *The Columbiad* must seem tedious and outmoded to a modern reader, they bespeak a concern for values derived from the historical experience of their writers.

The sets of values supported by Mather and Barlow are distinguishable though not fully separable. Mather points repeatedly to the virtues of faith demonstrated through conversion, humility in the form of self-abasement and submission to God's will, and charity. These are supported by reason as an aid to the understanding of the divine will, commitment to work and to good works, self-discipline, a sense of community and civic duty, and deference to an orthodox elite consisting of ministers and magistrates. Although the passive virtues of humility and charity are ordained, the active military virtues of resolution, fortitude, and combativeness are also needed by the soldiers of the Lord in their never-ending war with Satan.[27]

Barlow, a spokesman for mutually supportive "civil rights" and "social virtues" (II, 541), is an apostle of reason, of the intellect as it is nourished and supported by a sense of duty, justice, and liberty. In addition to "all rights that Britons know" (II, 546), Barlow stands for the revolutionary virtues of liberty, equality, and brotherhood as a goal of world-wide progress. Unlike Mather, who loves righteous violence and looks forward to the conflagration that will purge the sinful world, Barlow is a pacifist.

Also unlike the Puritan, who must submit his will to God's, Barlow believes that his virtues can be achieved only through the exercise of the will of the enlightened individual, acting in concert with his fellow citizens in a democratically organized society.

The contrasting otherworldly religious doctrine of Mather, tempered by prudential considerations, and the secular progressive philosophy of Barlow have both contributed in many ways to the continuing definition of values in American society—a process reflected in American literature, especially in writings identified with the epic tradition. Not the least of their legacies is a common persistence in aspiration.

---

bility is in part a not entirely secularized theory of the fall of man. See Frank Kermode, "Dissociation of Sensibility," *Romantic Image* (New York, 1957), pp. 138–161.

27. In his *Diary,* Mather quite often thanks God for the defeats which He has given to Mather's enemies (as in I, 405). He also reports on having preached on "Military Duties" to the Artillery Company of Middlesex (*Diary,* I, 132).

Franklin's Massacre of the Hessians

WALTER BLAIR

A comparison between Benjamin Franklin's "The Sale of the Hessians" and historical facts about the battle which the highly praised satire treated throws light on the author's rhetorical methods.

The Declaration of Independence voiced the dislike of Americans for the British policy which "The Sale" impugned near the end of a long list of injuries, usurpations and oppressions with which the signers charged George III: "He is at this time transporting large Armies of foreign Mercenaries to compleat the works of death, desolation and tyranny, already begun with circumstances of Cruelty & perfidy, scarcely paralleled in the most barbarous ages, and totally unworthy of the Head of a civilized nation." The tone attests to the bitterness caused by news that German mercenaries had been hired to aid his majesty's forces. Within days of the signing of the Declaration, a Connecticut newspaper was making a prediction that the "native ferocity" of the largest contingent of hirelings, the Hessians, "heightened and whetted, by the influence and malice" of the king, "will exhibit such a sense of cruelty, death and devastation, as will fill those of us who survive the carnage, with indignation and horror; attended with poverty and wretchedness."

Franklin helped formulate the Declaration and signed it in July 1776. He had time to read some of many fulminations like the one in the *Norwich Packet* before he left Philadelphia on 26 October and sailed to Paris to serve as a commissioner. He was in Paris, therefore, in March 1777 when news reached him about the military engagement which had taken place in Trenton, N.J., the previous 26 December.

Having been pushed off of Manhattan Island and having avoided annihilation by sheer good luck, the Americans under Washington had retreated through New Jersey across the Delaware River into Pennsylvania. The general himself wrote that unless things took a turn for the better, "I think the game is pretty nearly up."

Scanty intelligence reports had it that between two and three thousand Hessian troops, and no British troops, were holding Trenton. With daring born of desperation, Washington planned to have Continental forces cross the Delaware at McConkey's Ferry above Trenton on Christmas night, march in two columns to opposite ends of the town's main streets and attack the next morning. As the operation proceeded, many things went wrong: the river was high and flowing fast, ice-blocks cluttered it, a strong wind blew; the crossing was hard. Instead of arriving, as planned, before daybreak, the militia men were delayed until eight o'clock in the morning.

But some things worked in the Continentals' favor: Colonel Johannes Rall, the German commander, had swallowed propaganda about American weakness and disbelieved warnings. Rampaging winds, rain, sleet, and snow cut down visibility. The roar of the storm covered the sound of firings at the picket post. So after all, the attack was a surprise; a few shots threw Rall's forces into disorder; Washington's men won a quick victory and were able, with few or no losses, to withdraw across the river with guns and a great many prisoners.

Franklin dated "The Sale of the Hessians," "Rome, February 18, 1777," and a subhead indicated that it was a letter "from the Count de Schaumbergh to the Baron Hohendorf, commanding the Hessian troops in America." "On my return from Naples," the count begins, "I received at Rome your letter of the 27th December of last year. I have learned with unspeakable pleasure the courage our troops exhibited in Trenton, and you cannot imagine my joy on being told that of the 1,950 Hessians engaged in the fight, but 345 escaped."

Unjustified though it was by the men's defeat, the count's patriotic pride in their "courage" seems normal. But the cause for his additional "joy"—that of 1,950 men "but" 345 escaped—alerts attention. So the next jarring note catches a reader's eye—the word *just* in the sentence that follows: "There were just 1,650 men killed. . . ." Inevitably, the question arises: What kind of a man is this who is delighted to learn that few of his countrymen escaped from a battlefield and that a large number were killed?

The question is soon answered: The count, a Hessian, has recruited those troops and is to be paid blood money for every man killed. And Hohendorf's careful report is going to show that instead of the 1,455 men that the British say were killed, 1,605 actually were; therefore instead of the 483,450 florins they claim they owe him, he'll rake in 643,500 florins. As the letter continues, signs mount that the count is a heartless monster. Not only is he sure, says he, that his correspondent will straighten out Lord North's figure on the corpses; he's also sure that he'll see to it that the British quibble that a hundred wounded shouldn't be paid for "as dead" is disposed of according to instructions given in Cassel:

> . . . you will not have tried by human succor to recall the life of the unfortunates whose days could not be lengthened but by the loss of a leg or an arm. That would make them a pernicious present, and I am sure they would rather die than live in a condition no longer fit for my service. I do not mean by this that you should assassinate them;

we should be humane, my dear Baron, but you may insinuate to the surgeons with entire propriety that a crippled man is a reproach to their profession, and there is no wiser course than to let every one of them die when he ceases to be fit to fight.

Here, in other words, is a 1777 version of profitable euthanasia without any threat of suits for malpractice.

The count's next instructions suavely suggest that more killings—of new recruits he'll soon send—will tickle him no end. For these slaughters, he's able to produce highly moral justifications and classical precedents:

Don't economize them. Remember glory before all things. Glory is true wealth. . . . A battle gained without costing the conqueror any blood is an inglorious success, while the conquered cover themselves with glory by perishing with their arms in their hands. Do you remember that of the 300 Lacedaemonians who defended the defile of Thermopylae, not one returned? How happy should I be could I say the same of my brave Hessians!

At this point, the count notices an awkward implication: The brave Spartans had been led by their king, and since he'd "perished with them," to complete his parallel de Schaumbergh should hurry overseas, lead his recruits in battle, and have the pleasure of being gloriously annihilated. He quickly thinks up unassailable reasons for failing to take this appealing opportunity: "things have changed, and it is no longer the custom for princes to go and fight in America for a cause in which they have no concern." Besides: Someone has to stay in Europe to collect payment for each Hessian killed. And the count himself has to be there to replace troops lost—a tougher and tougher job since men are becoming scarce and have to be supplanted by boys.

The count can suggest, though, two more ways that casualties—and therefore payments—can be increased: (1) When men suffer from dysentery, don't cure them. Such men are likely to be cowards; "they pay me as killed for all who die from disease, and I don't get a farthing for runaways." (2) Prolong the war, thereby giving more men a chance to die gloriously.

These measures, the count confides, are particularly desirable since "I have made arrangements for a grand Italian opera, and I do not wish to be obliged to give it up." The nobleman cheerily ends with a pious prayer: "Meantime I pray God, my dear Baron de Hohendorf, to have you in his holy and gracious keeping."

The count's greedy and hypocritical maunderings don't give the slightest hint of what historians agree was the chief fact about the Trenton attack. This victory, following an unrelieved run of Continental defeats and hardships, in fact was a welcome turning point in the war: it restored

Washington's prestige as a commander, brought desperately needed re-enlistments and lifted the hopes of patriots. The omission was understandable since Franklin, with the task of cajoling France into giving his countrymen military and economic aid, would have been a fool to play up heartening circumstances when writing for a French and continental audience. (The piece was first published in French.)

Just as understandably, the satire made the most of a repulsion that the Old World shared with the Americans. Frederick the Great of Prussia had written his friend Voltaire that anyone "out of my school . . . would not have sold his subjects to the English as one sells cattle to be taken to the slaughter house. . . . Such conduct is motivated only by selfish greed." One Landgrave's agent had called his job of negotiating a treaty of subsidy "hateful." And even some members of the British Parliament had called the practice of hiring mercenaries to fight freeborn Englishmen "unthinkable." Franklin therefore attacked a practice that was widely disliked.

To do this, he used techniques that not long before had been deployed with tremendous impacts by two British satirists—Daniel Defoe and Jonathan Swift. James Franklin had carried from London to Boston writings by this pair and shelved them in his library. His younger brother read their rhetoric and their fiction, praised them often and admittedly imitated them. Defoe in "The Shortest-Way with the Dissenters" (1702) and Swift in "A Modest Proposal for Preventing the Children of Poor People in Ireland from Being a Burden to their Parents" (1729)—famous and characteristic satires—had a character who was a scoundrel (to use Swift's word) "insinuate" his own malignancy by nakedly exposing horrible attitudes and urging inhuman acts. Both documented the despicable qualities of their assumed characters by having them use many mundane touches that appeared to be factual. Swift, wrote Hippolyte Taine, "marks the dimensions, and so forth, like a good engineer and statistician, omitting no trivial and positive detail. . . . In this he had no equal but Defoe." Franklin similarly hits disreputable practices by having a hellhound write a bland letter crammed with details and figures which attest to the calculating villain's heartlessness.

A comparison between fairly well established facts about the Battle of Trenton and the "facts" in the baron's letter suggests, furthermore, that Franklin used faculties which Defoe once praised himself for having—"miraculous fancy and lively invention."

Precisely what the commissioner read or heard in Paris about the affair at Trenton is anybody's guess. On the scene or near it, soon after the event, reports of course left something to be desired. A Yankee private who qualified for a remedial composition course wrote in his diary the day of the attack: "This morning at 4 a clock we set off with our Field pieces and Marched 8 miles to Trenton whare we ware attacked by a Number of

Hushing [Hessians] and we Toock 1000 of them besides killed some. Then we marched back and got to the River at Night and got over all the Hushing." Colonel Carl Leopold Burmeister of Cassel, stationed in New York, on 27 December 1776 wrote that when "more than 10,000 rebels" had surprised the Hessians at Trenton: "They were badly treated and made prisoners, losing their guns, colors, and all equippage." Four hundred, he had learned, managed to escape: "Many officers escaped and are sick, but many others died with Colonel Rall, though I cannot furnish at this time a list of the killed and wounded."

Figures on which historians now agree fairly well are: 1,436 Hessians in the engagement; 412 escapees; 918 captives (including officers); 22 killed; 84 wounded. Compared with these, figures given by the private and the German colonel, understandably, aren't too accurate. But compared with the figures that the count flings around they are miracles of precision.

Since a Count Schaumberg did represent George III in hiring German mercenaries, Franklin took his letter writer's name from actuality. Otherwise it is impossible not to believe that he played very fast and loose with available information, whatever it was. Granted, he may have received somewhat inaccurate reports. But it is quite incredible that, thanks to prodigious good luck, every snippet of information that came to him was as incorrect as "the count's" or that every single figure he set down reached him so handily distorted to help show up the count as greedy, sanctimonious, calculating, and cruel:

(1) Manipulated by rumor or—much more likely—by Franklin, the number of Hessians swells from 1,436 to 1,950; escapees shrink from 412 to 345; the number of the wounded grows from 84 to 100; the 918 captives (who in fact got very humane treatment) completely vanish; and—most striking of all—the 22 killed mysteriously pile up to 1,605. Each distortion multiplied the casualties or minimized the number not harmed. Each therefore enlarged the villainy of the count who was responsible and who not only profited from disasters but gloated over them.

(2) What about the count's happy discovery that the English ministry's claim is inaccurate, and therefore he's not to be paid 483,450 florins for the deaths of 1,455 Hessians but 643,500 florins for 1,605 men killed? The count is living in a fool's paradise. His mathematics are cockeyed. He thinks he can get 401 florins per corpse when the British rate is 332. But that's not his worst miscalculation. Bernhard A. Uhlendorf, who studied the treaties that set payments for the use of German mercenaries, finds that the one signed in Hesse-Cassel on 15 January 1776 and applicable to the men stationed in Trenton provided that Baron von Schlieffen (and not, incidentally, Count de Schaumbergh) "was to receive virtually £110,000 annually for twelve thousand men until one year after his troops had returned to Cassel." Since "Schaumbergh" made such a big thing of collect-

ing for cadavers, what Uhlendorf found out about this possible source of income is even more interesting: "The treaty . . . did not contain the blood-money clause, that is, the clause relative to payments to be made to the German prince for killed, maimed and wounded," at all. So neither 332 florins nor 401 florins per corpse, and neither 483,450 florins nor 643,500 florins for the total number of killed warriors was forthcoming: the recruiter of the mercenaries killed in Trenton wasn't to get a single florin.

Franklin's procedure, it is clear, was essentially that of Defoe and Swift —flinging around hordes of details and piles of statistics, whether they have been shakily based upon actuality or conjured up out of thin air, and indicating they have been set down by an unmitigated rascal to his discredit and that of his allies. In the words of Moses Coit Tyler, this work "displays, with marvelous subtlety and wit, that sort of genius which can reproduce with minute and perfect verisimilitude the psychological processes of some monstrous crime against human nature,—a crime which it thus portrays both to the horror and the derision of mankind." And a comparison of the count's "facts" with historical actualities shows that a wild imagination greatly helped Franklin make the processes vivid and disgusting.

Since I relate Franklin's technique to that of characteristic American humor elsewhere, I'll merely glance at one relationship here in conclusion. It seems to me relevant to recall Norris W. Yates's authoritative definition of the American tall tale: "a fantastic yarn rendered temporarily plausible by the supporting use of realistic detail." Thanks to Franklin's inventiveness, doesn't this apply pretty well to "The Sale of the Hessians"?

References

Authoritative discussions of the Battle of Trenton as part of the American Revolution: Robert W. Coakley and Stetson Conn, *The War of the American Revolution* (Washington, D.C., 1975), pp. 50–52; Douglas Southall Freeman, *George Washington, a Biography* (New York, 1951), IV, 291–324, 374–379; Piers Mackesy, *The War for America 1775–1783* (Cambridge, Mass., 1965); and Samuel S. Smith, *The Battle of Trenton* (Monmouth Beach, N.J., 1965).

Useful reports on the Hessians and their part in the war: Carl Leopold Baurmeister, *Revolution in America, Confidential Letters*, ed. Bernhard A. Uhlendorf (New Brunswick, N.J., 1957), pp. 3, 28, 78; Ernst Kipping, *Die Truppen von Hesen-Kassel im amerikanischen Unabhaengigkeitskrieg 1776–1783* (Darmstadt, 1965), and *The Hessian View of America 1776–1783* (Monmouth Beach, N.J., 1971).

The best biography of Franklin continues to be Carl Van Doren, *Benjamin Franklin* (New York, 1938). Valuable critical studies include Richard Amacher, *Benjamin Franklin* (New York, 1962); Lewis Leary, "Benjamin Franklin," which Professor Leary kindly let me read in manuscript in 1975; Bruce I. Granger, *Benjamin Franklin, An American Man of Letters* (Ithaca, N.Y., 1964); Larzer Ziff, "Introduction" to *Selected Writings of Franklin* (New York, 1959) and *Puritanism in America* (New York, 1973). Professor Amacher gave a version of this paper careful scrutiny and the author helpful suggestions.

A perceptive survey is James Sutherland, *Daniel Defoe: A Critical Study* (Cambridge, Mass., 1971). The same author's "Forms and Methods in Swift's Satire," in *Jonathan*

Swift: A Dublin Tercentenary Tribute (Oxford, 1967), pp. 61–77, was invaluable. So were Edward W. Rosenheim, *Swift and the Satirist's Art* (Chicago, 1963), and Wayne Booth's discussions of both Defoe's irony and Swift's "A Modest Proposal" in *A Rhetoric of Irony* (Chicago, 1974).

A Well-Wrought Crockett: Or, How the Fakelorists Passed Through the Credibility Gap and Discovered Kentucky

JOHN SEELYE

"Half-horse, half-alligator," Davy Crockett is an amphibian likewise where studies in American folk literature are concerned: his upper half is identifiable as a historical figure, a colorful politician from the Tennessee backwoods, while his hinder parts are obscured by mythic waters, the Mississippi River. And as with the great river, the effect is to enlarge, and by enlarging, to distort. A politicized version of Daniel Boone, Crockett in his own day represented a distinct stage in the development of subliterary types: where Boone was shaped into an epic hero, a champion of national expansion into the Ohio Valley, Crockett emerged as a much more complex expression of the American spirit, a braggart buffoon who was martyred at the Alamo. Half hero, half horse's ass, Crockett even as a practical politician found himself torn between local and national interests, and the literature he inspired is divided into authentic and spurious anecdotes, with a great deal of questionable material in between.

Walter Blair early on enumerated six separate identities for this Krishna of the American folk pantheon, and threw up his hands over the task of distinguishing between the "real" and the "legendary" parts. Blair opted for celebrating the legend, letting the other half slide, and his decision, coming at the end of the thirties, pretty much sums up the attitude of scholars who dealt with Davy Crockett during that decade, like Blair's co-workers, Franklin J. Meine, Constance Rourke, and Richard M. Dorson. This uncritical period begins with Rourke's *American Humor* (1931), and ends with Ben A. Botkin's *Treasury of American Folklore* and Blair's *Tall Tale America*, both published in 1944 and given an added degree of chauvinism thereby. Blair's book, subtitled "A Legendary History of Our Humorous Heroes," in effect enlisted Crockett—along with the likes of Mike Fink, Pecos Bill, John Henry, Paul Bunyan, and Joe Magarac—in the war effort, "native American" supermen set in motion to smash the Nazi menace. Like World War II itself, this act of massive cultural naiveté would not be repeated.

As early as 1930, professional students of folklore had discovered the extent to which, in the case of the ballad of John Henry, commercialization had polluted traditional wellsprings. And by 1950, a number of so-called folk figures celebrated by Walter Blair were turning out to be artificial creations, hokum heroes invented by journalists and publicists with not even a remote connection to any popular oral tradition. In 1939, in *Davy Crockett: American Comic Legend*, Richard Dorson enthusiastically lumped his champion in with Pecos Bill and Paul Bunyan as native American versions of European mythic types, but by the end of the next decade Dorson made a distinction between folk- and what he called "fake" lore, which last was associated with Botkin's popular *Treasury*. The most egregious example of fakelore hero was Paul Bunyan, whose very size symbolized the giantism of the hoax, for as Daniel Hoffman demonstrated in 1952, the legend had more to do with the ledgers of a lumber company than with loggers' tales told around the campfire.

In 1956 there appeared James Atkins Shackford's *David Crockett: The Man and The Legend*, which in very strong terms dismissed "the mythological Crockett" celebrated by Blair and Dorson. Moreover, in a lengthy series of appendixes, Shackford turned a merciless gaze on the printed material from which Rourke and the rest derived their "folk" hero: Only *The Narrative of the Life of David Crockett*(1834) was dependable, Shackford opined, for the other books were either doubtful in origin or posthumous attempts to capitalize on the hero's notoriety. And as for the comic *Crockett Almanacs*, from which Rourke drew much of her most colorful material, and which Dorson anthologized as his *Legend*, Shackford dismissed them as a "gargantuan hoax . . . part of the exploitation of his renown which yet goes on . . . that point, I think, at which a low type of literary exploitation joined hands with the economic need of inferior literary ability." That is, though there was a very real and genuinely heroic historic David Crockett, the Davy of the almanacs (and Rourke) was a hokey hero sprung from the printer's font.

Shackford's sentiments remained a matter of opinion, however, until 1973, when Joseph Arpad's "The Fight Story: Quotation and Originality in Native American Humor" appeared in *The Journal of the Folklore Institute*. For Arpad demonstrates the extent to which the earliest of the Crockett almanacs were inspired by a popular play, *The Lion of the West*, the hero of which, Nimrod Wildfire, was conceived by James K. Paulding and modeled loosely after the Davy Crockett of burgeoning public notoriety. Concentrating on Wildfire's "fight story," a monologue which was widely circulated in newspapers of the day, Arpad traces it back not to an oral source but to Paulding's own *Letters From the South* (1817). Arpad assumes that Paulding got the original story (about a fight between a boatman and a waggoneer) from some "local storyteller," but the earlier analogues that he cites come also from printed, not oral, sources, all of which are presented as eyewitness accounts by literate (and literary) travelers. Behind this tradition there may lie an oral or even folk tradition, but the evidence gathered by Arpad necessarily promotes a strictly literary metamorphosis, a sequence in which the popular and mass-produced Crockett of the almanacs represents a final stage. A significant icon in this evolution is the picture of Crockett on the cover of the *Davy Crockett Almanac* for 1837, a woodcut copy of a widely circulated picture of Nimrod Wildfire as played by James H. Hackett, twin images printed side by side (or back to back) in Arpad's article.

Richard Dorson included this iconographic metamorphosis in his discussion of Crockett's place in *America in Legend* (1973), where he concedes that the almanac stories represent a move from folk anecdote to "popular literature": "Hack writers in Eastern cities hammered out fanciful escapades for the annual almanac issues . . . yarns [that] constitute a subliterature rather than a folklore." Dorson maintains however that the almanac-makers' Crockett represents "a transition not a sharp break" in the evolution of folk to popular hero, and shows how a number of the almanac stories derive from European folktales and myths. But so, one might respond, does the story of Rip Van Winkle, yet Irving's "Hudson-River tale" does not appear in *America in Legend*. Still, Dorson's revised view of the Crockett almanacs must be regarded as a major development in folklorist scholarship, for it was the "grandiose" phase of the Crockett almanacs on which Dorson, along with Blair and Rourke, had chiefly relied for the tallest of the Tennessean's tales, stories which now must be regarded as largely fakelore.

A point has been reached, apparently, in which the difference between Shackford's opinion and Dorson's concerning the authenticity of the Crockett almanacs is negligible. No longer regarded as directly derived from folk tales, the Crockett almanacs are seen as an early version of popular literature: relying on oral conventions, the comic "legends" were the invention of literary hacks who consciously introduced mythic (archetypal) elements. Though Dorson does not make the point, we can see that from superheroes like Davy Crockett to supersleuths like Nick Carter and on to Superman himself, there is a continuity which has its origins in the ur-hero, Hercules. In America, this is the Kentucky connection, but the men who made it, whatever the nature of their sources, were, like Paulding and Irving, well aware of the Old World analogues. Fakelorists of considerable acumen, they discovered long before Paul Bunyan hove into view the literary potential of the American forest, whether as scenery or as the stuff of crudely cut engravings and the paper they were printed upon.

Henry Nash Smith in *Virgin Land* and Richard Slotkin in *Regeneration through Violence* have variously charted the literary metamorphosis of Daniel Boone, the prototype of subsequent "myths," whose heroic advent was the work of John Filson, who in 1784 celebrated the feats of the Long Hunter by way of promoting Kentucky real estate. With some help perhaps from Daniel Bryan's Miltonic *Mountain Muse* (1813), Boone found his way into an apostrophe in Byron's *Don Juan*, from whence he was elevated by the talents of Fenimore Cooper to literary apotheosis as Leatherstocking. Cooper's creation undoubtedly encouraged a long line of popular biographies of Boone, such as the one written by Timothy Flint in 1833, so that by the end of the nineteenth century the Long Hunter and a host of fictional counterparts had become familiar figures in the Beadle Dime Novels. Much as Davy Crockett became a woodcut ventriloquist's dummy for Whig interests, so Leatherstocking served as a spokesman for Cooper's conservative Jeffersonianism, and Walt Disney's resurrected Crockett may be seen as a wilderness prophet heralding John F. Kennedy's New Frontier. This ulterior dimension has a sinister slant, for in America the wilder versions of pastoral have a radically reactionary bias. Designed for popular consumption, these literary sharpshooters are the invention chiefly of a moneyed elite, and the "legendary" Davy Crockett like the literary "Jack Downing" may, like the wit and wisdom of Abraham Lincoln and Mark Twain, be traced to Whiggish origins.

This is particularly true of *An Account of Col. Crockett's Tour to the North and Down East* (1835), an attack on the Democrats with which Crockett himself had little connection, and the spurious *Col. Crockett's Exploits and Adventures in Texas* (1836) is at once fiercely chauvinistic and anti-Jacksonian, a curious compound of expansionism and conservatism that matches the paradoxicalness of Whig politics in the southwest. But even the two books either authorized or in part authored by Crockett, the *Sketches and Eccentricities of Colonel David Crockett* (1833) and *The Narrative of the Life* (1834), known generally as Crockett's *Autobiography*, seem to have been designed to further his political career. Though Crockett disclaimed any connection with the *Sketches* in his introduction to the autobiography, which he said was written to correct the many errors in the other book, Shackford is convinced that the first-published account of Crockett's exploits was compiled with his connivance. The Tennessee Congressman most certainly acted ambivalently where Paulding's play was concerned, for though he graciously accepted the author's statement that no conscious caricature was intended, there is a tradition that he once publicly returned from his theatre box Hackett's congé of acknowledgment. If Shackford is right, and Crockett did authorize the *Sketches and Eccentricities*, then the link Arpad has established between the book and the play suggests that the Congressman was willing to benefit from notoriety which—as he later discovered to his dismay—he seems to have confused with fame.

Though copyrighted by "Davy Crockett," and after 1835 in the name of his heirs, not even the earliest Crockett almanacs have been traced to Crockett himself. The initial number was printed in 1834 (for the year 1835), and given his repudiation that year of the comic version of his life and adventures, we may be sure Crockett would have regarded any such continuation of the *Eccentricities* version with displeasure. The first four issues of the Crockett almanacs, all bearing a Nashville imprint, most certainly derive from the 1833 collection of anecdotes, and, like that book, seem to have been inspired by the popularity of Paulding's play. Nimrod Wildfire has no Whiggish coloration, but is distinguished by a native American chauvinism that is, if anything, Jacksonian in its hues, and so also with the bulk of the *Sketches and Eccentricities,* which are hunting stories for the most part, and lack the anti-Democratic bias revealed in the last pages of the book. The almanacs, as the penultimate stage in this evolution, preserve the sugar and throw away the pill. Totally lacking in definable party politics, the Nashville almanacs continue to portray the wilderness sporting life, and differ from the *Sketches and Eccentricities* in a general coarsening of tone and broadening of humor, with Crockett serving as often as a butt of jokes as their perpetrator. Thus the fight story stressed as the genetic literary link by Arpad appears with a significant variation in the first number of the Nashville series: not discussed by Arpad, this version involves Crockett's amorous adventures with the mistress of a stagecoach driver. Though caught at the worst possible moment by the driver, Crockett is victorious in the fight that follows, but acknowledges he never told *this* story to "Mrs. Crockett," nor did Dorson include it in his *Legend.*

The only episode in the Nashville almanacs having the faintest political implication is the appearance, in the second number, for 1836, of "Ben Harding, Member of Congress from Kentucky," who relates his "Early Days, Love and Courtship." But what follows has nothing to do with politics and even less with the historical Ben Hardin (*sic*), a colorful Whig politician from Bardstown. "Ben Harding's" autobiography is a compressed reprise of Crockett's almanac adventures, and includes an enlistment under Jackson at New Orleans and a rough and tumble courtship with "one Betsey Blizzard." Hardin in fact never served in the army and was, unlike Crockett, a member of the relatively genteel middle-class gentry of southwestern society. His nineteenth-century biographer, Lucius P. Little, places Hardin between Crockett and John Randolph as being halfway between the backwoods screamers and the tidewater aristocracy. Randolph himself fastened the epithet "Old Kitchen Knife" on Hardin, claiming that his speaking style was both rough-honed and deep-cutting, and the chosen instrument is symbolic, being not the bowie knife associated with the wilder parts of the west but a domestic implement.

Though lacking a college education, Hardin was a learned man and a witty raconteur, whose biography is pieced out by Little with the kinds of anecdotes that made him a local celebrity if not a national one. He belonged to that middling class of professional men who were more apt to be the authors of southwestern humor than the central figures in it, circuit-riding men of the law who maintained an uneasy peace with the predominantly Jacksonian population of the southwestern states. As Little acknowledges, "the comic almanac maker of his day made Mr. Hardin the unwilling vehicle for communicating jokes rather broader than he ever indulged in the most unreserved moments" (288). This considerably understates the situation. By 1839, "Ben Harding" had become the "editor" and "publisher" of the Nashville almanacs, and continued in that capacity long after the Crockett almanacs dropped the Tennessee association, figuring in many stories as the boon companion of the rambunctious Colonel. However, it is not as a Kentucky congressman that he figures in 1839 and afterwards, but as a stereotyped American version of Jack Tar, a sailor who first meets "Kurnel Krockett" while "cruising down the Massippy [sic] on a raft." Hearing of the Colonel's "disease" in Texas, and having in the meantime suffered a "game leg and a short hip" that made him "unseaworthy," Harding "went on a cruise down into Kentuck, and there . . . cum across the Kurnel's papers." Out of respect for the "old Kurnel," Ben announced in the almanac for 1839 that he will continue his good work, that he will "cruize about among the gravers and printers in person," seeing to it that "everything [is] done ship-shape and Bristol fashion."

By 1841, in the last of the almanacs bearing the Nashville imprint, Harding had grown a wooden leg and established contact once again with Davy Crockett, who was alive and as well as could be expected while working in the Mexican mines. Instead of dying at the Alamo, Crockett had been taken prisoner, and he writes his old friend Harding in the hope of obtaining the funds necessary to effect his escape. In 1843, by which time the Crockett Almanacs were being published by Turner and Fisher in New York (as well as other eastcoast cities), "Harding" had been corrected to "Hardin," and the sailor-editor is still trying to raise the money "for getting Crockett out of the mines." But there he remains, increasingly a hostage to political fortunes, for under the Turner and Fisher imprint the almanacs took on a definably expansionist note. In the 1843 number, there appears a letter from Crockett expressing chauvinistic anxiety on the Oregon question, and in 1845 he declares himself as being "like my salt-water friend, Ben Hardin, of the rale American grit, and like him I go for Texas and Oregon, clar up to the very gravel stone, for they both belong to Uncle Sam's plantation." It is these Turner and Fisher almanacs that are chiefly responsible for the "grandiose" stage of the Crockett "legend," overblown exaggeration in harmony with the expansionist mood expressed throughout, a jingoism with a crudely racist, even genocidal, bite. Mexicans and Cubans are depicted as degenerate outlaws, Indians are "red niggers," and Negroes are tacitly accepted as handy victims of wrath, being ape-like caricatures of humanity. In sum, under the "editorship" of Ben Harding / Hardin the Crockett almanacs begin to express a spirit that is closer to the dark side of Jacksonianism than to the Whig élan.

Commentators have noted the strategic differences between the earliest and later Crockett almanacs, and though the genuineness of the Nashville imprint has been questioned, as a grouping the first four Nashville "Crocketts" have a definitive uniformity of design, attested to by Franklin J. Meine in his 1955 edition of them. An important register of the distinction to be made between early and later almanacs is found in the woodcuts that were a constant feature. Where the Nashville imprints contain anonymous illustrations notable for charm and naiveté, bold even primitive designs whose archaic qualities evoke native American folk art, under the aegis of Turner and Fisher the pictures are executed (and signed) by professional craftsmen, and evince the same tendency toward grandioseness that characterizes the anecdotes they were designed to accompany. Though less crude than the pictures in the Nashville almanacs, the Turner and Fisher illustrations are far more ugly, an increase in grotesqueness matching the violence and bigotry of the tales.

As Shackford observes, the chief motivation seems to have been economic opportunism, a willingness to pander to the American propensity for mayhem that would thenceforth remain a constant factor in the popular or mass marketplace. Though the expansionist ideology expressed by the Turner and Fisher almanacs did not accord well with the Whig platform during the 1840's, the commercial spirit was thoroughly Whiggish, and it is notable that Turner and Fisher were the publishers during this same period of such obvious Whig documents as *Gen. Zachary Taylor's Old Rough & Ready Almanac for 1848*. In fact, as Milton Drake's bibliography suggests, almanacs were, when openly political, generally in support of Whig candidates. But though printers and publishers were loyal to the Whig cause, they were willing to pander to the prejudices of Jacksonian democracy, expressing hostilities of a sectional and racial sort which, as a legendary mix, is much closer to the American monomyth isolated by Richard Slotkin in *Regeneration through Violence* than to the earliest anecdotes associated with Davy Crockett. Since this element is introduced by Ben Harding / Hardin's appearance as sailor / editor, that advent perhaps deserves more study than it has hitherto received.

Several Ben Harding stories are included in Dorson's anthologized *Legend,* and Constance Rourke gives him passing mention, but the congressman turned sailor as either a folk or fake figure has generally been neglected. Moreover, the Crockett "legend" in its telling by Rourke or in descriptions by Blair and Dorson does not include the Colonel's survival in the Mexican mines. Though obviously a fictional convenience, a device allowing for further Crockett stories even after the "Kurnel's papers" gave out, the Mexican mines business is no less "legendary" than the stories which the situation permitted. It is, however, less heroic than having Crockett die at the Alamo, and one suspects that modern scholars of folklore have yielded to the same chauvinistic impulse governing much of the production of the original Crockett stories. So also with Ben Harding / Hardin, who is if anything more "legendary" than Crockett—because almost entirely fictitious—and who figures in more tall tales than Mike Fink. Yet Walter Blair and Franklin Meine pay him little attention, and he is not included in Blair's roundup of "folk" heroes in *Tall Tale America,* though one would think that such a belligerent tar would have been of great service against his old adversaries—people of any color but white. Perhaps because he is a sailor, Ben Harding / Hardin was exempted from consideration by folklore scholars of the 1930's, who were chiefly concerned with legends generated by the frontier, the mythic matter that occupied the popular mind after the Civil War to the exclusion of all others. Having generated a considerable maritime literature, on both elite and popular levels, American writers after the war gave in to the frontier necessity, a phenomenon matched and in part accounted for by the decline of the United States as a major sea power during those years. But the rediscovery of Melville's novels in the 1920's was accompanied by no equivalent interest in maritime folklore.

Moreover, Ben Harding / Hardin is chiefly of interest here because of his Kentucky connection: his appearance as "editor" of the Crockett almanacs occurs at just that point variously described by Shackford and Dorson when the anecdotes left the sphere of "oral" or "folk" creation and became early manifestations of "popular" literature. The authenticity of even the earliest Crockett stories as "folk" literature is still open to question, but there is no denying that under the aegis of Ben Harding / Hardin the "legend" became consciously manipulated for profit. Though taking his name from an historical figure, moreover, Ben Harding / Hardin is a stereotyped literary creation, a sailor sprung from the decks of Cooper's sea-going romances. As a "folk" figure, then, he is ascertainably "fake," and is therefore an important addition to that growing pantheon of phony heroes, being a giant's step toward Paul Bunyan. To understand the full implication of this fact, however, we need to consider two important questions: (1) Why was Ben Harding transformed from a Kentucky congressman to a tar? and, (2) What is a sailor doing on the Mississippi River?

The first question can be relatively easily, though conjecturally, answered. Ben Harding/Hardin was first introduced to the almanac audience in the year after Crockett's death—in the second "Nashville" imprint —and though Crockett is the medium, Harding's first words are suggestive: "As the public seems to be very anxious to hear all about my friend Colonel Crockett, I don't see no reason why I should not make some stir in the world too, as we are both members of Congress. I have long had an intention to write my life, and tell about the wild varmints that I have killed, and how I got to be elected member of Congress, and all that." What follows, again, bears no relation to the historical Hardin but is imitative of Crockett's adventures. It seems reasonable to assume that the editor of the "Nashville" almanacs felt it was necessary to find a replacement for the martyred Tennesseean, and hit upon the happy idea of introducing the Kentucky Whig as a convenient substitute. As the misspelling of the Kentuckian's name and the fictitiousness of his adventures suggest, the editor had no real knowledge about Ben Hardin, but then Crockett in the almanacs is increasingly identified as a Kentuckian, suggesting that the pervasive influence of Paulding's fictional character was more powerful than any geopolitical reality.

Whatever the reasons for the editor's creation of a Crockett replacement, the idea died in the same issue in which it was born. Perhaps Hardin did not wish to undergo the painful process of becoming a folk hero, which had meant for Davy Crockett first the loss of his office and then of his life. Being a lawyer, Hardin had the means at his disposal for objecting in an effective manner, and being a Kentuckian he had other resources to draw upon also. Whatever the reason, when Ben Harding next appeared it was as a sailor, and as a sailor he remained, editing the almanacs and having adventures of his own and with Crockett on the Mississippi and in foreign climes. This second appearance was in the "Nashville" almanac for 1839, and later in that same number the opening account of the initial meeting between the backwoodsman and the sailor is considerably expanded upon, once again in the words of Crockett:

I was laying asleep on the Mississippi one day, with a piece of river scum for a pillow, and floating down stream in rail free and easy style, when all at once I was waked up by something that cum agin my ribs like it was trying to feel for an opening into my bowels. So I just raised my head to see what kind of a varmint was sharpening his teeth agin my ribs, and seed it was something that lookt so much like a human cretur that I was half a mind to speek to it. But it had a tail to its head about as big around as my arm and as long as a hoss pistle. The cretur was floating on three kegs fastened to a log, and held a pole in his hand that he had punched me with in the ribs, when I fust woke up. His trowsers was made of white sail cloth, and they was so wide about the legs that I knowed he had stold 'em from some big fat feller, for they didn't fit him no more than my wife's raccoon skin shift would fit the fine ladies in Washington. He had on light thin shoes with big ribbons in 'em and a painted hat with another big ribbon in that. So then I concluded rite off he had ben robbing a Yankee pedlar and got away all his flashy trumpery. Says I, 'Stranger, I take it you are a human by the looks of your face, but you are one of the greatest curosities I've seen in these parts. I don't wonder you wake me up to look at ye.' 'By the devil!' says he, 'the thing has got the use of lingo like a Christian. I thought I had spoke a catfish. Where are you cruising, old rusty bottom? You are the queerest rigged sea craft that I ever saw on soundings or off.' 'You infarnal heathen,' says I, 'I don't understand all your stuff, and I spose you are fresh down this way. But I'll have you understand that I'm a snorter by birth and eddycation, and if you don't go floating along, and leave me to finish my nap I'll give you a taste of my breed. I'll begin with the snapping turtle, and after I've chawed you up with that, I'll rub you down with a spice of the alligator.' With that he looked as mad as a shovel full of hot coals, and he took a long string of tobakkur out of his pocket, and arter he had bit off a piece long enough to hang a buffalo, he roared out, 'I'll shiver your mizen in less time than you can say Jack Robinson, you fresh water lubber! You rock crab! You deck sweeper! swab!' Says I then, for my steam begun to get rather obstropolous, 'I'll double you up like a spare shirt. My name is Crockett and I'll put my mark on your infarnal wolf-hide before you've gone the length of a panther's tail further.' With that he roared right out a laffing, and I was so astonished, I held my breath to see the cretur laff on the eve of a battle, but I soon seed the reeson of it, for he stooped down and reached out his hand, and says, 'tell me for God's sake, old fogy, are you the feller that makes them allmynacks about cruising after panthers and snakes and swimming over the Mississippi?' Says I, 'I'm a roarer at that bizness that you've mentioned, stranger. Going to Congress and making allmynacks is my trade.' 'Give us your flipper then, old chap,' says he, 'I woodn't hurt a hare of your head for the world. Isn't there a grog shop here on the coast, for by G—— I'll treat you if I sell my jacket. I'd give two weeks allowance if our boson was here—Hurra! three cheers for old Crockett! He used to read your allmynack to us on the

DAVY CROCKETT'S ALMANAC.

18   I leave this rule for others, when I'm dead,
      "Be always sure your right, then go a-head."
      CALENDARS CORRECT FOR THE
      ENTIRE UNION, THE TERRITORIES,
      TEXAS, AND BRITISH PROVINCES.   45

BOSTON:

PUBLISHED BY JAMES FISHER, No 71 COURT STREET;

PUBLISHER OF JUVENILE WORKS, TOY BOOKS, &C., &C.

forecastle, for d'ye see, I can't read. I got my larning under the lee of the long boat, and swear my prayers at a lee earing in a gale o' wind. But I can read pikturs to a d——n, and I could spell out your crocodile's tails from their heads when I see 'em drawed out in your book.'

The anecdote continues, with Crockett taking Harding home with him for dinner and the old sailor drinking whiskey and telling "such stories about what he had seed as made the gals dream o' nights for a fortnite arter he was gone; and as I spose the reader would like to hear some of 'em, I think I shall put 'em in print." But the main point of the story is contained in the quoted portion above, which is rendered at length because it is a significant variation of the fight story which Professor Arpad views as the central link between *The Lion of the West*, the *Sketches and Eccentricities*, and the Crockett almanacs.

For this hostile meeting between the backwoodsman and the sailor, unlike the violent encounters between Davy Crockett and riverboat men on the Mississippi, does not end in a bloody fight. Instead, the two antagonists become friends because of Harding's flattering overtures, a reversion of the conventions that is a meliorating device: the fight story is being consciously manipulated so as to emphasize the friendly mingling of salt water and fresh, signalling the entrance of Ben into Davy's world. Unlike Crockett's other antagonists, who end by acknowledging his superior strength but go their separate ways, Ben will remain. He will become not only Davy's companion but his equal, in effect a maritime equivalent and counterpart to the "Kentuckian." The symbolic implication of this union is clarified by the cover of a Crockett (Turner and Fisher) almanac for 1845, the issue that contains Davy's imperialistic sentiments concerning Oregon and Texas, for the picture is a monumentally chauvinistic composition including a spread eagle and a pediment featuring a melee between white men and red, as jingoistic and Jacksonian a composition as one could possibly conceive. Yet there is a Websterish and Whiggish cast to this emblem also, for the back-to-back bond of sailor and frontiersman expresses the mystic idea of Union, the kind of politics of compromise that did not admit to the physical impediment of the Alleghanies.

By 1845, the publication of the almanacs was openly associated with northeastern cities, and Ben-the-Sailor is likewise an east coast (seaport) figure. His appearance in the "Nashville" almanacs, in 1839 and afterwards, therefore suggests an eastern influence, even an eastern place of publication. Further evidence corroborating this possibility is found in the first almanac "edited" by Harding, a gruesome full-page woodcut entitled "The Pirates Head, As drawn by Ben Harding," illustrating the sailor's account of one of his seagoing (anti-Hispano-American) adventures. An identical woodcut (reproduced at the right) may be found in

The Pirates Head,
As drawn by Ben Harding. See Page 24.

The Pirates Own Book, where it is entitled "the head of Benevides stuck on a pole." First published in Boston in 1837 by Samuel N. Dickinson, this compilation of maritime mayhem was reprinted up and down the eastern seaboard frequently thereafter, and has been credited to Charles Ellms, an illustrator-editor residing in Boston in the 1830's and 40's. The *Pirates Own* was produced anonymously, but Ellms's name appears on later collections of similarly nautical material, including *Robinson Crusoe's Own Book* (1842) and *The Tragedy of the Seas* (1841), sensational nonfiction embellished with crude woodcuts similar to those that make up much of the Nashville almanacs' rough-hewn appeal.

Moreover, in *Crusoe's Own Book* there appears verbatim a story about "Mike Shuck[well], the Beaver Trapper" that was printed in the first Nashville almanac, and though we cannot put too much weight on this particular link—given the propensity of anthologists to gather material from various sources—the use of the "Pirates Head" picture does suggest a certain printshop propinquity. Equally suggestive is the claim of Ellms's publisher, Dickinson, that his firm originated the Crockett almanacs. The statement, according to Clarence Brigham of the American Antiquarian

Society in a letter to Franklin Meine in 1950, appears "on the back page of a pink cover which Dickinson issued, wrapped around his two publications of the *Old American Comic* and the *People's Almanac*, in that way issuing them as a pair with a general title of *Almanacs for 1844*":

> About ten years since, the first Comic Almanac that was ever published, was the American Comic. The idea was a novel one, and not more than two seasons had passed before a covetous spirit brought into the field other Comic Almanacs. A few years later and the Crockett Almanac was started, by us, and we thought the idea quite as novel as that of the Comic. But one season passed before Crockett Almanacs sprang up spontaneously, almost, in different parts of the Union.[1]

Addressed to "The Editorial Fraternity," the publisher's statement goes on to complain about the cheapening of price—and quality—of his competitors' almanacs, but the pertinent part of the statement is contained above. "Ten years since" is not quite accurate, for the *American Comic* almanac was first published, in Boston, in 1831 (for 1832). Moreover, the statement may have been merely a publisher's self-praising blurb. But the Crockett connection becomes somewhat stronger when one realizes that both the *American Comic* and the *People's* almanacs first appeared over Charles Ellms's name, and were published by him until 1839, when they were taken over by Dickinson. Given this genesis, Dickinson certainly had the right to claim priority for these two almanacs, and given that right, we may give some credence to his claim for having originated the idea for the first Crockett almanac. Most important, such a possibility puts the "Nashville" imprint square in the heart of the northeast, suggesting that Charles Ellms not only originated "Ben Harding" but the "Davy Crockett" celebrated by folklorists of the 1930's.

A quick comparison between the *American Comic Almanac* and the Nashville imprints would seem to disprove any such assumption, for the title of Ellms's first comic almanac appears to be a contradiction in terms: as "American," it is distinctly British in derivation, with an emphasis on puns, witticisms, and exaggerated, nonsensical illustrations, which are quite sophisticated in execution for the most part. True, this is characteristic of much "American" humor of the day, as much "American" literature in the 1830's bore the impress of Scott and Goldsmith, a derivativeness that makes the sudden appearance of native humor all the more fresh and startling. But if we turn to Ellms's other almanac, the *People's* (first published in 1833), we pick up a very strong trace of American

---

1. I should like to thank Mr. Marcus A. McCorison, director of the American Antiquarian Society, for providing me with a copy of this letter, which is quoted by Franklin J. Meine in his edition of the first four "Nashville" almanacs. The illustrations in this chapter are reproduced with the permission of the American Antiquarian Society.

pungency. Like Ellms's maritime collections, the *People's* (as its very title suggests) is designed for a low level of literacy, and contains largely sensational and not comic material. But so do the earliest of the Nashville imprints, which give equal space to stories of hunting and adventure as to backwoods humor, interspacing these narratives with encyclopedic accounts of American wildlife. The *People's Almanac* follows a similar practice, and though the fauna, like the settings for the anecdotes, are exotic and not native, the layout of the publication, the style of the woodcuts, and the obviously popular appeal may be compared to the first four Crockett almanacs bearing the Nashville imprint.

Moreover, there appears in the first number of *The People's Almanac* a woodcut that provides the most conclusive link between Ellms's acknowledged publications and the "Nashville" almanacs. Illustrating "the ferocity of alligators," it is a picture of an encounter between an alligator and a very large snake. This same woodcut, with strategic alterations, was used in the Crockett almanac for 1836, the first Nashville imprint in which Ben Harding appears, illustrating Ben's "method" for killing alligators. This is Harding the Kentucky congressman, not the sailor, but the association of man and beast does put additional meaning on Ben's declaration in 1839 that though he cannot read, he understands pictures, "and could spell out your crocodile's tails from their heads when I see 'em drawed out in your [Crockett's] book." Like the other evidence linking Ellms to the Nashville imprints, this is circumstantial, but until similar correspondences between the first Crockett almanacs and other popular productions are detected, the iconographic evidence points directly to Charles Ellms as the originator of the Crockett "legend" in one of its most influential avatars, an early stage in its "folkloric" history. We can only lament that Ellms's letter book in the collections of the American Antiquarian Society covers the period 1833–34 only, giving out during the critical year in which he, in my opinion, undertook the publication of an American almanac which is comparable to *Poor Richard's* as a contribution to our popular literature.

There is in that regard one letter sent by Ellms that is particularly suggestive.[2] Written to a bookseller on October 4, 1833, it announces the publication of "The Hickory Almanac," which would be "a political work and advocate Mr Van Burens [*sic*] election to the Presidency," but which would also "contain a number of fine engravings and be perfectly respectable":

> The engravings will be many of them Historical such as the view of the battles of Bunker Hill & New Orleans, Portraits of Jefferson and

2. Quoted here with the permission of the American Antiquarian Society, Mr. Marcus A. McCorison, Director.

An Alligator choked to death.

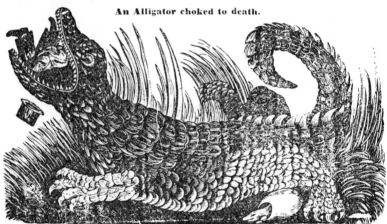

other distinguished men of the democratic Party. It will be edited by
a man who was in favour of Jackson when he was first nominated for
the Presidency, in opposition to John Quincy Adams and Cra[w]ford—
But there will be some views of scenery and nautical history so as to
instruct and amuse all readers—I think you might sell a great many
if you had your name in the imprint. It will be continued annually
with new Engravings executed expressly for the work.

As with a number of his other proposals, Ellms was overly optimistic concerning the future of the "Hickory Almanac," which was never published.
Instead, perhaps, he hit upon the idea of a comic almanac that would

profit from the rage for the eccentricities of another man "who was in favour of Jackson when he was first nominated for the Presidency" but who later reneged, and by that act lost his congressional seat and gained a permanent place in our pantheon of popular heroes.

Though hardly "perfectly respectable," the Crockett almanacs most certainly were designed "so as to instruct and amuse all readers" of whatever party. As in Ellms's first almanac, the short-lived *United States Working Man's* (1831), his democratic sympathies were completely in keeping with Whig rhetoric as voiced by Webster and Everett in their speeches to organizations of "working men," being designed to encourage greater productivity and programs of self-help. Thoroughly apolitical, the earliest Crockett almanacs were the products of commercial considerations, and seem to have been created in New England, as the introduction of the spurious "Ben Harding" certifies. Divorced from any direct contact with the trans-Alleghany zone, Ellms and his co-workers relied on Paulding's play and the *Sketches and Eccentricities* for their initial inspiration, then allowed their imaginations freer play as the "legend" gained momentum. Ellms's most distinctive contribution to American humor seems to be the wonderful woodcuts that give the Nashville almanacs their "folk" flavor, but in this graphic dimension there is evidence of metamorphosis also. Thus the cover for the first Nashville imprint differs little from the *Comic Almanac* designed and published by Ellms the year before. It is with the second and subsequent covers that the "myth" begins to shape the matter, but as with the Crockett trimmed in wildcat fur for 1837, the Kentucky connection remains both a derived and a literary one.

Whether Charles Ellms or some anonymous hack was responsible for creating the "legendary" Ben Harding we will probably never know, but as a Boston-bred attempt to manufacture a maritime, east coast equivalent to the Southwest's Davy Crockett, the colorful sailor attests even further to the literary origins of our "popular" myths. Moreover, as an agent important to the transition from the comic tradition derived from Paulding's play to the increasingly violent mode developed by Turner and Fisher, Ben Harding bears witness that the movement had more to do with creating and then holding a popular audience than with the recording of authentic folk stories. As in pornography, an appetite having been created must be fed increasingly bizarre variations upon a basic situation, and as in an adventure series on television, the settings and stories become increasingly exotic and unlikely. So *Wagontrain* sows Samurai warriors on the Great Plains and Davy and Ben and Huck and Tom have wild adventures amongst pirates and Injuns. These matters deserve further study, but any such investigation should at the start divest itself from the unquestioning acceptance of the Crockett almanacs as "folk" material.

"Go Ahead!"

Davy Crockett's
ALMANACK,
OF WILD SPORTS OF THE WEST,
And Life in the Backwoods.

CALCULATED FOR ALL THE STATES IN THE UNION.

NASHVILLE, TENN. PUBLISHED BY SNAG & SAWYER.

As early as Joel Barlow's *Vision of Columbus*, the rise of a national literature in America was informed by a self-consciously "native" mythology, an eclectic mingling of American materials and classical, biblical, and, more latterly, folk motifs imported from the Old World. So Washington Irving, in shaping his Hudson River stories, gave mythic substance to regional settings by drawing on German *Volksagen*, and what was going on in the almanacs of the 1840's is an ephemeral version of what was happening in novels now regarded as classic examples of the genre. At the one end we have Cooper's Leatherstocking Tales, which took the "legend" of Daniel Boone and adapted it to the historic romance as established by Sir Walter Scott—in effect developing an American literary counterpart to the legendary Rob Roy, being a Robin Hood in buckskins. At the other end we have *Moby-Dick*, in which the dreary, monotonous facts of whaling were elevated to a Gothic romance starring a mad captain whose epical heroics bear a closer resemblance to the deeds of Perseus than to the real-life adventures of a Yankee whaler.

Both Cooper and Melville were aware of and borrowed materials from the marginal zones of American literature, in the hope perhaps of gaining the widest possible readership. Of the two authors, Cooper was by far the more successful in capturing a popular audience, and it is interesting to note that when, in 1840, he returned to the adventures of Leatherstocking after the hiatus of more than a decade—during which time the "legend" of Davy Crockett was created—Cooper mixed his maritime and wilderness genres, giving his backwoods Pathfinder an old salt, Charles Cap, for companion, and in Jasper Western the fresh-water sailor, he created a hybrid of the two stereotypes. If Cooper was inspired to do so because of the advent in 1839 of Ben Harding as Crockett's sea-going friend, the match was paradoxical, for it was Cooper who, in *The Prairie*, gave Leatherstocking a partner called Paul Hover, a Kentuckian bee-hunter who embodies many of Davy Crockett's "legendary" characteristics. Since the Congressman from Kentucky first appeared on the national scene in the year that Cooper's novel was published, we may doubt any direct connection—even though the bee-hunter becomes a successful candidate for Congress. But when Richard Penn Smith set about, in 1836, to arrange for Crockett's apotheosis at the Alamo, he seems to have kept this coincidence in mind, for on the way to his tragic appointment with destiny, the Tennessee hero was given a bee-hunter as guide. Such arrangements suggest that our premier mythic terrain, the trans-Mississippi West, was from the beginning a creation of the East, being almost entirely a territory of the literary imagination.

How Emerson, Thoreau, and Whitman Viewed the "Frontier"

GAY WILSON ALLEN

I

No American in the nineteenth century, no matter where he lived, could escape some influence of the "frontier" (the thin line separating an established settlement and the uninhabited wilderness), whether from experience, hearing or reading about it, or as myth in folklore and literature. This, I assume, we can take for granted. But the ways in which the influence was felt and its effects upon a given individual, especially a writer or artist, were as varied as the history of the settlement of the North American continent by the Europeans who arrived intermittently from 1607 until around 1890, when the frontier virtually disappeared, and Frederick Jackson Turner, looking back, formulated his theory.[1]

At the age of twenty Ralph Waldo Emerson shared the belief of most of his countrymen that his own nation was morally superior to all others. He wrote in his *Journal* on April 8, 1823: "Separated from the contamination which infects all other civilized lands this country has always boasted a great comparative purity. At the same time, from obvious causes, it has leaped at once from infancy to manhood; has covered & is covering millions of square miles with a hardy & enterprizing population. The free institutions which prevail here & here alone have attracted to this country the eyes of the world."[2]

However, some "patriots" feared that the nation had grown *"too fast for its virtue & its peace."* In support of this view, Emerson added: "In the raw multitudes who lead the front of emigration men of respectability in mind & morals are rarely found—it is well known."[3] Notice that he says *emigration*, meaning the migration from the settled eastern seaboard to the unsettled, or sparsely settled, West. Of course, like every New Eng-

1. "The Significance of the Frontier in American History," read at the summer meeting of the American Historical Association, Chicago, 1893; reprinted in *The Frontier in American History* (New York, 1920); paperback, New York, 1962.
2. *The Journals and Miscellaneous Notebooks of Ralph Waldo Emerson*, ed. William H. Gilman et al. (Cambridge, Mass., 1960–), II, 115.
3. Ibid.

lander, he admired the *immigrants* who had come from despotic Europe seeking freedom in the New World—though later he would have ambivalent feelings about the ignorant and destitute Irish who would come to escape famine and British exploitation. But in the 1820's some descendants of the earlier settlers, who had not been able to succeed in the older settlements, were moving westward, and Emerson was not sympathetic with them:

> The pioneers are commonly the offscouring of civilized society who have been led to embark in these interprizes by the consciousness of ruined fortunes or ruined character or perchance a desire for that greater license which belongs to a new & unsettled community. These men & their descendants compose the western frontier population of the United States and are rapidly expanding themselves. At this day, the axe is laid to the root of the forest; the Indian is driven from his hut & the bison from the plains;—in the bosom of mountains where white men never trod, already the voice of nations begins to be heard —haply heard in ominous & evil accents.[4]

We see that what particularly alarmed Emerson was that these ruffians were destroying the forests, the Indians, and the buffalo—in short, destroying nature. "Good men desire," he declared, "& the great Cause of human nature [i.e., humanity], that this abundant & overflowing richness wherewith God has blessed this country be not misapplied & made a curse. . . ."[5] He called the exploiters "an accursed tribe of barbarous robbers." He feared that the machinery of Government, acting upon "the territory at so great distance," would be feeble and ineffective; that "the Oracles of Moral law and Intellectual wisdom in the midst of an ignorant & licentious people will speak faintly & indistinctly."

Boston in 1823, where Emerson was teaching school at the time, was a stronghold of Federalism, and he was recording as his own convictions what John Quincy Adams, for instance, was saying.[6] The Federalists did not object to expanding the American nation, but they wanted it to be orderly, legal, and remunerative to the national treasury. The lands should be sold, not given away, or taken over by squatters. But by the following year, when J. Q. Adams became president in a controversial election, the migration was becoming about as impossible to control as a tidal wave. Henry Adams in his *History* says of this period, "From Lake Erie to Florida, in long, unbroken line, pioneers were at work, cutting into the forests with the energy of so many beavers, and with no more

---

4. Ibid.

5. Ibid., p. 116.

6. Brooks Adams in his introduction to Henry Adams' *Degradation of the Democratic Dogma* (New York, 1919) summarizes the political philosophy of John Quincy Adams.

express moral purpose than the beavers they drove away."[7] Of course this historian was biased in favor of his Federalist ancestors, yet the beaver comparison is apt. Everyone thought the natural resources unlimited, and the pioneers destroyed with abandon. Cooper in his novel called *Pioneers*, published the year of Emerson's *Journal* entry, described the mindless destruction. Wild pigeons, for example, flew over in flocks so dense they darkened the sun. For sport, settlers shot them down with a cannon. About a century later the last wild pigeon died in the Cincinnati Zoo.

Emerson believed as strongly as anyone that American writers must create a literature to match the country's fabulous natural resources. Oliver Wendell Holmes called Emerson's "American Scholar" address a declaration of American literary independence.[8] "We have listened too long to the courtly muses of Europe," Emerson declared. Every man should "plant himself indomitably on his instincts. . . . We will walk on our own feet; we will work with our own hands, we will speak our own minds."[9]

This was the very attitude of independence which Turner regarded as the spirit of the frontier. And many of Emerson's statements can be quoted—especially out of context—to confirm this interpretation. "My book should smell of pines and resound with the hum of insects,"[10] he exclaims in "Self-Reliance"—though of course he did not have to go to the frontier to find pines and insects. He also admired savages for their health and strength. "What a contrast," he says in this same essay, "between the well-clad, reading, writing, thinking American with a watch, a pencil and a bill of exchange in his pocket, and the naked New Zealander, whose property is a club, a spear, a mat and an undivided twentieth of a shed to sleep under!"[11] Emerson might have thought of a no-less-sturdy American Indian, or a "Mountain Man" of the Rockies—tougher even than the Indian—or tanned pioneers crossing the great plains in covered wagons. He did admire such courage and tenacity as they displayed, and in "The Poet" he lamented that "we have yet had no genius in America, with tyrannous eye, which knew the value of our incomparable materials, and saw, in the barbarism and materialism of the times, another carnival of the same gods whose picture he so much admires in Homer. . . ."[12] But he himself was not that modern Homer. Whitman, his confessed disciple, would attempt to be. Why not Emerson? The answer lies in part in his moral revulsion against the frontier movement.

---

7. Vol. I, Chap. VI, of *History of the United States during the First Administration of Thomas Jefferson* (New York, 1889); reprinted in Great Seal Books (Cornell, N.Y., 1955), p. 127.
8. *Ralph Waldo Emerson* (Boston, 1885), p. 115.
9. *The Complete Works of Ralph Waldo Emerson* (Boston, 1903–1904), I, 114–115.
10. Ibid., II, 58.
11. Ibid., p. 84.
12. Ibid., III, 37.

In time Emerson somewhat outgrew his early Federalism, but he would always hate Andrew Jackson almost as much as John Quincy Adams did. He did not take a lively interest in the election of 1828, but each year that Jackson served as president increased his bitterness. He wrote his brother William in 1829, "We are fallen on evil days. That word Country [i.e., Nation] must make us blush or lament."[13] He was in New York visiting his brother during the political campaign of 1834, and witnessed the rowdy parades, boastful speeches, and even riots. Though he was disgusted with the conduct of both parties, he regarded the Democrats (whom he called "Tories") as "the *bad* party." Their banner displayed good professions, such as "Down with corruption!" but he thought they should read, "Evil be thou my good!"[14] Yet if the Whig party (which had succeeded the Federalist) should lose— "which God avert!"—he believed that the "law of compensation" would set in: "Let the worst come to the worst & the Whig cause be crushed for a season & the Constitution be grossly violated[,] then you should see the weak Whig become irresistible."[15] Not, of course, very good prophecy.

Emerson had less faith than Whitman in the virtue or sound judgment of the common man, though he supported the democratic processes of government, and thought they could be made to work. What he believed with all his soul was that every man has innately a moral conscience which will guide him wisely in all his conduct if he will listen to it. The chief intent of nearly all Emerson's speeches and writings was to teach men to listen to their inner voice, which he believed to be the voice of God. Every man has an instinct for good, but only a few live up to it. As late as 1850 Emerson wrote in his Journal: "My quarrel with America, of course, was that the geography is sublime, but the men are not; that the inventions are excellent, but the inventors, one is ashamed of; that the means by which events so grand as the opening of California, Texas, Oregon, & the junction of the Oceans, are effected, are paltry, the filthiest selfishness, fraud, & conspiracy."[16]

By the time Emerson lectured in the 1850's on the prairies of Ohio, Illinois, and Wisconsin, the actual frontier had moved farther west, but he met people who had either been pioneers or were still close to them in spirit. At St. Louis he took a surprisingly deterministic view, blaming the environment, especially the river, for the stunted humanity: ". . . this Mississippi River that warps the men, warps the nations, they must all obey it, chop down its woods, kill the alligator, eat the deer, shoot the wolf, 'follow the river,' mind the boat, plant the Missouri-corn, cure, &

13. *Letters of Ralph Waldo Emerson*, ed. Ralph Rusk (New York, 1939), I, 274.
14. *Journals*, IV, 332.
15. Ibid., IV, 334.
16. Ibid., XI, 284.

save, & send down stream the wild foison harvest tilth & wealth of this huge mud trough of the 2000 or 10000 miles of river."[17] No one had a day's leisure, with mud up to his knees, and his collar perpetually dingy with coal dust. "How can he be literary or grammatical?"[18]

Yet Emerson, who valued grammar and a clean collar, admired the independence and courage of these tough men. They carried themselves like kings: ". . . I notice an extraordinary firmness in the face of many a drover, an air of independence & inevitable [firm] lips, which are worth a hundred thousand dollars. No holding a hat for opinions."[19] And yet the politicians who represented them in the statehouses were "truckling & adulatory." This was the curious contradictory legacy of the frontier.

In 1840 Emerson correctly declared, "In all my lectures, I have taught one doctrine, namely, the infinitude of the private man."[20] But he did not mean that all men are God-like; rather that they have an unlimited possibility of becoming more spiritual and stronger moral influences. In *Nature* he said that "a man is a god in ruins."[21] And in another place, "man is the dwarf of himself."[22] Skipping for the moment the transcendental theology of these statements, it is pertinent to say that Emerson attributed all of men's shortcomings and failures to their being out of harmony with nature. Though his doctrine was ultimately metaphysical, it also applied—and still applies, I think—in a practical sense. In the poem called "The Sphinx," Nature, "the universal dame," taunts the poet with man's condition:

> "But man crouches and blushes,
>   Absconds and conceals;
> He creepeth and peepeth,
>   He palters and steals;
> Infirm, melancholy,
>   Jealous glancing around,
> An oaf, an accomplice,
>   He poisons the ground.["][23]

The poet insists, however, that man can be redeemed, for "The fiend that man harries / Is love of the Best." Yet heroic effort is needed: "To vision profounder, / Man's spirit must dive." Because Emerson loved the "sublime geography" of America, he was grieved at its abuse by the mindless hordes of pioneers; hence his anomalous attitude to the movement which Whitman regarded as heroic and epic. Such events as the California Gold Rush aroused Emerson's indignation and scorn, as when he said: "If

17. Ibid., p. 528.
19. Ibid.
21. *Works*, I, 71.
23. *Works*, IX, 22.

18. Ibid.
20. Ibid., VII, 342.
22. Ibid.

a man is going to California, he announces it with hesitation; because it is a confession that he has failed at home."[24]

II

Edwin Fussell in his admirable study *Frontier: American Literature and the American West* (1965) devotes a whole chapter to Henry David Thoreau, in which he shows this paradoxical writer's fascination with the words *frontier, west,* and *wilderness*.[25] Thoreau was forever punning on these words, and at times was so ironical that the reader scarcely knows how to take him. In the famous essay called "Walking" he says, "even I am leaving the city more and more, and withdrawing into the wilderness. . . . I must walk toward Oregon, and not toward Europe. And that way the nation is moving, and I may say that mankind progress from east to west."[26] From these remarks one might think Thoreau was ready to take to the Oregon Trail himself. But actually he never had the slightest inclination to do so. In his first book, *A Week on the Concord and Merrimack Rivers,* he displayed his semantic game: "The frontiers are not east or west, north or south; but wherever a man *fronts* a fact, though that fact be his neighbor. . . ."[27] Thoreau continues: "Let him build himself a log house with the bark on where he is, *fronting* IT, and wage there an Old French war for seven or seventy years, with Indians and Rangers, or whatever else may come between him and the reality, and save his scalp if he can."[28]

For the actual western frontier Thoreau had some of Emerson's antagonism. He frequently made sarcastic remarks about foolish and selfish men drawn to California by the Gold Rush. In a personal letter to Harrison Blake (February 27, 1853) he declared: "The whole enterprise of this nation, which is not an upward, but a westward one, toward Oregon[,] California, Japan &c, is totally devoid of interest to me, whether performed on foot or by a Pacific railroad. . . . It is perfectly heathenish—a filibustering *toward* heaven by the great western route."[29] His "heaven" lay in a different direction. In a merry passage on exploration in the conclusion to *Walden* he advised, "explore your own higher latitudes."[30] Men fleeing to Oregon or California were not doing that—were, in fact, probably fleeing from themselves.

24. *Journals,* XI, 71.

25. *Frontier: American Literature and the American West* (Princeton, N.J., 1965), chap. 4.

26. *The Works of Thoreau,* ed. Henry Seidel Canby (Boston, 1937), p. 668

27. Quoted by Fussell, p. 178.

28. Ibid.

29. *The Correspondence of Henry David Thoreau,* ed. Walter Harding and Carl Bode (New York, 1958), p. 296.

30. *Works* (Canby), p. 457.

Thoreau's masterpiece, *Walden*, contains the best—and trickiest—examples of his metaphysical frontier. Fussell says he played at being a pioneer,[31] and that is true, but he played the game on such a multi-level chessboard that to say this is oversimplifying. Like the pioneers, he cleared a space in the woods, built a cabin with his own hands, and lived for two years and two months with the pond and the hoot owls for companions. Emerson owned the land, so it might be said that he was a squatter, except that he had permission. This hut was only a mile from Emerson's house, and he walked the railroad ties frequently to the village post office—and his mother's kitchen. Furthermore, he built the hut with second-hand planks instead of logs, and plastered the inside—hardly a frontier home.

It is easy to satirize Thoreau's "pioneering" and his experiment in economy, and various critics have done so, from James Russell Lowell[32] to Leon Edel.[33] He made himself vulnerable by his elaborate bookkeeping, leading many readers to think that his object was to show how little work a man needed to do to support himself. Actually, Thoreau worked very hard at Walden Pond, but not, as Edel says, at hoeing his beans,[34] which he gave a minimum of attention; he worked at "exploring his higher latitudes" and writing a masterpiece of prose, much of it devoted to some of the most acute criticism of the contemporary American life-style. He said that most of his fellow townsmen wasted their time, their energy, and their moral force in "keeping up appearances," i.e., in accumulating property which brought them neither happiness nor moral and intellectual improvement. He thought they conducted themselves like Henry Adams' pioneer-beavers, and probably most of them did.

Thoreau was fascinated by the wilderness, but not for the same reason that the pioneers were. His travels have often been belittled because he said facetiously that he had traveled much in Concord. But he did make three trips to the Maine wilderness, part of which was still frontier country, and part completely uninhabited, except by moose, bears, and other wild animals. He made the first trip in September 1846, having left Concord, Massachusetts, on August 31.[35]

At Bangor a relative joined Thoreau, and they walked and boated a hundred miles up the Penobscot River, five miles past the last cabin, and then through virgin forest to Mt. Ktaadn, the second highest mountain in New England. In Thoreau's opinion this wild and unsettled region

---

31. Fussell, pp. 191 ff.

32. "Thoreau's Letters," *North American Review*, October, 1865; revised, *My Study Windows* (Boston, 1871).

33. *Henry D. Thoreau*, University of Minnesota Pamphlets, No. 90 (Minneapolis, 1970).

34. Ibid., p. 9.

35. *The Maine Woods*, in *The Writings of Henry David Thoreau* (Boston, 1895), III, 1.

was more interesting than any he could reach "by going a thousand miles westward."[36] There were already over two hundred and fifty sawmills on the Penobscot and its tributaries, but the loggers had not yet reached the Ktaadn forests, though their mission seemed to be, as Thoreau said, "like so many busy demons, to drive the forest all out of the country, from every solitary beaver-swamp and mountainside, as soon as possible."[37]

On the West Branch of the Penobscot Thoreau and his companion, following a dim footpath, occasionally came to a log house, usually five to ten miles from its nearest neighbor. One of these was "Uncle George" McCauslin's. He entertained them with "true Scotch hospitality," and Thoreau found him

> A man of dry wit and shrewdness, and a general intelligence which I had not looked for in the backwoods. In fact, the deeper you penetrate into the woods, the more intelligent, and, in one sense, less countrified do you find the inhabitants; for always the pioneer has been a traveler, and, to some extent, a man of the world; and, as the distances with which he is familiar are greater, so is his information more general and far reaching than [that of] the villagers. If I were to look for a narrow, uninformed, and countrified mind, as opposed to the intelligence and refinement which are thought to emanate from cities, it would be among the rusty inhabitants of an old-settled country, on farms all run out and gone to seed with life-everlasting, in the towns about Boston, even on the high-road in Concord, and not in the backwoods of Maine.[38]

Thoreau employed "Uncle George" and his bateau to guide them to Mt. Ktaadn and back to McCauslin's house. For Thoreau it was an almost idyllic experience, which he described with unaffected enjoyment, without the mannerisms and comic posturing in *Walden*. His companions climbed partway up Ktaadn with him, but he went to the top alone. For the first time he realized how "primeval, untamed and forever untamable *Nature*" is. He felt "the presence of a force not bound to be kind to man . . . here not even the surface had been scarred by man. . . ."[39] In his awe of non-human nature and disgust for destructive human beings Thoreau reminds one of Robinson Jeffers.[40]

During this trip Thoreau met few Indians, only some drunken hunters from Indian Island, where the whole Penobscot tribe had settled and was trying to adopt the ways of the white man. "In the progress of degrada-

---

36. Ibid., p. 3. 37. Ibid., p. 4.
38. Ibid., p. 28. 39. Ibid., p. 94.
40. In "Science," for instance, "introverted man" has "bred knives on nature [and] turns them also inward. . . ."

tion," Thoreau observed, "the distinction of races is soon lost."[41] But the Indians had not been dispossessed of their forest, and they still visited it to hunt when they felt like it. Yet they were fast losing their savage culture without finding anything better to take its place. Thoreau's strongest impression of the Maine wilderness at this time was that "we have advanced by leaps to the Pacific, and left many a lesser Oregon and California unexplored behind us."[42] Beyond Indian Island travel was still by bateau and canoe, "and sixty miles above, the country is virtually unmapped and unexplored, and there still waves the virgin forest of the New World."[43]

Seven years later, about the same time of the year, Thoreau made his second trip to Maine,[44] during which he paddled up the Chesuncook in a birchbark canoe. This time he and his companion employed an Indian guide, Joe Aitteon, "a good-looking Indian, twenty-four years old, apparently of unmixed blood, short and stout, with a broad face and reddish complexion. . . ."[45] He was illiterate, but Thoreau found him intelligent and completely at home in the woods—that is, so far as finding his way and knowing the habits of the wild animals; he admitted his inability to survive in the wilderness, as his ancestors had done, without a pack of supplies. Joe demonstrated his hunting skill by killing and butchering a moose, but Thoreau found the whole procedure highly offensive: "This afternoon's experience suggested to me how base or coarse are the motives which commonly carry men into the wilderness. The explorers and lumberers generally are all hirelings, paid so much a day for their labor, and as such they have no more love for wild nature than wood-sawyers have for forests. Other white men and Indians who come here are for the most part hunters, whose object is to slay as many moose and other wild animals as possible."[46]

Thoreau thought it strange "that so few [people] ever come to the woods to see how the pine lives and grows and spires. . . ." By "pine" he meant, of course, the white pine, which could grow to six feet or more in circumference, tall and straight to its towering tip. To Thoreau, there was "a higher law affecting our relation to pines as well as to men. A pine cut down, a dead pine, is no more a pine than a dead human carcass is a man."[47] The logger or lumberman no more knows the pine than the extractor or user of whale-oil knows the whale, or the ivory hunter the elephant. "Every creature is better alive than dead, men and moose and pine trees, and he who understands it aright will rather preserve its life

41. *Maine Woods*, III, 105.   42. Ibid., p. 111.
43. Ibid   44. Ibid., p. 112.
45. Ibid., p. 120.   46. Ibid., pp. 161–162.
47. Ibid., p. 163.

than destroy it." He pronounced the pine "as immortal as I am, and per-chance will go to as high a heaven, there to tower above me still."[48]

Thoreau visited a loggers' camp, where thirty men were going and com-ing; in winter, a hundred lodged there, he was told. It seemed to him like a war camp, for the "war against the pines, the only real Aroostook or Penobscot war."[49] But the men seemed to think more about eating than war, and he supposed it must have been the same with Homer's warriors. They did not seem heroic to Thoreau. And after the loggers would come the settlers, who would continue the destruction. "The civilized man not only clears the land permanently . . . and cultivates open fields, but he tames and cultivates to a certain extent the forest itself. By his mere presence, almost, he changes the nature of the trees as no other creature does."[50]

The pioneer of ecology, George Perkins Marsh, was United States Min-ister to Turkey at the time Thoreau was making these trips to the forests of Maine, and he would not publish his epochal book, *Man and Nature*, until 1864, two years after Thoreau's death.[51] These two New Englanders should have known each other. While living in Europe Marsh became con-vinced that the real cause of the decline of the Roman Empire was the ecological destruction by the Roman soldiers, who lived off the country and left depleted soil as well as destitute people in their wake. Thoreau could have taught the Vermont ecologist that the same effects could be observed in his own country after the warriors against the forest had left maimed and dead white pines on the fields of their victories; or to put it more generously, Thoreau could have corroborated Marsh's own observa-tions in Vermont.

Although unaware that he was anticipating a new science, Thoreau made specific observations that ecologists would discover later. For ex-ample, he noted that "the surface of the ground in the Maine woods is everywhere spongy and saturated with moisture."[52] Not until the twen-tieth century would Americans learn what the loss of this moisture could do to the soil, vegetation, and people. Thoreau observed also that after a forest fire the second growth of trees was not another stand of white pines, but poplars, huckleberry bushes, and other shrubs. "We have as yet," he wrote, "had no adequate account of a primitive pine forest." He surmised that Maine would soon be like Massachusetts—and he might have added

48. Ibid., pp. 164–165.
49. Ibid., p. 173.
50. Ibid., p. 205.
51. For a good summary of Marsh's life and writings, see Franklin Russell, "George Perkins Marsh," in *Makers of Modern Thought* (New York, 1972), pp. 310–319. *Man and Nature* (1864), rev. as *The Earth as Modified by Human Action*, 1874.
52. *Maine Woods*, p. 206.

that the eroded soil of his state was a major cause of emigration to the ever-receding western frontier. "We seem to think that the earth must go through the ordeal of sheep-pasturage before it is habitable by man." He questioned "the virtue of making two blades of grass grow where only one grew before. . . ."[53]

Thoreau was not so foolish or impractical as to think that the advance of the frontier could be stopped, leaving pristine nature unmarred by human aggression. But he was an early Conservationist—or more accurately, a Preservationist.[54] He advocated "national preserves, where no [Indian] villages need be destroyed, in which the bear and panther, and some even of the hunter race, may still exist, and not be 'civilized off the face of the earth.' . . ."[55] These preserves would be "for inspiration and our own true recreation," and he might also have invoked his metaphysical "higher law" which made the white pine as immortal as he. Or Emerson's "occult relation" between plants, animals, and men. That relation may still not be fully understood today, but we are learning that in destroying other forms of life we destroy ourselves. This principle was the basis of both Emerson's and Thoreau's antagonism to the American "pioneers."

Thoreau's third trip to Maine in the summer of 1857[56] was perhaps his most enjoyable one, though it mainly confirmed previous impressions of the frontier and the wilderness. At Oldtown he was able to engage the most renowned Indian guide in the state, Joseph Polis, who lived up to his reputation. Joe Polis lived in a white two-story house, well furnished and surrounded by fruit trees and a well-kept garden. In his birchbark canoe he took Thoreau and his unnamed companion to the Allegash Lake, by way of Moosehead, and returned by the East Branch of the Penobscot. Thoreau soon respected and admired Polis, and wrote down the Indian names of plants, animals, and places which Joe gave him. Not surprisingly, he found on the East Branch that "things are quite changed since I was here eleven years ago. Where there were but one or two houses, I now found quite a village, with saw-mills and a store. . . ."[57] A few "solitary pioneers" still lived in the woods, and Thoreau thought they were better off than "the helpless multitudes in the towns who depend on gratifying the extreme artificial wants of society and are thrown out of employment by hard times!"

The Penobscot Indians seemed to be even more social than the whites:

53. Ibid., pp. 207, 208, 210.

54. "Conservationists" want to conserve and control the use of natural resources; "Preservationists" want to leave the wilderness in its natural state. See Roderick Nash, *Wilderness and the American Mind*, rev. ed. (New Haven, 1973), esp. chap. 6.

55. *Maine Woods*, p. 212.

56. Ibid., p. 214.

57. Ibid., p. 393.

> Ever and anon in the deepest wilderness of Maine, you come to the log-hut of a Yankee or Canada settler, but a Penobscot never takes up his residence in such solitude. They are not scattered about on their islands in the Penobscot, which are all within the settlements, but gathered together on two or three,—though not always on the best soil,—evidently for the sake of society. I saw one or two houses not now used by them, because as our Indian Polis said, they were too solitary.[58]

However, though these Indians were becoming settlers themselves, they were not aggressive like the whites. It was the white settlers who were depleting the natural resources. They had built dams along the St. John River to make it flow toward Bangor, thus "turning the forces of nature against herself, that they might float their spoils out of the country. They rapidly run out of these immense forests all the finer, and more accessible pine timber, and then leave the bears to watch the decaying dams, not clearing nor cultivating the land, nor making roads, nor building houses, but leaving it a wilderness as they found it."[59] But not quite, one might add; and Thoreau here uses "wilderness" in a pejorative sense. He was perhaps too indifferent to the economic cause of this devastation of nature. "The chopper fells trees," he commented drily, "from the same motive that the mouse gnaws them,—to get his living. You tell me that he has a more interesting family than the mouse."[60] But Thoreau was evidently skeptical of this statement. One must admit that his ecological wisdom was in part fortuitous, a side result of his dislike of mass-man, and his preference for the natural forms of life which man devours in his insatiable hunger.

III

Walt Whitman saw no conflict between man and nature, because his sympathy was for mass-man, or man *en masse*, to use his own phrase.[61] As a boy he was fond of the outdoors on Long Island, and in old age he wrote some interesting nature-notes in *Specimen Days*.[62] But real wilderness he never knew from experience. The closest he ever came to the frontier was on parts of his trip in 1848 to New Orleans by stagecoach through the West Virginia mountains and then by steamboat down the Ohio and Mississippi rivers. He returned by way of the Mississippi, the Great Lakes, and the Hudson River.[63] On seeing the Platte Canyon in

---

58. Ibid., pp. 399–400.   59. Ibid., p. 312.
60. Ibid., p. 313.   61. See poem, "One's-Self I Sing."
62. *Prose Works 1892*, ed. Floyd Stovall (New York, 1963), I, 143ff.
63. Described in "Excerpts from a Traveller's Note Book," reprinted in *Uncollected Poetry and Prose of Walt Whitman*, ed. Emory Holloway (New York, 1921), I, 181–190.

Colorado on a trip he took in old age he exclaimed, "I have found the law of my own poems."[64] But as either autobiography or poetics, this is as obscure as his intent to speak in his poems with the "rectitude and insousiance of the movements of animals and . . . the sentiment of trees in the woods. . . ."[65]

In his early manhood Whitman was a Jacksonian Democrat and a faithful believer in "manifest destiny." He was thrilled by the visions of the hordes of restless Americans moving across the Mississippi, invading, taking possession of, and "civilizing" the western lands. He marched with them in imagination, though his actual knowledge of the frontier was limited to reports of the explorers, such as John C. Frémont,[66] and the speeches of the expansionist politicians. In an editorial in the Brooklyn *Eagle*, January 22, 1847, he declared: "This Republic—with its incalculable and inexhaustible resources, lying for thousands of miles back of us yet, and not possibly to be developed for ages and ages—*wants the wealth of stout poor men who will work* more than any other kind of wealth."[67]

Because he believed the western lands to be "inexhaustible" for "ages and ages," Whitman championed unrestricted immigration of the poor from Europe. His only regret was that they did not "penetrate immediately into the interior—to the 'far West' if possible—and settle down in an agricultural way."[68] It is well known, of course, that many did not, especially the Irish during the potato famine in Ireland, because they did not have the means of providing themselves with transportation and food for the trip.

Whitman also believed that "the boundless democratic free West" would eventually "outtopple in means, extent and political power, all the rest of this Republic. . . ."[69] As an ardent supporter of "free soil," he looked to the West to undermine slavery, economically and politically, and thus *save* the nation for freedom and democracy. He also thought that "the Atlantic States, with a rush after wealth, and the spread among them of effeminating luxuries, need a balance wheel like that furnished by the agricultural sections of the West."[70]

During the 1856 presidential campaign, when both political parties (or three, if we count the American or "Do Nothing") refused to face honestly

---

64. *Prose Works 1892*, I, 210.

65. Preface 1755, reprinted in *Leaves of Grass*: Comprehensive Reader's Edition, eds. Sculley Bradley and Harold W. Blodgett (New York, 1966), p. 717.

66. Frémont led an expedition to the Wind River Range of the Rocky Mountains in 1842, and published a report in 1843; a second expedition to the Oregon and California country in 1843–44, and a third in 1845 from Salt Lake to California.

67. Reprinted in *Gathering of the Forces*, ed. Cleveland Rodgers and John Black (New York, 1920), I, 163.

68. Ibid., p. 164.   69. Ibid., p. 26.

70. Ibid.

the issue of slavery and "free soil," Whitman envisioned the kind of man he thought could save the nation, an almost clairvoyant forecast of the "Rail-Splitter" who did appear four years later: "I would be much pleased to see some heroic, shrewd, fully-informed, healthy-bodied, middle-aged, beard-faced American blacksmith or boatman come down from the West across the Alleghanies and walk into the Presidency, dressed in a clean suit of working attire, and with the tan all over his face, breast, and arms; I would certainly vote for that sort of man, possessing the due requirements, before any other candidate."[71]

The previous year in his preface to the first edition of *Leaves of Grass* Whitman had also projected the American poet as "a bard . . . commensurate with" his people, *incarnating* "its geography and natural life. . . ." This bard would "flood himself with the immediate age as with the vast oceanic tides."[72] That Whitman himself did this all critics now agree, and the age with which he flooded himself was the age of his nation's expansion into the West. Though he had seen the West only in imagination, he sprinkled "Song of Myself" with images of the frontier, the Oregon Trail, the Great Plains, and the Rocky Mountains. I quote a few examples:

> Alone far in the Wilds and mountains I hunt,
> Wandering amazed at my own lightness and glee,
> In the late afternoon choosing a safe spot to pass the night,
> Kindling a fire and broiling the fresh-kill'd game,
> Falling asleep on the gather'd leaves with my dog and gun by my side.
>
> . . . .
>
> I saw the marriage of the trapper in the open air in the far west, the bride was a red girl,
> Her father and his friends sat near cross-legged and dumbly smoking, they had moccasins to their feet and large thick blankets hanging from their shoulders,
> On a bank lounged the trapper, he was drest mostly in skins, his luxuriant beard and curls protected his neck, he held his bride by the hand,
> She had long eyelashes, her head was bare, her coarse straight locks descended upon her voluptuous limbs and reach'd to her feet.[73]

Among the many roles the poet plays in this poem is that of

> A Kentuckian walking the vale of the Elkhorn in my deer-skin leggings, . . .

---

71. "The Eighteenth Presidency!" ed. Edward F. Grier (Lawrence, Kansas, 1956), p. 21.
72. Preface 1855 (see note 65 above), pp. 711, 726.
73. *Leaves of Grass* (Reader's Ed.; New York, 1966), p. 37. Subsequent page references noted parenthetically are to this edition.

A boatman over lakes or bays or along coasts, a Hoosier, Badger, Buck-
    eye; . . .

Just how far Whitman could carry his myth of the Western Pioneer,
and how little it had to do with historical reality, may be seen in the
rousing, marching poem "Pioneers! O Pioneers!" (p. 229):

> Come my tan-faced children,
> Follow well in order, get your weapons ready,
> Have you your pistols? have you your sharp-edged axes?
>   Pioneers! O Pioneers!
>
> For we cannot tarry here,
> We must march my darlings, we must bear the brunt of danger,
> We the youthful sinewy races, all the rest on us depend,
>   Pioneers! O Pioneers!
>
> O you youths, Western youths,
> So impatient, full of action, full of manly pride and friendship,
> Plain I see you Western youths, see you tramping with the foremost,
>   Pioneers! O Pioneers!

The poet sees the advance of the American frontier as only an episode
in the history of the human race, but still a high point in that evolutionary
march: "Have the elder races halted? . . . We take up the task eternal. . . .
We debouch upon a newer mightier world. . . ."

> On and on the compact ranks,
> With accessions ever waiting, with the places of the dead
>   quickly fill'd,
> Through the battle, through defeat, moving yet and never stopping,
>   Pioneers! Oh Pioneers!
>
>   . . . .
>   All the pulses of the world,
> Falling in they beat for us, with the Western movement beat,
> Holding single or together, steady moving to the front, all of us,
>   Pioneers! O Pioneers!

This poem was written in 1865, and apparently Whitman regarded the
outcome of the recent fratricidal war as another advance of the "Pioneers,"
though he alludes to it only in praise of the "mighty mother mistress," the
"fang'd and warlike mistress." In the context of *Drum-Taps*, where this
poem was first published, the "mistress mother" is the American nation,
which has survived the divisive war to the advantage, in his opinion, of
the human race. Now the "daughters of the West" must never be divided
again: ". . . in our ranks you move united, / Pioneers! O Pioneers!"

Unlike Henry Adams, Whitman never thought of these "pioneers" as omnivorous beavers destroying the primeval forests, or as Thoreau's field mice gnawing the bark to satisfy their hunger. Rather they were a brave and heroic army conquering nature for the good of mankind, creating an archetypal democracy. Remembering Emerson's shudders over man's poisoning the ground, and Thoreau's protests over the destruction of centuries-old trees, it is interesting to analyze Whitman's "Song of the Redwood-Tree." (It was written, by the way, during the second Grant administration.)

The "song" is the redwood's death chant. The tree is being cut down by the lumbermen, and the poet in fantasy hears the

> . . . crackling blows of axes sounding musically driven by strong arms,
> Riven deep by the sharp tongues of the axes, there in the redwood forest dense,
> I heard the mighty tree its death-chant chanting.   (p. 206)

The choppers and the teamsters do not hear it, only the poet. The tree sings that it too has "consciousness" and "identity," feels that it has "grandly" filled its place in nature, and must now abdicate for "a superber race," one long predicted. (The syntactical context would suggest that the redwood abdicates for a new race of trees, but the theme of the poem makes it clear that the "race" is human.)

A Conservationist or a Preservationist must find the logic of this poem maddening. The tree not only accepts annihilation, but glories in being "absorb'd, assimilated" by these superior creatures who will "really shape and mould the New World, adjusting it to Time and Space" (p. 208). They are impelled by the "hidden national will," which will breed a higher type of humanity than the world has ever known. This, of course, is only an expression in poetic symbols of the theory which the literary nationalists began shouting after the War of 1812, culminating in Whitman's 1855 preface. But I know of no other literary work which so naively reveals the American national consciousness of the nineteenth century—though with most of the people it was probably an unconscious drive. But whether conscious or unconscious, it made the plunder of their natural resources inevitable—and tragic, courting hubris, as we can now see.

> The fields of Nature long prepared and fallow, the silent, cyclic chemistry,
> The slow and steady ages plodding, the unoccupied surface ripening, the rich ores forming beneath;
> At last the New arriving, assuming, taking possession,
> A swarming and busy race settling and organizing everywhere,

> Ships coming in from the whole round world, and going out to the
> whole world, . . .   (p. 209)

These words are in roman type, to distinguish them from the tree's
song, printed in italics. Thus the poet himself says these activities are
"the means, the implements" to fullfill the promise of a thousand years,
which is a "new society . . . proportionate to Nature." The poem ends,
therefore, with the poet's prophetic vision:

> Fresh come, to a new world indeed, yet long prepared,
> I see the genius of the modern, child of the real and ideal,
> Clearing the ground for broad humanity, the true America, heir of
>   the past so grand,
> To build a grander future.

The poet says nature lay "fallow" until the pioneers came and used or
improved it by clearing the land, damming the rivers, building cities; in
brief, harnessing the forces of nature for human use. Whitman achieved
in this poem his great ambition to be the poetic spokesman of his nation.
Exploiting nature to improve the standard of living has always been the
national goal. It seemed not only good to most Americans, but almost a
fulfillment of their "manifest destiny." And no one who is not a complete antihumanist would think of stopping all consumption of nature's
products. In fact, it is the nature of living forms to consume and digest
other living forms.

Fortunately, today many thoughtful men and women think there is a
limit to this process of consumption, and if we have not quite reached it,
we are at least on the outskirts of it. Faced with this portentous situation,
we find it difficult to see our frontier history in the self-flattering manner
of Turner and Walt Whitman. Even Thoreau's misogynistic warnings
begin to seem like better prophecy than Whitman's.

But is not the real solution the one Ralph Waldo Emerson preached
in his transcendental way?—and for that reason little understood and less
heeded: namely, *man must achieve a true balance with nature.* The ecologist tells us what that means. Emerson, of course, says that more than
science is needed: a redemption of the soul of man. To understand fully
what he means by *soul* would take us into theology and metaphysics, but
the basic application of his doctrine is simpler than the concept. "The
reason why the world lacks unity," says Emerson in *Nature*, "and lies
broken and in heaps, is because man is disunited with himself. He cannot
be a naturalist [which I take to mean one who understands nature] until
he satisfies the demands of spirit."[74] Again, spirit is metaphysical, but

---

74. Emerson, *Works*, I, 73–74.

Emerson adds that the first demand of spirit is love. So I paraphrase: Until men learn to love and respect nature, of which they are a part—so that they must respect themselves and each other—, they cannot mend their broken world. For an American this means to repair the damage done to nature during and as a consequence of our frontier history: damage to forests, soil, streams, animals, etc., including the displaced aborigines. The fact that today there are many vigorous voices advocating "conservation" and "preservation"[75] shows that we are turning from the views of Whitman in "The Song of the Redwood-Tree" to Emerson's in *Nature* and Thoreau's in *The Maine Woods*.

---

75. Nash (see note 54 above) discusses the major voices and lists (pp. 274–288) the more important publications. The American Indian is also being studied with new respect: see *Teachings from the American Earth: Indian Religion and Philosophy*, ed. Dennis Tedlock and Barbara Tedlock (New York, 1975).

Hawthorne's Sketches and the English Romantics

RICHARD HARTER FOGLE

Hawthorne's sketches are perhaps too numerous, interspersed as they are among the tales of his three collections, to have been appreciated at their full value as compositions. As a whole, they are strongly unified, very highly wrought, and remarkably harmonious. "The Old Manse," for example, is a little masterpiece of controlled atmospherics and gradation, covered, as its main metaphor affirms, with an almost imperceptible luminous veil. The delicate charm of these sketches was no doubt considerably responsible for the mild and affectionate popularity which Hawthorne enjoyed in his own time up to *The Scarlet Letter,* and of which he was inclined to complain. It may be a bar to our reception of them today, and the sketch itself, like its relative the personal essay, has largely ceased to be an acceptable genre. In some instances, too, his titles repel us. Who can take seriously a work by the name of "Little Annie's Ramble"?

Also, we are perhaps inclined to remember best the sketches that are over-filled with finespun conceits and ingenuities, like "A Virtuoso's Collection," and to overemphasize the trivialities in them. As with Hawthorne's tales, however, his sketches are almost invariably firm, architecturally strong, and self-consistent. Harmonious in themselves, they are consequently unique and original, with a central life of their own. And, however light they may appear, they are essentially serious and responsible. As Allen Tate has somewhere remarked, Hawthorne was a very considerable abstract thinker, and he usually had weighty concerns in mind.

His sketches are securely moored to actuality, but more visibly than his fictions they are speculations, explorations in the world of mind and spirit, and thus are exercises in imagination. They look to the "inward sphere," the dreams, the desires, the unfulfilled aspirations of the soul, the impalpable shadows and mutations of consciousness and their mysterious origins. Hawthorne is cautious and controlled; he is aware of more than he cares to tell or could indeed express. He reflects at the end of "The Old Manse," "How narrow—how shallow and scanty too—is the stream of thought that has been flowing from my pen, compared with the broad tide of dim emotions, ideas, and associations which swell around me from that portion of my existence! How little have I told!"

"The Haunted Mind" takes up the romantic theme of dreaming and imaginative creation. Like Coleridge, Hawthorne considers the physical causes of creative dreaming, but his theory is more literary and less literal and rationalist than Coleridge on the topic. To the latter a dream is the imagination's interpretation of physical sensations, internal and external, whereas Hawthorne supposes a state of ideal receptivity after the first heavy sleep, in a condition between sleeping and waking. The two are agreed in specifying that the mind in dream fuses opposite extremes, and is subtly suspended between them. To Coleridge dream, like art, is illusion, a midpoint between delusion and actual experience. Hawthorne also conceives it as illusion, but thinks of it as a crucial moment between sleeping and waking, which partakes of insights derived from both. "You find yourself, for a single instant, wide awake in that realm of illusion, whither sleep has been the passport, and behold its ghostly inhabitants and wondrous scenery, with a perception of their strangeness such as you never attain while the dream is undisturbed." Dream brings to light a subterranean layer denied to ordinary consciousness, by excluding the external world and the will. There is an interim when one is within the dream and yet outside it, able to compare, to bring the critical process to bear upon the dream experience in a complex fusion of opposites. With its perception of strangeness, it is a romantic insight into the relation of unusual with usual, forming an imaginative truth. Thus to Keats, "The Imagination may be compared to Adam's dream—he awoke / and found it truth."

In Hawthorne this "moment of truth" resembles an experience he describes elsewhere, in which by a sudden inadvertent glance one catches nature unawares, stripped of her veil. It is an accidental, sidelong look, but a reward of many vain efforts to penetrate her mystery. Both Coleridge and Keats see the danger as well as the magic of dreaming, and Hawthorne perhaps more than either. The dream-state accentuates both pleasure and pain, the light and the darkness; and we are powerless to choose and avoid. For Hawthorne the buried corpse is always lurking, in the depths of Judge Pyncheon, or beneath the Temple's marble floor in "The Lily's Quest"; nor is it absent from the haunted mind of his dreamer:

> In the depths of every heart there is a tomb and a dungeon, though the lights, the music, and revelry above may cause us to forget their existence, and the buried ones, or prisoners, whom they hide. But sometimes and oftenest at midnight, these dark receptacles are flung wide open. In an hour like this, when the mind has a passive sensibility, but no active strength; when the imagination is a mirror, imparting vividness to all ideas, without the power of selecting or controlling

them; then pray that your griefs may slumber, and the brotherhood of remorse not break their chain.

So in Coleridge the lovely dream-garden of "Kubla Khan" has its lesser-known counterpart in "The Pains of Sleep," among which are

> Thirst of revenge, the powerless will
> Still baffled, and yet burning still!
> Desire with loathing strangely mixed
> On wild or hateful objects fixed.
> Fantastic passions! Maddening brawl!
> And shame and terror over all!
> Deeds to be hid which were not hid,
> Which all confused I could not know
> Whether I suffered, or I did:
> For all seemed guilt, remorse or woe,
> My own or others still the same
> Life-stifling fear, soul-stifling shame.

"What if Remorse," asks Hawthorne, "should stand at your bed's foot, in the likeness of a corpse, with a bloody stain upon the shroud?" And the burden may be heavy enough without positive remorse of conscience. "Sufficient, without such guilt, is this nightmare of the soul; this heavy, heavy sinking of the spirits; this wintry gloom about the heart; this in-distinct horror of the mind, blending itself with the darkness of the chamber." The indistinctness is important to the horror, as it would generally be in Hawthorne, as the sign that reality has been lost. It may be said in passing that indistinctness is an element of the deathlike acedia that Coleridge often describes, for example in his "Dejection: An Ode."

In "The Haunted Mind" the "nightmare of the soul" is the negative of the imaginative state, which is "an intermediate space; where the business of life does not intrude; where the passing moment lingers, and becomes truly the present; a spot where Father Time, when he thinks nobody is watching him, sits down by the wayside to take breath." If Keats with his habitual concreteness had described Coleridge's nightmare the results would have been literally hair-raising; as it was, Keats's dream of the imagination had its nightmarishness. He is obliged to reflect, amid the gorgeous images of his "Epistle to John Hamilton Reynolds,"

> O that our dreamings all, of sleep or wake,
> Would all their colours from the sunset take:
> From something of material sublime,
> Rather than shadow our own soul's day time
> In the dark void of night.

Imagination uncontrolled is "a sort of Purgatory blind." As with Hawthorne, nightmare will come:

> Few are there who escape these visitings,—
> P'rhaps one or two whose lives have patent wings,
> And thro' whose curtains peeps no hellish nose,
> No wild-boar tushes, and no Mermaid's toes.

In "The Haunted Mind" two hours of the night are to be spent "in that strangest of enjoyments, the forgetfulness alike of joy and woe." It is no doubt coincidental that Madeline, Keats's greatest dreamer, in "The Eve of St. Agnes" precedes her dream-vision of Porphyro by a period of oblivion, her soul

> Flown, like a thought, until the morrow-day;
> Blissfully haven'd both from joy and pain;
> Clasp'd like a missal where swart Paynims pray;
> Blinded alike from sunshine and from rain,
> As though a rose should shut, and be a bud again.

To sum up, dream is to Hawthorne as to Coleridge and to Keats a special version of imagination, allied with the unconscious mind, an indispensable element of reality. Hawthorne is most fearful of straying in the dark chambers of the soul, since of the three he is most deeply engaged with guilt and evil. Though an acute and courageous explorer, he has the sharpest sense of danger in the offing.

"A Select Party" and "The Hall of Fantasy" also affirm the romantic faith in imagination—cautiously, as is the case with "The Haunted Mind." The "Party" is held by a "Man of Fancy" at "one of his castles in the air." Only the Select are at home here; to the unfit "it was unreal, because they lacked the imaginative faith. Had they been worthy to pass within its portals, they would have recognized the truth, that the dominions which the spirit conquers for itself, among unrealities become a thousand times more real than the earth whereon they stamp their feet." The Hall of Fantasy is likewise fragile, giving "the impression of a dream, which might be dissipated and shattered to fragments by merely stamping the foot upon the pavement." Nevertheless, "with such modifications and repairs as successive ages demand, the Hall of Fantasy is likely to endure longer than the most substantial structure that ever cumbered the earth."

Both sketches are Shelleyan in their insistent emphasis upon the paradox of solid insubstantiality, or the permanence of evanescence. Their locales resemble the airy palace of Queen Mab, or the chariot of the moon in *Prometheus Unbound*, whose "wheels are solid clouds, azure and gold." Thus Hawthorne's castle in the air, whose strong foundations and massive walls were "quarried out of a ledge of heavy and sombre clouds," and irradiated with "a flood of evening sunshine." The Hall is a place of dreams, wishes, projects, and aspirations. Primarily it is a Palace of Art, lighted "through stained and pictured glass, thus filling the hall with many-colored radiance"; "its inmates breathe . . . a visionary atmosphere." It is reminiscent, indeed, of Shelley's "dome of many-colored glass," which "stains the white radiance of Eternity," especially as the "white sunshine of actual life" must needs be borne in mind amid its "gorgeous and bewildering light."

It recalls as well the stained-glass window of Keats's "Eve of St. Agnes." Keats's "casement high and triple-arch'd" is the medium of imaginative faith, in which Madeline appears transfigured, "a splendid angel newly dress'd / Save wings, for heaven." What we see of the Hall is what art conveys, the "manifest content" of the dream. "In its upper stories are said to be apartments where the inhabitants of earth may hold converse with those of the moon; and beneath our feet are gloomy cells, which communicate with the infernal regions, and where monsters and chimeras are kept in confinement and fed with all unwholesomeness." The main hall, however, the abode of the poet, contains the essential truth for those few who are capable of seeing it. Mere dreamers, fanatics, and vulgar projectors are deluded by it, "because they mistake the Hall of Fantasy for actual brick and mortar, and its purple atmosphere for unsophisticated sunshine. But the poet knows his whereabouts, and therefore is less likely to make a fool of himself in real life." None may live always in the Hall of Fantasy, but a choice few "possess the faculty, in their occasional visits, of discovering a purer truth than the world can impart among the lights and shadows of these pictured windows."

"The Hall of Fantasy" is essentially a romantic affirmation, but it is insistent upon the separation of imagination and art from total life. The problems of this relation are ever-present to the English romantic poets as well, but not so steadily in the forefront as they are to Hawthorne, who has always in mind the possibilities and the perils of going astray. Keats, who makes the greatest phrases in praise of imagination, poetry, and art, shares Hawthorne's worries about their roles, and expresses them in his tortured *Fall of Hyperion*. "Fanatics have their dreams," says Keats, "wherewith they weave / A paradise for a sect." "Poesy alone can tell her dreams," and dreams more largely, but he is not able to distinguish entirely among the fanatics, the poets, the mere dreamers, and the men of active good will.

To Hawthorne "there is but half a life—the meaner and earthlier half—for those who never find their way into the hall." The artist, as we have seen, is most at home there, but it belongs to the reformer too, and the prophet. As to these, "Many of them had gotten possession of some crystal fragment of truth, the brightness of which so dazzled them that they could see nothing else in the wide universe." Yet with all their delusions, the hall has endowed them with some inkling of true light. "Far down beyond the fathom of the intellect the soul acknowledged that all these varying and conflicting developments of humanity were united in one sentiment. . . . My faith revived even while I rejected all their schemes." Keats, and of course Shelley, also shared this faith. There is a hint here of Shelley's vast Demogorgon in *Prometheus Unbound,* his symbol for Necessity, or what must be from the nature of things. Demogorgon lives in a cave far underground, in Hawthorne's words, "Far down beyond the fathom of the intellect." He represents the unconscious, in Shelley's optimistic notion of it; he is the eternal and fundamental reality of man, his foundation. He is a very democratic conception of Necessity; it is preordained in basic truth and the structure and the movement of history that the tyrant Jupiter must fall before him. Hawthorne's Hall of Fantasy is a democratic and optimistic place. It is to be noted that in its center there is a fountain, and that "a strange vivacity is imparted to the scene by the magic dance of this fountain, with its endless transformations, in which the imaginative beholder may discern what form he will." It is remarked that its water is in some instances "known to have intoxicating qualities." So has the potent realm of Demogorgon, and its "mighty portal,"

> Whence the oracular vapour is hurled up
> Which lonely men drink wandering in their youth,
> And call truth, virtue, love, genius, or joy,
> That maddening wine of life, whose dregs they drain
> To deep intoxication; and uplift,
> Like Maenads who cry loud, Evoe! Evoe!
> The voice which is contagion to the world.

Shelley's "intoxication" is more clearly beneficent than Hawthorne's, but there is a resemblance between the two.

The function of the Hall of Fantasy is to prefigure an ideal immortality. It is the land of the legitimate desires of the human heart, and it keeps men in the way of salvation by spiritualizing (a frequent word with Hawthorne) the grossness and opacity of actual existence. The castle in the air which is the setting for "A Select Party" is similar to it, containing as it does the realizations of unrealized aspirations and plans. The most striking of the guests at the party is the American Genius of prophecy, so long looked forward to. This castle is lighted by harnessed meteors covered with evening mist, a combination that provides "the brilliancy of a powerful yet chastened imagination," artistically concealing what is irrelevant and discordant. This light "seemed to hide whatever was unworthy to be noticed and give effect to every beautiful and noble attribute."

In this castle there is a moonlight room of unrealized possibilities. The light itself is "the aggregate of all the moonshine that is scattered around the earth on a summer night while no eyes are awake to enjoy its beauty." Its principal feature is "a multitude of ideal statues, the original conceptions of the great works of ancient or modern art, which the sculptors did but imperfectly succeed in putting into marble; for it is not to be supposed that the pure idea of an immortal creation ceases to exist." Hawthorne speculates elsewhere in this fashion: both in his notebooks and in *The Marble Faun* sculpture is said to be a moonlit art, and in "An Aesthetic Company" (*The Marble Faun*) the trial sketches and cartoons of the old masters are preferred to their completed paintings, as closer to the original inspiration. Likewise the "pure idea" is triumphant in the tale of "The Artist of the Beautiful," where, although Owen Warland's master creation is destroyed he is able to view its destruction unmoved: "He had caught a far other butterfly than this." But the entire passage calls Shelley to mind.

The unseen moonlight is like the poet in the first act of *Prometheus Unbound*, whose ethereal musings are an earnest of future good, however irrelevant and insubstantial they appear:

He will watch from dawn to gloom
The lake-reflected sun illume
The yellow bees in the ivy-bloom,
Nor heed, nor see, what things they be;
But from these create he can
Forms more real than living man,
Nurslings of immortality!

The Platonic distinction between the idea or inspiration and the imperfect execution of it is widespread in romantic thought. Romantic criticism habitually tries to work back from the object of art to its vital source. Something of the power of "Kubla Khan" arises from the contrast of the poem with the vision it tries to express:

Could I revive within me
Her symphony and song,
To such a deep delight 'twould win me,
That with music loud and long,
I would build that dome in air,
That sunny dome! those caves of ice!

This view of poetry and art is particularly prominent in Shelley, to whom "the most glorious poetry that has ever been communicated to the world is probably a feeble shadow of the original conceptions of the poet."

Correspondingly, another room contains "works which the author only planned, without ever finding the happy season to achieve them." These include among others the conclusion of Coleridge's *Christabel*. Every author, it is said, "has imagined and shaped out in his thought more and far better works than those which actually proceeded from his pen." In yet another "noble saloon" the pillars are "solid gold sunbeams," so that "the room was filled with the most cheerful radiance imaginable, yet not too dazzling to be borne with comfort and delight," and added to this are "many-colored clouds of sunrise" and scattered rainbows. All this is again decidedly Shelleyan: what the room contains is also perhaps Shelleyan, "Like an unbodied joy whose race is just begun," and typical of Hawthorne too, for "whatever means and opportunities of joy are neglected in the lower world had been carefully gathered up and deposited in the saloon of morning sunshine." Hawthorne was consistently romantic in believing that his time had turned away from many legitimate pleasures in its quest for mental and material profit; the nineteenth century had become too wise and too sad, as he said both early and late.

Hawthorne's sunrise and rainbows are Wordsworthian as well as Shelleyan; they evoke the "Ode on Intimations of Immortality," which he seems to have known very well. Two points about the "Ode" are especially relevant: its use of light and its theme of immortality. As in Hawthorne's sketch there is a rainbow, and there is the glory, the splendor, the radiance of sunlight, which fade into "the light of common day." Wordsworth's poem has not wholly satisfied some students of metaphor and symbol: when we follow the course of his sun from dawn to dusk his afternoon is a bit of a letdown. Also, he apparently concedes a little too much with his

> What though the radiance which was once so bright
> Be now forever taken from my sight?

His theme is continuity, "what has been must always be." All our experience is valuable and essentially imperishable, if only we are capable of realizing its oneness, and if we can refrain from breaking the vital links of our experiencing by arbitrary and artificial exclusions. But the poet comes dangerously close, it would seem, to permitting a lapse in continuity himself.

To say this, however, is to forget that the "Ode" is about intimations of immortality. Its image-patterns are inevitably incomplete in themselves; they cannot properly be self-contained, since their function is merely to point towards the theoretical limit of eternal being, which is limitless. Wordsworth once remarked that no one could thoroughly grasp his poetry who failed to understand its infinitude—and the "Ode on Intimations of Immortality" is a notable instance of his meaning. So it was also with Hawthorne. In his sketches and elsewhere his references to providence and immortality are too consistent and emphatic to pass by. They occur in his writing both early and late (the *English Notebooks*, for example), and they cannot be dismissed as merely conventional. Like Wordsworth in his "Ode," he was perhaps inclined to concede a little too much to "the light of common day," almost to the point of self-contradiction. He can envision imaginative syntheses, as in his picture of the American Genius, but he will not stay with them. There is always something beyond, another perspective.

As has been mentioned, the most notable guest at the Select Party is the American Genius to come. American as he is, he has many of the marks of Wordsworth's ideal poet, or Shelley's. He is properly lonely and obscure, "a young man in poor attire, with no insignia of rank or acknowledged eminence." A little unusually for Hawthorne, he reconciles warm sensibility with power of thought: in his eyes is "such a light as never illuminates the earth save when a great heart burns as the household fire of a grand intellect." The American Genius "dwells as yet unhonored among men," but is destined for "triumph over all the ages." He is, in short, a compendium of the romantic poets' conception of the ideal romantic poet. This being so, it is interesting to reflect that in "Hawthorne and His Mosses" Melville identifies the Genius with Hawthorne himself.

"A Select Party" and "The Hall of Fantasy" emphasize the mingled magic and danger of the world of imagination and fancy; and it has been suggested earlier that Keats among the romantics is most like Hawthorne in his worries about the proper relationship of this world to reality. His enigmatic *Lamia* is a case in point. The supernatural Lamia creates her own "hall of fantasy," an enchanted palace, for her lover Lycius, and they abide in it in perfect happiness until Lycius insists upon relating it to the world outside, to the destruction of both Lamia and himself. The poem is not easy to interpret, but it is at any rate clear that Lycius fails to grasp the relationship of art to life. Lamia has created an artistic illusion, which her lover shatters from failure of insight. Unlike Melville's Bartleby, he does not know where he is. In Hawthorne's two sketches it is the peculiar power of the poets and artists that they do know where they are.

"The Toll-Gatherer's Day" is a study of time and eternity in which the toll-gatherer himself is a Wordsworthian figure, mildly wise, while the stream of travellers, as in Shelley's *Triumph of Life*, represents flux, motion, illusion, and dream. At the end of the day the lighthouse and the stars stand forth in eternity, "mingling reveries of heaven with remembrances of earth." The sketch manages to suggest Wordsworth and Shelley and at the same time decidedly express Hawthorne's own cautious and delicate explorations. His Wordsworthian toll-gather is ambivalent in his sensitivity. Amid life's strong current he is still, he sees without acting, and the full heat of the day, the center of the dusty thoroughfare, would be too much for him.

"Sights from a Steeple" is Shelleyan in its comprehensive perspective, and particularly in looking upward to "the very zenith," where "the ethereal azure . . . appears only a deepened shade of nothingness." It contains, too, a study of clouds while a storm is gathering, and builds to the crescendo of the storm itself, with a final rainbow of hope. The strategically located spectator is a "spiritualized Paul Pry" invisibly seeing and knowing all. In its aerial contrasts and its breadth of vision it resembles Shelley's light-perfused "Lines Written Among the Euganean Hills," and something as well that Shelley does not give, but can be found in Coleridge's poem "This Lime-tree Bower My Prison." "Sights from a Steeple," as does the Coleridge piece, presents a development as well as a change of light and object. It is cyclical and shaded.

"Sunday at Home" likewise calls to mind the complex, imperceptible motion and development of light and shade in Coleridge's "Lime-tree Bower." Its dominant image, the sunlight on the church spire, traverses a cycle of slow change "from morning to night." In Hawthorne's own canon its transfigured Sunday morning is like the opening of "The Minister's Black Veil," and both are Shelleyan in their radiance. Coincidentally, there are two Blakean touches in "Sunday at Home." We have no indication that Hawthorne knew Blake, and the point is worth making only because there are more important resemblances elsewhere. However this may be, Hawthorne's churchgoing children are like flowers or butterflies, as Blake's orphans of the first "Holy Thursday" are "flowers of London town"; and Hawthorne's sympathetic reflection upon blacks who might pray to be white makes one think of "The Little Black Boy."

"Night Sketches," like others mentioned here, a visionpiece, is Shelleyan in its use of darkness and space. As Shelley reaches out, so Hawthorne's "farthest star that stands sentinel on the borders of uncreated space" is like "the soul of Adonais" a limit, or the meeting-place of spiritual and physical worlds. "Night Sketches" is a study in dream-like fancy, whose setting is the border between inward and outward, the strange and familiar, in musings before a homely fire, which merges at the conclusion of the sketch by way of a lantern in the darkness into the "lamp of Faith, enkindled at a celestial fire." The conclusion of Shelley's *Adonais* is in its elements the same, although Shelley is far more intense.

The Romanticism of Hawthorne's sketches resembles the Romanticism of Coleridge, Wordsworth, Shelley, and Keats, though it is not identical with it, just as the poets are not identical with each other. In all of them, however, are the same opposing urges. One is toward the synthetic and consummate symbol, which somehow manages to pack everything into one; or more elegantly, to convey the universal by a particular; or Emersonianly, the All by means of the Each. The other urge is toward infinity, and therefore indeterminacy of pattern. These opposite tendencies are present in Hawthorne, although not in precisely the same proportions as in either the Romanticism I have specified or in any individual Romantic. Hawthorne commits himself less fully to the synthesizing symbol, and he is frankly tentative; he seeks nice adjustments, and he is continually aware of possible modifications by particular contexts and circumstances. Ordinarily he understands rather than imagines syntheses. He employs Romantic symbols critically and eclectically, without surrendering his intellect to them: invariably propositions awaken his mind to counter-propositions.

The Poet as Theme Reader: William Vaughn Moody, a Student, and Louisa May Alcott

GEORGE ARMS

For English 22 at Radcliffe, William Vaughn Moody wrote this comment on a first fortnightly theme, a reminiscence by a student who had read *Little Women* and later met its author:

> A charming theme, both in spirit and treatment. It has the unmistakable note of sincerity, and has at times an imaginative and pathetic quality which touches and convinces the reader. On the other hand the phrasing is often weakly conventional, giving a note of false sentiment which is in sharp contrast with the pervading atmosphere. It could be shortened by the omission of unnecessary details and a more rigid economy in language. Your style is apt to degenerate into diffuseness. Your sentence structure is not always good, too much being crowded into one sentence, and the parts being strung together with loose connectives
> Rewrite.
>
> W. V. Moody.[1]

Before we turn to the theme itself, Moody's teaching of English 22 deserves a brief review.[2] Graduating from Harvard in 1893, he studied for his M.A. in the following year. In the year after that, he taught in the advanced composition course under the direction of Lewis E. Gates at Harvard and Radcliffe. This was the year that Frank Norris (whose themes were read mostly by Herbert V. Abbot, though some by Gates) and Gertrude Stein (whose themes were read mostly by Moody) were enrolled in English 22. Stein's extant essays have been printed, the fortnightly ones with Moody's comments and marginal entries.[3] The comments usually

---

1. The comment and theme are owned by the author of this article. Moody's criticism and his later marginal commentary are printed with the kind permission of Frederick J. Fawcett, 2nd. Republication of all manuscript materials printed in this article requires the same permissions as are indicated here and elsewhere.

2. Moody's career at Harvard receives extended treatment in Maurice F. Brown, *Estranging Dawn: The Life and Works of William Vaughn Moody* (Carbondale, Ill., 1973). I am also indebted to Mr. Brown for help on many problems.

3. Rosalind S. Miller, *Gertrude Stein: Form and Intelligibility* (New York, 1949). Of the forty-seven themes printed, seven are fortnightlies with extended commentary, of

run the same length as that on the essay about Louisa May Alcott, though the marginal notations are less frequent, somewhere between seven and twelve as against the thirty in the Alcott theme. Rosalind S. Miller, the editor, thinks that Moody did less than full justice to Stein, largely because of his attachment to the genteel tradition. To a degree she is right, for Moody objects to treating "a morbid psychological state" or to "the cold-blooded methods of laboratory analysis" or to an "analysis of the girl's reaction" as "unpleasant." But more usually Moody concerns himself with style, point of view, structure, and mechanics. In comparing Stein's writing in English 22 with that of Norris, James D. Hart finds her "immature in ideas and techniques," apparently endorsing her course grade of C and Norris' B+ at midyear with a final A.[4]

Besides Stein's, the only other set of Moody-corrected themes that I have located are eight fortnightlies by Wilhelm Segerblom filed in the Harvard University Archives.[5] Segerblom was evidently not a man with literary interests, so that Moody's treatment of his work provides sharp contrast with that of Stein. Little marginal notation appears (an average of four entries an essay), suggesting that Moody regarded Segerblom as unlikely to improve his style. The general comments on the extant essays are, however, with one exception close to the hundred-word range that seems standard with Moody, though they strike me as harsher than Segerblom's workmanlike if unadorned prose deserves. On the first theme, an amusing report of a laboratory experiment that miscarried, Moody explodes, "This theme has not much literary value," but later concedes its "considerable merit of perfect clearness and directness of statement." When in "Theme No. 6" Segerblom attempts a story of a widow's change from squalor to salvation through the gift of a geranium, Moody leads off, "This would make a very good tract for a Flower mission, though to the unregenerate mind the effect seems hopelessly in excess of the cause." Ultimately the teacher and student come to guarded terms in the "connected work" of five sequential themes, of which happily we have the whole set—an argument for the Viking colonization of North America and its influence on the first voyage of Columbus. Mostly Moody regards the sequence with respect, allowing rather less solid documentation than I think a teacher

which six are read by Moody. Of the remaining forty, two are rewritten fortnightlies and the rest are daily themes.

4. James D. Hart, ed., *A Novelist in the Making* (Cambridge, Mass., 1970), pp. 13 and 15. The forty-four extant themes by Norris are all dailies, all but seven relating to *Blix, McTeague,* and *Vandover and the Brute.* Mr. Hart's introduction includes an illuminating description of English 22.

5. William W. Whalen, of the University Archives, has generously searched the English 22 essay files for those corrected by Moody and has found only this set. Quotations are with the permission of Mr. Fawcett (see n. 1) and of the Harvard University Library. Segerblom (1872–1941) taught chemistry at Phillips Exeter Academy from 1899 to 1937; author of several books, he also published many articles and pamphlets.

would today. On the final essay of both the sequence and course he begins his comment, "You bring together a very considerable body of evidence and marshall it on the whole effectively." But he concludes his paragraph by advising Segerblom that he must learn to organize "if you expect to go on with work of an expository nature."

On the whole, then, though the evidence constitutes a small sampling, the general consensus that Moody read his student's essays with care and perception is substantiated. That he did not detect genius in Stein or appreciate the interests of Segerblom are the lapses of distinguished critics as well as of teachers of writing. How many themes he usually corrected I have not been able to find out. As he wrote Robert M. Lovett on April 25, 1895, "You will forgive me for not sooner answering your kind letter, when you call to mind your early morning and midnight coping with the English 22 fortnightly." [6]

At this time Lovett and Robert Herrick were trying to persuade Moody to come to the University of Chicago, where indeed he became an instructor following his year at Harvard. About his early teaching there we have at least two accounts, a booklet by Grace N. Veeder, who took his English 4 in the fall of 1896, and a typescript by Charlotte Wilson, who took his course in the summer of 1898.[7] As one might expect from former students who were moved to write about him, both reminiscences are tributes to his effectiveness as a teacher. Mrs. Veeder has printed her class notes, which suggest that English 4, a "Course of Daily and Fortnightly Themes," was modeled closely on English 22. To the four kinds of writing in English 22—"Description, Narration, Exposition, and Argument"— Moody apparently added a fifth, "Persuasion." But as the surviving themes by Norris and Stein suggest, neither course adhered closely to these rhetorical genres. Perhaps more openly than at Harvard, Moody turned the direction of English 4 toward creative writing or literary criticism: the class notes report Moody's reading from submitted essays, but more frequently from novelists (as George Eliot, Meredith, and Thackeray) and poets (as Browning, Keats, and Tennyson). On one occasion Moody compared sonnets with daily themes and may have suggested that the students could write sonnets as an alternate for themes. As Veeder suggests, the course was "artistic" and not as systematic as English 3.

But it is time to turn to the author of the essay on Louisa May Alcott, the literary subject of which may partly have caused Moody to call it "charming." Her name was Florence Phillips, and except for what she says

---

6. Daniel G. Mason, ed., *Some Letters of William Vaughn Moody* (Boston, 1913), p. 23.

7. Grace N. Veeder, *Concerning William Vaughn Moody* (Waukesha, Wis., 1941), 19 pp.; Charlotte Wilson [Baker], "The Gift" (ca. 1913), 6 pp. Both works have been courteously supplied by Jane Colokathis, of the John Regenstein Library, University of Chicago. I have not tried to locate themes done at Chicago that were corrected by Moody.

of herself in the reminiscence, I have not found out much about her. Since she was a Special Student, the Radcliffe College Archives have only a little information.[8] Born in 1864, she had attended Miss Annie Brown's School in New York City, and between 1892 and 1895 she took one or two courses each year at Radcliffe, receiving a grade of B in English 22 (about halfway between Stein's C and Norris' B+/A) for the fall semester of 1894. The date of her death is still to be established: the alumnae directory lists her as deceased in 1926, but the preceding directory of 1922 gives her address as 245 West 76 Street.

In transcribing Miss Phillips' essay (her first fortnightly, October 10), I have used standard editorial symbols to show Moody's corrections, written in red ink: square brackets for comments (usually written in the margins but here placed after the matter to which they apply), pointed brackets for cancellations (by lining through, by parentheses, or by circling), vertical arrows for insertions, and italics for underlining. Phillips' manuscript, a model of neatness, has been transcribed exactly as she wrote it. In order to avoid confusion with Moody's corrections, her relatively few cancellations and insertions (about a dozen) have not been recorded. Mostly in the first paragraph Miss Phillips makes some insertions (definitely in her own handwriting), cancellations, and parenthetical markings in pencil— also unrecorded. It seems likely that she penciled these changes in response to Moody's direction, "Rewrite"; and their appearance mostly in the first paragraph suggests a conference with Moody before she made her revised draft.

My Romance.

The lowest drawer of my desk is seldom unlocked, and it is never opened by any ⟨other than⟩ ↑one but[9]↓ myself. For there I keep my few cherished possessions, the *"death in life" relics of my experience* [A trifle ornate]. Far back and quite at the bottom of my drawer there is a little book. ⟨.⟩ ↑. T↓ the brown covers are faded, and the gilt letters of the title are worn with age. A few letters tied together with a string of white ribbon, and a blue silk marker with the words "Remember me" in faded lettering, lie between the *tinged* [Ambiguous] pages ⟨of the volume.⟩ On the ⟨only remaining⟩ title page a verse is written in a child's cramped hand, and over the headings of the chapters and on the margins of the leaves there are sentences like these,—"Jo is a dear splendid tom-boy," "how good that Beth got well," "what a good

---

8. Elizabeth Shenton, Assistant to the Director, the Arthur and Elizabeth Schlesinger Library, Radcliffe College, has kindly provided me with information on Florence Phillips in the archives. Inquiries in the usual places have not yielded further knowledge of her, and I would of course welcome a fuller biography from someone who knew her.

9. Moody wrote "except" before "but" and cancelled it.

time they did have," "I love aunt Jo better than anyone *almost*."¹⁰

The *almost* was significant to me, *it symbolized my mother* [Inexactly phrased]. Soon after she had made me a gift of the book, ↑and↓ while I was still a very little girl, my mother died. And my aunt, to whose care I was left, did not give presents except on Christmas and on birthdays. Two books a year will not make a library grow fast, and *if they would*, those *new books were not always* [Not clear] the kind I liked. ⟨And⟩ my gifts ↑moreover↓ no longer bore the dear inscription "With mothers love." So my oldest friends remained my dearest for two reasons, because they were associated with the memory of my Mother, and because I had no others that I liked as well [Repetition of idea—Condense the paragraph].¹¹

I found refuge from all my little sorrows, ⟨and I shared all my little joys⟩ [Disturbs the idiom.] in the companionship of *"Jo" and "Polly"* [Be more definite]. These friends were as real to me as any in life. I pictured them in other scenes than those in the stories, and when I walked with my aunt on the avenue bright with shops and busy life I often imagin*ed myself one of my favorites* [Not clear]. I tried to imitate their virtues. I learned all that I could about Boston, where they lived; and one day I learned something that troubled me. I heard a lady say that the Boston people were cold, stiff in manners, that all the women ⟨there⟩ wore eye glasses and walked with a hop-skip-and-jump, that they aped the English and were not at all like New-Yorkers. My governess was English ⟨,⟩ ↑.↓ I¹² tried to picture "Jo", "Meg", "Rose", or even "aunt Jo" like ⟨my governess⟩ ↑her↓ ,¹³ *with spectacles, and ejaculating* [Not quite smooth] "fancy" every now-and-then ⟨;⟩ ↓.↑ I found it impossible to walk with a hop-skip-and-jump. So finally I concluded that my friends were not that sort of people, and thus healed the painful sense of separation from them *caused by these peculiarities* [Inexact]. "Little Women" was once more my Bible, and the brown house on the outskirts of Boston, the home of the March family, was my Mecca, toward which I often looked from my window in an uptown street *in the metropolitan city*. [Circumlocutory]

One day, with mingled feelings of regret and superior wisdom, such as children feel when they learn that Santa Claus is not Santa Claus

---

10. The underlining of "almost" here and in the next paragraph is by Phillips.

11. Moody's vertical line from "remained" through "as well" applied these remarks to the whole passage.

12. Here, as usually elsewhere, in correcting run-on sentences Moody writes over the comma with an "x," which I have transcribed as a period. On this occasion he writes over the "I" of the essay with his own "I"—obviously the result of habit in capitalizing the first letter of a new sentence.

13. Phillips had deleted "her" with its uncertain antecedent and inserted "my governess," while Moody cancels "my governess" and restores "her." Students seldom win!

⟨but that their parents is Santa,⟩ the thought came to me that "aunt Jo" was Miss Alcott, that Miss Alcott created my people, and that she didn't look like "Jo" or "Polly" but was grown up and probably *quite* [?] serious. I pictured her a sunny, motherly woman with soft brown hair and eyes like my Mothers.¹⁴ Every bit of *news* [?] concerning her that I could find ⟨was⟩ ↑I↓ treasured. One day an article written by ⟨herself⟩ ↑her↓ about her ↑own↓ early life appeared in St. Nicholas, with a wood-cut portrait.¹⁵ How I hovered over that article, and how *blitherly* [Best word?] I framed the wood-cut likeness of my friend in a cardboard frame, the ⟨corners tied together⟩ with blue ribbons.

My affection for Miss Alcott did not lessen when I entered my teens, and my dearest hope and constant faith was that I should see her some day,—some day when I grew up and could do as I liked. At length I did *grow up, for my* [Logical?] brother married. And then I knew the time had come for me to see Miss Alcott. I felt that if I could catch a glimpse of her as she passed her door it would sooth my injured feelings for the loss of my brother, and straighten the general crookedness of the world. Permission to pass a month in *Boston* with a friend once obtained it was not long before I found myself riding out of the Grand Central Station toward *Boston*, [Repetition]¹⁶ the city of my dreams [Diffuse].¹⁷

I knew that Miss Alcott's home was in Concord, and I had pictured that village on a hill overlooking Boston; a ⟨sort of⟩ ↑an↓ Arcadian place where many wise and lovely beings lived together. It was, therefore, ⟨rather⟩ disappointing to be obliged to take the train to reach it. My friend and I went there one fair June morning. At the Concord station a one armed man with a carry-all was waiting for pilgrims, and *we were* at once *driven* [Avoid passive constructions] to Miss Alcott's home. Our ⟨guide and⟩ driver proved loquacious, and ⟨he⟩ did not object to the questions showered upon him. We soon learned, with a sense of relief, that Miss Alcott was not in Concord; that she was a plain woman who didn't "put on airs", and that she had a smile like a sunbeam. He told us sundry other things about Mr. Alcott who was living, and Emerson and Thoreau who were dead, but these accounts did not interest me very much. I was absorbed in what I saw as we drove about under the tall Elms: there was the beloved river where ⟨"⟩ Jo ⟨"⟩ met Apollyon ↑,↓ there was the hill that the "little

14. An apostrophe in "Mothers" appears probably in pencil, here omitted as a late correction. See also n. 23.
15. Not located. Phillips may have confused the *St. Nicholas* sketch with one in *The Youth's Companion*, but that has not been located either.
16. Moody has drawn a line between the first underlined "Boston" and the second.
17. A vertical line applies "Diffuse" to the whole sentence.

pilgrims climbed", and there was "the square brown house" where my beloved ⟨"⟩ March ⟨"⟩ family once had lived. I pictured ⟨"⟩ Jo ⟨"⟩ reading in the friendly old apple tree which grew in the garden of Miss Alcott's early home ⟨;⟩ ↑.↓ I fancied "Meg" singing in the parlor of the old brown house to "Beths" accompaniment ⟨;⟩ ↑.↓ ⟨and⟩ "Mrs. March's" motherly face seemed to look out from one of an upper window, and I heard her cheery voice call "girls, girls *have*[18] you pocket handkerchiefs," and a gay, girlish laugh ring, as two little figures disappeared down the unpaved street *through the mists of long ago* [Sentimental and conventional]. I spent a long, blissful day roaming about the green, sweet-smelling village, full of *summer sights and sounds* [Quotation?], *till a shower blew up* [Destroys unity of sentence]. We were obliged to seek shelter from the big drops, and as we waited under a blooming chestnut tree, some one in a house nearby played the second movement of Chopin's "Funeral March"; the familiar, ⟨beloved⟩ melody mingled with my ⟨half⟩ dreamy thoughts, and made a fitting close to one of the happiest days of my life.

A few *days* after my eventful *day* in Concord, a lady waiting on the wharf at Nonquitt for the small steam-tug which conveyed passengers from New Bedford, may have been annoyed by two eager faced girls trying to stare her out of countenance. Why I knew Miss Alcott at first sight I never felt quite sure, for she did not much resemble her photographs, that I had seen. [Remodel / Not well massed][19] ⟨And⟩ while we sailed across the bay, in the sunset, I had pictured Miss Alcott strolling on the beach, humming ⟨"Three Fishers" or some other⟩ ↑a↓ sea-song, for it was a romantic evening, *the air soft and* salt [Syntax], and the blue bay ⟨quite⟩ [Inexact use] tumbled with little waves. But the moment that I saw the plain, *almost English-governess-like looking* [Awkward] woman on the Nonquitt wharf I I [*sic*] knew she was Louisa Alcott. The ↑?↓[20] tall figure, the fine head, the deep arch of the brows about the eyes, and the simple hat and gown ⟨in those days of fuss and feathers,⟩ marked her ⟨with a distinction that was⟩ unmistakabl ⟨e⟩ ↑y↓ [Diffuse]. Yet my disappointment at first was keen, for she did not look like the image I had cherished so fondly in my imagination. And when I was left alone in my room at the hotel, I threw myself in a disappointed heap on the bed moaning ↑,↓ " ↑I↓ ⟨i⟩s *that* my dear aunt Jo ⟨."⟩ ↑?"↓

18. The underlining is by Phillips.
19. A vertical line probably applies the comment to the passage from "Why I knew" through "Nonquitt wharf."
20. An illegible word is inserted at this point in a somewhat darker ink than is usual in the essay and in handwriting probably not that of Phillips. Underlining of "that" at the end of the paragraph is by Phillips.

Miss Alcott had a cottage at Nonquitt, near the sea, but she took her meals at the hotel, and by some happy chance we were placed at her table. How my heart beat when that first night at supper the *tall form "came down upon us"* [?]. I looked out of the opposite window steadily through that meal, and I left the table with my berries ⟨quite⟩ untasted. But I watched for her on the piazza, and when she passed out of the door, stopping to speak to an old lady, I felt a rush of sympathy and love. No, she was not the handsome woman I had pictured so fondly in the old days, glowing with health and life ⟨, that⟩ ↑. That↓ Miss Alcott belonged now to the cycle of departed fairy Kings and Queens. The real Miss Alcott was a dignified woman, past fifty, with a sad, careworn face and absent eyes. People said that she had faded since her Mother's death, ten years ago, and that she was suffering from the effects of overwork. But the beautiful head with its wealth of dark chestnut hair, and the strength and refinement in her expression and movements gave her a Queenly [No cap?] presence. Her smile was like sunshine, it transfigured her face; *and latter I often caught glimpses* of the *droll, tender woman beloved by so many girls and boys* [Anticlimax—Also destroys the unity of your sentence].

One day, when I had been sitting opposite her at meals a full week, she spoke to me. And then one evening I found myself in her tiny parlor;—I was too excited by the event to sleep much that night! I haunted her steps at a respectful distance day ⟨by⟩ ↑after↓ day. A few times I met her on the cliffs, and one afternoon I sat by her side under a friendly tree which grew near her door. For her sake I braved the snakes, and ruined my clothes, in quest of water lilies, and ⟨I⟩ went alone into the tall wheat fields to gather crimson lilies. And how shy and glad I felt when she guessed my secret and said one morning, with a kind and penetrating glance, "are you the good fairy who leaves flowers on my doorstep"? I did not dream of telling her that I had come all the way from New York for the purpose of seeing her, but she guessed I wanted something, and one evening I had a long talk with her. She listened to my little tale of perplexities [Very charming][21] with sympathy, and something of amusement I think, her eyes turning often from my childish face *toward the summer sea.* That night when she kissed me I whispered "I shall never love anyone as I do you," and I never shall, ⟨in the same way.⟩ [This jars upon me as a false note of conventional sentiment. Find a fresher phrase][22]

---

21. Moody's vertical line applies "Very charming" to the whole passage beginning with "sleep much that night!" toward the start of the paragraph.

22. Moody's comment may apply only to the cancelled phrase, but it begins where he underlines "toward the summer sea"—otherwise unexplained.

The month soon passed and I was called home. I saw Miss Alcott twice the following winter; and at Christmas I sent her roses. One March night my brother gently broke the news to me that Miss Alcott was dead. I took my little book then, my mother's gift, the dear volume of "Little Women", from its nook on the book-shelf, and I put it away with a few letters in the bottom drawer of my desk. I felt that some warmth had gone forever from my life; I knew that a beautiful spirit had passed from this world, and that my little romance was ended.

I must apologize for making this theme longer than it should be, and shall try to keep within the limits in future.

We have already seen how Moody commented on the essay. Certainly he is justified in speaking of a touch of "false sentiment," especially in view of the writer's age when she wrote it—thirty years or well beyond that of the average undergraduate. And he is right too on the conventional phrasing, the diffuseness, and the loose connectives.[23] As for his asking the author to rewrite, his request is not unusual. Of the six Stein essays he read, he asked her to rewrite all or parts of three, though he gave her a choice of revising on one of these; and of the eight Segerblom themes he wanted rewriting of all or parts of three, but gave a choice of revising or rewriting three others, perhaps because he felt that rewriting would do no good.

But to return to his response to the Phillips essay on Alcott, one wonders whether Moody knew any of Alcott's books (he was born in the same year that the second part of *Little Women* appeared) and whether he had the ambivalent attitude toward it and its sequels generally held in the literary community. Finally, Moody might have entertained the possibility (as I have) that the meeting with Alcott was a fictional projection on Phillips' part—the coincidence of their being seated at the same hotel table perhaps going too far in this delightful fantasy!

Whatever Moody's knowledge of *Little Women*, Phillips knew the book well, as the most specific allusions—Jo meeting Apollyon on the river and others on the Concord visit—bear out. Though Polly appears in *An Old-Fashioned Girl* (1870), she is properly paired with Jo, since she has many of Jo's characteristics. Jo as an aunt does not emerge until *Little Men* (1871), third in the series, though she is technically an aunt (since her sister Meg has twins) in *Little Women* itself, and her persona merges with the

---

23. Like most theme readers, Moody does not catch everything. Most notably he is casual about missing apostrophes and irregular capitalization. Though he corrects most run-on sentences, they do not upset him as much as they still upset many.

author's increasingly, as the six miscellanies entitled *Aunt Jo's Scrap-Bag* (1872–1882) remind us. The girl Rose plays a part in *Eight Cousins* (1875), fourth in the series, and the main part in its sequel *Rose in Bloom* (1876). While some *Little Women* devotees may object to Phillips' notation "how good that Beth got well" in view of her dying in the second part of the novel, she does survive an attack of scarlet fever in the first part, when everyone has given up hope of her living.

As I suggested, I have speculated from time to time on the actuality of the meeting of Phillips and Alcott. It has seemed so fitly fortuitous that I am partly sorry to have verified it as a fact through the discovery of three letters from Alcott to a "Florence,"[24] who turns out definitely to be the writer of the essay. The three letters[25] deserve printing for their bearing on the Phillips-Alcott relationship and for the additional insight they provide of Louisa May Alcott in her final years.

Alcott almost certainly wrote the first letter of December 26 in 1885, acknowledging the Christmas gift of roses mentioned at the end of the Phillips essay. Main evidence for dating is the reference to *The Alcott Calendar for 1886*, which would have been marketed in the holiday season of late 1885 and which may have reproduced the Walton Ricketson bas-relief.[26] Though it is tempting to regard those roses as having been sent on Christmas, 1887 (the Christmas before Alcott's death on March 6, 1888), Phillips telescopes the time in her essay. As for the two winter visits of which she writes, one suspects that they came after the gift, perhaps in response to the letter of thanks, or again, with the fusion of time in the essay, that they may have been in separate years.

Dec. 26*th*

Dear Florence.

Many thanks for the roses & the Xmas wishes. Both were very sweet & pleasant to receive on that day, & I hope came from a happy, busy girl who begins to find her efforts & hopes blossom into contentment & peace of mind.

---

24. The discovery owes to the careful search of the Alcott papers at the Houghton Library by Mrs. Richard B. Currier, of the Manuscript Department. She has also identified for me the Alcott diaries of 1885, 1886, and 1887. Though no references to Florence Phillips appear in them, they provide background for these later years. I am also indebted to John C. MacLean, of Orchard House, Concord, for carefully reading and describing the 1888 diary.

25. Printed here by the kind permission of the Louisa May Alcott Association and of the Houghton Library.

26. Raymond L. Kilgour, *Messrs. Roberts Brothers Publishers* (Ann Arbor, Mich., 1952), p. 227, describes the calendar as containing "Louisa's portrait and views of Concord homes." I have not been able to locate a copy. Though the Ricketson bas-relief was to appear as the frontispiece of *Jo's Boys*, published about October 9, 1886, the announcement that "The bas-relief is done" hardly suggests book publication, but appearance in the calendar seems possible.

I have been poorly for some time, but keep about & am not quite a drone. We are in B. you know, & the boys & Mrs P.[27] enjoy it very much.

Lulu is losing her teeth & looks like a little granny, but is well & busy with school & play.

Have you had an Alcott Calender? If not let me send you one. They go very well & Fred is very fine with his first literary success.

The bas-relief is done, & people like it. Mr R. prefers softness to strength so has missed what I like best, but the old lady looks young & amiable, & as she was some ten or fifteen years ago. Are you going to have one?

I wish I had something *very* lovely to send you, but perhaps a very earnest wish for help & happiness is what you would like best, & much love

from your *friend*

L. M. A.

Further support that the letter of December 26, 1885, is the first of the three comes from a less intimate tone than appears in the other letters, though this is the only one in which Alcott sends her love. The dating, especially in conjunction with the next letter, sets the latest possible year for Phillips' visit to Nonquitt as 1885. That year is also likely, since it seems more in keeping with the time that the young woman would not have traveled alone to Boston until she was twenty-one, which she had just become.[28] Under "May & June" the 1885 diary notes that Alcott settled in a little cottage with Lulu and her governess, most likely on June 20, with later entries indicating that she stayed until August 8. Though Lulu and the governess are not mentioned in the theme, it may be expected to focus on Louisa May Alcott alone. However, quite possibly the visit could have taken place anytime beginning in 1881, when Alcott first went to Nonquitt; and Lulu, the daughter of Alcott's sister May, who had died soon after her daughter's birth in 1879, would have been with her aunt since the first Nonquitt summer.[29]

The second letter follows on June 10, 1886, with the year established by Alcott's 1886 diary entry under "June" that shows her to be at Mt. Wachusett and to have just read Hedge's new book. The letter also points to the

---

27. Mrs. Anna Alcott Pratt and Louisa May Alcott's two nephews, John Sewall Pratt Alcott (whom his aunt adopted on July 10, 1887) and Frederick Alcott Pratt.

28. The essay speaks of Louisa May Alcott as "past fifty" (she was born in late 1832) and notes her mother's death (late 1877) as "ten years ago." This chronology, a bit inconsistent, still allows 1885 as reasonable.

29. Madeleine B. Stern, *Louisa May Alcott* (Norman, Okla., 1950, 1971), pp. 283–284 and 292–294. The book has provided most of my biographical information, and in addition Ms. Stern has helped greatly by patiently providing further guidance.

Nonquitt visit as in 1885, for if Phillips had met Alcott the previous June, quite probably she wrote the next year with the hope of seeing her again. Interestingly, it reverts to the "perplexities" for which Phillips had sought advice one evening at Nonquitt, and invites further correspondence.

Mt Wachuset.
June 10*th*

Dear Florence,

Your kind letter finds me on the hillside trying to get strength for home cares & duties after a winter of illness & idleness.

Dont despair, my dear, one gathers strength from falls, & experience is a grand teacher stern as she seems.

I am a very despondent old soul, & nothing but duty & an ever growing faith in the great Helper keeps me from despair when year after year goes by with no record but suffering.

Pain is *my* teacher, & my lesson to give up, to wait & be cheerful, [ca. 2 letters missing].30 A serene soul can ma[ke] a feeble body ⟨of⟩ [un?] burden if it can only keep up high enough.

I am glad any words of mine help you, I wish I could set you a better example, but one's failures often serve others, & so have a use. I am not going to Nonquit this year but shall be here & at home.

No N.Y. nor any pleasure trips for me yet. I still hope but make no plans.

What are you reading? If you like German writers Hedge's new book "Hours with the German Classics" is good. I enjoyed it very much.

Write to me when you feel like it & tell me any troubles I can help. Keep hoping & trying, & be sure the strength & light will come, for no sincere effort is ever wasted.

With best wishes for a happy summer I am
affectionately yrs [signature clipped out]

The letter of December 7 cannot be dated with the certainty of that of June 10, but very likely it belongs to 1886 too. Alcott probably did not move into the Dunreath Place sanatorium in Roxbury until January 1, 1887, and she had begun the fall of 1886 at 10 Louisburg Square, where she had been the winter before. Though she was ill "with my dyspepsia" throughout 1886, it does not appear from her diaries that she was nearly as ill as in 1887, a year in which her almost daily entries read like a medical casebook of a woman painfully dying. Yet at the end of 1887 she

---

30. These brackets and the two pairs following mark the clipping of the signature on the verso of the sheet. In this letter and the next, standard editorial symbols show Alcott's few corrections.

rallied and could conclude that year with the comment: "A hard year, but over now. Please God the next be happier for us all."[31]

Dec. *7th.*

Dear Florence

I am always glad to hear from you, & to find that you are "creeping on," though I dare say I should think you were learning ↑to↓ walk fast if I saw you.

Being mortal we cannot expect to fly, & must content ourselves with a long slow climb, glad if each year we are one step higher than the last.

Watch, wait, *try* & leave the end to time sure that all will be well if we are patient, trusting & cheerful. It is hard for youn[g][32] people to believe th[at] *everything* has to wait, & in their hurry then are apt to help open the buds & so spoil them instead of letting them bloom as God pleases.

Find some poor people to help, even one girl to cheer up, or a child to clothe, & it will do you good. I'm very poorly with my dyspepsia & I cheer myself up by looking after a very destitute family, & giving them the food I cant eat. Try it.

We are in Boston where we were last winter, & Lulu is blooming and good with an excellent governess.

It *is* a comfort to know that out of my own experiences & trials I have extracted help or pleasure for others. I suppose that was why they were sent me. Write when you feel like it. With much hope & all good wishes yr friend [signature clipped out]

The letter of December 7, 1886, if I have correctly surmised the date, is the most exhortational of the three; yet it still has the quality of moving, especially in view of the troubled life of the older woman at the time. Probably Florence Phillips continued to feel the "warmth," to use her term at the close of her essay, even though the moralizing seems to me to tend toward the expedient ethic that becomes increasingly prominent in the *Little Women* sequels—"Be nice to others because you'll feel nicer yourself," to put it rudely. Still, here is a girl who, like so many of her generation, found in Jo, that "dear splendid tom-boy," a real liberation; and as a young woman she found in Jo's creator much of Jo herself, a "beautiful spirit," whom we admire for her resilience and humanity.[33]

31. Printed here by the kind permission of the Louisa May Alcott Association and of the Houghton Library.

32. Again the brackets mark the clipping of the signature on the verso.

33. Martha Saxton, *Louisa May: A Modern Biography of Louisa May Alcott* (Boston, 1977), takes a different view of both *Little Women* and its author: "Jo's development is a sweetly sentimental version of the journey everyone has expected to make" (p. 4). "[Alcott] was divided between the impulsive, outgoing, opinionated, large-spirited

But one regrets that the later fortnightly themes of Florence Phillips have disappeared along with Moody's comments. Whether under his sympathetic reading she achieved a less diluted "quality which touches and convinces the reader" we shall probably never know.

---

woman she was meant to be and the withdrawn, hostile introvert who kept that vital woman locked up" (p. 7).

The Tragedy of Self-Entrapment: Ellen Glasgow's *The Romance of a Plain Man*

C. HUGH HOLMAN

Allen Tate once called the early novels of Ellen Glasgow "premodern," seeing them as possessing "the irony of time and place out of joint . . . of social discrepancies."[1] But her eighth novel, published in 1909, when she was thirty-six, *The Romance of a Plain Man* is, I believe, a clear and reasonably distinguished example of what Tate calls a modern southern novel. I further believe that failure to recognize this "modern" element has tended to make its critics uncomfortable with the work.

Tate defines the primary change from the writing of the nineteenth-century South to that of the Southern Renascence as being "a shift from rhetoric to dialectic," a change from the writer as "the old Southern *rhetor* . . . who was eloquent before the audience but silent in himself" to the writer who carries on an argument within himself with the result that "the Southern dramatic dialectic . . . is resolved . . . in action."[2] *The Romance of a Plain Man*, although Glasgow's only first-person novel, presents such a dialectical struggle within its narrator-protagonist, and more important—and usually ignored by its critics—a dialectical view by Glasgow herself of the struggle which the action of the novel embodies, a view different from that of the narrator-protagonist.

The Romance of a Plain Man was in several respects a significant departure in Glasgow's career. At the ages of twenty-four and twenty-five she had published her first two novels *The Descendant* and *Phases of an Inferior Plant*. Then in 1900, with the publication of *The Voice of the People*, she had begun what proved to be her major and persistent novelistic project, a multivolumed "chronicle of manners . . . integrated by the major theme of social transition" and forming "a social history of Virginia."[3] It had been followed by *The Battle-Ground* (1902) and *The Deliverance* (1904), additional panels in her growing record of social change in Virginia. Then during and immediately after a period of great emotional turmoil—of what precise nature the biographers have remained

---

1. "A Southern Mode of the Imagination," in *Essays of Four Decades* (Chicago, [1968]), p. 582.

2. Ibid., pp. 590, 591, 592.

3. Ellen Glasgow, *A Certain Measure* (New York, 1943), pp. 66, 30.

uncertain—she had published *The Wheel of Life* (1906) and *The Ancient Law* (1908), works which she considered inferior.[4] *The Romance of a Plain Man* was for her a return to her former power after this emotional disorder which she attributes in her autobiography, *The Woman Within*, to the unhappy affair with the mysterious "Gerald B—." Blair Rouse says accurately that *The Romance of a Plain Man* represents the "beginning of a period of more rewarding productivity."[5] and certainly the works which immediately followed it—*The Miller of Old Church, Virginia*, and *Life and Gabriella*—represented her best work before *Barren Ground*, in 1925.

The Romance of a Plain Man enjoyed a moderate success in the marketplace; it sold over 23,000 copies in its first seven months and, all told, there were at least nine American and British impressions.[6] It received a good press on publication, but later critics have been mixed in their reactions to it; some, like Blair Rouse and me, have liked it very much, but more have followed Frederick P. W. McDowell's lead who saw in it "her talent at its thinnest."[7] Glasgow herself is partly responsible for this equivocating view; in *A Certain Measure* she confined her essay on the novel largely to personal reminiscences about its Richmond setting, apologies for her use in it of a first-person male narrator, and defenses of the last half of the book.[8] She did not include it in the eight-volume Old Dominion Edition, although she did include it in the twelve-volume Virginia Edition. But in large measure, the critics' problems with *The Romance of a Plain Man* result from failing to understand her method and the nature of her irony in this work, from not recognizing the skillful use she makes of women characters as historical embodiments, and from reading it as a rhetorical statement rather than a dialectical study.

The Romance of a Plain Man is the story of Ben Starr, a very poor Richmond boy who by persistent effort and intelligence rises from grocery delivery boy to tobacco factory worker to investor and banker and finally is offered the presidency of the South Midland and Atlantic Railroad, the major railway system of the South. In one sense, this story, laid between 1875 and 1908, is the account of an Horatio Alger hero's rising to greatness through the ranks in the impoverished South immediately after the Reconstruction period. It is this aspect of the novel upon which most critics

---

4. She twice selected novels for collected editions of her works, but did not select these two works either time.

5. *Ellen Glasgow* (New York, 1962), p. 64.

6. William W. Kelly, in *Ellen Glasgow: A Bibliography* (Charlottesville, Va., 1964), pp. 32–35, lists eight impressions; however, I am working from a 1910 Doubleday, Page impression not in Kelly's listing.

7. *Ellen Glasgow and the Ironic Art of Fiction* (Madison, Wis., 1960), p. 31.

8. Probably she was still arguing against George Brett, of The Macmillan Company, who had made her rewrite the last half of the novel before publishing it. See E. Stanly Goldbold, Jr., *Ellen Glasgow and the Woman Within* (Baton Rouge, La., 1972), p. 86.

have centered their attention, and they have tended to see the parallel—but in no way conflicting—story of Starr's worship of, love for, and marriage to Sally Mickelborough over the opposition of her family and the society of Richmond as simply one aspect of the poor boy's rise to fame and fortune. This second story, however, is the dialectical center of the novel, and, however accurate the broad historical outline of events in the building of a New South through the banking and railroad interests may be—and Stanly Goldbold, himself an historian, declares it to be accurate[9]—Glasgow's most significant historical attitudes are expressed through Ben Starr's relation to Sally Mickelborough, her maiden aunts the Misses Bland, and the aristocratic society of Richmond to which she belongs.

When he is a small boy, an arrogant Sally Mickelborough tells Ben that he is "common," and he resolves quietly to be worthy of her. He plays with her as a child in "the enchanted garden" of her large house on Old Church Hill, a garden which becomes for him a permanent symbol of a gracious, old, and closed order, one he can enter only by permission, not by right. He later says: "I saw always in my imagination the enchanted garden, with its cool sweet magnolias and laburnums, and its great white columns from which the swallows flew, with short cries, toward the sunset."[10] When he begins to be a financial success, he addresses himself to being worthy eventually to claim her hand, interpreting that worth largely in terms of the influence and power which money can bring and the things which he can give her. When he confesses this ambition, she confesses her affection and admiration for him and insists that there is no need to wait. Over the protests of her family and the objections of their friends, they are married. Ben continues his desperate and time-consuming struggle to acquire wealth and power and to achieve the other of his great ambitions, which is to be the president of the South Midland and Atlantic Railroad, of which his principal benefactor, General Bolingbroke, is president. As he devotes more and more of his time to his business affairs, particularly during and after a great financial crash which wipes out his financial fortune and for a time makes him and Sally very poor and struggling people—almost certainly the Depression of 1893—Sally finds that the man whom she had married because of her admiration for his power and energy, for his courage and determination, and whom she loves dearly, is unable to offer her a sufficient portion of his life to make her own life satisfying. She turns in what is clearly an innocent manner to the continuing worship of a former and rejected suitor, George Bolingbroke, who is an almost total personification of the manners, the grace, the tradition, and the charm of the aristocratic South, but who has no profession, does little

9. Goldbold, pp. 252–253.
10. Ellen Glasgow, *The Romance of a Plain Man* (New York, 1910), p. 113.

actively in the world, lives upon the wealth and power which his uncle General Bolingbroke has created, and devotes himself with a single-minded devotion to what might almost be called the worship of the southern woman, personified in Sally Mickelborough. This worship proves to be effective as an act of friendship both to Ben and to Sally, but it is not able to restrain Sally's growing discontent with the way of her life, and when finally her health is seriously undermined and she flees to a country estate accompanied by George, it is on the day when the telegram arrives telling Ben Starr that he has been elected president of the South Midland and Atlantic Railroad. He rushes to her side in the country with the whole situation at last clear in his mind, with the need to choose between his two major ambitions—his love for Sally Mickelborough and his desire that his life shall be bound permanently to hers and his desire for the strength and power which the railroads accurately represented in the late nineteenth-century South. The choice that he makes is to refuse the presidency of the railroad and go with Sally on a long trip which will begin the slow recuperation of her health and the restoration of their marriage.

Glasgow says that *The Romance of a Plain Man* "parallels *The Voice of the People* in my social history of Virginia. Both volumes deal with the rise of the working man in the South, but the point of view is dissimilar and the theme is approached from opposite directions. In *The Voice of the People*"—the story of the rise of a poor farm boy to the governorship of the State of Virginia—"I was writing objectively, of the 'poor-white' farmer in politics, and in *The Romance of a Plain Man*, I was treating, subjectively, the progress and decline of modern industrialism."[11] The parallel between the objective telling of Nicholas Burr's story in *The Voice of the People* and the subjective telling of Ben Starr's story is important, for it is in that subjective story, the story of the inner emotional life and the choices made within that emotional life that the key to the meaning, the method, and the value of *The Romance of a Plain Man* truly lies. Equally important is her statement that she, in tracing the rise of the working man, is tracing "the progress and decline of modern industrialism," for its decline is a significant element in *The Romance of a Plain Man*.

Ellen Glasgow has been severely criticized for giving the novel an ending that is viewed as sentimental. Edward Wagenknecht, usually an admirer of Glasgow's work, for example, says that *The Romance of a Plain Man* has "a sentimental and evasive ending, with Ben quite unconvincingly relinquishing the goal of all his striving to devote himself, at long last, exclusively to her [Sally]."[12] The criticism is unjust. The choice that Ben Starr makes is actually, in terms of the movement of history, between the

---

11. Ellen Glasgow, *The Woman Within* (New York, 1954), pp. 180–181.
12. *Cavalcade of the American Novel* (New York, 1952), p. 272.

Old South and the New, and the time is the first decade of the twentieth century. In many respects the pattern of southern history in this century is the product of that choice, an emotional election of the Old South values over those of the New South, repeated thousands of times by men of power and influence. The actual choice was frequently made in terms of the black man, for it was out of such choices that Jim Crow laws and Grandfather clauses were made; it was out of such choices that the arch-conservatism of southern politics in the first half of this century came, and it was out of such choices at last rejected that the modern South has taken shape. If the Sally Mickelborough story in *The Romance of a Plain Man* is, as I believe it is, a fable of history, a retelling in miniature of the rise of the middle class, it is also a retelling of the way in which that middle class was torn between the ideals and forms of an aristocratic society which it admires but cannot understand and the demands of a new and vigorous world which it must follow if that world is to come fully and healthily into being. As Ben Starr sensed, even as a struggling boy, "the air . . . was already full of the promise of the industrial awakening, the constructive impulse, the recovered energy . . . in which I . . . was to have my part." [13] He knew also "instinctively that my future triumphs would be in a measure the overthrow of the things for which he [General Bolingbroke, his aristocratic benefactor] and his generation had stood. The manager's casual phrase 'old families,' had bred in me a secret resentment, for I knew in my heart that the genial aristocracy . . . was in reality the enemy." [14] Ben Starr's choice is that of heart over head, that of the wistful poor boy still lost in the dream of the "enchanted garden," but as a parable of history it is tragic. That Ellen Glasgow should encompass that grave and finally grim choice in a gentle and appealing love story in which the attractive and pleasant heroine is in a sense the embodiment of the darker side of the choice which the post-Reconstruction South faced is, I think, the problem which has led the critics examining the book to fail to appreciate the skill with which it is constructed.

I think what Glasgow is doing here is what she did in a number of her fictional social histories, and it is what Faulkner was also to do in his long legend of Yoknapatawpha County—that is, to present historical movements not through a record of large historical events but rather through their representation in smaller units, a synecdochal process by which Ben Starr becomes not only himself, a unique individual rising from the lowest levels of the middle class to positions of power, but also a representative form of a large historical movement. Sally Mickelborough represents much that is strong, good, appealing, and delightful about the aristocratic Old

---

13. *The Romance of a Plain Man*, p. 88.
14. Ibid., pp. 108–109.

South. To Ben Starr, she is the embodiment, the virtual avatar of the
" 'something else' " that distinguished her class, of "this humour, this
lightness, and above all this gallantry, which was so much a part of the
older civilization."[15] Glasgow said of her in *A Certain Measure* that she
was "a mingling of all those characteristics we used to think of as especially
Virginian,"[16] and Sally and her friends from the higher classes of Richmond society represent the whole class of which they are a part. The story of
her life—that is, of her surrender to the forces of innovation and energy
which the post-Civil War world demanded—represented the momentary
fascination of that aristocracy with the energy and power of the New South.
General Bolingbroke represented the way in which some members of that
aristocracy had maintained their position while working vigorously with
the new middle class and even aiding it as he aided Ben Starr. Yet Sally
comes to see, as Glasgow herself said on one occasion, that "progress more
fatal than poverty, destroyed the lingering charm of the old culture."[17] I
believe that it was her awareness that she had caught large historical
movements in private and personal stories that led Ellen Glasgow to say,
when she reread *The Romance of a Plain Man* thirty years later, that it
was "an authentic rendering of unwritten history."[18]

The historian Henry Steele Commager has said, "It was the revolution
of opinion that Miss Glasgow traced—especially feminine opinion . . . the
society of . . . [Virginia] was never so dependent on money as that of the
northern cities, [thus] it was not so vulnerable to the assaults of new
wealth."[19] Indeed in *The Romance of a Plain Man* the embodiment of
attitude and opinion is essentially feminine. The clearest expression of
the attitude of Richmond aristocracy is that of Miss Mitty and Miss Matoaca Bland, Sally Mickelborough's aunts, total embodiments of the aristocratic traditions of a world that is already past. Miss Mitty will not tolerate
Ben Starr, for his father was a working man, and who someone's father is
is for Miss Mitty more important than character or accomplishment. Miss
Matoaca, an active woman suffragist, a feminist pamphleteer, who dies in
a march for women's rights, has turned to this active statement of conscience in the world as a result of the frustrations of a society which has
maintained a double standard of sexual purity for its men and women.
She was in love with General Bolingbroke when he was young, but she
declined his hand when she learned that he was impure in his sexual relations. She has turned now to an insistence upon woman's equality, and

15. Ibid., p. 363.
16. *A Certain Measure*, p. 74.
17. Ibid., p. 73.
18. Ibid., p. 72.
19. *The American Mind: An Interpretation of American Thought and Character
Since the 1880's* (New Haven, 1952), p. 66.

yet she cannot see that that same principle of equality should guarantee to Sally Mickelborough a freedom from the very tradition which has driven Miss Matoaca to make what appear to her and her sister to be such desperate gestures of conscience. She was, as Ben Starr said, "herself the slave of an ancestry of men who oppressed women, and women who loved oppression . . . a gallant martyr to the inequalities of sex, who still clung, trembling, to the inequalities of society. . . . She would go to the stake . . . for the cause of womanhood, but she would go supported by the serene conviction that she was 'a lady.' "[20] George Bolingbroke becomes a feminized aristocrat not because he lacks masculinity, although he does lack force, but because he subjects himself totally to the whims of a pampered feminine world and does not see that in a sense that subjection betrays the very women whom he worships.

Ellen Glasgow used the old traditional culture of Richmond and of Virginia with affection, however amused that affection may be, and she began early in her career to move from her positive approval of the triumph of the middle class to a growing sense of loss at what it destroyed. The course she took between old and new ways is one familiar to students of attempts to deal with the forces operating in the past, whether in the work of novelists like Sir Walter Scott or the critical theories of Georg Lukács. Historically-minded writers are likely to be fascinated with and emotionally wedded to a past which inevitably is leaving, while they applaud the new world being born, and in their work to follow a familiar course from revolution to reaction, from espousing the new to lamenting the passage of the old. *The Romance of a Plain Man* stands in the middle of this process for Ellen Glasgow, and it embodies in as nearly perfect a balance, I believe, as she ever achieved, the middle course which heroes of historical novels have taken from Scott to Allen Tate.[21]

One of the primary glories and difficulties of *The Romance of a Plain Man* is its choice of the first-person narrative point of view and the use to which Miss Glasgow puts that choice. She acknowledged that the use of a male narrator in the novel presented "almost insurmountable disadvantages," but she said, "My intention was to write a romance of the ordinary, and to treat, with a faintly satirical flavour, a series of adventures in the democratic society of our time." She chose, therefore, to tell the story "from within, and to combine the participant and the narrator."[22] This narrative point of view was associated, she believed, with "heroic enterprises," and its choice established a tone of gallantry for a

20. *Romance of a Plain Man*, p. 206.

21. See Georg Lukács, *The Historical Novel*, trans. Hannah and Stanley Mitchell (Boston, 1963) and Alexander Welsh, *The Hero of the Waverley Novels* (New Haven, 1963).

22. *A Certain Measure*, pp. 70–71.

novel which was to be a "romance of the ordinary." I am reminded of a very traditionally inclined member of my household to whom, when the book was new, I loaned a copy of John P. Marquand's *The Late George Apley* fearing that he would be offended by its satiric attack upon his values, only to find that he regarded Apley and his account as beautiful and profoundly true. I think something of this sort has taken place with a number of critics reading *The Romance of a Plain Man*.

Even the title established this basic irony. *Romance* is used in the medieval sense of a narrative of the deeds of a swashbuckling aristocratic hero, but *Plain Man* is Ellen Glasgow's term for one of the plain people, as opposed to good families. Actually the young Ben Starr is more than once referred to as "poor white trash."[23] Both the title and the basic attitudes and problems of emotional allegiance for the authors are similar in *The Romance of a Plain Man* and *A Connecticut Yankee in King Arthur's Court*. Glasgow depended on the discrepancy in using a point of view associated with heroic enterprises to recount a romance of the ordinary, confident that, as she expressed it, it would "lend a sharper edge and occasionally ironic tone to this realistic romance of an average man of good will."[24] It is lost on the critic who fails to see the irony implicit in the point of view.

Even those of us not of a phenomenologist persuasion tend to classify writers by the common characteristics of their collective works, and we have long ago classified Ellen Glasgow as primarily a verbal ironist and praised her for a felicitous, witty, but overly self-conscious style. When, as in *The Romance of a Plain Man*, her irony is not in the direct verbal constructs of her style but in the relationship of that style to her subject matter, when it is structural, a function of the narrative point of view rather than the literal written words, we tend to miss it, as we do in *The Romance of a Plain Man*, and therefore to feel that the book has a peculiar flatness and lack of wit.

Ben Starr is made into what Wayne Booth calls an unreliable narrator, yet he is in a sense a naive narrator, since both Glasgow and the reader understand him and his situation better than he does. This kind of dramatic irony is peculiarly present in the case of one of the most mechanical characters in the book, Ben's sister Jessy, whose eyes are so firmly fixed upon the material things of this life, upon money, advancement, clothes, the outward symbols of success, that she becomes both a little ridiculous and a little repulsive. Ben dislikes Jessy's materialism intensely without ever realizing that he is himself caught in exactly the same materialism and that, though in his case the complications are enormously greater, he

---

23. *Romance of a Plain Man*, pp. 20, 82.
24. *A Certain Measure*, p. 71.

consistently makes in regard to his beloved Sally the same kinds of choices that he thoroughly condemns in his sister.

The point of view has been criticized because there is very little detail, very little historical fact, and very little technical information about business and industry in a story told by a man who was deeply caught up through much of the time of action of the book in these very things. McDowell says, "Such a tale is sentimental when, as here, business success and failure are only vaguely related to economic milieu, and when the drive for financial power is an insistently mentioned fact rather than an imaginatively recreated reality. . . . Miss Glasgow's failure, however, to discuss the disturbingly close alliance between the railroad interests and the Democratic political machine in Virginia in the early twentieth century detracts from the verisimilitude and significance of the novel."[25] Yet it can be argued with equal force that the book is not about business at all but that business, industry, and politics are subsidiary to the fundamental choice which Ben Starr must make between two irreconcilable attitudes toward life and history. Indeed, while the inclusion of a larger amount of material on the technical aspects of business, industry, and politics might satisfy those who want to see the book as grounded firmly in the specific events of history, it could be done only at the cost to the book of its primary synecdochal value as a record of a choice which the New South made. One is reminded that in Fitzgerald's *The Great Gatsby*, Nick Carraway, who is a bond salesman in New York City, tells us, "Reading over what I have written so far, I see I have given the impression that the events of three nights several weeks apart were all that absorbed me. On the contrary, they were merely casual events in a crowded summer, and, until much later, they absorbed me much less than my personal affairs,"[26] which consisted largely of selling bonds. William Dean Howells' *The Rise of Silas Lapham*, although one of its major moral decisions hinges upon the business dealings of Lapham, tells us remarkably little about business, business techniques, and almost nothing about the paint industry on which Lapham's fortune rests. Blair Rouse is only partly correct when he argued in Glasgow's defense that she was interested not in the details of business but in "the *effect* of the business struggle on individuals."[27] Indeed I think she is not truly interested even in this effect but rather in the opportunity of choice which successful business endeavors force upon the protagonist.

Among those books which have been cited as examples of stories that somehow parallel *The Romance of a Plain Man* and might have been in Glasgow's mind—and they include the Horatio Alger books and Dickens'

25. McDowell, pp. 90, 91.
26. F. Scott Fitzgerald, *The Great Gatsby* (New York, Scribner's Library Edition), p. 37.
27. Rouse, 68.

Great Expectations[28]–should be added Henry James's *The American*, a book remarkably similar from a plot standpoint, though not in its ultimate meaning. Both the James novel and *The Romance of a Plain Man* have self-made protagonists who rise through unusual intelligence and industry to great business leadership in the period after the Civil War. Both these protagonists are ignorant of aristocratic values and traditional methods but are deeply enamoured of them. Both feel that in a sense money and financial success are keys to the acquisition of these cultural values. Both are rejected by families who disapprove of the union of their young women with these crass nouveau riche protagonists. Both ultimately fail in maintaining both the aristocratic dream and the financial success. Here the difference between the two novels becomes most pronounced, for Christopher Newman renounces the right to revenge, gives up the dreams of European culture, and goes back home, whereas Ben Starr makes exactly the opposite choice and renounces the raw energy which has given him his strength and power and embraces the life pattern of his aristocratic wife.

Viewed in this ultimate sense *The Romance of a Plain Man* is a skillfully contrived and effective narrative in which the self-made man, through the dreams of rewards and glories which are in a sense forbidden to him and which he thinks he can get only through energy and money, steadily and completely entraps himself in an emotional and psychological situation fraught with tragic possibilities. At the end of the story the answer Ben Starr gives to the dilemma that confronts him is indeed a tragic answer, for the self-entrapment has been so complete that there is no way out that is not either individually or historically destructive. To have embodied this kind of statement about the history of her region in a novel that is on the surface the love story of a self-made man is no small accomplishment. In writing *The Romance of a Plain Man*, Ellen Glasgow embodied in her characters and the action of her novel no simple rhetorical assertion but a dialectical examination of the complex issues of a moment of significant historical choice. The resulting book deserves from us a kind of attention different from that which we have been giving it.

---

28. Edward Wagenknecht, "*Great Expectations* and Ellen Glasgow," *Boston University Studies in English*, III (Spring, 1957), 57–60.

The Socialist and Socialite Heroes of Upton Sinclair

L. S. DEMBO

In *The Radical Novel in the United States* Walter Rideout defended the long, didactic conclusion of Upton Sinclair's *The Jungle* by maintaining that the turn of the hero, Jurgis Rudkus, to socialism was carefully prepared for: Sinclair conducted Jurgis "through all the circles of the workers' inferno" and attempted to "show that no other savior except socialism exists."[1] The point is worth elaborating for it is crucial to an understanding of what Sinclair achieved in *The Jungle* and what he failed to achieve in most of his other novels.

Now, without the specifically socialist conclusion, Jurgis' story would be that of a naturalist man in a naturalist world. His repeated insights into the harsh terms of life in Packertown are never in themselves enough to free him. He arrives in America, for instance, with a naive faith in the ways of the world and a pride in his own powers; in reaching the inevitably disastrous decision to buy a house, he reasons: "Others might have failed at it, but he was not the failing kind—he would show them how to do it. He would work all day, and all night, too, if need be; he would never rest until the house was paid for and his people had a home."[2] He eventually gains an understanding of his situation: "He had learned the ways of things about him now. It was a war of each against all, and the devil take the hindmost. . . . You went about with your soul full of suspicion and hatred; you understood that you were environed by hostile powers that were trying to get your money and who used all the virtues to bait their traps with" (p. 87).

This disillusionment does not make a socialist out of Jurgis. Quite the contrary, he accepts the state of affairs around him as a permanent reality, a given to which he must adapt himself. It is the naturalist, not the socialist, who declares the world a hopeless jungle. Thus Jurgis, still confident in

---

1. *The Radical Novel in the United States, 1900–1954, Some Interrelations of Literature and Society* (1956; rpt. New York, 1966) pp. 35–36. For an account of Sinclair's difficulties in completing the novel see Leon Harris' *Upton Sinclair: American Rebel* (New York, 1975) pp. 75–77. Harris points out that Sinclair was never satisfied with any of the several conclusions he had written.

2. *The Jungle* (New York, 1906), pp. 57–58.

his powers, goes no farther than determining on personal survival and the
protection of his immediate family. His encounter with unionism teaches
him that he has "brothers in affliction, and allies. Their one chance for
life was in union, and so the struggle became a kind of crusade" (p. 107).
But this sentiment, embryonic to begin with, does not withstand the despair that overtakes him as he lies convalescing from an injured ankle.

It is in the misery of his imprisonment for assaulting his wife's seducer,
however, that the vision of the world as a jungle in which all that matters
is personal survival overwhelms Jurgis. Sinclair makes it explicit that frus-
tration and rage, not social consciousness, underlie Jurgis' "rebellion":

> These midnight hours were fateful ones to Jurgis; in them was
> the beginning of his rebellion, of his outlawry and his unbelief. He
> had no wit to trace back the social crime to its far sources—he could
> not say that it was the thing men have called "the system" that was
> crushing him to the earth. . . . He only knew that he was wronged,
> and that the world had wronged him. . . . And every hour his soul
> grew blacker, every hour he dreamed new dreams of vengeance, of
> defiance, of raging, frenzied hate.   (p. 192)

This response is as far as Jurgis can go; on the death of his son, the last
member of his immediate family, he can feel only the same kind of rage:
"There should be no more tears and no more tenderness; he had had
enough of them—they had sold him into slavery! Now he was going to be
free, to tear off his shackles, to rise up and fight . . . he was going to think
of himself, he was going to fight for himself, against the world that had
baffled him and tortured him!" (pp. 253–254).

Thoroughly disillusioned but still unenlightened—trapped by ignorance
as well as rage—Jurgis gains a temporary respite by fleeing to the country-
side, but returns to a life of street crime and, when the opportunity presents itself, political corruption. Nor is he averse to strikebreaking, an
activity that earns for him, for the first time in the novel, Sinclair's sarcasm.

Regarded from a socialist point of view, Jurgis is the very man who,
because of his sufferings, can appreciate the truth once it is made known
to him. His conversion is explained in the same oration that illuminates
him:

> there will be some one man whom pain and suffering have made
> desperate. . . . And to him my words will come like a sudden flash of
> lightning to one who travels in darkness. . . . The scales will fall from
> his eyes, the shackles will be torn from his limbs—he will leap up with
> a cry of thankfulness, he will stride forth a free man at last! A man
> delivered from his self-created slavery! A man who will never more
> be trapped—whom no blandishments will cajole, whom no threats

will frighten; who from to-night on will move forward, and not backward, who will study and understand, who will gird on his sword and take his place in the army of his comrades and brothers. (pp. 361–362)

An important point is easily overlooked in the flow of the rhetoric: revelation is only the first step in a socialist education; it must be followed by hard study and experience. The conclusion of *The Jungle* is optimistic not simply because it envisions a socialist victory at the polls, but because it marks the socialization of a man who without the doctrine would be wholly lost.

Never committing himself to a specific social theory, Zola emphasizes the baffling multiplicity of socialist solutions and at the end of *Germinal* he sends his hero, Lantier, off to Paris still uncertain of the path he should follow. Nothing is clear but the grim possibility of anarchic and apocalyptic uprising—the one sure means of ushering in a new world. Committed to socialism, Sinclair is anxious to show the diversity in socialist thought only to indicate that, contrary to the stereotype, socialists have no "cut-and-dried program for the future of civilization." And he does go on to list the fundamental principles on which all socialists agree. For Zola, "heredity" was as crucial an influence on character as environment: that fact was expressed in the belief that there existed a jungle within as well as without. Sinclair believed there was no jungle within except that created by the jungle without, that there was a specific criterion for enlightenment, and that socially conscious men, using rational means, could bring about change.

Unfortunately, the men and women who Sinclair believed met these standards—his heroes and heroines—frequently turn out to be not proletarians or foreigners but upper-class Americans. The implications of this preference are startlingly evident even in *King Coal* (1917), an account of conditions in the unorganized coal industry that was intended to be another muckraking bombshell. The trouble with this novel is not that it insists on presenting socialist propaganda in the guise of literature; to the contrary, it is socialist merely by inference. Its real failure lies in its focussing upon the experiences of an upper-class hero (Hal Warner, a mine owner's son who decides to spend a summer, disguised, in a mining camp not owned by his father, and soon finds himself championing the miners' causes). As he was to do in many of his succeeding novels, Sinclair, though intent on exposing the oppression of the working class by an avaricious and tyrannical capitalism, chooses as his means of narration the romantic clichés of popular fiction. The education of Hal is so simplistically and obviously rendered that *King Coal* cannot be justified by one's calling it a *Bildungsroman*. Although it is probable that Sinclair felt he could better enlist the sympathies of the bourgeois reader by presenting the story as he did—and in 1917 he may indeed have been right—an account of the heroic adventures and the noble, self-sacrificing behavior of a clear-eyed, red-blooded, rich young American among a group of downtrodden, confused, often inarticulate, and impotent foreigners not only appeals to the worst kind of sentimentality but confirms more prejudices than it dispels.[3]

"The book," comments Sinclair, "gives a true picture of conditions and events. . . . Practically all the characters are real persons, and every incident which has social significance is not merely a true incident, but a typical one. The life portrayed in *King Coal* is the life that is lived today by hundreds of thousands of men, women and children in 'this land of the free.' "[4] This description may be accurate enough from a journalistic point of view but only from that point of view. Unlike the characterization in *Germinal*, or even in *The Jungle*, for that matter, that in *King Coal* is superficial and stereotypical. We are presented with a "representative" old Slovak, an Italian anarchist, a fiery Irish maid with an alcoholic father, and others—all of whom emerge precisely in their typicality, just as do the municipal and mine officials and their police.

We see these characters mostly through the eyes of a twenty-year-old youth, who is sensitive but inexperienced and still limited by many of the prejudices of his class. Sinclair seems to have a broader vision than his hero; here is his treatment of Hal's initial encounter with the poor:

> He had come with love and curiosity, but both motives failed here. How could a man of sensitive nerves, aware of the refinements and graces of life, learn to love these people, who were an affront to his every sense—a stench to his nostrils, a jabbering to his ear, a procession of deformity to his eye? . . . After all, what were they fit for, but the dirty work they were penned up to do? So spoke the haughty race-consciousness of the Anglo-Saxon, contemplating the Mediterranean hordes, the very shape of whose heads was objectionable.   (p. 21)

3. In his highly sympathetic book, *Upton Sinclair, a Study in Social Protest* (New York, 1930), Floyd Dell points out the dubious use of aristocratic heroes in *Metropolis* (1908) and *The Moneychangers* (1908). Although he sees this approach in *King Coal* as a disability, he still finds the novel a "brilliant" success. I am not saying that after Jurgis Rudkus Sinclair wholly abandoned the proletarian as a central character—Jimmy Higgins, the "typical" Socialist worker in the novel bearing his name (1919), being a case in point. There is a difference, however, between a "central character," depicted as a victim or a pawn or an Everyman, and a "hero," depicted as a leader or an especially endowed person.

The opinion that Sinclair was aiming *King Coal* at a bourgeois audience, whom he hoped to waken to the conditions of the miners, should be qualified. Publishing many of his own works and selling them at a low price, Sinclair apparently had a working-class audience as well (see Dell, pp. 181–183).

4. "Postscript," *King Coal* (New York, 1917), p. 384. Further page references to this edition will be noted parenthetically in the text.

Sinclair obviously disapproves of this attitude, but when Hal learns better, what does he learn?

> Thus, as always, when one understood the lives of men, one came to pity instead of despising. Here was a separate race of creatures, subterranean gnomes, pent up by a society for purposes of its own. . . . Coal would go to the ends of the earth, to places the miner never heard of, turning the wheels of industry whose products the miner would never see. It would make precious silks for fine ladies, it would cut precious jewels for their adornment, it would carry long trains of softly upholstered cars across deserts and mountains; it would drive palatial steamships out of the wintry tempests into gleaming tropic seas. And the fine ladies in their precious silks and jewels would eat and sleep and laugh and lie at ease—and would know no more of the stunted creatures of the dark than the stunted creatures knew of them. Hal reflected upon this, and subdued his Anglo-Saxon pride, finding forgiveness for what was repulsive in these people—their barbarous jabbering speech, their vermin-ridden homes, their bare-bottomed babies.   (pp. 22–23)

The speciousness of this passage is apparent in almost every line. The mine-owner's son finds "forgiveness" for the people whose exploitation has made him the "superior" person he is! It is easy enough for him to deride the "fine ladies" on "palatial steamships," quite another for him to realize that he is no less implicated. All of Hal's fine heroics on behalf of the poor —including his imprisonment in his bid to become checkweighman (a representative of the miners who makes certain that each man is credited by the company with the proper weight of coal he has dug)—are, without this knowledge, little more than adolescent adventures.

What is more, this lack makes Hal's heroism dangerously misleading. Because he is "educated" and "American," he is chosen as a leader and spokesman, and we are led to believe that he alone, acting on his own initiative, has the consciousness and capability to take effective action. Even the organizer from the miners' union is relegated to a passive role. As for most of the miners, we learn, "it was impossible to work so hard and keep . . . mental alertness . . . eagerness . . . and sensitiveness." This may well be true, but the activities of a Hal Warner, disguised as Joe Smith, are, from any social perspective that goes beyond romantic sentimentalism, irrelevant.

Hal persuades his college classmate, Paul Harrigan, son of the owner of the mine in which he is working, to order the superintendent to expedite rescue operations after an explosion (the mine had been sealed to prevent further property damage) and eventually, on the advice of union representatives, convinces his fellow-workers not to go ahead with their planned strike. After these exploits, he decides to return to his normal life and to marry the spoiled girl to whom he had been engaged; even from the beginning he had spurned the love of the Irish working-class girl whom he now leaves, as he leaves all his summer working-class friends, "with more than a trace of moisture in his eyes."

Sinclair means all this quite seriously; throughout the entire novel Hal's idealism and nobility are contrasted with the insensitivity and avarice of his relatives, friends, and the institutions they control. But because it lacks the sophistication and insight to develop the full implications of class relations, the work fails in social vision. Because it creates a stereotyped hero and not a character who undergoes an authentic moral development, it fails as a novel and remains at best a piece of muckraking journalism, at worst a sentimental tale.

A decade after he published *King Coal*, Sinclair wrote an exposure of the oil industry (*Oil!*, 1927) and once again chose to tell the story of an upper-class boy, this time Bunny Ross, the son of an oil magnate, who is torn between a devotion to his father and to a working-class friend, Paul Watkins, who perpetually is victimized by and reveals the horrors of the capitalist system in America. Bunny lives a dual life: captivated by the romance of oil exploration and eventually involved with a movie star, he remains partly true to his class; still he engages in radical activities at the conservative college he attends and befriends and gives financial aid to a group of socialists. After his father dies, he gives himself over more fully to the radical cause by founding a labor college and offering marriage to a Jewish socialist girl.

Unlike *King Coal*, which centers upon the tyranny exercised over an isolated mining camp, *Oil!* is a sweeping novel that, covering Bunny's life from boyhood in the 1900's through his youth in the 1920's, includes as part of its background the First World War and the Allied invasion of Russia in 1919, as well as the election of Harding and the subsequent oil scandals. Sinclair also comments on religious superstition in capitalist America through the story of Paul Watkins' brother, Eli (modelled on Billy Sunday), "Prophet of the Third Revelation," who rises to wealth and power. As always, Sinclair can be effective in describing social injustice, but he is still heavy-handed and unconvincing in creating a hero.

Bunny, it is true, is portrayed as an ambivalent figure—and as such is neither an outright hero or villain. Sinclair is explicit about Bunny's deficiencies: his extreme dependence on his father, his inclination to "lean on others," and his general fecklessness. On the other hand, he supposedly possesses the same "nobility" as Hal Warner in *King Coal*; he is depicted as being one of the rare men of compassion of his class and this quality is meant to redeem him. But unlike George Orwell, for example, Sinclair is interested in declassment not as a psychological, social,

and ethical phenomenon but rather as a device for revealing the manners
and conduct of the two classes through sensitive eyes. Bunny is chiefly an
observer and sympathizer. Although he undergoes something of a socialist
education, he is never made to experience the hardships of an oil worker.
And like Hal, even when participating in radical activities, he holds the
trump card of his identity as the son of a member of the ruling class; although occasionally baited by the press, he is never really brutalized.

That Sinclair is himself aware of these weaknesses in the position of his
upper-class heroes is evident in *Boston* (1928), at once an account of the
Sacco-Vanzetti case and a novel about the social and moral education of
a Brahmin woman, Cornelia Thornwell, who, upon the death of her
wealthy and powerful husband, renounces her family (and all it stands
for) and attempts to transform herself into a working-class woman. This
so-called runaway grandmother does, in fact, undergo all the hardships
that an unskilled worker in a New England cordage factory in 1917 would,
but it is still not enough, as she learns in an argument with a French
socialist:

> "Understand me, Comrade Thornwell, it is good of rich and cul-
> tured ladies to take an interest in the exploited workers; but you
> suffer always from the fact that you can't possibly realize how they
> actually feel."
> "Don't forget, Comrade Leon, I worked for a year and a half in a
> cordage plant, and lived on the wages."
> "I know. . . . and I never heard anything like it. But all the same,
> if you will pardon me, it wasn't practically real, because if you had
> been ill or out of a job, you'd have gone back to your family; it wasn't
> psychologically real, because you always knew you could, and you had
> the moral support of knowing you were a lady. No worker has that. . . .[5]

This revelation does not prevent Cornelia from committing herself to a
socialist view of the world, nor does it in any way detract from Sinclair's
obvious admiration for his heroine and her real-life models. What helps
make her a sympathetic figure, not only to Sinclair but, insofar as she is
credible at all, to his readers, is precisely what is lacking or at least un-
emphasized in the other heroes: a strength of character that perhaps goes
deeper than politics or doctrine, and manifests itself in her desire to see
and act upon the truth as it reveals itself, a quality that goes against the
grain of her entire Brahmin upbringing in which decorum, maintained
by repression and hypocrisy, is the chief value in social conduct, especially
among women. Her education through the long ordeal that begins with
her flight and culminates in the execution of Sacco and Vanzetti is in-

---

5. *Boston* (Long Beach, Cal., 1923), p. 231.

tended to be that of the reader as well. *Boston* is Sinclair's *Vérité*, Sacco and Vanzetti, his Dreyfus. Like Zola, he argues for "objectivity" and historical accuracy in the reconstruction of the circumstances. "An honest effort," he tells us, "has here been made to portray a complex community exactly as it is. The story has no hero but the truth." And he continues, "I wish to make clear that I have not written a brief for the Sacco-Vanzetti defense. I have tried to be a historian. What I think I know, I have told the reader. What is uncertain, I have so portrayed—and have let the partisans of both sides voice their feelings and beliefs. My book will not satisfy either side completely; both have already expressed dissent—which I take to mean I have done my job" (p. vi).

But this statement scarcely characterizes a novel which, for all the research behind it, is impelled not by detachment but moral outrage. One can concede, I suppose, that Sinclair does explore certain morally ambiguous areas—as, for example, the dilemma into which Lee Swenson, the experienced, tough, radical lawyer, leads Cornelia when he informs her that she (and she alone) has the power to destroy the prosecution's case against Sacco and Vanzetti if she'll commit perjury; the implications and ramifications of this problem occupy Sinclair for several pages. Nonetheless, we neither expect nor find any sympathy whatsoever for those who have brought Sacco and Vanzetti to trial (the "rulers" of the Commonwealth of Massachusetts) or any hostility toward those who would defend them. By a "complex community," then, Sinclair in no way means one toward which, or in which, moral neutrality can have any place. What he does mean is a society divided into the oppressors and their henchmen and the oppressed; the former contains frequently antagonistic groups, such as the Back Bay aristocracy and the wealthy and politically potent Irish, but their commercial, legal, political, and social interactions are reducible to the common motives of avarice and lust for power. The latter are the poor, chiefly Italian, who are invariably portrayed in a favorable light; they are not Zola's Parisian poor (*L'Assommoir*) or his land-hungry peasants (*La Terre*). Whereas in Zola, family life on all social levels is dominated by envy and greed and therefore is in a state of disintegration, in Sinclair, Italian family life stands in ideal contrast to that of the Brahmins. Tolerance, generosity, kindness—an openness to life—characterize the relationships of the Brinis, with whom, as a boarder, Cornelia finds more than adequate compensation for the hardships she must endure as a laborer.

If Sinclair has presented an oversimplified image of the Italian family, it is not necessarily out of sentimentality that he has done so. Such an image logically underscores the view that, along with self-interest, an almost psychopathic paranoia marked the "American" attitude toward the Italians, all of whom it held to be potential bomb-throwing anarchists.

Accordingly, Bartolomeo Vanzetti, whom Sinclair describes as a man of words rather than action, emerges as the perfect Italian hero, a saintly man incapable of taking any life, to say nothing of gunning down the paymaster of a shoe factory.

What is ironic in all this is that the socialist view of the anarchists— that is, the one expressed by Pierre Leon in his argument with Cornelia— actually justifies the anxieties of the capitalists who wish to jail, deport, or execute the "whole lot of them":

> All militant anarchists believe in bombs. Not all make them. . . . But the faith calls for it. . . .
>
> What you have to get clear is the central doctrine of anarchism, that property used for exploitation is theft. That makes capitalist society a gigantic bandit-raid, a wholesale killing; any killing you have to do to abolish it, or to cripple it, always is a small matter in comparison.   (p. 233)

That Vanzetti as a dedicated anarchist could have committed the crime with which he has been charged is a possibility that Cornelia cannot accept—nor, in a sense, can Sinclair himself, since the effectiveness of his attack on the Commonwealth—the capitalist state—depends on Vanzetti's innocence, not only as a bandit but as a bomber. Equally important is that such innocence—carrying with it an inability to act—reaffirms the notion, ubiquitous in Sinclair's work, that the oppressed cannot save themselves—that somehow their salvation, if attainable at all, requires the appearance of enlightened American aristocrats who renounce or rebel against their class.

The wealthy, clean-cut American, sympathetic to the socialist cause but accustomed to privilege and material comfort, was to remain Sinclair's favorite hero to the end. Not only does he reappear in the simple propaganda piece about the Spanish Civil War, *No Pasaran*, but he is elaborated throughout the eleven-volume Lanny Budd series, Sinclair's epic and chronicle of the period 1913–1949. Written between 1940 and 1953, these novels can scarcely be called proletarian literature since they deal mostly with the haute bourgeoisie, the aristocracy, high government officials and leaders and with the diplomatic and political history of the West. Fascism, Nazism, and finally world communism emerge as the central evils; capitalism is attacked for generating these forms of tyranny or, at least, making it possible for them to flourish. Except for one episode concerning the slums of pre–World War I London, there is no attempt to delineate consistently the conditions that inspired the muckraking novels.

From the start Sinclair's reviewers were sensitive to the aesthetic weak-

nesses of the series.[6] Pedantry, sentimentality, and an irritating facetious-
ness permeate the entire work. Wholly unaffected by the stylistic innovations of the twentieth century, Sinclair writes in what is often the worst
rhetoric of another age. His treatment of personal relations, including
Lanny's pallid romances, is superficial and contrived and the dialogue of
his characters often banal and awkward. He is repetitious to the point of
distraction, not only in his recitation of facts or his use of epithets for
his characters, but in the plotting itself. (Lanny's adventures fall into
basic types that appear cyclically: the interviews with political leaders,
the rescue of prisoners or victims of the fascists, the participation in
seances, art agent dealings, dealings with socialists. The many visits to
Hitler or Roosevelt are identical in form, if not in actual subjects discussed,
as are the other adventures within their categories.) Yet all these weaknesses conceded, there is no denying that Sinclair does have a genius for
recreating historical events and portraying a seemingly endless variety of
actual public figures. These portraits are not the ironic or idealized sketches
that one finds in Dos Passos but convincing if limited life studies. In
addition to Hitler and Roosevelt, Lanny Budd, playboy, art agent, and
presidential spy, has protracted or numerous dealings with most of the
major and many minor Nazi officials, Harry Hopkins, Hearst, Truman,
Churchill, Laval, Petain; he has illuminating encounters with hundreds
of others, including English, French, German, Italian, and Spanish aristocrats, industrialists, generals, scientists, and politicians. This plethora and
scope led one reviewer to argue that Lanny was "an all-seeing eye, not
a dramatic hero." From the viewpoint of technique Lanny is perhaps
a device, but that does not mean we can avoid judging his character
or considering his development as a socialist sympathizer and its actual
significance.

The illegitimate son of Robbie Budd, an American munitions maker,
and his first love, Mabel Blackless (called Beauty), whose marriage had
been prevented by the Budd family, Lanny is born and raised on the
Riviera by his socialite mother. He comes under the sway of his father,
who visits him often and exposes him to his Darwinian views of society
in the hope that Lanny will eventually take his place in the family business. Thus, justifying his trade, Robbie plants the seeds of a capitalist
philosophy: " 'Men hate each other. . . . They insist upon fighting, and

---

6. One of the best commentaries on Sinclair's weaknesses both in the Lanny Budd
series and in general can be found in S. Gorley Putts, *Scholars of the Heart* (London,
1962) pp. 87–109. Jon A. Yoder also has a good account of the Lanny Budd novels in his
useful survey of Sinclair's life and career as a socialist writer, *Upton Sinclair* (New York,
1975). Yoder sees the problems of contemporary liberalism as the central theme of the
series, as well as of *Boston*.

there's nothing you can do about it, except learn to defend yourself. No nation would survive for a year unless it kept itself in readiness to repel attacks from greedy and jealous rivals. . .' " (WE, p. 39).[7] He sees the First World War as a "war of profits," in which the steel men were "selling to both sides, and getting the whole world into their debt" and international industrialists in general "had taken charge of the war so far as their own properties were concerned" (WE, p. 280).

But Lanny finally is convinced no more by his father's conclusions than by those of his uncle, Jesse Blackless, the spokesman for violent world revolution: "The uncle and the father agreed upon the same set of facts, and they even drew the same conclusion—that nobody ought to be patriotic. The point where they split was that Robbie said you had to stuff your pockets, because you couldn't help it, whereas Uncle Jesse—Lanny wasn't sure what he wanted, but apparently it was to empty Robbie's pockets!" (WE, p. 281). Repudiating them both, Lanny sees himself at the age of eighteen, after his experiences at the peace conference, as "the man who loved art and beauty, reason and fair play, and pleaded for these things and got brushed aside. It wasn't his world! It had no use for him! When the fighting started, he'd be caught between the lines and mowed down" (WE, p. 635).

Still, as he grows older, he continues to make discoveries that won't allow him peace of mind with his own class: "No longer an innocent child, he looked about him at the idlers of this Côte d'Azur and they had ceased to appear glamorous. He saw gambling and drinking and assorted vices, and what seemed to him an orgy of profitless activity . . . when he went into the great cities he was made sick by the spectacle of human degradation. . ." (BTW, p. 443). The young Spanish socialist, Raoul Palma, urges him into making his first commitment: "He was ready to teach a class in the [socialist] night school, and one in the Sunday school. He would tell the workers of the Riviera and their children about the great war which was already growing dim in the world's memory; he would try to explain to them the forces which caused it, and what they could do by their collective efforts to prevent another such calamity from breaking upon their lives" (BTW, p. 593). If this sounds both presumptuous and ludicrous, it is pure Sinclair and we are meant to take it seriously. Lanny will eventually come to doubt his effectiveness, but having married the heiress Irma Barnes, who will prove to be a reactionary, he is unable, even if he so desired, to do any more: "Lanny Budd found himself in the midst of a social whirlwind, and it would have been cruelly unkind of him not

---

7. *World's End.* For convenience I have used the paperback edition (Curtis Books, New York, n.d.). References have been made to the following volumes under their abbreviations: BTW (*Between Two Worlds*), DT (*Dragon's Teeth*), PA (*The Presidential Agent*), OSS (*O Shepherd, Speak!*), RLB (*The Return of Lanny Budd*).

to like it. Once more the ladies were in charge of his life, and what they considered proper was what he did" (DT, p. 224).

Content to roll through life "in a well-cushioned limousine," Lanny is confronted in the years 1933–1937 with the accession to power of the Nazis and the advent of the war in Spain. Through his boyhood friend, Kurt Meissner, pianist, composer, Prussian aristocrat, and Beauty Budd's former lover, he had come to know and love pre-Hitler Germany; he is fluent in the language and seems to be as much at home in upper-class German society as he is in French and English. In aiding another long-time friend, the Jewish speculator Johannes Robin, one of whose sons has married Lanny's step-sister, to escape, Lanny is given a direct insight into the realities of the new regime, and the fate of another son, Freddi, only increases Lanny's horror.

His commitment now takes the form of financial aid to a Socialist underground, whose representative, Trudi Schultz, a dedicated young Socialist and art student, Lanny makes several trips to Berlin to meet. Irma, who has grown less and less tolerant of his leftist activities, unsuspectingly accompanies him on one of his trips, and though she consents, in an emergency, to help smuggle Trudi, threatened by the Gestapo, out of the country, she has had enough. Characteristic of Lanny's double life is that part of the escape plan includes a prearranged visit to Hitler at Berchtesgaden, and here Irma's voluntary declaration of her admiration for the Nazis precipitates Lanny's final decision to divorce her.

What is thematically important in all this is that it signals the first real moral crisis in Lanny's life, and this crisis is accentuated when it becomes apparent that not only Irma, but most of Lanny's friends and acquaintances—the aristocracy and the ruling classes of western Europe, along with powerful groups in the United States, see in fascism and Nazism only a bulwark against the "Bolshevik menace." In *Wide Is the Gate* (vol. 4) ("Wide is the gate, and broad is the way, that leads to destruction") this thesis is dramatized repeatedly and offered as the basic reason that the Nazis were unchecked in the thirties. Whether talking to French industrialists, Spanish landowners, or highborn persons in the British Foreign Service, Lanny, when he is later gathering political information, knows just what politics will ingratiate him most quickly. But when he is sincere, as he must be with his father, now building aircraft, when after his experiences in Spain he comes to argue for a pursuit plane for the loyalist government, he finds himself in a hopeless deadlock with his own family. Robbie's intransigence, his bitter opposition to the Republican forces is a graphic enough demonstration of the chasm that has opened between Lanny and his class.

Whatever the depth of his commitment, Lanny, as it turns out, finds himself in a position that requires his continued existence as one of the privileged. As a "presidential agent," charged by Roosevelt with learning the intentions of the rich and powerful of Europe, he poses as a Nazi sympathizer pursuing his trade as an art agent. Aside from contact with Raoul Palma and the Cote D'Azur Socialists, his only connection with the movement is through his continued relationship with Trudi Schultz, who refuses to give up hope that her husband, though captured by the Gestapo, is still alive, and, from Paris, slavishly devotes herself to composing anti-Nazi propaganda to be smuggled to German workers. Lanny, after a less than romantic courtship, marries her, admires her, and, when she is kidnapped by Gestapo agents in France, moves heaven and earth to locate and rescue her, until he is given confirmation of her death in Dachau.

With the exception of Rick (Eric Pomeroy-Nielson), another boyhood friend, who was crippled while flying for the R.A.F. during World War I and has become a liberal journalist and playwright, there are few members of the aristocracy with whom Lanny can express his real feelings. As he is to reflect after the Nazis are defeated, "He had been living in the enemy's country, not merely physically but ideologically; he had been living capitalism and luxury, while cherishing democracy as a secret dream" (OSS, p. 348). The fact remains, however, that despite some mental anguish and the personal risks involved in espionage, Lanny is never called upon to make any real sacrifices, never suffers unduly, and never abandons the habits, instincts, and outlook of the man of privilege. He tells Trudi that the force of property is "so overwhelming that only a small fraction of mankind has any chance of resisting it. I am not sure if I myself am among this number; I feel myself struggling in a net, and just when I think I am out of it I discover that another fold has been cast over my head and I am as helplessly entangled as ever" (WITG, p. 423). This is a genuine insight, but its implications are not pursued. To Sinclair, Lanny is a wholly creditable hero whose essential high-mindedness is seriously presented: "No, he was not a Socialist, he didn't know enough to say what he was, but he knew human decency when he met it, and he had learned what it was for a modern state to be seized by gangsters and used by them to pervert the mind and moral sense of mankind" (BTW, p. 382). Lanny always speaks for "human decency," for the sound mind and moral sense of mankind. Thus, even though Sinclair has created a dichotomous position for his character, one that invites further inquiry into his motives and behavior, the subtleties involved have no part in Sinclair's design.

For example, it is of no thematic consequence that Lanny is a man who lives to ingratiate himself with others and that deception and manipulation are second-nature to him; that he is sanctimonious, condescending, and passionless; that his charm, his "famous smile," his ready wad of cash, his inside knowledge, his possession of credentials with intimidating signatures are his chief means of getting along in the world. Perhaps affected most by Trudi's kidnapping, and then not because he loved her but because he felt guilty for not having loved her enough (again the Moral Hero), he emerges physically and emotionally unaltered from every perilous adventure he has had, including torture by the Russians after the war. It is true he has risked much in helping relatives, friends, and allies escape from Germany, but he is wholly capable of turning down an appeal by strangers without much more than apt reflection on the sadness of the situation and perhaps a "tear in his eye."

The lack of psychological dimension in Lanny's character is no mere technical failing; it is a reflection of Sinclair's view of the world, which to its core is rationalistic and moralistic. Here is an example of his philosophizing:

> Presumably . . . Providence or God wanted each human to do his best; and for Lanny that could only mean a great deal of puzzling or worrying. Perhaps this puzzling and worrying was part of the process God meant for each of the two billion creatures to go on striving until it learned to think more clearly, and so to organize and cooperate with its fellows. . . . Why couldn't they have learned to cooperate from the beginning? Why couldn't they have been born with enough sense in their heads—instead of with a desire to dominate and oppress, to rob and kill. . . . If they were ever going to stop dominating and oppressing, robbing and killing, it would be because some among their number had sufficient intelligence to persuade others to settle down and produce wealth for themselves instead of trying to take it away from their neighbors.   (PA, p. 558)

"Think more clearly, and so to organize and cooperate," "sufficient intelligence to persuade others"—these ideals are clearly the inspiration for the kind of liberal socialism that Sinclair espouses. They assume a simple human psychology and ethos in which reason and passion, intelligence and stupidity, are easily distinguishable from one another, as are good and evil, and they are founded on the hope that men can change themselves and the world by rational decision. One of the major problems, as formulated by Rick as early as the round of futile international conferences after World War I, is that of education and communication:

> There just wasn't enough intelligence on the poor tormented planet; not enough statesmanship, not enough ordinary decency. The people weren't able to control the forces which modern industrialism had created; they didn't even have the means of getting the facts. There were a few honest papers, but they reached only a small public; the big press was in the hands of the big interests, and told the people whatever suited the purposes of the masters of steel and munitions and oil.   (BTW, p. 148)

This passage, of course, expresses Sinclair's own purposes throughout a lifetime of writing.

Although, whatever its relation to capitalism, fascism presented its own forms of oppression and required a shift in perspective, it made a Manichean view even more credible. With the emergence of the Nazis, dragons appeared on the earth and dragon-slayers would have to be called upon to eradicate them: "It was Lanny's fond dream that the whole people were wiser than any self-appointed leaders; that if they could once get power and keep it, they and the products of their toil would no longer be at the mercy of evil creatures spewed up from the cesspools of society. So long as such existed, so long as they could seize the wealth of great nations and turn them to fanaticism and aggression, they had to be fought. . ." (OSS, p. 210). Elsewhere, Lanny reasons, "It was really not the German people who were perpetrating [the atrocities of Nazism], but a band of fanatics who had seized a nation and were perverting its youth and turning them into murderers and psychopaths. Germans would awaken someday as from a nightmare and contemplate with loathing and dismay the crimes that had been committed in their name" (PA, p. 640). In this view, "evil" is not in the normal order of things and certainly not within oneself; it cannot belong to a whole people but only to the fanatics among them or to specific "creatures" who can be so designated. Wholly "other," it can be isolated and fought by the forces of reason and the men of "human decency."

These sentiments are perhaps more adequate as a call to action than as an explanation of the Nazi phenomenon. They are, in fact, too simplistic even for Sinclair's own portrayals of Nazi officials. In his dealings with these figures Lanny is so often caught up with them as personalities, that he must remind himself that they are perpetrators of atrocity. They come from all walks of life, represent a variety of temperaments, and more often than not are "typical" Germans. Ironically, one of the most fanatical of them is Lanny's old friend, Kurt Meissner.

The defeat of the Nazis did not, of course, satisfy Sinclair's moral sense; after bringing the series to a conclusion with *O Shepherd, Speak* (vol. 10) in 1949, he added a new volume in 1953, *The Return of Lanny Budd*, a work permeated with the attitudes of the Cold War. The Shepherd to whom Sinclair is referring is Roosevelt, whom Lanny has adulated and whose death he sees as leaving the world without strong moral leadership.

Having for over a decade regarded the idea of "the Bolshevik Peril" as a Nazi-propagated illusion, Lanny, after a flirtation with pacifism, now embraces it as a religious truth. The moral conflict that engages him is not between socialism and capitalism but between democratic socialism and revolutionary socialism, which Sinclair translates into a holy war between democracy and tyranny. Thus, explaining his view of the world situation to Truman, Lanny begins with what appears to be a straight-forward socialist critique (Truman has asked what the U.S. has done to alienate the Soviet Union):

> "What we have done . . . is to be a bourgeois nation, the biggest and richest in the world. Our affairs are run by immensely wealthy capitalists who choose dummy legislators and tell them what to do. The capitalists are automatically driven by the forces of an expanding economy to reach out to every corner of the earth for raw materials and markets. We take these by purchase where possible, but where we encounter resistance we are ready to use force. By this means we reduce all colonial peoples to the status of peons and we keep them there."

Instead of pursuing the logic of this argument, Lanny shifts the grounds of his attack and becomes ironic:

> "But now come the heroic Bolsheviks, the followers of the Marxist-Stalinist line, calling upon the awakening proletariat to arise and expropriate the appropriators. I don't know whether you understand that jargon, Mr. Truman, but you have to learn it, because that is what we have to face the balance of our lives."
>
> "I have heard it, Mr. Budd, but it is hard to make it real to myself."
>
> "It is just the realest thing going. It is being recited day and night by tens of thousands of inspired fanatics. They are teaching it to millions; they are teaching it to the young, and in one generation more there will be whole countries full of people who have never heard anything else and who take it just as seriously as you take the Gospels according to Matthew, Mark, Luke, and John."   (RLB, pp. 119–120)

After more of this palaver in which Lanny draws a picture of hate-filled hordes using every possible means to bring about the destruction of the United States, Truman concludes that the country will have to rearm, but that having a large army will not be incompatible with social progress. Lanny goes away happy.

That the ideal of social progress per se is uppermost neither in Sinclair's mind nor his hero's at this time becomes all the more obvious when it is expressed by another sympathetic character, Professor Charles T. Alston, New Dealer, foreign policy expert, and general insider. Speaking on the radio program sponsored by Lanny and Laurel's "Peace Foundation"—now sounding the alert on World Communism—he argues, "The only possible chance of defeating Communist dictatorship is by setting up industrial democracy by constitutional methods in which our political freedoms would be retained. That is one way we can gain and keep the support of the masses and bring the Red dictatorships to defeat" (RLB, p. 163).

Lanny's half sister, Bessie, always strong in her views, becomes in this volume one of the Communist "fanatics" against whom Lanny supposedly scores point after point in bitter debates (though she is too far gone to realize it), whom he sorrowfully denounces to the FBI as an espionage suspect, and whose long-suffering husband, Hansi, he not only sets free but provides with a more suitable mate. In his arguments with Bessie, Lanny seems never really to answer her charges but rather presents counter-charges about Communist methods that are meant to be unanswerable. He has, in short, ceased being merely a bore and has himself become a zealot whose anti-Communist preaching fills several hundred pages. The conclusion of the Lanny Budd series in a grand peroration brings Sinclair's career full circle, a story of the triumph of moral ardor over the art of fiction.

Ezra Pound and the Attainment of Imagism

BERNARD DUFFEY

There is evidence that when Ezra Pound arrived in London in the fall of 1908 he was ready to inaugurate a poetic career. During the three months or so in Venice which had intervened between his discharge from the faculty of Wabash College and his appearance in the English capital, he had employed a Venetian printer to put together the seventy-two-page volume, *A Lume Spento* (he translated the phrase, "With Torches Quenched"), which would be his first book of poems. He promptly dispatched some forty copies to his father in Philadelphia with instructions to begin a campaign toward securing American publication for the book. "The American reprint," he urged, "has got to be worked by kicking up such a hell of a row with genuine and faked reviews that Scribner or somebody can be brought to see the sense of making a reprint. I shall write a few myself and get someone to sign 'em." [1] A copy of *A Lume Spento* had gone to William Carlos Williams for his reaction, and Pound's friend seems to have felt the work to be dangerously idiosyncratic. Pound had replied, "But, mon cher, would a collection of mild, pretty verses convince any publisher or critic that *I* happen to be a genius and deserve audience?" [2] And he proceeded to outline his idea of his work.

> To me, the short so-called dramatic lyric—at any rate the sort of thing I do—is the poetic part of a drama the rest of which (to me the prose part) is left to the reader's imagination or set in a short note. I catch the character I happen to be interested in at the moment he interests me, usually a moment of song, self-awareness, or sudden understanding or revelation. And the rest of the play would bore me and presumably the reader. I paint my man as I *conceive* him. Et Voila tout!
>
> (pp. 3–4)

The letter contained one other emphasis. "Then again you must remember I don't try to write for the public. I can't. I haven't that kind of intelligence" (p. 6). Such a letter leaves little doubt that, despite his

---

1. Quoted from Donald Gallup, *A Bibliography of Ezra Pound* (London, 1963), p. 21.
2. *The Letters of Ezra Pound*, ed. D. D. Paige (New York, 1950), p. 4. Page references following in parentheses are to this volume.

Browningesque inclination toward dramatic monologue, Pound had set out to be an independent, self-defining poet from the beginning.

The letter also suggested that at least some part of *A Lume Spento* had been written during his months at Wabash where the flamboyance of his personality had roused a distrust capped by his befriending a stranded actress, and so had resulted in his dismissal. "If anybody stuck *you* in Indiana for four months," he said to Williams, "and you didn't at least *write* some unconstrained something or other, I'd give up hope for your salvation" (p. 5). Beyond such generalized rebelliousness, however, Pound's letter had begun to outline a specific sense of his writing, one I will be arguing here that culminated in the definitions of Imagism he arrived at in 1913 and, in doing so, formulated in short compass a highly complex sense of his own poetic ends and means.

Pound himself would often speak slightingly of Imagism in later years, and some of his critics, notably Hugh Kenner in *The Pound Era*,[3] have been inclined to dismiss the matter as essentially a side issue in the story of his evolution. Kenner himself proposed a centering of Pound's poetic impulses in his association with the Vorticist activity of 1914–1915. Donald Davie, arguing in a related direction, also characterized Pound's involvement with Imagism as "spectacular, brief, and tangential."[4] It seems, however, that Pound's own disavowals may have been more forcibly affected by his anger at the misuse he felt Amy Lowell and others had made of his program than by any basic alteration in his own thinking, and that perpetuation of them is misleading. Toward supporting this conclusion, my present purpose will be to read Pound's early critical writing in some detail and to urge that Imagist ideas were present from its beginning. During its course they ramified toward an overall view of the nature and value of poetry, and at a certain moment, they were put together to make a clear, consistent, and durable formulation of Pound's most basic poetic commitment.

That formulation appeared in the famous "manifesto" in *Poetry* magazine[5] consisting of a short letter Pound had largely prepared for his friend F. S. Flint to sign urging "direct treatment of the 'thing,' whether subjective or objective" along with the exclusion of any language "that did not contribute to the presentation," and rhythmical composition "in sequence of the musical phrase, not in sequence of a metronome." To these stipulations, Pound, in his own name, added a longer list of recommendations headed off by his definition of an image as ". . . that which presents an

---

3. Berkeley and Los Angeles, 1971. See especially the chapter on "Imagism," pp. 173–192.

4. *Ezra Pound, Poet as Sculptor* (New York, 1964), p. 36.

5. F. S. Flint, "Imagisme," and Ezra Pound, "A Few Don'ts By An Imagiste," *Poetry*, I (March, 1913), 198–206. The page reference following in parentheses is to this volume.

intellectual and emotional complex in an instant of time." He referred his meaning of "complex" to the "newer psychologists such as Hart," and, after this rather casual gloss, went on to more particular definition giving the image independent and sufficient existence in its own right: "It is the presentation of such a 'complex' instantaneously which gives that sense of sudden liberation; that sense of freedom from time limits and space limits; that sense of sudden growth, which we experience in the presence of the greatest works of art" (p. 205).

To come back to beginnings, the London of 1908 in which Pound arrived was itself showing some signs of readiness for a degree of poetic innovation, or even of program. The general literary scene had been subject to larger or smaller shock waves as early as the advent of Rossetti and Swinburne in poetry, Hardy in fiction, and Shaw in the drama. In an editorial in his *Poetry Review* of 1912 Harold Monro continued the story by noting that, after Swinburne in poetry, came the generation of the nineties, "John Davidson, Francis Thompson, W. E. Henley, W. B. Yeats, William Watson, Lionel Johnson, and Ernest Dowson."[6] But, his judgment ran, "Our impression of the period is one of a poetry stunned by fact" (p. 248). The root cause of such paralysis he located in a radically new element in English awareness. "In 1871 *The Descent of Man* was published, and henceforward the Victorian manner of thought, the honest doubt, and mild groping toward infinity, became, in the face of new revelation, harmlessly ridiculous" (p. 247). Finally, such dispersal of established convention, followed by the failure of the fin de siècle to establish a new mode, meant that "poetry entered virginal upon the twentieth century, and the poets of today find themselves suddenly emerging from a transition period, a strange world about them, a broken tradition behind, and a new one in the future to create" (p. 248).

There were other signs of enlarging awareness besides Monro's. "The revolution of the word began, so far as it affected the men who were of my age in London in 1908, with the LONE whimper of Ford Madox Hueffer,"[7] Pound always insisted, and Hueffer's moral was that poetry must be at least as well written as prose. It is true that the *English Review* which Hueffer (later, Ford Madox Ford) was to begin editing in 1908 would briefly become a center for vitality and discipline in English writing, but also T. E. Hulme would assemble the Poets' Club in 1908 which met for a year or two to hear Hulme call attention, among other things, to what he called "the image." Hulme had been commenting on William James, Henri Bergson, and Remy de Gourmont in the *New Age* as early as 1909 and following with particular interest the revolt they bespoke against any

---

6. "The Nineties," *Poetry Review*, I (June, 1912), 247. Page references following in parentheses are to this volume.

7. *Polite Essays* (Norfolk, Conn., [1939]), p. 50.

rationalistic domination of thought. His concept of the image was especially linked with Bergson's argument for the reality of time as "duration,"
and for "intuition" as the faculty by which such reality could be appre-
hended. The connection would be made explicit, and public, by 1911 as
in that year Hulme commented in print on a book of poetic theory by
Tancrède de Visan, a follower of Mallarmé, applying Bergsonian thought
to symbolism: "Life is a continuous and unanalysable curve which cannot
be seized clearly. It can only be got at by a kind of central vision as opposed to analytic description. This central vision expresses itself by means
of symbols. M. Visan would then define Symbolism as an attempt by
means of successive and accumulated images to express and exteriorize
such a central lyric intuition."[8] In still another quarter, and in the literary
column he called "Books and Persons" and signed as "Jacob Tonson,"
Arnold Bennett opined in 1908 that Robert Bridges and W. B. Yeats were
the two best among contemporary poets,[9] and in the words of Osbert
Burdett both were noted for their innovation, Bridges in "metrics" and
Yeats as a "Symbolist."[10]

The idea of poetic "symbolism" added a real but somewhat unaccount-
able seasoning to the English poetic air. In opening his own "Recent
Verse" column in the *New Age* in 1908, F. S. Flint began with an epigraph
from Mallarmé. "In truth, there is no prose; there is the alphabet, and
there are verses more or less compact, more or less diffuse." Flint went on
to pose his own avant-garde standards by citing Poe's charge against the
reality of the long poem and urging that conventional poetic form did
"not sustain anyone who is not a genius." He concluded that "a poet
should listen to the instinctual rhythm within him."[11] Flint was to re-
iterate his sense of needed innovation as his column proceeded on through
the two years-odd of its duration to argue that "the only common relationship of the new writers is to the anarchy of their times, out of which they
have sprung and which they reflect" (p. 449), and that the pressing need
of English poetry was for "a revaluation of all poetical values."[12] In
February of 1909 he gave condescending notice to "a little plaquette of
verse by members of the Poets' Club" (p. 327). The following week he
was chided by T. E. Hulme for his judgment, but he was also invited to
inspect the club at first hand and to join it if he wished. This Flint pro-

8. "Book of the Week," *New Age*, IX (Aug. 24, 1911), 401.
9. *New Age*, IV (Dec. 3, 1908), 112.
10. "The Last Ten Years in English Literature," *New Age*, III (June 13, 1908), 136
and (July 4, 1908), 191.
11. "Recent Verse," *New Age*, III (Aug. 15, 1908), 312. The page reference following in
parentheses is to this volume.
12. "Recent Verse," *New Age*, IV (Nov. 26, 1908), 96. The page reference following in
parentheses is to this volume.

ceeded to do, entering the group at about the same time that Pound was to be drawn into it.

Pound's earliest critical writing was not immediately affected by such lines of thought, however. It was, instead, to begin drawing together a complex innovative position of its own. He had given a set of lectures at the Regent Street Polytechnic in London on "The Development of Literature in Southern Europe," and, following the same path toward quick publication blazed by his poetry, he had this material in book form in the summer of 1910 as *The Spirit of Romance*, published by Dent. His task as lecturer had been largely expository and descriptive, a tracing of poetic expression in the languages of Provence, Tuscany, northern France, Spain, and Portugal, with a chapter on medieval Latin lyric, the general subject in which he had specialized both as undergraduate and graduate student. Through this process, however, his account also kept a critical argument in view which, concluding his chapter on Villon, he applied in summary to the main line of the verse he had been describing, one he rooted in the pervasive "realism" of romance expression. "Dante's vision is real, because he saw it. Villon's verse is real, because he lived it; as Bertran de Born, as Arnaut Marvoil, as that mad poseur Vidal, he lived it. For these men life is in the press. No brew of books, no distillation of sources will match the tang of them."[13] Such argument in fact drew on two shaping ideas: those of the "Romance" tradition as a path leading to the discovery of literary vigor and a notion of literary vigor, in turn, made dependent on the act of intensely felt and recorded life.

Such thinking was to be a controlling power throughout the book. In an opening comment on Ovid, Pound noted that the *Metamorphoses* "has the clarity of French scientific prose" (p. 15). Ovid's art, "before Browning, raises the dead and dissects their mental processes" (p. 16). His chapter on Arnaut Daniel praised the troubadour who had been honored by Dante as a poet "not content with conventional phrase, or with words which do not convey his exact meaning," (p. 25) and one, consequently, whom Dante had esteemed for "maestria" (p. 133). Following his subject into its Tuscan flowering in Guido Cavalcanti and Dante himself, Pound noted a change from Provençal origins. "The cult of Provence had been a cult of the emotions; and with it there had been some, hardly conscious, study of emotional psychology. In Tuscany the cult is a cult of the harmonies of the mind." But it was still the qualities of directness and presence which had prevailed; ". . . this virtue it ever has, it is not rhetorical, it aims to be what it is, and never pretends to be something it is not" (p. 116).

Pound's long chapter on Dante clung persistently to the same critical

---

13. *The Spirit of Romance* (Norfolk, Conn., [1953]), p. 178. Page references following in parentheses are to this volume.

theme. He characterized the *Commedia* as "the journey of Dante's intelligence through the states of mind wherein dwell all sorts and conditions
of men before death," and the Italian's journey became a symbol of "mankind's struggle upward out of ignorance into the clear light of philosophy"
(p. 127). Likening the famous fourfold range of Dante's meaning to the
complexity of a mathematical synthesis of particulars into a single logical
unity, Pound used an extended comparison he was later to salvage and
repeat in his "Vorticism" essay of 1914, but he also went on to more particular specification. Beauty in Dante was like that of Whistler's painting,
less the source of immediate impact on the reader than of a power by
which, after absorbing it, "one finds new beauty in natural things" and so
is admitted "to a deeper knowledge, to a finer perception of beauty" (p.
154). Like Wordsworth, Dante had feeling for nature, but "he describes
the actual sensation with more intensity," and Dante stood in sharp contrast to Whitman's "catalogues and flounderings" (p. 155). In language,
Shakespeare was "more beautifully suggestive," Dante "more beautifully
definite" (p. 158). Like Arnaut Daniel's, Dante's "vividness" depended
greatly on comparison to a "particular phenomenon." Underlying all was
"the great sub-surge of his truth and his sincerity" (p. 163).

The Spirit of Romance could be surveyed at greater length, but its
insistence on vivid and sharply felt experience and expression would only
repeat itself the further. Villon, thus, was a poet who "never lies to himself; he does not know much, but what he knows he knows; man is an
animal, certain things he can feel" (p. 169). The simplicity and realism of
the Spanish *Poema del Cid* was superior to the more ornate and conventional *Song of Roland*. Even the philosophy of Richard of St. Victor attained a state of poetry; "not because of its floridity, but because of its
intensity" (p. 116). Finally, Pound concluded, poetry by its vividness might
well be more closely related to "the best of music, of painting, and of
sculpture, than to any part of literature which is not true poetry." Matthew Arnold's standard for poetry as a "criticism of life" was blasphemy
against both poetry and life itself. "Poetry," to the contrary, "is about as
much a criticism of life as a red-hot iron is a criticism of fire" (p. 122).

The Spirit of Romance was a study in literary history rather than a
program for poetic composition, but it clearly gathered itself around a
sense of the responsibility primary for composition. Its repeated insistence
on directness and intensity was a plainly delineated move, this early, toward establishing what would become the first principle of Imagism.

Pound's critical and theoretical writing burgeoned in the years between
1910 and 1913. He contributed a growing number of short pieces to the
literary press and in addition published three more substantial items following *The Spirit of Romance*. In 1911 he made his own debut in the

New Age, the vigorously independent socialist weekly whose purchase by A. R. Orage in 1907 had created the review of "politics, literature and the arts" where Hulme and Flint, along with other innovating notables on the London scene, had already appeared. In a series of articles called "I Gather the Limbs of Osiris" and published between November, 1911, and February, 1912, Pound returned to poetry of the past, particularly to Arnaut Daniel this time, but now to fashion a more explicitly stated critical position out of it.[14] Also in 1912 he printed in *The Quest* magazine of London an essay to be called "Psychology and the Troubadours" which in 1932 and afterwards, appeared as a new fifth chapter in *The Spirit of Romance*. Late in the year a second series of essays, "Patria Mia," also appeared in the *New Age*.

Since 1908, he had brought out five small volumes of verse.[15] Much writing had in fact been carried forward from one book to the next, and the whole was strongly marked by Pound's sense of the literary past. It may well have seemed that his poetry was growing repetitious of the note he had first struck in *A Lume Spento*. As sympathetic a reviewer of *Exultations* in 1909 as F. S. Flint could complain that "if Mr. Pound could only forget his literature he would exult to more purpose."[16] *Canzoni* drew even sharper criticism in 1911 and, particularly, a pointed personal objection from Ford Madox Hueffer against its sometimes elaborate archaism.[17]

The "Osiris" essays, however, did not wholly preempt new ground. Much of their content, like that of *The Spirit of Romance*, was given over to translating and commenting on older poetry, but in the process a number of critical points emerged. Chief among these was the need Pound now expressed for revision of current poetry in a twofold direction. On the one hand lay the familiar argument, ". . . we must have a simplicity and directness of utterance." But this position was now expanded to advocate an utterance which also "is different from the simplicity and directness of daily speech, which is more 'curial,' more dignified." There were few fallacies, Pound thought, "more common than the opinion that poetry should mimic daily speech."[18] He was to provide a friendly review of Hueffer's volume of verse, *High Germany*, in the *Poetry Review*, but in it he also took exception. "Mr. Hueffer is so obsessed with the idea that the language of poetry should not be a dead language, that he forgets it must be the

14. Reprinted in Ezra Pound, *Selected Prose 1908–1965*, ed. William Cookson (New York, 1973), pp. 19–43.

15. *A Lume Spento* (1908); *A Quinzaine for This Yule* (1908); *Personae of Ezra Pound* (1909); *Exultations of Ezra Pound* (1909); *Canzoni of Ezra Pound* (1911).

16. "Verse," *New Age*, VI (Jan. 6, 1910), 234.

17. See Noel Stock, *The Life of Ezra Pound* (New York, 1970), p. 103.

18. *New Age*, X (Feb. 15, 1912), 369. The page reference following in parentheses is to this volume.

speech of to-day dignified, more intense, more dynamic, than to-day's speech as spoken." [19]

The argument of the "Osiris" series dwelt further on points that suggested how a poetically "curial" speech might best be sought. In treating Daniel's work, as in his consideration of the Anglo-Saxon "Seafarer" which opened the series, Pound announced that he was seeking "a new method in scholarship," an emphasis on the "luminous detail in history," one that generated "a sudden insight into circumjacent conditions, into their causes, their effects, into sequence, and law," and the essay was not long in converting such "luminous detail" from a historical to a poetic context. In addition to the historian, Pound argued, "the artist seeks out the luminous detail and presents it. He does not comment. . . . As scholarship has erred in presenting all detail as of equal import, so also in literature, in a present school of writing, we see a similar tendency" (p. 130). The sense of reality he sought was not that of orthodox realism. Just as the language of mere daily life diminished the force of poetry, so a literature that aspired only to the experience of daily life would find its force spent, its "curial" resonance and suggestion occluded.

As the decade proceeded, this concept would turn out to have large consequences for Pound's sense of poetry. The idea of the "luminous detail" is clearly a first effort at defining what he would later call the "image," as it indeed called for an "intellectual and emotional complex" and one implying freedom "from time limits and space limits; that sense of sudden growth, which we experience in the greatest works of art." And one need not press the concept too hard to see in it also a beginning of the very sense of history that would be emerging in *The Cantos* by the decade's end as an aestheticizing of Pound's loyalties and antagonisms into moments intensely if not always clearly suggestive of special meaning, an argument that would seek to alter history by Imagist methods from the recording and interpreting of fact to make of it something more like high drama, one suddenly revealing the nature of the forces animating it. The process had found echo as far back as Pound's 1908 letter to Williams affirming the "moment of song, self-awareness, or sudden understanding or revelation" by which a dramatic character or, now, a dramatic situation, made itself resonant with implication.

The sense of image toward which Pound was moving was one, again, seeking "intellectual and emotional complex" as its substance. Good writing was always what he called "efficient" writing. But this did not mean that good writing was sparse in meaning. Imagist "efficiency," rather, and in contrast to the flatness and "dailiness" of realism, sought "revelation" or luminous moment. This had been the drift of argument throughout

19. *Poetry Review*, I (March, 1912), 133.

the "Osiris" essays, and in their course it was developed into a number of other particulars.

Later in 1912, Pound's essay on "Psychology and the Troubadours" carried the argument to greater length. His subject was the familiar pre-occupation with the langue d'oc and its poetry, but for the first time the question now drew him to the obsessive subject of troubadour poetry, that of chivalric love and its celebration. Such seeming conventionality was in fact now to reveal unsuspected thrusts toward the sense of "liberation" and "sudden growth" that Imagism also would seek.

Troubadour poetry, he held, shared with Greek myth a participation in what he proposed "as a sort of permanent basis in humanity,"[20] an act that in his summary would sound much like the direct and intuitive participation in the Bergsonian flux which Hulme had been advocating for poetry and one, further, that Hulme identified with the advent of symbolism. Hulme's interest in symbolism, however, appeared to be something rather different from the linguistic and transcendental emphasis of chief concern to Mallarmé and his circle. Hulme had been particularly taken with Visan's book applying Bergson to symbolist theory, and during the same month he reviewed that work he also supplied a second review to the New Age treating the later and still living French symbolist author, Remy de Gourmont. Delior, the work's author, particularly stressed the philosophic materialism implicit in Gourmont's thought, its emphasis on human life as a biological phenomenon existing wholly in its physical processes and one for which "ideas" or intimations of a mental or spiritual realm were never more than secondary manifestations of physical being. The emotions of love, in particular, were biological and, within those limits alone, psychological. Hulme, nevertheless, saw Gourmont as a spokesman also for symbolism, but such symbolism, now, was necessarily a phenomenon contained within the Bergsonian realm of duration as it was likewise wholly contained within a physical universe. In particular, said Hulme, Gourmont "sees life essentially, as the necessity to procreation, try to disguise it how we may, and art is one of the forms of the sexual instinct."[21]

Pound too sought a common ground for the mixture of physical and spiritual he identified in troubadour poetry, and, with a more traditional imagination than Hulme but with no less emphasis, he too drove toward a sense of physical ambience by resorting to an ancient doctrine he imputed to Greek myth and to troubadour poetry alike, that of the correspondence of microcosm and macrocosm. As microcosm, man contained in himself what Pound called both "sun" and "moon," the light both of the

20. The Spirit of Romance, p. 92.
21. New Age, V (July 8, 1909), 219.

ordinary and the extraordinary. The saint or seer was one who in fact and in flesh experienced the sacred, a union of force between physical and spiritual poles. As one example, the monk "develops at infinite trouble and expense the secondary pole within himself" and so "produces his charged surface, which registers the beauties, celestial or otherwise, by contemplation." In a second case, that of the lover, "which I must say seems more in accord with 'mens sana in corpore sano,' the charged surface is produced between the predominant natural poles of two human mechanisms. Sex is, that is to say, of a double function and purpose, reproductive and educational."[22] To write imaginatively and out of the truth of awareness would be to apprehend the macrocosm by vivid apprehension of the microcosm. Intuitive seizure of the part could provide intuitive illumination of the whole. "We have about us the universe of fluid force, and below us the germinal universe of wood alive, of stone alive. Man is—the sensitive part of him—a mechanism, for the purpose of our further discussion a mechanism rather like an electric appliance, switches, wires, etc." (p. 92). Hulme had also emphasized Gourmont's claim that one should never hesitate "to introduce science into literature or literature into science,"[23] and Pound's description of man as "mechanism" here seemed more akin to Hulme's feeling for the living texture of "durée" than to any more rationalistic scheme. Wood was "alive," stone was "alive," and man's openness to such life was like that of a conductor of electrical impulse.[24]

If Hulme had found such "symbolist" poetry to be a potentially liberating and validating power in modern writing, its force thus was a suprarationalistic but still wholly natural one, and Pound shared in that line of argument. The center of consciousness, he urged, lay in what "Greek psychologists" had called "the *phantistikon*," the image-making faculty. One kind of mind "is like soap-bubbles reflecting sundry patches of the macrocosmos," and such accidental and superficial reflection of reality was unimportant. With others, however, consciousness might be "germinal." "Their thoughts are in them as the thought of the tree is in the seed, or in

22. *The Spirit of Romance*, p. 94. The page reference following in parentheses is to this volume.

23. *New Age*, V (July 8, 1909), 219.

24. There are signs indicating that Pound's attachment to this line of thought remained with him for several years at the least. *A Lume Spento* had contained such poems as "The Tree" or "La Fraisne" recording the poet's sense of union with living trees leading to supra-rational intuition. Several years later Pound would record of his first meeting with Arnold Dolmetsch, the musician and maker of musical instruments, his sense that he had, in metamorphosed fact, encountered the figure of Pan. "The undeniable tradition of metamorphosis teaches us that things do not remain always the same, they become other things by swift, unanalysable processes" ("Affirmations I: Arnold Dolmetsch," *New Age*, XVI [Jan. 7, 1915], 246). Pound's phrase here echoes Hulme's rendering of Bergson's sense of flux as "a continuous and unanalysable curve." See p. 5 above.

the grass, or the grain, or the blossom. And these minds are the more poetic, and they affect mind about them, and transmute it as the seed the earth. And this latter sort of mind is close on the vital universe. . . ."[25]

Pound thus had arrived at an agreement with what may be called a natural symbolism and, in doing so, had defined the reality within which Imagist perceptions could claim substantive, intuitive worth. He shared ground with Hulme's feeling for Bergson and Gourmont. The Imagist aim in poetry would not be only for "efficiency," for "luminous detail" as such, it would also include mind's knowing such event as revelation *within* the flux of experience. "There is," Pound argued, "in what I have called 'the natural course of events' the exalted moment, the vision unsought or at least the vision gained without machination" (p. 97). Richard of St. Victor had suggested that "by naming over all the most beautiful things we know we may draw back upon our minds some vestige of the heavenly splendor" (p. 96). Dante had done something of the sort by preceding the movement of the *Divine Comedy* into the *Paradiso* with his six cantos of vivid and moving description of the earthly paradise (p. 140). In Pound's view of the matter, to succeed in such effort was to make all there was of heavenly revelation available to the earthly eye. The goal of poetry must be the attainment of the most pointed, most illuminating revelation available to human sight.

If, in all this, "Psychology and the Troubadours" seemed to run beyond Imagist definitions, the link between them, that of hewing to a universe of vital meaning, may be suggested from a brief essay entitled, in odd spelling, "Prologomena," appearing in the February, 1912, *Poetry Review*. In its compass, Pound was once again seeking to justify his continued absorption in the past. To this end, he epitomized his argument in a four-point "credo" within the essay that in itself repeated four times over the "naturalness" of the virtue he sought for, its relation to living force, just as in his troubadour essay he had come down so strongly on the sensitivity of that poetry to the implications of its naturally supernatural world.

The "credo" first professed belief in "an absolute rhythm," one which corresponded "exactly to the emotion or shade of emotion to be expressed," an intimate union, that is, between poetic means and substance and so between form and implication. The second heading was that of "Symbols." Repeating here his feeling for a naturalness paralleling Dante's harmony of idea with precise natural fact, Pound announced, "I believe that the proper and perfect symbol is the natural object." If a secondary suggestion was present, it should appear "so that a sense, and the poetic quality of the passage, is not lost to those who do not understand the

---

25. *The Spirit of Romance*, pp. 92–93. Page references following in parentheses are to this volume.

symbol as such, to whom for example a hawk is a hawk." Revelation lay more in particulars than in transcendental gesture. Technique, in turn, was "the test of a man's sincerity," without which any claim to revelation must be hollow, and the "trampling down of every convention that impedes or obscures the determination of the law, or the precise rendering of the impulse." Finally, "some poems may have form as a tree has form, some as water poured into a vase." Form might be symmetrical or not, but it must accurately apprehend and shape its subject.[26] The drift of the whole argument was summed up, finally, near the conclusion of the "Osiris" series itself, to which Pound referred in "Prologomena," and which was appearing during the same time in the *New Age*. "For it is not until poetry is 'close to the thing' that it will be a vital part of contemporary life. As long as the poet says not what he, at the very crux of clarified conception, means but is content to say something ornate and approximate, just so long will serious people, intently alive, consider poetry as balderdash."[27]

In September of 1912 Pound's "Patria Mia" series began appearing in the *New Age*. Its chief concern, of course, was the state of American writing, along with implications for American art in general. What appeared in it was considerably briefer and differently pointed from the content of the small book Pound would seek to make under the same title by conflating this material with a later set of *New Age* essays,[28] and the "Patria Mia" of the *New Age* particularly emphasized the importance of freedom, culture, and discipline to American expression. Its concluding argument gathered up much of the force of the whole eleven articles as it moved toward establishing Whitman as representative of an American character in poetry possessed of great potential achievement. "It is, as nearly as I can define it, a certain generosity; a certain carelessness, or looseness, if you will; a hatred of the sordid, an ability to forget the part for the whole, a desire for largeness; a willingness to stand exposed."[29] In displaying such spirit, Pound argued, Whitman spoke for a certain venturesomeness and devotion to freedom, which were the most admirable and useful of American traits. "One may not need him at home," Pound cautioned, "but if one is abroad; if one is ever likely to forget one's birth-right . . . one can find in Whitman the reassurance."

---

26. *Poetry Review*, I (Feb. 2, 1912), 75.
27. *New Age*, X (Feb. 15, 1912), 369.
28. The volume, *Patria Mia*, was not to be published until much later. Its manuscript had been sent to a small Chicago publisher, Ralph Fletcher Seymour, but was lost during a reorganization of his business. It was eventually recovered by Seymour and appeared in 1950. The Seymour text is reprinted in Pound, *Selected Prose 1909–1965*, pp. 101–146.
29. *New Age*, XI (Nov. 14, 1912), 36. The page reference following in parentheses is to this volume.

But the Poundian and Imagist drive for a parallel sort of freedom needed complement, one figured forth in this case by a second American, the painter Whistler. His message was essential. "It was, in substance, that being born an American is no excuse for being content with a parochial standard" (p. 36), a view that Pound would seek tirelessly to impose on Harriet Monroe's eclectic hospitality in *Poetry*. Whistler was the "martinet" American art, especially, needed, and the Imagist manifesto in *Poetry* was in effect a redaction of his lesson for emerging American expression.

By the end of 1912, thus, I would argue, a broad ground had been prepared from which the Imagist prescriptions would take their character, and from which Pound could develop his argument of "The Serious Artist" later in 1913[30] that artists constituted "the antennae of the race." The value of direct and vivid expression had been described in a major current of poetry flowing from the late Latin to Villon. The force of that stream had been summed up in the doctrine of "the luminous detail." Such luminosity had been related to a combined physical and mythological doctrine of intuition which itself roughly agreed with aspects of both Bergson's and Gourmont's thinking as linked to the needs of contemporary expression by T. E. Hulme. The statement of the program itself was drawn up for and published in a new, hopeful American literary venture. In all this, Pound had prepared a prescription for authenticity in poetry related to past and present both, and one finding force and value where, he would hold, life revealed itself most tellingly.

The formalizing of Imagism in March of 1913 was a focussing of the whole development of Pound's thinking over a period of five years, one clearly the opposite of accidental or trivial in its relation to his concerns and one difficult to dislodge from a position at the center of his thought about his own art. The formulation had hardly been arrived at, however, before dissension from his program began to manifest itself. His anthology, *Des Imagistes*, appeared in 1914. Its publication had been more a lucky accident, however, than the result of dependable circumstances, and when Amy Lowell appealed to certain of Pound's associates to allow her to assume responsibility for continuing the anthology, and coupled her offer of support with freedom from Pound's stringent taskmastering, a number of them turned against what they now saw as an overbearing narrowness in his program. Pound's efforts in behalf of his cause had not flagged. He had assembled its first volume and had secured its publication. He had, furthermore, prepared a much larger statement of Imagist aims and ideas than could be fitted into *Poetry*'s limited space. In August of 1914, however, Pound and the original Imagist group had parted, and, he wrote

30. *New Freewoman*, I (Oct. 15, 1913), 162.

Harriet Monroe, he was retitling the Imagist essay as "Vorticism."[31] It would appear the next month in the *Fortnightly Review*.

The event was Pound's first plain avowal of his abandonment of the Imagist cause. What "Vorticism" was to mean to him is too complex a subject to more than glance at here, but it was not easy to separate from the central Imagist principles he was to repeat in defining it. It is worth noting that his adoption of the new label would be announced in an essay still holding to his term *Imagisme* and still centered in the same emphases that had marked his earlier critical writing. At its end, he proposed a definition for what he now wanted to call a "vortex," but that definition itself began by identifying the old and new language. "The image is not an idea. It is a radiant node or cluster; it is what I can, must perforce, call a VORTEX, from which, and through which, and into which, ideas are continually rushing."[32]

The term Pound had originally coined had been seized upon by a group hostile to him, and it became necessary to find a new term. In the place of "Image," consequently, there would be "Vortex." There would be no change, however, in his concept of the poetic unit, a "primary pigment" that was still the rendering of an "intellectual and emotional complex in an instant of time." Most notably, Pound the Vorticist would now reach out for a better sense of his poetry's relation to other arts (a concern, however, that had been noted as early as 1910 in *The Spirit of Romance*) just as Imagism had been concerned with the relation of it to a literary complex. That new effort, an Imagism writ larger, would dominate the Vorticist program.

31. See Ellen Williams, *Harriet Monroe and the Poetry Renaissance* (Urbana, Ill., 1977), pp. 132–133.
32. Quoted from Richard Ellmann and Charles Feidelson (eds.), *The Modern Tradition* (New York, 1965), p. 152.

The Harlem Renaissance: One Facet of an Unturned Kaleidoscope

DARWIN T. TURNER

Geraldine's brash cry, "What you see is what you get," is appropriate comment on the tendency of many Americans to fix their attention on only a particular aspect of Black life in America—usually the most spectacular aspect. If they would twist the base of the kaleidoscope of Black life, the multicolored fragments would rearrange themselves into different patterns, some of them startlingly different. But few viewers choose to adjust the kaleidoscope.

As a result, out of the many patterns of Black life during the 1920's, the dominant image emblazoned on the vision of America is the Harlem Renaissance. By the same process, from the Harlem Renaissance itself, a Jazzed Abandon has become the most memorable spectacle. James Weldon Johnson's description of reactions to Harlem summarizes the legend of the Harlem Renaissance:

> It is known in Europe and the Orient, and it is talked about by natives in the interior of Africa. It is farthest known as being exotic, colourful [*sic*], and sensuous; a place of laughing, singing, and dancing; a place where life wakes up at night. This phase of Harlem's fame is most widely known because, in addition to being spread by ordinary agencies, it has been proclaimed in story and song. And certainly this is Harlem's most striking and fascinating aspect. New Yorkers and people visiting New York from the world over go to the night-clubs of Harlem and dance to such jazz music as can be heard nowhere else; and they get an exhilaration impossible to duplicate. Some of these seekers after new sensations go beyond the gay night-clubs; they peep in under the more seamy side of things; they nose down into lower strata of life. A visit to Harlem at night—the principal streets never deserted, gay crowds skipping from one place of amusement to another, lines of taxicabs and limousines standing under the sparkling lights of the entrances to the famous night-clubs, the subway kiosks swallowing and disgorging crowds all night long—gives the impression

that Harlem never sleeps and that the inhabitants thereof jazz through existence.[1]

Johnson continued, "But, of course, no one can seriously think that the two hundred thousand and more Negroes in Harlem spend their nights on any such pleasance."[2] So we too can say, "Surely, no one seriously thinks that this picture or even the entire 'Renaissance' constitutes the totality of the patterns housed in the kaleidoscope of Black life during the 1920's, the decade of the 'New Negro.'"

Even if one examines only the literary portraiture of the decade, one discerns more than a single image as the minute, tinted mirrors arrange and rearrange themselves into diverse patterns reflecting the actuality of Black life or reflecting the psyches of the Black and white artists who depicted that life. A knowledgeable individual twists the instrument to view the primitivism depicted by such white authors as Julia Peterkin, Eugene O'Neill, Sherwood Anderson, Dubose Heyward, Mary Wiborg, and William Faulkner, or the exotic abandon simulated by Carl Van Vechten. But a slight adjustment reshapes those images into the cultural elitism revealed by Van Vechten and cherished by W. E. B. DuBois. Another adjustment reveals the integrationist optimism of Langston Hughes, or the pan-Africanism of W. E. B. DuBois, or the Black nationalism of Marcus Garvey. Examine rural southern Blacks from the perspectives of Peterkin, Heyward, Faulkner, and Jean Toomer; or scrutinize the urban northerners of Toomer, Claude McKay, Rudolph Fisher, Langston Hughes, and Countée Cullen. Smile at the enthusiastic and naive Carl Van Vechtens, Mabel Dodges, and other white patrons as they prance about with their trophies collected on safaris into the Black jungles; then scowl at the lynchers painted by Claude McKay and photographed by Walter White. Admire the "patient endurance," with which William Faulkner colored his Dilsey; but do not overlook the militant impatience that inflames McKay's poetic voice. Consider the African nationalism vaguely sketched by Cullen, Hughes, and McKay; but compare it with Hughes' poetic demands for American integration and McKay's impressionistic sketches of the damnable siren, America, that fascinates, challenges, and captivates Blacks. Excite yourselves with sexual abandon garishly painted by Van Vechten, Anderson, McKay, and Toomer; but study also the conservative, often frustrated Blacks portrayed by Jessie Fauset and Toomer. Weep for the impotent failures depicted by O'Neill and Paul Green; but rejoice with the bold, determined aspirants of Fauset and Fisher.

---

1. James W. Johnson, *Black Manhattan* (New York, 1968; originally published, 1930), pp. 160–161.
2. Ibid., p. 161.

Beyond the literary spectrum, the images are equally diverse. The decade of the 1920's was ushered in by the triumphant return in 1919 of the highly decorated Black 369th Infantry, which marched from the docks, down Broadway, and through Harlem, led every step of the way by James Europe's jazz band. But the decade was ushered in also by the "Red Summer" of 1919. In that year alone, according to historian John Hope Franklin, approximately twenty-five race riots throughout the nation spilled blood on the streets of the democratic land that, less than a year earlier, had won the war (so Americans said) that, President Wilson boasted, would end all wars and would safeguard democracy. Jazz was in vogue: such Black musicians as Duke Ellington and Fletcher Henderson attracted thousands of excited people to hear their bands, and Louis Armstrong gained new fans with each performance. But poverty was in vogue also: Black migrants who could not find jobs and older residents who had lost theirs to a new influx of whites gave rent parties, which remained joyous as long as no one remembered that the only reason for the party was the inability to pay the rent. Occupants of Harlem for less than a decade, Blacks were buying homes for residence and for profit on a scale rivaling the stock market speculations of their white contemporaries; but hard times had already established residence in the South, as Waring Cuney revealed in "Hard Times Blues":

I went down home
About a year ago
Things looked so bad
My heart was sore.
People had nothing
It was a sinning shame,
Everybody said
Hard times was to blame.

Great-God-A-Mighty
Folks feeling bad,
Lost all they ever had.

Sun was shining fourteen
Days and no rain,
Hoeing and planting
Was all in vain.
It was hard times, Lawd,
All around,
Meal barrels empty,
Crops burnt to the ground.

Great-God-A-Mighty
Folks feeling bad,
Lost all they ever had.

Skinny looking children
Bellies poking out,
Old pellagra
Without a doubt,
Old folks hanging 'round
The cabin door
Aint seen things
This bad before.

Great-God-A-Mighty
Folks feeling bad,
Lost all they ever had.

Went to the Boss
At the Commissary Store,
Folks all hungry
Please don't close the door,
Want more food, little time to pay.
Boss man laughed
And walked away.

Great-God-A-Mighty
Folks feeling bad,
Lost all they ever had.

Landlord coming 'round
When the rent's due,
Aint got the money
Take your home from you.
Takes your mule and horse
Even take your cow,
Says get off this land
You no good no how.

Great-God-A-Mighty
Folks feeling bad,
Lost all they ever had.

For Black folks, and many rural whites, times were bad—at the very height of the Jazz Age when Scott Fitzgerald's sheiks, flappers, and Gatsbys were staging their most lavish parties. Blacks were not naive about the times. With the assistance of Walter White, a Caucasian-looking Black, the N.A.A.C.P. launched its three-decades-long campaign against lynching. The *Messenger*, a Black newspaper, advocated socialism as the only solution to the economic problems of Black Americans; and *The Crusader*, another Black newspaper, denounced American bigotry in tones that a subsequent generation would believe originated in the 1960's. Recognizing the inability of nonunionized workers to withstand the arbitrary practices of the bosses, Black workers struggled to enter or establish unions: in the Brotherhood of Sleeping Car Porters, A. Philip Randolph created the most enduring of them all. Scorning any hope for Black economic or political power in the United States, Marcus Garvey, a West Indian, enlisted thousands of new followers who wished to sail the Black Star Line back to Africa. Ironically, Garvey, an actual Black from an island, won more power and financial support in America than Eugene O'Neill ever envisaged for his Emperor Jones, a fictional Black American who seizes control of a Black island.

Such awareness of the multiplicity of patterns of Black life during the 1920's justifies a reexamination, necessarily brief and somewhat superficial, of the Harlem Renaissance, particularly the literary Renaissance—to determine the reasons for its image as Jazzed Abandon, to trace more closely the more serious themes of the literature, and to reassess the significance of the Renaissance.

If we of the 1970's picture Black life in the 1920's as a riotous night-club tour, we cannot blame the best-known white writers for our misconception. Ironically, although Blacks became so popular as a subject that almost every prominent American author of the decade featured them in at least one major work, most of these authors ignored the Harlem scene in their literature. Such obvious neglect prompts speculation about the reasons: Were the authors describing the Afro-Americans they knew best? Or were they deliberately creating Black characters who would contrast with, and perhaps obscure, the image of the proud Renaissance Blacks?

Of course, in 1920, when O'Neill's *Emperor Jones* appeared, the Harlem Renaissance was less than a flutter in the heart of Alain Locke, the Black philosopher and cultural historian who named that era. O'Neill cannot be accused of ignoring what he could not have been expected to see. Situating his Black on a Caribbean island, O'Neill showed how fear, stripping away civilized veneer, reduces a man—in this instance, a southern Black—to a primitive.

The contrast between the Renaissance and O'Neill's work, however, appears in *All God's Chillun Got Wings* (1924). This drama, necessarily set in the North, describes the pathetic relationship between a Black man, who aspires to be a lawyer, and the "fallen" white woman whom he marries. The woman, betrayed and deserted by a white lover, marries the

Black but becomes insane—or more insane, according to your view. The Black fails to become a lawyer partly because his wife, not wanting him to succeed, interferes with his study. The more crucial reason for his failure, however, is that whenever he is examined by whites, he forgets whatever he knows. In 1924, the year the play appeared, Jessie Fauset and Walter White published the first Black novels of the decade: *There Is Confusion*, which centers on the lives of middle-class Blacks in Philadelphia, among them a Black graduate of a white medical school, and *The Fire in the Flint*, a protest against lynching. For three years, Black musicals had been the rage of Broadway theater. BLACK was in, by 1924. The next year *Survey Graphic* would focus an entire issue on the "New Negro," James Weldon Johnson would hail Harlem as the capital of Black America, others would call it "Mecca." Despite these events, O'Neill provided New York theatergoers with a Black protagonist whose aspirations exceed his ability. Whatever O'Neill's reasons for the theme, the choice of an actor to portray the protagonist could not have been more ironic. The Black who panics when examined by whites was played by Paul Robeson, all-American football player (I believe that he was the first Black selected by Walter Camp as an All-American), a twelve-letter man in athletics, and a Phi Beta Kappa graduate, who earned one of the highest academic averages in the history of Rutgers University.

The spectacle of Black failure was continued by Paul Green, a North Carolinian who wrote more plays about Blacks than any other white person during the decade. In 1926 Green won the Pulitzer Prize for *In Abraham's Bosom*, a drama in which Black Abe McCrannie, during Reconstruction, tries futilely to establish a school for Blacks. In the same year, 1926, W. E. B. DuBois, editor of *The Crisis*, the voice of the N.A.A.C.P., continuing a practice intended to encourage Black scholarship, published the pictures of the year's Black college graduates. Within a few years, DuBois would proudly announce that the large number of graduates prohibited his publishing the pictures of all.

Another memorable drama of the decade was Dubose Heyward's *Porgy*, now an American "classic," a story of a Black and crippled junk dealer, who strives to win Bess, a fallen woman, from Crown, a bad, bad man. Perhaps the most appropriate evaluation of the drama comes from W. E. B. DuBois, who insisted that he did not object to the play. Then, sniffing delicately from the rarified atmosphere surrounding a New England Brahmin who was a Ph.D. graduate from Harvard and had been a graduate student at Heidelberg, DuBois explained that, although he did not doubt that Heyward's Blacks existed in Charleston, South Carolina, he regretted Heyward's failure to portray the educated Blacks DuBois associated with when he visited that city.

During the 1920's William Faulkner foreshadowed his future stature with *The Sound and the Fury*, located primarily in Mississippi, with a glance at Cambridge, Massachusetts. Faulkner's major Black character in this novel is Dilsey, prototype of "the Black who endures." Like Green and O'Neill, Faulkner probably had not read Alain Locke's introduction to *The New Negro* (1925). Locke asserted: "Sentimental interest in the Negro has ebbed. We used to lament this as the falling off of our friends; now we rejoice and pray to be delivered both from self-pity and condescension. The mind of each racial group has had a better weaning, apathy or hatred on one side matching disillusionment or resentment on the other; but they face each other today with the possibility at least of entirely new mutual attitudes."[3]

The decade ended with a production of the extraordinarily popular *Green Pastures* (1930) by Marc Connelly. Based on Roark Bradford's *Ol' Man Adam and His Chillun*, the drama seems to retell the Old Testament from the perspective of a Black child at a church fish-fry. The narrator is not a child, however; he is an adult.

However distorted their vision of Blacks may have been, well-known white American authors of the 1920's cannot be blamed for the exotic image of the nightclub Black. That image comes from Blacks themselves and from a few whites who identified themselves as promoters of Blacks or as sympathizers.

The image may have begun with *Shuffle Along* (1921), a brilliant and popular musical, written and directed by four Blacks—Flournoy Miller, Eubie Blake, Noble Sissel, and Aubrey Lyles. In the same year, *Shuffle Along* was succeeded by *Put and Take*, another musical by a Black—Irving C. Miller, who also produced *Liza* (1923), which was followed in the same year by *Runnin' Wild* by Miller and Lyles. The beauty of Afro-American chorus girls such as Florence Mills and Josephine Baker, the exotic foreign settings, the gaiety and the frenzy of these musicals and their successors may have cultivated in Broadway audiences a taste for particular depictions of Black life. Furthermore, these musicals may have created an image difficult to change.

Although it is located in the South, Sherwood Anderson's *Dark Laughter* (1925) conjures up the image of a joyful, untroubled people who, themselves freed from the need to read Freud, laugh gently at frustrated whites, who repress their own sexual desires. The image of joy continues in Carl Van Vechten's novel, *Nigger Heaven* (1926), set in Harlem. Although Van Vechten later proclaimed his desire to familiarize white readers with a cultural Black society which gives soirées and speaks French, he glamorized the Scarlet Creeper, a "sweetman" (gigolo), and he depicted Black night life with an excitement certain to allure readers.

---

3. Locke, "The New Negro," *The New Negro* (New York, 1968), p. 8.

The exoticism and gaiety appear in the works of Black writers themselves. Even Countée Cullen, known to subsequent generations as a somewhat prim purveyor of high art, contrasted the warmth of Blacks with the coldness of whites, wrote atavistically of the African rhythm inherent in the walk of a Black waiter (in *Color*, 1925), and rhapsodized the wildness of the African heritage.

In his first collection, *The Weary Blues* (1926), Langston Hughes not only created jazz / blues poems but also wrote with an exuberance tending to promote the image of an uninhibited people:

Dream Variation

To fling my arms wide
In some place of the sun,
To whirl and to dance
Till the white day is done.
Then rest at cool evening
Beneath a tall tree
While night comes on gently,
    Dark like me,—
That is my dream!

To fling my arms wide
In the face of the sun,
Dance! whirl! whirl!
Till the quick day is done.
Rest at pale evening. . . .
A tall, slim tree. . . .
Night coming tenderly
    Black like me.[4]

Black novelists also contributed to the image of an uninhibited people whose lives are exotic whirls. In *Home to Harlem* (1928), Claude McKay, a Black West Indian, drowned social protest in a flood of night life—prostitutes, sweetmen, jazz, night club fights—as he told the story of a Black deserter from the armed services who searches through Harlem for the prostitute whom he loves. Succeeding novelists, such as Rudolph Fisher (*The Walls of Jericho*, 1928) and Wallace Thurman (*The Blacker the Berry*, 1929), seemed almost compelled to include irrelevant nightclub scenes as though they had become clichés of Black life.

It should not be wondered then that W. E. B. DuBois, editor of *The Crisis*, reserved sections of several issues to question whether writers and publishers shared his fear that Black writers were being encouraged to

4. Hughes, *The Weary Blues* (New York, 1926).

create derogatory pictures of Blacks. Seriously concerned about respectable images of Blacks, DuBois, more than two decades earlier, had rationalized their enthusiasm as a primitivism promoted by the experience of slavery, a primitivism which would be modified when Black Americans matured into the sophistication of Euro-American society. Now that his "Talented Tenth" seemed to promote spectacles of frenzy, however, DuBois suspected that their desire to publish persuaded them to ignore the truth of Black life and to pander to whites by creating images designed to titillate.

Beneath the surfaces of gay abandon during the 1920's, however, are more somber issues, more sober themes which should be examined more closely. The same writers who seem to rejoice in the enthusiasm of Black life also sounded what Langston Hughes described as "the sob of the jazz band"—the melancholy undertone of Black life, ever present but sometimes unheard by those who fail to listen carefully.

Claude McKay pictured a Harlem dancer who guards her soul from the lascivious image suggested by her dance (*Harlem Shadows*, 1922), and Langston Hughes described the weariness of a jazz pianist (*The Weary Blues*, 1926). In *The Walls of Jericho* (1928) Fisher overshadowed the scenes of night life with a quieter depiction of the romance of two working people of Harlem. Thurman tempered his scenes of night life and dances in *The Blacker the Berry* by revealing that some Blacks visited dance halls not to gorge themselves with gaiety but to discover companionship to ease their loneliness. In the same novel a white Chicagoan confirms his impression that the exotic savagery of Harlemites is grossly exaggerated by their white press agents. While his actress-sister revels in what she considers the barbaric splendor of the Black club they visit, the Chicagoan sees a generally decorous behavior which assures him that Harlemites are no wilder than the Blacks he has known in Chicago (and perhaps not as wild as the whites in either city). Countée Cullen asserted that he wrote *One Way to Heaven* (1932) to counter Carl Van Vechten's *Nigger Heaven* by showing the humanity of Black life in Harlem. In scene after scene, Cullen balances superficial exuberance with sober explanation: The enthusiasm of a religious revival does not obscure the fact that in attendance also are some morally respectable Blacks who are not swept away by the emotion. The heroine, a morally circumspect, hard-working woman, has attended several revivals to which she has been indifferent. A male's illicit love affair is ascribed partly to the nature of the wandering male and partly to a desire to find companionship because his wife, who has become a religious fanatic, is engaged in an affair with Jesus.

These more serious vestiges of Black life in America should not be ignored when one considers the literature of the Renaissance; for, far from being mere entertainers, many Black writers regarded literature as a means of seriously examining problems of living. Moreover, they did not restrict their examinations to problems of Blacks in an adversary relationship with white society. Almost from the first they were concerned with issues which might be considered universal if American critics were more willing to discover universality in the lives of Black people.

The interest in human conditions appears in Jean Toomer's *Cane* (1923), the work of the Renaissance which is the best known and the most highly respected in academic circles. Toomer delineates many protagonists whose difficulties do not depend primarily upon their ancestry: Karintha has matured too soon sexually; Carma lives in a society which pretends that a woman should become sexless if her husband does not live with her; Esther cannot reconcile her sexual urges with the education by a society which has taught her that "good" girls do not feel such urges; John, in "Theater," cannnot adapt his idealized romanticizing into a satisfactory relationship with an actual woman; Dorris, in "Theater," dreams of a companionship that will provide a real substitute for the artificiality of the theater; Muriel, in "Box Seat," fears to defy the little-minded, social regulators of the world; Avery finds it more pleasurable to be supported by men rather than to labor as a teacher in a normal school. The problems of these individuals may be complicated or intensified by their condition as Blacks in America, but the problems would exist regardless of their race.

Jessie Fauset, the too little-known author of *There is Confusion* (1924), *Plum Bun* (1929), *The Chinaberry Tree* (1933), and *Comedy: American Style* (1933), contrived her novels to focus on the problems of Blacks whose lives are not continuously affected by their interrelationships with whites. Most often their problems derive from their ambition or from a society excessively willing to evaluate individuals according to false criteria. In *There is Confusion*, for example, an ambitious young Black protagonist disrupts and nearly destroys the people around her because she tries to regulate their lives according to her delusions. Because she believes that people should not marry outside their class, she interferes with her brother's romance with a young woman whose family background is different. Doing "the right thing," by withdrawing from the relationship, the second young woman then rushes into an unfortunate marriage. Because the protagonist believes that suitors must be trained into suitably devoted servants, she refuses to apologize to the man she loves even though she is wrong. After he apologizes in order to effect a reconciliation, she delays a response with the deliberate intention of causing him to learn that he cannot win her too easily. She begins to realize her error only when he, jolted by her rebuff, proposes to a woman who offers him affection without reservation.

In stories which she published during the 1920's, Zora Neale Hurston of Florida explored such an "in-group" issue as the manner in which townspeople affect individuals by forcing them to act out of character in order to maintain the respect of the mob ("Spunk"). In addition, she vividly revealed the problems which disturb male-female relationships: the alienation which develops when a naive wife is seduced by a traveling salesman ("The Gilded Six-Bits"); the tragic consequences when a self-centered husband who has exploited his wife tries to replace her ("Sweat").

Black dramatists, such as Willis Richardson and Georgia D. Johnson, prepared domestic dramas for the Black community: the tensions between a man and his improvident brothers-in-law ("The Broken Banjo"); the pathos of a situation in which a child is permitted to die because the mother favors the healing power of faith above that of man's medicine.

In such ways as these, Black people of the Renaissance explored serious issues involving Black people but not deriving primarily from the racial ancestry or from their relationship with whites. This statement, however, should not encourage a fallacious assumption that the Black writers evaded their racial identity or ignored problems which do derive from interracial conflict. To the contrary, Black Renaissance writers frequently expressed concerns which strikingly anticipate major themes identified with the revolutionary Black Arts writers of the 1960's: a search for and affirmation of ancestral heritage, a feeling of alienation from the white Euro-American world; a presentation of and protest against oppression; and even militant defiance of oppression.

Just as Black Arts writers of today affirm their African heritage, so many Renaissance writers sought identity through identification with an ancestral past. Jean Toomer sought identity derived in part from the consciousness of the slave South and Africa (*Cane*, 1923, and "Natalie Mann"). As I have pointed out earlier, Countée Cullen proclaimed that the sober teachings of Christian civilization could not curb the memories and the urges which linked him with Africa ("Heritage"). Langston Hughes found pride in identification with a race so old in human history that it had lived when rivers were young ("The Negro Speaks of Rivers"). Although some of these ancestral searches may seem rhetorical rather than actual, although some of the thoughts of Africa are sufficiently atavistic to promote a concept of exotic primitivism, the quests respond partly at least to Alain Locke's urgings that Black artists search for subject and style in an African tradition.

For the Black American writer of the 1920's, however, the search for ancestry proved more difficult than for white Americans. Some Blacks, ashamed of their ancestry as slaves and as descendants of Africans whom they judged to have been savages, attempted to evolve more respectable ancestry from identification with former masters. In *There Is Confusion* (1924) Jessie Fauset suggested the problems sometimes posed by the quest for European ancestry. Moreover, Blacks who wished to affirm a Black heritage were forced to identify with a continent rather than with a particular tribe or nation. Hence, the identification sometimes became intellectual and abstract rather than personal. The problem is suggested by Hughes:

Afro-American Fragment

So long,
So far away
Is Africa.
Not even memories alive
Save those that history books create,
Save those that songs
Beat back into the blood—
Beat out of blood with words sad-sung
In strange un-Negro tongue—
So long
So far away.

Subdued and time-lost
Are the drums—and yet
Through some vast mist of race
There comes this song
I do not understand,
This song of atavistic land,
Of bitter yearning lost
Without a place—
So long,
So far away
Is Africa's
Dark face.

Failure to establish psychological identity with the Black heritage and corresponding awareness of exclusion from the European heritage sometimes produced a sense of alienation comparable to that expressed by Black Arts writers today. The feeling resounds vividly from McKay's "Outcast."

For the dim regions whence my fathers came
My spirit, bondaged by the body, longs.
Words felt, but never heard, my lips would frame:
My soul would sing forgotten jungle songs.
I would go back to darkness and to peace,
But the great western world holds me in fee,
And I may never hope for full release,

While to its alien gods I bend my knee.
Something in me is lost, forever lost,
Some vital thing has gone out of my heart,
And I must walk the way of life a ghost
Among the sons of earth, a thing apart;
For I was born, far from my native clime,
Under the white man's menace, out of time.

The serious themes that Renaissance writers explored most frequently, as might be expected, are protests against oppression. The presence of such themes has been obscured by three facts: (1) many readers remember the glamorous gaiety and forget the serious comments; (2) some protests appear as brief asides rather than fully developed explanations; (3) some protests seem mild because, rather than directly assaulting whites, they adumbrate the manner in which external oppression causes Blacks to oppress themselves. The way that serious protest can be ignored is evidenced by the customary reactions of casual readers to McKay's *Home to Harlem* (1928), which appears, even in this paper, as a prototype of a Black work that promotes exoticism. The vividly exotic spectacles blind many readers to McKay's presentation of such facts as the following: During World War I many Black soldiers who enlisted to fight for democracy were restricted to service as laborers; during the 1920's some Harlem clubs, whether owned by whites or Blacks, discriminated against Blacks by refusing them admission—except as entertainers or waiters; in many occupations Black workers surrendered their dignity to the caprice of white supervisors.

It is true that no *Native Son* burst from the Renaissance to denounce American oppression. But Walter White's novel *The Fire in the Flint* (1924) decries the brutality of lynchings, as does Claude McKay's "The Lynching." Toomer's "Blood-Burning Moon" and "Kabnis" (*Cane*) reveal the powerlessness of Blacks to protect themselves from white brutality: a successful self-defense summons the lynch mob as quickly as a murder would.

Much more prevalent is the Renaissance writers' tendency to attack oppression indirectly by showing how it causes Blacks to turn against themselves. Because color, as an evidence of African ancestry, was a shibboleth of whites against Blacks, many Blacks used color as a criterion of intragroup evaluation. In *The Blacker the Berry* the protagonist, because of her dark skin, suffers within her family, in school and college, and in efforts to secure employment. Yet pathetically, as Thurman shows, the heroine cherishes the same criteria which have victimized her. She desires only men who are of lighter complexion and Caucasian appearance; and she undervalues herself, believing for a time at least that her Blackness is an ineradicable blot upon her record. In *Comedy: American Style* (1933) Fauset censured a Negro mother who values her children according to the degree of their approximation to Caucasian appearance. Walter White's *Flight* (1928) and Nella Larsen's *Passing* (1929) show the dilemmas of heroines who, repressed by the conditions of life as Blacks, attempt to improve their lot by passing for white.

In ironic repudiation of the images of Blacks as amoral beings, Jean Toomer repeatedly stressed the necessity for middle-class Negroes to liberate themselves from conscious imitation of the restrictive morality of Anglo-Saxons. "Esther," "Theater," and "Box-Seat" all reveal the frustrations of Black people who, desiring social approval, repress their emotions, their humanness. In "Kabnis" Carrie K., fearing censure by others, represses her instinctual attraction to Lewis. Paul ("Bona and Paul," *Cane*) loses a female companion because of his self-conscious desire to explain to a bystander that the relationship is not lustful. Toomer's most fully developed attack on middle-class morality appears in the unpublished drama "Natalie Mann." Mert, a school teacher, dies because she perceives too late that she must enjoy passion fully without concern for society's censure. Natalie, the protagonist, develops to this awareness only through the assistance of a Christ-like male who himself has experienced the rebukes of the middle class.

Toomer was not the only writer to question the excessive effort of Blacks to conform to the standards presumed to be those of whites. The protagonist in Walter White's *Flight* is forced to leave town and, temporarily, to deny her race because Blacks will not permit her to forget that she has had a child out of wedlock: her lover's proposal of abortion so diminished him in her esteem that she refused his subsequent efforts to marry her.

During the 1920's few writers reacted militantly to oppression with the kind of rhetoric for which Black revolutionary literature became notorious during the 1960's. There are several reasons. A generally optimistic faith that talented Blacks soon would merge with the mainstream muted rhetorical violence and violent rhetoric. Furthermore, publishers during the 1920's did not permit the kind of language and the explicit description of violent action which became almost commonplace in later decades. Third, the publishing houses were controlled by whites. It should be remembered that much of the Black revolutionary literature of the 1960's issued from Black publishers of poetry and in Black community drama.

Under the circumstances it is not surprising that the militant reaction often was expressed as self-defense, as in Claude McKay's well-known "If We Must Die" (*Harlem Shadows*). Less frequently came prayers for destruction, as in McKay's "Enslaved" (*Harlem Shadows*). Most often the militancy is a proud hostility toward whites. At the end of *Flight* the male protagonist learns why his father abhorred whites: they had deprived him of inheritance by refusing to recognize him as their offspring. In turn he refuses to permit an elderly white to ease his own conscience by making a monetary donation while continuing to ignore the blood relationship.

I cannot conclude without reassessing the significance of the literary Harlem Renaissance. If it is remembered for expression of gaiety rather than for the serious concerns of the Black authors; if it was a movement which involved only talented artists in one segment of the Black American population; if it reflects primarily the life of only one part of one city inhabited by Blacks; if it evidences little awareness of such a significant issue for Blacks as DuBois' dreams and promotions of Pan-Africanism and even less awareness of or respect for Marcus Garvey's Back-to-Africa movement—if the literary Renaissance is so limited, does it merit serious study? Was it, as Harold Cruse has suggested, an era to be examined only as a pathetic example of a time when Black artists might have established criteria for their art but failed to do so? Was it, as W. E. B. DuBois stated and as LeRoi Jones insisted more forcefully later, a movement that lost validity as it became a plaything of white culture? In fact, is the very attention given to it by historians of Black culture evidence of the willingness of Blacks and whites to glorify, or permit glorification of, inferior art by Blacks?

Each of these allegations has partial validity. But such objections based on idealistic absolutes fail to consider the actual significances of the literary Renaissance. First, in no other decade had Black novelists been afforded such opportunity for publication. If fewer than twenty original, non-vanity-press novels appeared between 1924 and 1933, that figure nevertheless exceeded the number published by American commercial houses in all the years since the publication of the first Black American novel, William Wells Brown's *Clotel* (1853). Even the Depression and the closing of some outlets could not dispel the new awareness that possibilities existed for Blacks who wished to write novels. The field was open to many writers, not merely to the individual geniuses—the Paul Dunbar or the Charles Chesnutt of an earlier decade. This productivity, as well as the later success of Richard Wright, undoubtedly encouraged such novelists as Chester Himes, Ann Petry, Frank Yerby, and William G. Smith, who developed during the late 1930's and early 1940's.

The literary examples and inspirations were not limited to the novel. Only a few serious Black dramas reached Broadway, but the enthusiastic establishment of Black community theaters during the 1920's furthered the creation of a Black audience for drama and promoted awareness of the need for writers to create material for that audience.

Perhaps the productivity in poetry had less significant influence because Blacks previously had found outlets for poetry—the national reputation of Paul Laurence Dunbar was known by Blacks. Moreover, poetry was still to be considered an avocation which one supported by revenue derived from a stable vocation. But there was hope that Black writers might be able to sustain themselves partly through grants, for Countée Cullen had established a precedent by winning a Guggenheim fellowship for his proposal of a poetry-writing project.

Of final benefit to future writers was the mere fact that entrées had been established. A Langston Hughes or Wallace Thurman or Countée Cullen or, later, an Arna Bontemps knew publishers and knew other people who might be able to assist prospective authors. In all these senses, the Renaissance was not a rebirth but, in very significant ways, a first birth for Black Americans in literature.

A second significance of the literary Renaissance is its inspiration for African and Caribbean poets such as Léopold Senghor, Aimé Césaire, and Léon Damas who, a generation later in the 1930's and 1940's, promoted Negritude, a literary-cultural movement which emphasized consciousness of African identity and pride in the Black heritage. More than a decade after the Negritude writers, newer Black American writers of the 1960's looked to African Negritude for inspiration. Thus, both directly and circuitously, the Renaissance promoted Black American literature and Black consciousness of future decades.

Finally, the Renaissance has importance as a symbol. In many respects, the actuality of a culture is less important than the myth which envelops and extends from that culture. The memory that Black Americans had been recognized and respected for literary achievements, as well as other artistic achievements, established awareness that there could be a literary culture among Blacks. If the memory faded rapidly from the consciousness of white America, it did not fade from the minds of Blacks responsible for continuing the culture among their people. Marcus Garvey did not succeed in restoring Black Americans to Africa; consequently, he is remembered as a dream that faded. But the Renaissance, for Black Americans and others, has gained strength as the mythic memory of a time when Blacks first burst into national consciousness as a talented group that was young, rebellious, proud, and beautiful.

The Novels of Carl Van Vechten and the Spirit of the Age

DONALD PIZER

Carl Van Vechten's first novel, *Peter Whiffle*, appeared in 1922 and his seventh and last, *Parties*, in 1930. Van Vechten is thus a novelist of the twenties in that all his fiction was written during that decade. Of course, Van Vechten had several successful vocations in fields other than fiction both before and after the twenties. For much of his early career, from his arrival in New York in 1906 until the publication of *Peter Whiffle*, he was an influential music critic and essayist; his later years, until his death in 1968 (at the age of 88), are notable for his photography and for his efforts in promoting collections of literary and cultural archives.[1] Nevertheless, there are a number of reasons, besides accident of publication date, for the association of Van Vechten and his major work with the 1920's.

Several of his best novels chronicle either in authorial asides or miniature essays the taste and interests of the decade from the conventional to the avant garde. In particular, if one wishes to know what people of advanced sensibility were reading in the 1920's, or how they decorated their homes, or what music they listened to or pictures they admired, Van Vechten's fiction is a full and sure guide. His novels communicate as well a sense of the leading personalities of the day. Van Vechten was an inveterate name dropper, and figures such as Max Eastman, Big Bill Haywood, Gertrude Stein, and Theodore Dreiser—to say nothing of leading opera singers and entertainers—appear briefly or are mentioned in passing. Several of his more substantial fictional characters are thinly disguised portraits of major cultural figures of the period: Edith Dale in *Peter Whiffle* is Mabel Dodge Luhan, and David and Rilda Westlake in *Parties* are Scott and Zelda Fitzgerald. A great bon vivant and literary entrepreneur, Van Vechten is also identified with the twenties because of his many efforts to further the careers and reputations of his contemporaries among the "clever people."[2] He was an early supporter of James Branch Cabell and

---

1. There is no biography of Van Vechten, but see the biographical portions of Edward Lueders, *Carl Van Vechten* (New York, 1965).

2. See Edward Lueders, *Carl Van Vechten and the Twenties* (Albuquerque, 1955), Bruce Kellner, *Carl Van Vechten and the Irreverent Decades* (Norman, Okla., 1968), and Van Vechten, *Fragments from an Unwritten Autobiography* (New Haven, 1955).

was among the first enthusiasts of Elinor Wylie's fiction, leading (so the semi-apocryphal story goes) a torchlight procession in New York to celebrate the publication of *Jennifer Lorn*. He knew Joseph Hergesheimer well, and it was he who was the principal organizer of a "gathering of the forces" in Richmond in the spring of 1924, when he, Elinor Wylie, and Hergesheimer were guests of the Cabells.[3]

These various involvements by Van Vechten in the social and literary life of the time are of interest but are nevertheless little more than footnotes to the cultural history of the decade. Moreover, Van Vechten's depiction of the twenties in his fiction appears to be superficial because it can be identified with a number of the more obvious characteristics of the myth of the Jazz Age. His characters are for the most part well-to-do New Yorkers whose lives are occupied with parties and sex, and his prose is mannered, light, and witty. His fiction therefore appears to be related to the self-conscious immorality of a well-publicized but essentially minor phase of the life of the twenties, and Van Vechten himself appears to be an occasionally amusing but essentially slight chronicler of this phase.

This impression of slightness is due in part to Van Vechten's comic style (a problem I shall return to later) and in part to a failure to recognize that his fiction as a whole expresses a large-scale interpretation and vigorous defense of the spirit of the age. Van Vechten's novels, arranged in order of interior chronology rather than in order of publication,[4] are as follows:

Title	Setting (place)	Setting (time)
The Tattooed Countess (1924)	Maple Valley, Iowa	1897
Peter Whiffle (1922)	New York, Paris, Florence	1907–1919
The Blind Bow-Boy (1923)	New York	Contemporary
Firecrackers (1925)	New York	"
Nigger Heaven (1926)	Harlem	"
Spider Boy (1928)	Hollywood and Santa Fe	"
Parties (1930)	New York, London, Paris	"

The seven novels thus divide into four interpretive subgroups within the historical period of the late 1890's to the "present" of the late 1920's. *The Tattooed Countess* and *Peter Whiffle* deal with the origin of the spirit of

---

3. Emily Clark, *Innocence Abroad* (New York, 1931), pp. 141, 167.

4. Van Vechten's novels are almost always discussed in order of publication. Even Edward Lueders, whose 1965 *Carl Van Vechten* contains the fullest account of Van Vechten's novels, proceeds by order of publication. This consideration of the novels by date of appearance has often resulted in an impression of indirection in Van Vechten's work as a whole. Oscar Cargill's remark, in his *Intellectual America* (New York, 1941), p. 509, is characteristic: "Shifting enthusiasms explain each and all of Van Vechten's novels."

the twenties while *The Blind Bow-Boy* and *Firecrackers* are Van Vechten's principal rendering of this spirit. *Nigger Heaven* and *Spider Boy* contribute to an understanding of two distinctive characteristics of the period, while *Parties* is a finely focused portrait of the nature of the decade at the moment of its death.

The belief that Van Vechten's novels contain a coherent and consistent view of the twenties is supported by the presence of a number of both major and minor characters in more than one novel. Van Vechten suggests by this device that his novels, though disparate in plot and setting, have a controlling center—that the imagination which peopled one novel is still present in another and that thus all seven novels, because they focus in one way or another on the meaning of the age, have an underlying and consistent historical vision. Van Vechten's two most important reappearing characters are Gareth Johns and Campaspe Lorillard. Gareth Johns is a young man rebelling against midwestern village life in *The Tattooed Countess* and a successful but embittered and world-weary novelist in *Firecrackers*, *Nigger Heaven*, and *Parties*. Campaspe is the central figure in Van Vechten's two major New York novels, *The Blind Bow-Boy* and *Firecrackers*. The two figures characterize two generations of "free spirits" in the 1920's, the older and the younger. Johns' hardness and cynicism reveal the soul-destroying compromises and cruelties required of those who rebelled in the nineties, while Campaspe's poise and equanimity reveal the benefits of the earlier struggle for those who came of age in the twenties. In addition to Johns and Campaspe, a number of other characters appear from novel to novel. Clara Barnes, the complacently untalented opera singer, is in *The Tattooed Countess* and *Peter Whiffle*; the Countess seeks to rekindle the passions of youth in *The Tattooed Countess* and dies loveless in *Firecrackers*; and Paul Moody, Zimbule O'Grady, and Edith Dale represent various characteristics of New York life in *The Blind Bow-Boy* and *Firecrackers*, and appear in other novels as well.

The Tattooed Countess is Van Vechten's most autobiographical novel.[5] Like one of its principal characters, Gareth Johns, he too had rebelled against the limitations of midwestern small-town life of the late 1890's and had escaped to a larger world. The novel is therefore an interpretation both of the shape of Van Vechten's career[6] and of the more general cultural and literary movement which in the twenties came to be called "the revolt from the village."

---

5. In the discussion which follows, page references to Van Vechten's novels in my text are to the following editions: *Peter Whiffle* (New York: The Modern Library, 1929); *The Blind Bow-Boy* (New York: Knopf, 1925); *The Tattooed Countess* (New York: Knopf, 1924); *Firecrackers* (New York: Knopf, 1925); *Nigger Heaven* (New York: Grosset & Dunlap, 1928); *Spider Boy* (New York: Knopf, 1928); *Parties* (New York: Knopf, 1930).

6. See Lueders, *Carl Van Vechten*, pp. 21–22.

Into the smug yet repressed Iowa town of Maple Valley comes the Countess Nattatorrini, born Ella Poore in Maple Valley fifty years earlier. The Countess' sensuous, self-indulgent, expansive, and freedom-loving nature crystallizes the suspiciousness, ignorance, and narrowness of the town. She loves beauty and art and cannot live without passion, while the town is proud of its new waterworks and of the prospect of a new terminal. So gradually her initial mixed sentiments of nostalgia, distaste, and curiosity toward Maple Valley turn to hate and rebellion, and those of the town toward her shift from pride to anxiety to contempt. At its simplest the novel thus contrasts two sets of values—those of provincial America and those of "decadent" Europe. But it also implicitly contrasts two moments in time—the fictional "now" of the 1890's when rebellion must be escape to Europe, and the real "now" of the twenties when New York has replaced and indeed surpassed Europe as a haven of freedom and when not a few but a large number of young men have rebelled against the stifling moralism and cultural barrenness of provincial America and have sought freedom and fulfillment elsewhere.

The theme of escape dominates the depiction of the relationship between Gareth and the Countess. Ella is attractive to the seventeen-year-old Gareth because of what she represents and what she can give him. She is art and freedom and Europe in the sense that her wealth and her need for him will help him achieve these prizes. Above all she symbolizes Paris, the city of freedom. As she speaks of Paris, Gareth realizes that "People there seem to be able to be themselves, to do what they want to do, to live for love or whatever it is they want to live for" (p. 224). In Maple Valley, however, the "narrow prejudices of [the] town, based on complete ignorance of life," prevent one from being what one is (pp. 129–130). The Countess realizes the consequences of this repression of an entire generation and prophetically cries out, "You'd better look out! You don't know what you're doing to the next generation. They won't stand it; no one with any brains would stand it! They'll revolt! They'll break loose! You'll see . . ." (p. 130).

But Gareth is not the "next" generation; he is the present, and his rebellion, because it is an exceptional occurrence and because of the strength of the forces arrayed against him, can only be achieved with a certain ruthlessness. In addition, as it would seem from *Peter Whiffle*, this early generation of rebels frequently mistook the voguishly avant garde for self-expression. In *Peter Whiffle* Van Vechten again sketches a young man who has rebelled against his family and a safe career in a midwestern town and is seeking to be an artist. But as Van Vechten's mock biography of Peter unfolds we realize that Peter's enthusiasms are both a satiric history of various literary and art vogues from 1907 to 1919 and an explanation of the failure of American writers of this period to achieve a major and distinctive literature despite their rebellion and freedom.

At first Peter is drawn to the mannered fin-de-siècle decadence of Gautier, Huysmans, and Wilde. "Subject is nothing," he declares; "form, style, manner" are everything (pp. 48–49). He writes nothing, however, and when his "biographer" next encounters him he has been converted by *Sister Carrie* and is attempting to write a novel about "a little Jewish girl, who works in a sweat-shop. She has one blue eye and one black one. She has a club-foot, a hare-lip, and she is a hunch-back" (p. 116). This interest is followed by brief flirtations with cubism, with the new psychological novel, and with an Arthur Machen mysticism and morbidity. His quests for the new and extreme exhaust Peter, and he dies young without having written a word during his lifetime. But he has at least discovered the error of his pursuit, as he tells his biographer toward the end of his life. His was too cerebral a view of literature, and he was therefore too much and too easily influenced by the ideas of others. "You must search the heart; the mind is negligible in literature as in all other forms of art. Try to write just as you feel and you will discover that your feeling is greater than your knowledge of it" (p. 232).

This conventional romantic aesthetic has little intrinsic interest. It is of some importance, however, as an interpretation of the weaknesses in a particularly flat period in American literature by one who himself participated in the period. Rebellion and freedom are not enough, Van Vechten implies, if they cannot be cultivated as vehicles of true self-expression. If a writer merely adopts the radical formulas of his time, his work will be sterile. Thus, in two very different novels—the first an evocation of an American small town of the 1890's, the other a caricature of the avant garde enthusiasms of the following generation—Van Vechten intimates that the twenties were to be a period in which rebelliousness came of age in art forms and life styles which were above all dedicated to the cultivation and celebration of individual distinctive temperaments.

This suggestion is confirmed by the two novels which Van Vechten devotes to a dramatization of the principal values of the age, *The Blind Bow-Boy* and *Firecrackers*. Both novels are dominated by Campaspe; out of her actions and musings there emerges a code of life which transcends her and becomes that of an entire generation. On the surface, the code is one of personal license for those who have the wealth and leisure to do as they wish without regard for conventional opinion or morality. Campaspe's tastes and interests, however, are in fact of a cultivated hedonism, of an elegant and imaginative sensuality. Like Elinor Wylie, Van Vechten celebrates not mere sensation but rather the life of feeling pursued as an expression of one's deepest self. Thus, Campaspe is interested primarily in those who are "natural," who are above all themselves in the expression of their desires, whatever the "decadence" of their lives.

The plot of *The Blind Bow-Boy* rests upon the distinction between the natural and the derivative and imitative in character. Harold Prewett, the novel's ostensible protagonist, finally rebels against the life of middle-class respectability which his father desires him to accept because this life is being imposed upon him by deception. He tells Alice, his "good" wife (whom he has been deceived into marrying), that Campaspe and her decadent set are at least "clean. They didn't know what it was all about, but they were natural and real while all you rotters have been playing parts" (p. 201). He realizes that he has been weak, and therefore susceptible to trickery, because he has been "afraid of life" (p. 231) and has not known himself. Seeking to correct both of these deficiencies, he undertakes an "experimental" life of emotional involvement with those who do know themselves and are not afraid to express themselves in their lives—first with Zimbule O'Grady and then, at the close of the novel, with the Duke of Middlebottom.

Out of Campaspe's self-knowledge and Harold's gradual understanding of the need for self-knowledge, there emerges in *The Blind Bow-Boy* a code of life which asks that experience be faced openly and that it be pursued in the direction which one's temperament determines. One does not rebel because others are doing so, and one does not reject rebellion because others find it repugnant. One expresses one's nature and one's own preferences, whether this leads toward the establishment of a summer opera season in New York (one of the burlesque incidents in the novel) or toward a life of pleasure or a life of work. So Campaspe has done and so Harold learns to do.

In *Firecrackers* this code faces a major challenge in the personality and philosophy of Gunnar O'Grady. Ennui is one of the threats to a life of elegant pleasure not bolstered by a conscious hedonism. Paul Moody, Harold's "wastrel" amoral guide in *The Blind Bow-Boy*, has married a wealthy older woman and is bored and restless despite having all he desires. There appears the mysterious Gunnar—initially in the guise of a furnace repairman—whose grace, beauty, and joy seem to proclaim the benefits of a life of purpose and work. Paul is converted by Gunnar's example to seek employment, and others in Campaspe's circle are analogously affected. Campaspe herself is drawn into the struggle because of the ineffable charm and appeal of Gunnar. Nevertheless, she recognizes the paradoxical harmfulness of Gunnar's doctrines. She tells him that it is wrong to seek to change Paul: "However unconsciously, he had realized himself very neatly, very completely, I thought. I still think so. It may not have been a very big self, or very important self, but it was Paulet's *own*" (p. 99). She does not, she explains to Gunnar, believe in "beneficial" changes in one's basic character. All we can do is "to drag an unsuspected quality out of its hiding place in the unconscious. If it is there, *in us,* it can neither be virtue nor vice. It can only be ourselves. Whatever it is, if we admit that it belongs to us, we need it to complete ourselves" (pp. 99–100). Campaspe's ideal of freedom to be oneself rather than to be "good" is complemented by her ideal of freedom in love. Again Gunnar is the principal challenge to this freedom, for his notion of love is of high seriousness and total possession. In this instance it is Campaspe herself who is threatened, since like everyone else in the novel she is drawn powerfully by the mysterious aura of beauty and strength emanating from Gunnar. She falls in love with him, and as long as he refuses to admit his love for her and seeks instead to escape, she is imprisoned by her love. But when at last he surrenders to his passion, she is free. For with the consummation of their love, she can move on. "Promiscuity" for Campaspe is therefore a way of maintaining her freedom, of not being bound or imprisoned by an emotion, of continuing to live the experimental rather than the prescribed life.

Campaspe's "victory" over Gunnar is not the triumph of flightiness and moral laxness over commitment and high seriousness. Rather, it is the victory of the ideals of choice and freedom over the limitations imposed on one's temperament by the estimable but straitjacketing ideals of productive work and romantic passion. As Campaspe realizes at the close of *The Blind Bow-Boy,* her life is negative in that she seeks always to start afresh rather than to hold and to cultivate. But though "only the present occupied her," "it delighted her to remember that the present was as blank as a white sheet of paper" (p. 260). Openness and delight—these are the keys to Campaspe's "philosophy"—though these terms perhaps disguise the strength and earnestness of their own kind necessary to fulfill her experimental ideal.

Nigger Heaven and *Spider Boy* are obviously though superficially works of the twenties in their subject matter. The primitive vitality of Harlem, particularly as expressed in singing and dancing, and the tinsel make-believe of Hollywood were heavily publicized centers of attention during the decade. Van Vechten's manner in the two novels—his sympathetic portrayal of black life and his burlesque satire of Hollywood—aptly reveals his attitude toward these contrasting worlds. Yet both novels are clearly related to Van Vechten's portrayal of the underlying spirit of the age in that both deal with areas of life in which it is almost impossible to achieve the sense of identity and the freedom of choice which Gareth and Harold seek and which Campaspe has gained.

The principal characters in *Nigger Heaven* are two educated and cultivated Harlem blacks, Mary Love and Byron Kasson. He wishes to be a writer, she wishes to feel rather than merely understand the emotional openness and strength of black life. But their education has alienated them. Mary realizes that "she had lost or forfeited her birthright, this primitive birthright which was so valuable and important an asset, a birthright that all the civilized races were struggling to get back to . . ." (p. 89). And Byron finds that he cannot write about Harlem life because he does not know it and cannot feel it. Both find that they cannot discover who they are or what they feel because their natures have been shaped by their condition and their condition is a rootless wandering between two worlds.

In *Spider Boy*, Ambrose Deacon, a successful but shy and naive New York playwright, discovers that in Hollywood no one is himself, no one has an identity other than his Hollywood "role." All the stars behave as "stars" and are temperamental, all the studio magnates are crude, unimaginative, and money-grubbing, all the directors megalomaniacs, and so on. Since Ambrose is a writer, no one can accept that he does not wish to write for Hollywood (he has been "abducted" there on his way to Santa Fe), and the plot of the novel centers on the burlesque irony that Ambrose's reluctance brings him higher and higher offers. Assumption and action in Hollywood are thus shaped entirely by role playing, and the product of this universal failure in identity is a gross caricature of art, the film "Spider Boy."

Parties brings the decade to a close in the sense that it was written soon after the crash. But the novel is also a summary and reprise of Van Vechten's interpretation of the twenties. *Parties* evokes the surface glamor of the age in a series of extended drinking sessions in speakeasies, restaurants, hotels, and private bars by a group of wealthy and irresponsible New Yorkers. The revelers are dominated by three characters who represent the meaning of the trope that life is a party. The Gräfin discovers in parties the life she always desired but never had. In her seventies, parties to her are an expression of her delight in youth, in doing what she wants to do, and in the sparkle and tinkle of life; she thus blossoms and flourishes. She is the last and one of the most appealing of Van Vechten's figures who are themselves and act firmly on that basis without regard for convention. As Rilda enviously notes, "She is so simple and so direct and it's so wonderful of her to know what she really wants" (p. 80). From this self-knowledge she derives great strength despite her age and slightness. "Her vitality was enormous, a bright flame that flared up inside her wrinkled but not unsightly substance" (p. 148). The Gräfin is the spirit of Campaspe rendered both paradoxical and mischievous by its presence in a little old lady who resembles a Dresden doll.

For Rilda and David Westlake, the other two principal characters in the novel, parties are an escape from the prison of their possessive love. They too echo Campaspe, but now the Campaspe of much of *Firecrackers* who found her freedom constrained by her love for Gunnar. So Rilda and

David writhe and squirm within a love which expresses itself as jealousy, self-torment, and the desire to wound, and so they seek in the drunkenness and promiscuity of parties a release from their pain. The party is thus a reflective symbol both in this novel and in all of Van Vechten's fiction, since it is what an individual brings to a party which determines its meaning for him. The party as a symbol of life sums up Van Vechten's central vision of experience while contributing to the possible misinterpretation of that vision. For though it may appear that the tinkle of ice in glasses and the hum of conversation represent the decadent triviality of the age, in truth it is the opportunity for self-discovery and self-expression within the freedom of a "party" which more correctly mirrors Van Vechten's image of life in the twenties.

Van Vechten stated this view of the decade explicitly in *Parties* in his description of the Lindy Hop, a dance similar to the party in its seemingly self-indulgent decadence. The Lindy Hop, Van Vechten notes, is a dance which "is Dionysian, if you like, a dance to do honor to wine-drinking, but it is not erotic" (p. 185). Rather, "it is a celebration of a rite in which glorification of self plays the principal part" (p. 184), and it therefore has value and importance as an "expression of self so often denied human beings" (p. 187).

Van Vechten's major theme in his fiction is the need for the individual to discover and express his temperament. To succeed in this commitment to self, as Gareth and the Countess learn in the 1890's and as the Westlakes learn in the twenties, is difficult and often impossible. Obstructing this attempt to achieve self-discovery are not only the barriers of conventionality and propriety but a host of more particularized social and personal handicaps ranging from provincial narrowness to the imprisoning effect of unfulfilled or overpossessive love. No wonder that Campaspe and the Gräfin are Van Vechten's only fully triumphant figures and that beneath the bright laughter of the parties in his novels there often sounds a note of despair and defeat.

In one of her long meditations in *The Blind Bow-Boy*, Campaspe expresses her distaste for the "heavy" fiction of such writers as Waldo Frank, Theodore Dreiser, and John Dos Passos.

> How was it possible [she thinks] to read an author who never laughed? For it was only behind laughter that true tragedy could lie concealed, only the ironic author who could awaken the deeper emotion. The tragedies of life, she reflected, were either ridiculous or sordid. The only way to get the sense of this absurd, contradictory, and perverse existence into a book was to withdraw entirely from reality. The artist who feels the most poignantly the bitterness of life wears a persistent and sardonic smile. (p. 160)

Of the characteristics of the "ironist" which Campaspe notes, the "sardonic smile" is Van Vechten's most readily observed fictional mannerism. As authorial presence he is the aloof dandy in tone, above the occasion yet willing to share in its absurdity. He achieves this effect of ironic distance in a number of ways. His playful allusions to real people and events, his exotic and occasionally lugubriously esoteric diction, his use of a "high" style to describe sexually titillating moments, his deadpan delivery of outrageous opinions—all contribute to a sense of an author who is not taking himself, his material, or his readers very seriously. His bold display of wit also suggests a willingness to introduce a sardonic sparkle for its own sake—that is, as a reflection of authorial brilliance. Indeed, Van Vechten's wit is to many readers the most striking immediate effect of his novels; it ranges from the open salaciousness of the comment in *The Blind Bow-Boy* that one of Zimbule's lovers had her "name tattooed on his person so cunningly that it can only be deciphered under certain conditions" (p. 135) to the sly bitchiness of the remark in *Parties* that "it is impossible to persuade people not to go to a party in New York, particularly if they are uninvited and English" (p. 63).

Not that all of Van Vechten's novels are equal in the extent of their surface glitter. The three works set outside cosmopolitan New York—*The Tattooed Countess, Nigger Heaven,* and *Spider Boy*—are less flamboyant in style and wit than Van Vechten's New York high-life fiction. Some of the details of village taste and life in *The Tattooed Countess* are rendered tongue in cheek, but for the most part this novel is the most conventional of Van Vechten's works in form and style. Van Vechten in this instance seems to have decided that historical recreation required a degree of "ordinariness" in fictional method if the substance of the recreation was to be considered "truthful." The same motive appears to inform his method in *Nigger Heaven,* since the intent of that book was in part sociological—to render truthfully a frequently misunderstood segment of American life. In *Spider Boy,* though plot and incident are often almost surrealistically absurd, prose style and narrative voice are curiously flat (and even dull). It is thus *Peter Whiffle, The Blind Bow-Boy, Firecrackers,* and *Parties* which reveal Van Vechten at his most playful, contrived, and mannered.

At the center of Van Vechten's comic mode is the ironic paradox which reveals the absurdity of life. For example, he is fond of depicting the misadventures of a naive or innocent figure in a sophisticated setting in order to dramatize the absurdity of conventional belief and value. Harold in *The Blind Bow-Boy,* Gunnar in *Firecrackers,* Ambrose in *Spider Boy,* and the Gräfin in *Parties* are figures of this kind. (In *The Tattooed Countess* the knowing and worldly Countess returns to unsophisticated Maple Valley with somewhat the same effect.) Like most ironists, Van Vechten is determined to reveal that nothing is what it seems to be. But he also moves irony toward paradox because his irony seeks to dramatize the opposition between the essential self and what the individual seems to value or desire; thus the contradictions of life. At the close of *Parties*, Hamish says of Rilda and David, whose love would appear to be a bond but in fact is destroying them, "They are incomprehensible. Stranger and stranger. Paradoxes. Contradictions" (p. 245).

Paradox is thus at the heart of the central action in most of Van Vechten's novels and is the source of the ironic tone binding plot, characterization, and setting. For example, the Countess is in fact being exploited (and will later be cruelly discarded) by the "innocent" youth she appears to be seducing; Harold will revolt not against the immorality of Campaspe and her set but against his father's "moral" intrigue; and Ambrose's naiveté and shyness are mistaken for shrewdness because he is in a world where innocence is unknown and sharp dealing universal.

Van Vechten's principal symbol of the paradoxes of life, a symbol which pervades and unites his fiction, is New York City.[7] New York to Van Vechten is a city of richness, variety, and diversity, a city of the unexpected and the possible in every range of life, from its ever-changing architecture, seasons, and inhabitants to the parties which concentrate and epitomize these qualities of the city. As Van Vechten wrote in *Parties*, "The city of New York is difficult to describe or understand save in terms of paradox, and so, perhaps, it is more satisfactory for those who may, to instinctively feel the metropolis rather than to attempt to comprehend her" (p. 137). So two of the major threads of Van Vechten's fiction—his affirmation of the instinctive and felt life and his belief that at the heart of feeling is paradox—unite in the symbol of New York. And so *Parties* itself is the supreme example of Van Vechten's art in that it is a novel in which the contradictions of life are dramatized in the mixed motives and temperaments of a party.

Of Van Vechten's seven novels, three are too weak or slight to warrant more than brief discussion as independent works. *Peter Whiffle* is too closely related to the form of the familiar essay as successfully cultivated by Van Vechten in the early portion of his career. Its hoax device, its first person narrator, its leisurely told anecdotes and set pieces (such as the account of a young American's first visit to Paris), all suggest the source of the novel in an idea which was then translated uneasily into fiction. And the idea itself, once we realize that it revolves around the demonstration that Peter's artistic impotence stems from his search for the avant garde, becomes repetitious and eventually cloying. *Peter Whiffle* contains some

7. For an extended discussion by Van Vechten of the theme of New York as paradox, see his essay "La Tigresse," in *In the Garret* (New York, 1920), pp. 263–271.

delicious literary parody, but this is not enough to make the novel work as fiction.

Whereas *Peter Whiffle* is insubstantial beneath its froth, *Nigger Heaven* is too "heavy" in theme and manner. The principal weakness of the novel is not that Van Vechten attempts to depict the full range of Harlem life, from pimps and racketeers to lawyers and artists. The novel could survive this sociological effort if all else were well. But in seeking to present a major tragedy of modern black life, Van Vechten adopts a dull and hackneyed love plot as his vehicle. Stripped of its Harlem setting, the love story of Mary and Byron is sentimental and lugubrious. High-minded starving young writer and equally noble and self-sacrificing young girl fall in love. She tries to help him with money and advice, but he is too proud to accept her aid. Wounded by his failures and by what he believes to be her pity and condescension, he takes up with a lascivious siren. Misunderstandings and complications follow and all ends in tragedy. The novel does not rise above this plot. As in a popular historical romance, only the local color and some of the minor characters have life.

Spider Boy, like *Peter Whiffle*, is limited by the obviousness of its principal theme—in this instance, a demonstration of the bad taste and elephantine egos of Hollywood. Van Vechten's satire is one dimensional and his Gulliver-like central character too shallow. Despite some high-spirited burlesque incidents, *Spider Boy* is his least successful novel.

The Tattooed Countess, the first of Van Vechten's major novels which I will discuss at some length, is not only conventional in form but also, by 1924, in subject matter and theme. *Winesburg, Ohio* and *Babbitt* had by then appeared and the "revolt from the village" was an acknowledged and widely publicized literary movement. Indeed, Van Vechten's contribution to the movement is less radical than either Anderson's or Lewis's, since *The Tattooed Countess* lacks both the experimental form of *Winesburg* and the almost surrealistic caricature of *Babbitt*. The novel opens with the Countess surreptitiously smoking a cigarette in the women's lavatory of the Overland Limited on her way to Maple Valley; it ends with the report of her departure several months later. In the interval she has been lionized by the town because of her "successes" abroad and has scandalized it because of her Bohemian ways. Most of all, she has assuaged, by means of the youthful Gareth Johns, the ache in her heart caused by the loss of her French lover.

The Tattooed Countess lacks the high style, the exotic characters, and the wit and naughtiness of Van Vechten's New York novels. Indeed, his tone is occasionally that of a nostalgic local colorist. Village types, occupations, pastimes, and tastes are characterized in detail and often with affection. Of course, this detail has a satiric center; like Mark Twain's Hadleyburg, the town is inordinately proud of itself. As one resident tells the countess, Maple Valley is "not as big as Paris yet, but it's newer" (p. 57). Nevertheless, the effect of much of this satire, as in the running joke of every resident describing at length to the countess the town's new waterworks, is more humorous than biting.

The sharp edge of Van Vechten's satire is felt more in the action and characterization of the novel than in its style and tone. All that is most vital in human nature, and particularly man's sexual nature, is hidden and suppressed by the residents of Maple Valley. Women sublimate sex into a hysterical religiosity, men secretly visit the immigrant girls of the town or the whores of nearby cities, and family life is a battlefield because of disguised or unacknowledged emotions. Lou, Ella's sister, is a warm, responsive woman who has been beaten into timid conformity by the town; the Colmans have an alcoholic father; the Johnses are bitterly divided because Gareth wishes to live his own life; and so on. The Countess is an anomaly in this setting of emotional repression because she has made her emotions her life and wears openly the scars of a life of feeling. In particular, she bears on her wrist a light tattoo commemorating her lost love, a "scar" which represents as well the commingled joy and pain of her many loves. Her values increasingly clash with those of the town as she realizes that what to her is "life"—love and sex and beauty—is to the town sin and idleness and thus must be hidden or disguised. "I am tattooed on my arm," she reflects bitterly, "while they are tattooed on their hearts" (p. 162).

The Tattooed Countess is most successful in Van Vechten's depiction of the relationship between Ella and Gareth. Theirs is no simple story of the seduction of a young man by an older woman but rather a subtly rendered account of a complex relationship. Initially, the Countess is drawn to Gareth because she needs a replacement for her French lover and because he is one of the few people in the town to show an interest in her and not merely to use her as a sounding board to enlarge upon the glories of the town. Gareth is drawn to the Countess because she can tell him about the world of art, ideas, and famous personalities that he wishes to enter. But gradually the relationship deepens and begins to reveal the essential nature of each character as well as the paradox at the center of the novel. Although the Countess appears to be a hardened woman of the world who is preying upon an innocent provincial youth, in fact it is Gareth who is hard and selfish and who is exploiting the Countess. He has already discovered in his experience with others in the town "that his interest in people depended entirely on what they had to give him" (p. 188), and the Countess is of great value because she can help him escape "this dull, sordid village" (p. 184). He is not drawn to her as a lover but he quickly senses that she wishes him to play this role. And so he muses:

The Countess could do everything, everything, that is, that he wanted. She had it in her power to reveal to him all that his imagination had taught him about art, life, and the world in general. In the beginning, she could perform the initial service of freeing him from the environment which until now had stifled him, take him away from this cursed town for ever, to set him down in a milieu where he might expand and grow. To this end he was willing to make primary sacrifices in the matter of taste. (p. 231)

But Gareth realizes that much of his appeal to the Countess lies in his supposed innocence and that she thus does not wish him to play an active role in their relationship, that "by far the greater part of her present feeling for him was created by her hope of conquering his imagined reluctance" (p. 229). With a calculated self-interest he permits himself to be seduced, all the while storing up a contempt for the Countess which will permit him to discard her (as we learn in *Firecrackers*) once he has finished using her; indeed, which will permit him to exploit their relationship still further by later writing a novel about it.

The response of the Countess to Gareth also is more than it appears to be. Gareth's beloved mother becomes ill and then dies during the summer the Countess is in Maple Valley. Gareth is both crushed and hardened by this blow. His mother is the only being he had ever loved, and his spirit now assumes a permanent coldness and bitterness. Yet he also needs warmth and comfort at this moment, and the Countess—who has no children—responds to his need with these emotions as well as with desire. "I will be everything to you," she tells him, "mother, mistress, wife. Tu es mon bébé!" (p. 260).

Although the Countess and Gareth are using each other, there is no degradation in this use. For each is also expressing a deep emotional need, and each is gaining emotionally from the relationship. It will all end in bitterness, but so do other kinds of relationship, kinds in which freedom is not gained and pain not relieved, even if only temporarily, by love. Thus, at the heart of what appears in style, form, and subject matter to be an anomalous work among Van Vechten's novels, there lies his central theme of the seemingly contradictory yet fertile ways in which the desire for freedom and the expression of need and temperament express themselves.

Whereas *The Tattooed Countess* rests on the conventionally rendered but deeply paradoxical relationship between the Countess and Gareth, *The Blind Bow-Boy* has a much more immediate ironic theme and form. From first to last the novel is a burlesque *Bildungsroman*. Harold's father tells him early in the novel: "You must see more of life and learn to live; you must learn to discount what you have been taught. In other words, you must learn to think for yourself, and become capable of *choosing* an occupation which will do you credit, which will be a reflection of your own personality and not of mine" (p. 15). But in fact the elder Prewett has so ordered the circumstances of the naive and inexperienced Harold's entrance into life that Harold will be forced to choose a way of life that is indeed a reflection of his father's personality. His plan is to throw Harold into a world of immoral licentiousness and thereby shock him into gladly accepting a safe marriage and career in the family cloak and suit business.

Initially Harold responds as his father anticipated. He is affronted and dismayed by the idleness, drinking, and casual sex of Paul Moody, Campaspe, and others of their set and turns in relief to the pursuit of the pure and ultrarespectable Alice. But gradually he comes to see that he has been deceived by others and deluded about himself—that his father and Alice have tricked him; that Alice's tastes are stuffy and colorless; and that he misses Campaspe and Paul when apart from them. He deserts Alice and after a brief period of indecision begins a new life of freedom and choice, of discovering who he is and what he wishes to do, first in a deliciously sensual affair with the beautiful and amoral Zimbule O'Grady and then in a trip to Europe with the Duke of Middlebottom.

This outline of *The Blind Bow-Boy* reveals little of the important role of Campaspe as guide and confidante of Harold and as "moral" center of the novel. Her elegant but independent taste in books, art, and interior decoration are the external signs of a temperament devoted to freedom. Hers is no flashy and noisy rebelliousness but rather an almost languid and obliquely expressed independence of mind and spirit. "Give me an intelligent hypocrite every time" (p. 72), she remarks at one point. In her relations with her friends, her children, and her husband (the ludicrously sentimental and insipid "Cupid"), she believes that she must not vigorously express her personality and "philosophy" and thereby perhaps shape their values. Rather, she seeks to be "different . . . with each of them" and thus, by reflecting "their respective temperaments," to play "the part of mirror" in their self-discovery (p. 132).

Another major figure in *The Blind Bow-Boy* is Zimbule O'Grady, the novice snake charmer whom Campaspe and Paul rescue from a Coney Island sideshow at the beginning of the novel. Like Harold she is young and inexperienced and like him she is absorbed into Campaspe's set for "instruction." But unlike Harold she has an animal freshness and openness and a simple delight in her own feelings and pleasure. She is similar in this respect to Campaspe, who "took quite as much pleasure in her body as she did in her mind. Was not her body, indeed, her chief mental pleasure?" (p. 99). And she differs from Alice, whose dreams rest upon "a little gray home in the east" (p. 106). Thus, the principal characters in *The Blind Bow-Boy*, as in *The Sun Also Rises*, fall into two distinct groups.

Campaspe, Paul, and Zimbule live dissolute lives but are true to themselves, while Alice, Harold's father, and Campaspe's husband are respectable but disguise their true feelings and seek to impose their conventionality upon others.

The language and incidents of *The Blind Bow-Boy* sparkle with Van Vechten's inventiveness at its boldest and most ingratiating. Perhaps something of this quality can be suggested by the character of Roland, Duke of Middlebottom, the genial homosexual who is recalled early in the novel by his former servant, Oliver Drains, who appears initially disguised as a sailor, who helps Campaspe organize a summer opera season in New York which consists of a single performance of a Stravinsky-like spectacle, whose family motto is "a thing of beauty is a boy for ever" (p. 117) and who is last seen with Harold strolling the deck of an ocean liner.

Toward the end of *The Tattooed Countess*, Van Vechten introduces a newspaper report of a meeting between the Kaiser and Tsar at which they pledge eternal friendship and peace. His implied point is that the moral hypocrisy of the age is not limited to middle America but is worldwide and that it will eventually lead to conflict and war. Political allusiveness of this kind is rare in Van Vechten's fiction, but even its occasional presence suggests a quality of mind which could seek, in *Firecrackers*, to write a novel of ideas with an almost allegorical symmetry.

Firecrackers opens with several characters suffering from ennui and nerves. The principal victims of this malaise are Paul, who has married an older woman for her money, and Consuelo, the precociously sophisticated ten-year-old daughter of Campaspe's sister. Into their lives comes Gunnar O'Grady, a mysterious young man who works at a series of jobs—furnace repairman, flower salesman, window dresser—with ease, grace, and intensity. His major vocation and avocation is acrobatics, and the perfect "balance" he achieves in this activity through his effort, skill, and absorption has the beauty and spirit of religious devotion. Paul and Consuelo are converted by the example and character of Gunnar—Paul to seek work for the first time in his life, Consuelo to herself become an acrobat. There is something ludicrously inept in these efforts: the light-minded and improvident Paul working as a stockbroker and advising others on their investments, the frail and ethereal Consuelo on the parallel bars. But Paul and Consuelo are nevertheless initially happy in their new faith. Campaspe, however, is troubled both by Gunnar and by the conversions of Paul and Consuelo, and the novel soon becomes a conflict between her and Gunnar—that is, between two opposing philosophies of life—for the "souls" of Paul and Consuelo.

Gunnar, we soon realize, represents the contemporary reemergence, in somewhat different form, of a Victorian ethic of perfection through effort. "Each of us is God," he tells Campaspe. "Each can be what he desires to make himself" (pp. 100–101). Thus man must seek through intensity of commitment to achieve perfection in whatever he undertakes. Campaspe has been confident enough in her own vision of life to contemptuously reject such mental health and self-improvement programs as those purveyed by "Swamis, Coués, or Freuds" (p. 126). She now perceives as well that though Gunnar's ideal has an appealing nobility and grandeur, it is "unnatural" and potentially harmful. Although she is attracted by Gunnar because "she had never before seen such great beauty in a face, physical, spiritual, and mental beauty, . . . yet she observed something else there, too, dimming the glory, a suggestion of hideous pain and incessant struggle" (p. 98).

The weaknesses in the ideal of work arise from its absolutism and its exploitability. The first is illustrated principally through Paul, the second through Consuelo. It is "unnatural" for Paul to work as a stockbroker because he cares neither for money nor business. He plays at this occupation, as he does with all life, and thus parodies rather than fulfills Gunnar's ideal. And Consuelo's governess senses the commercial possibilities of a regimen of acrobatics designed for those seeking relief from the anxieties of the modern world. Her chain of "clinics" is immediately and immensely successful. The most significant weakness in Gunnar's ideal, however, is revealed by Campaspe herself in her relations with Gunnar. He has left love and sex out of his "religion," and when he falls victim to these in the person of Campaspe, he feels himself burdened and defiled and runs away. In short, his high idealism is untrue to human nature, a quality which explains both its initial attraction and its inevitable pain and failure. And so again a Van Vechten novel turns on the belief that man must be true to his temperament—that the noble ideal of a Gunnar can imprison as fully as the conventional respectability of an Alice.

Firecrackers is more thematically explicit and tightly structured than Van Vechten's other major novels but this is not to suggest that its tone is gray or sombre. Although Gunnar himself is humorless, the remainder of Van Vechten's New York world—Campaspe, Paul, Consuelo, etc.—is rendered with his usual wit and panache. The novel is almost a repository of Van Vechten's most successful characters from earlier works, since not only do Paul and Campaspe reappear from *The Blind Bow-Boy* but also Gareth and the Countess from *The Tattooed Countess* and even (briefly) Edith Dale from *Peter Whiffle*. And some of the extended burlesque scenes reveal Van Vechten at his best—a vacuous New York cocktail party, for example, or the attempted seduction by Paul of Wintergreen Waterbury, a "simple child of Michigan" (p. 192) and a professional virgin of great fortitude. And as always in Van Vechten the novel gathers strength from its central paradox, in this instance that of the battle between the devil and an angel for human souls in which the "devil" is a latter-day amalgam of

Emerson and Carlyle and the "angel" is a cosmopolitan New York libertine.

Parties is probably Van Vechten's most significant and permanent work of fiction. Subtitled "Scenes from Contemporary New York Life," the novel consists of a series of parties at which a more or less integral "set" intermingle and interact to produce not a plot but rather an impression of a particular phase of contemporary life. The artistic method of *Parties* resembles that of atonal music and surrealistic art in that Van Vechten does not seek to impose order upon experience but rather to heighten an impression of the disharmony and disjunctiveness of experience, with the loud and discordant conversation of a party one of the principal means toward this effect.

Parties are the subject matter and theme of the novel. They occur in London, Paris, and New York for a full "season" of fall to spring and with a wide variety of participants. But basically there are three reappearing New York settings and a coherent group of celebrants. The places are the Wishbone speakeasy, Rosalie Keith's house, and the living room bar of the Westlakes' apartment. The principal participants are Rilda and David Westlake, their friend Hamish, the Gräfin and her protégé Roy Fern, the bootlegger Donald Bliss (who owns the Wishbone), Rosalie, Simone Fly, and the actress Midnight Blue.

The alcoholic party as a symbol of contemporary life has several meanings in the novel. It suggests on one hand the potential violence and physical debilitation of drinking to excess, and on the other the "exhilaration" and "pleasant glow" of drinking to precisely the right point where, for a moment, "every value is enhanced" (p. 123). To the Gräfin the party is indeed life enhancing and she finds in it friendship and gaiety and sparkle and openness. To David and Rilda the party is a narcotic addition, since they find in its drunkenness and enforced gregariousness an escape from their all-possessive love.

Parties contains almost all of the Jazz Age activities and preoccupations of Van Vechten's other novels—sexual promiscuity, homosexuality, alcoholism, Harlem, and Hollywood (through Midnight Blue)—but all appear with a sharper satiric edge than before. The Gräfin is now the sole remnant of a Campaspe-like ethic and power, while the Westlakes represent more fully than in any other Van Vechten novel the neurotic underside of a life of seeming pleasure and indulgence. Sex in particular in *Parties* is exploitative and self-aggrandizing, more a vengeance than a fulfillment. The darker tone of the novel is fully evident at one of Rosalie Keith's parties when a clairvoyant shatters the fragile self-protective masks of the guests by revealing the emptiness and shallowness of their essential natures. The structure of the novel also enforces through its circularity this theme of vacuity. The farcical "dream murder" of Roy Fern which opens the novel

(David wakes up believing he has killed Roy at a drunken party the night before) is confirmed at its close in Roy's death, largely because of David, during a drunken party. And "partying" itself has a life-deadening repetitious circularity, as David remarks at the party which closes the novel:

> Hamish and I will get drunk as usual this afternoon, and . . . we shall somehow manage to arrive at Rosalie's in time for dinner where, of course, we shall meet Rilda and . . . despite the fact we have purchased tickets to see Zimbule O'Grady in Buttered Toast, we shall spend most of the evening at Donald's and probably end up in Harlem. That is the life of our times in words of two syllables. I am not bitter about it. I accept it as the best we can do. (p. 260)

Parties maintains the high level of verbal wit, sexual farce, and satiric characterization of Van Vechten's other New York novels. But it goes beyond them in the brilliance of his evocation of the cacophony of New York—riveters hammering outside, loud drunken conversation within— and in the power of his use of the symbol of the party to suggest that gaiety is often not what it appears to be, that for many it is only a prison or a mask. *Parties* thus suggests that Van Vechten had come to accept fully a major corollary of his belief that self-discovery was the principal quality of the spirit of the age which he wished to communicate. For he now stressed that the superficially glamorous "scenes from contemporary . . . life" which were the context of self-discovery often disguised the "true tragedies" of mind and spirit which were inseparable from the pursuit of that ideal.

The Negative Character in American Fiction

TERENCE MARTIN

In response to a story which lamented the inadequate telephone service in Squaw Gap, North Dakota, William L. Guy, then governor of the state, wrote a letter to the editor of *The Wall Street Journal* on January 7, 1972. Many things a New Yorker might take for granted, he acknowledged, are lacking in Squaw Gap. Rather than "miles of abandoned tenement houses," one finds vistas of "buttes and ridges." Instead of an "oversized" telephone directory, one consults a book "that doesn't even have a yellow page." Compared to New York, Governor Guy admitted in his most sweeping concession, Squaw Gap has virtually "nothing": "It has no crime, no air pollution, no water pollution, no noise pollution, no racial tension, no civil disturbance, no congested highways, no congested airways."

In thus speaking up for the honor of Squaw Gap, Governor Guy strikes a note that runs deep into American history, beyond the familiar debate between village and city, to a time when Americans took a similar attitude toward Europe as a way of asserting a sense of pride in their new nation. Europe (so went the refrain) was decadent, polluted morally, victimized by tyranny, whereas America was unspoiled, possessed of a vaunted innocence. My interest in Governor Guy's remarks, however, is less in their substance than in their rhetorical stance. For Americans have long found a series of compelling negatives the surest way of claiming identity. Crèvecoeur, for example, prepares for his celebrated definition of the American in *Letters from an American Farmer* by saying that "here are no aristocratical families, no courts, no kings, no bishops, no ecclesiastical dominion, no invisible power giving to the few a very visible one; no great manufacturers employing thousands, no great refinements of luxury."[1] And the maverick Thomas Cooper explained in 1794 that America offered the emigrant a land with "no tythes nor game laws . . . no men of great rank, nor many of great riches." "Nor" do the rich have oppressive power—"nor" are the streets filled with beggars. "No where in America," he concludes, does one find wretchedness side by side with "luxurious parade."[2]

Such statements—and one could make an anthology of others like them—mark the difference between Old World and New by enumerating what

---

1. *Letters from an American Farmer* (London, 1782), p. 46.
2. *Some Information Respecting America* (London, 1794), p. 53.

is missing in the New. Their tone is dismissive, abruptly so; for the things dismissed are symbols of constraint which can be cancelled with each recurring negative—almost as if the rhetoric were staging a revolution of its own. Concomitantly, by extolling the nation for what it lacks, they demonstrate an impulse, perhaps a need, to negate in order to identify and possess. In essence they say, "What America does not have, it is." Such a distillation of meaning finds a direct analogue in a journal entry of Thoreau's in 1841. To express a sense of his individuality, Thoreau invokes studied negative cadences: "When I meet a person unlike me, I find myself *wholly* in the unlikeness. In what I am unlike others, in that I am." [3] Shortly after Thoreau's death in 1862 Emerson resorted to a startling series of negatives to describe the career of his contemporary. "Few lives contain so many renunciations," he wrote in his essay on Thoreau. He

> was bred to no profession; he never married; he lived alone; he never went to church; he never voted; he refused to pay a tax to the State; he ate no flesh, he drank no wine, he never knew the use of tobacco; and, though a naturalist, he used neither trap nor gun. . . . He had no talent for wealth, and knew how to be poor without the least hint of squalor or inelegance. . . . He had no temptations to fight against,— no appetites, no passions, no taste for elegant trifles.

A few paragraphs later Emerson adds—"No truer American existed than Thoreau." [4]

To be sure of what they were, Americans thus acquired a habit of asserting what they were not, both nationally and personally. The identifying myth of the American Adam emerged from a conviction of unlikeness and was articulated in purest form by the use of negative terms: a new paradise will flourish in the burgeoning nation, wrote Philip Freneau in "The Rising Glory of America,"

> by no second Adam lost,
> No dangerous tree with deadly fruit shall grow,
> No tempting serpent to allure the soul
> From native innocence. [5]

By negating the tree, the fruit, and the serpent, Freneau comes logically to the concept of "native innocence." And if the concept had a singular effect on the American's sense of himself in—or out of—world history, the negative rhetoric which produced it graduated to a remarkable career of its own. The protean function of such rhetoric can be epitomized by an

3. Perry Miller, *Consciousness in Concord: The Text of Thoreau's Hitherto 'Lost Journal' (1840–1841), Together with Notes and a Commentary* (Boston, 1958), p. 216.

4. *The Complete Works of Ralph Waldo Emerson* (Boston, 1903–1904), X, 454, 459.

5. *The Poems of Philip Freneau*, ed. Fred Lewis Pattee (Princeton, N.J., 1902), I, 82.

example from our own time which offers a disconcerting commercial reprise on Freneau's lines. In July, 1971, the *New Yorker* carried an advertisement for Swissair which invited the reader to visit Zurich, "a city with no slums, no strikes, no poverty, no unemployment, no raucous noise, no cliques of malcontents." Not only, we note, can Governor Guy defend Squaw Gap in terms of what it does not have; paradise can be relocated in Switzerland by the shrewd rhetoric of Madison Avenue.

Adaptable to diverse purposes, negative catalogues could likewise serve to express the feeling of some nineteenth-century American writers that a lack of tradition and legend posed a difficulty to artistic endeavor. In a memorable sequence of negatives, Henry James evoked the bleak social scene which, he felt, confronted Hawthorne in the 1830's.[6] Hawthorne himself, in his preface to *The Marble Faun*, explained that with "no shadow, no antiquity, no mystery, no sense of gloomy wrong," reality in America proved recalcitrant to the imagination of the romancer—and Irving, Cooper, and Margaret Fuller had already lamented in negatives the absence of what seemed congenial to their art. What these writers spelled out was the perilousness of their role in a nation that sought to discard prior experience in the interest of beginning again. What they and their contemporaries produced was a literature of astonishing vitality which transformed a habit of mind into an imaginative resource. In subtle and sophisticated ways, the negative impulse was carried far beyond the form of straightforward catalogues and made to function as a means of assessing the relationship of self to experience in a developing society. The final paragraph of Emerson's "The Over-Soul," for example, extends the cultural imperatives of "The American Scholar" to an absolute position: "Before the immense possibilities of man, all mere experience, all past biography, however spotless and sainted, shrinks away. . . . We not only affirm that we have few great men, but, absolutely speaking, that we have none; that we have no history, no record of any character or mode of living, that entirely contents us." Emily Dickinson's paradoxical credo that one knows best by not having ("Success is counted sweetest / By those who ne'er succeed") similarly demonstrates an attitude toward experience that demands negative formulation.

One of the most persistent manifestations of the tendency I have been describing can be found in fictional characters who enact the negative impulse—whose function it is to measure the world in which we live by the worlds in which they are unable to live. The best of these characters—among them Natty Bumppo, Huckleberry Finn, Isaac McCaslin, and Ran-

---

6. *Hawthorne* (London, 1879), p. 43.

dle Patrick McMurphy—exist in novels that virtually recapitulate the experience of America. And appropriately so, for the authentic negative character tends to play the role of original American in a socially insistent environment and thus to precipitate by contrast or collision the torrent of our history. Out of the differences in the novels themselves come variations in the role; but a genetic similarity, I believe, relates all such characters to the negative impulse which first sought identity in unlikeness.

James Fenimore Cooper's figure of Natty Bumppo stands as the classic example of a negative character in American literature. In *The Pathfinder* Natty says that he is a man with " 'neither daughter, nor sister, nor mother, nor kith nor kin, nor anything but the Delawares to love' " and thus defines himself by stipulating the personal and civilizing ties which he lacks.[7] What remains is a character whom Cooper defines—in the same novel—as a relative innocent, "a sort of type of what Adam might have been supposed to be before the fall, though certainly not without sin" (p. 143). Far apart in time and temperament is the figure of McMurphy in Ken Kesey's *One Flew Over the Cuckoo's Nest*. As the narrator, Chief Bromden, tells us, McMurphy is radically different from the other patients on the Big Nurse's ward because he has "No wife wanting new linoleum. No relatives pulling at him with watery old eyes. No one to *care* about, which is what makes him free enough to be a good con man."[8] Again, a negative rhetoric stipulates the absence of social and personal ties. What remains in this case is energy, the sudden release of outrageous energy into a starched and rigid fictional world.

Unlike Natty Bumppo, of course, McMurphy has only one life to give to his fiction. And *Cuckoo's Nest* moves swiftly to dispose of him in sacrificial victory. For Kesey introduces us to a negative character who is about to "*care*": during his six weeks on the ward McMurphy becomes deliberately encumbered with the shrunken men around him, willing to take on himself the burden of their struggle for manhood. Not that the transition from self-propelling freedom to responsibility for others takes place overnight. We are treated in the first half of the novel to the engaging spectacle of McMurphy challenging every restriction to his unbridled spirit, then—after he learns that he has been committed to the institution

---

7. *The Pathfinder*, illustrated from drawings by F. O. C. Darley (New York, 1869), p. 206. Subsequent page references to the Leatherstocking Tales will be from this edition of *The Novels of James Fenimore Cooper* and will be noted parenthetically in the text. The order of publication of the Leatherstocking Tales is *The Pioneers* (1823), *The Last of the Mohicans* (1826), *The Prairie* (1827), *The Pathfinder* (1840), and *The Deerslayer* (1841). The order according to Natty Bumppo's advancing age happens to be alphabetical: *Deerslayer, Mohicans, Pathfinder, Pioneers, Prairie*.

8. *One Flew Over the Cuckoo's Nest* (New York, 1973), p. 89. Subsequent page references to this edition of the novel will be noted parenthetically in the text.

—to his sobering decision to think only of his own release. But when Mc-Murphy commits himself to his fellow patients he thereby surrenders the negative qualities that originally defined him as a character.

Given the total conception of *Cuckoo's Nest*, there is no way to sustain the negative impulse that brought the primitive force of McMurphy into existence. To account for the hero's prior independence, Chief Bromden surmises that he has had to keep on the move in a twentieth-century America increasingly regulated by the Combine. A school "never" indoctrinated him, the Chief says, and the Combine "never" adjusted him socially "because a moving target is hard to hit" (p. 89). Mobility is thus a necessary condition of McMurphy's unencumbered status, a contemporary substitute for the sense of space which sustained earlier negative characters, ambivalent because of its tendency to yield the attributes of the "con man." In the controlled microcosm of the hospital, it faces an ultimate threat.

Throughout *Cuckoo's Nest* there is a sense of something lost—spontaneity, early happiness, a capacity for laughter. All such things belong to a forgotten world of freedom until they are resuscitated by McMurphy, the negatively created character who embodies, insists upon, and gives what the original world contained. As one might expect, McMurphy's force is registered most dramatically in the responses of the narrator. Thus, when he first shakes Bromden's hand the Chief reports that "It rang with blood and power. It blowed up near as big as his" (p. 24). Thus, too, the Chief attributes his rekindled optimism after the fishing trip to the fact that "McMurphy was teaching me": "I was feeling better than I'd remembered feeling since I was a kid, when everything was good and the land was still singing kids' poetry to me" (p. 243). But the fishing expedition signals the ending of the protagonist's career as a negative character. Tied now to the other patients, drained of the force he once possessed in abundance, the original McMurphy is virtually diffused among his comrades. He "doled out his life," as Chief Bromden says, "for us to live" (p. 245). The language of the novel encourages us to see him as a roughneck Christ figure: " 'Anointest my head with conductant,' " he says at shock therapy time; " 'Do I get a crown of thorns?' " (p. 270). And as the fishing trip gets underway the Chief observes that "McMurphy led the twelve of us toward the ocean" (p. 227).

In *Cuckoo's Nest* Kesey has introduced a negative character, plunged him into a world of intensified experience, and shown us that he combats a general diminution of self at the necessary expense of his original status —and thus of his life. Since it is the abiding function of such a character to measure, not to recast society, McMurphy's victory is neither literal nor final. Rather, it is a matter of legacy. As the Chief says, "The thing he was fighting, you couldn't whip it for good. All you could do was keep on whipping it, till you couldn't come out any more and somebody else had to take your place" (p. 303). With all his cartoon-like posturing, Mc-Murphy stands as a powerful example of the force and the fate of a modern negative character.

Not until he resurrected Natty Bumppo in *The Pathfinder* and *The Deerslayer* did Cooper feature him as what James Grossman calls "one of the great negative characters of literature."[9] Manifold signs of a negative conception, however, accumulate throughout the earlier Tales. In *The Prairie*, for example, Natty tells Ishmael Bush that he has " 'no regular abode' " (p. 24) and adds conventional metaphors of disengagement to a self-portrait drawn for Hard-Heart: " 'I have never been father or brother. The Wahcondah . . . never tied my heart to house or field, by the cords with which the men of my race are bound to their lodges' " (p. 344). More-over, during his elaborate death scene Natty announces that he is " 'with-out kith or kin in the wide world!' " (p. 475). In *The Last of the Mohicans*, he explains to Chingachgook that with " 'no kin, and . . . like you, no peo-ple,' " he is free to share the memory of Uncas (p. 442). And in *The Pioneers* he faces the most troublesome (and instructive) situation of all—that of an incipient negative character detained by loyalty in a region that has be-come inimicable to his temperament.

In *The Pioneers* Cooper introduces a Natty Bumppo who is bound by a prior obligation. He must remain near Templeton because of his ac-knowledged duty to Major Effingham. Never again does he come into a novel so encumbered, so tied to a place which is being transformed by time. Quite obviously, Templeton is not authoritarian in the manner of Kesey's hospital: the presiding figure of Judge Temple seeks to temper the extravagance of the settlers in a community still striving for social equilibrium; Oliver Effingham and Elizabeth Temple embody a legitimate promise for the future. Because of his allegiance to an earlier world, how-ever, Natty Bumppo becomes an anachronism in this novel, the futile an-tagonist of a progress to which Cooper is committed. Elizabeth Temple puts the matter bluntly: even " 'were we so silly as to wish such a thing,' " she says to an assenting Oliver, it would not be possible to " 'convert these clearings and farms again into hunting-grounds, as the Leather-stocking would wish to see them' " (p. 308). Inevitably, as one trapped in a linear movement of time, Natty Bumppo feels constraints. Inevitably, social forms operate to imprison him. The spectacle of Natty in jail and in the stocks symbolizes the position of the negative character (no matter how good) in society (no matter how benign). For the social conception and the negative conception are antithetical in nature. Neither can accommo-date the other.

---

9. *James Fenimore Cooper* (London, 1950), p. 148.

If the death of Mohegan diminishes Natty, that of Major Effingham releases him from his obligation to a defunct past and from the constrictions of a society that has grown up around him. He refuses the invitation of Oliver and Elizabeth to remain in the environs of Templeton because, as he says, " 'I'm formed for the wilderness; if ye love me, let me go where my soul craves to be ag'in!' " (p. 593). The " 'ag'in,' " I believe, is important. During the course of the narrative Natty has described Lake Otsego before Templeton as " 'a second paradise' " and has told Oliver of his two favorite places in the Catskills, both of which gave him the sense of being near " 'creation.' " He knows, in other words, " 'how often the hand of God is seen in the wilderness,' " and it is to the wilderness that he must go " 'ag'in' " (pp. 320–323). Intent on having Templeton pass to the best of the coming generation, Cooper has used Natty Bumppo as a foil throughout much of *The Pioneers*. A presocietal negative impulse accrues in the narrative, however, and receives formulation from Natty when he leaves the community. That Cooper (in the final sentence) describes the aging hunter as "foremost" in the band of pioneers "who are opening the way for the march of the nation across the continent" suggests the persistence of his social vision in this novel. He is reluctant, as it were, to send Natty Bumppo westward without a role that serves society in some way. But he has already conceived a negative character who yearns for the values of an original world; and he would ultimately give that character both Lake Otsego and the wilderness in the final novel of the series.

In *The Pioneers*, *The Last of the Mohicans*, and *The Prairie*, the evidence of Natty Bumppo's negative status comes exclusively from his own dialogue. The point is worth noting; for one of the distinguishing features of the final two Leatherstocking novels is that Cooper adds his narrative voice to the making of Natty's negative portrait. If Natty describes himself as without daughter, sister, or mother, it is the narrator who defines him as an Adamic figure. If a disappointed Natty tells Mabel Dunham that he " 'shall return to the wilderness and my Maker,' " it is the narrator who tells us that he "seemed to tear himself away" from Mabel "as one snaps a strong and obstinate cord" (*Path.*, pp. 506–507). And if the youngest Natty of all rejoices at the sight of a pristine forest with " 'not a tree disturbed even by red-skin hand . . . but everything left in the ordering of the Lord,' " it is the narrator who observes that "he loved the woods for their freshness . . . and the impress that they everywhere bore of the divine hand of their creator" (*Deer.*, p. 299). Cooper, in other words, joins forces with the resurrected Natty Bumppo, adopts—and even enlarges—his perspective, and presents him authorially as a character who functions negatively.

Cooper's emphasis on the uplifting virtues of nature in *The Pathfinder* and *The Deerslayer* becomes a significant part of a developing negative strategy. Uniquely affiliated with the wilderness, Natty Bumppo partakes of its original coherence and innocence—so much so that according to John F. Lynen "the landscape creates him, just as he, in turn, interprets it." [10] What we should bear in mind in adopting this perception is that these are Cooper's landscapes and that they augment the creation of Natty by means of a very traditional use of negative rhetoric. "Far as the eye could reach," writes Cooper in *The Pathfinder*, "nothing but the forest was visible, not even a solitary sign of civilization breaking in upon the uniform and grand magnificence of nature" (p. 289). The appeal of Glimmerglass in *The Deerslayer* comes from "the air of deep repose—the solitudes, that spoke of scenes and forests untouched by the hands of man" (p. 45). Blake Nevius has reminded us of the problems encountered by early nineteenth-century writers who sought to capture the effect of the American wilderness with such (negative) terms as *boundlessness* and *interminableness*. But Cooper, as Nevius demonstrates, had acquired by 1840 a "visual discipline" that allowed him to make effective use of scenic material. [11] Still, he describes by negation in both *The Pathfinder* and *The Deerslayer*. He tells us repeatedly what the wilderness is by telling us what it is not. He evokes (in *The Deerslayer*) a sense of timelessness, of a pristine "world by itself," by rhetorically cancelling out the signs of civilization. And he thereby creates a setting which validates the identity of a negative character who knew long before that he was " 'formed for the wilderness.' "

It took five novels to establish Natty Bumppo as the enduring negative hero. And the author who thought of calling the final Leatherstocking Tale "Judith and Esther, or, the Girls of the Glimmerglass" could hardly have been aware of all he was doing. [12] Nonetheless, during the course of these novels Cooper manages to create the prototype of the character who takes fictional form from a negative impulse. No matter their different situations, all such characters experience society as a constricting force. The tone may vary—as when Mark Twain reports in *Tom Sawyer* that "Huck Finn's wealth and the fact that he was now under the Widow Douglas's protection introduced him into society—no, dragged him into it, hurled him into it"—but the metaphors remain tellingly the same: "whithersoever he turned, the bars and shackles of civilization shut him in and bound him hand and foot." [13] Even the daily routine of a community thwarts the natural habits of the negative character. " 'I eat when hungry and drink when a-dry; and ye keep stated hours and rules,' " Natty Bump-

---

10. *The Design of the Present: Essays on Form and Time in American Literature* (New Haven, 1969), p. 187.

11. *Cooper's Landscapes: An Essay on the Picturesque Vision* (Berkeley, 1976), pp. 6–8, 100.

12. *The Letters and Journals of James Fenimore Cooper*, ed. James Franklin Beard (Cambridge, Mass., 1964), IV, 112.

13. *The Writings of Mark Twain*, Author's National Edition (New York, 1907–1918), XII, 286–287.

po says to Oliver and Elizabeth toward the end of *The Pioneers* (p. 503). Similarly, Huckleberry Finn tells Tom Sawyer that " 'the widow eats by a bell; she goes to bed by a bell—everything's so awful reg'lar a body can't stand it.' " And to Tom's objection that " 'everybody does that way,' " Huck replies (quite accurately), " 'I ain't everybody, and I can't *stand* it. It's awful to be tied up so.' "[14]

In *The Prairie* a momentarily wistful Natty Bumppo tells Paul Hover that if he could choose his " 'time and place again' " he would speak for " 'twenty and the wilderness!' " (p. 37). Resigned to his unlikeness in this novel, the aged Natty explains to Mahtoree that he came west " 'to escape the wasteful temper of my people' " (p. 264) and exempts himself from Le Balafré's charge of white cupidity by saying, characteristically, that he has never " 'coveted more ground than the Lord has intended each man to fill' "—that is, the ground on which he stands (p. 390). By the time of *The Prairie* Natty is self-defined as a landless man who has been able to shun a careless and grasping society because of the freedom afforded by the West. His death signals the end of the West as a sustaining refuge for the negative character, the need for a new strategy of survival. And when Cooper grants him a purified setting drawn to the specifications of " 'twenty and the wilderness,' " Natty enacts what became the essential reverie of the negative character—that of the freedom of a pre-adult world. As many critics have pointed out, Natty Bumppo regresses psychologically in the final two novels of the Leatherstocking series.[15] If Cooper juggles Natty's age in *The Pathfinder* so that he becomes old enough to be Mabel Dunham's father, he also makes him a boy who, as Mabel assures him, will dream again of hunting and trapping after his disappointment in love (p. 302). Following his refusal of Judith Hutter in *The Deerslayer*, he sits "playing with the water, like a corrected school-boy" (p. 592). The necessity for such regression balances its cost: what Cooper shows us is that childhood affords the ultimate protection against marriage. Since women are the bearers of culture in Cooper's fiction, since they provide what Nina Baym calls "the nexus of social interaction," to marry would be to form a per-petuating bond with society.[16] And societal bonds are what Natty Bumppo forever eschews.

The consensus is that Natty Bumppo weds the wilderness at the end of *The Pathfinder* and that the wilderness is, in Joel Porte's paraphrase of

14. Ibid., p. 288.

15. See, for example, Annette Kolodny's analysis of *The Pathfinder* and *The Deer-slayer* in *The Lay of the Land: Metaphor as Experience and History in American Life and Letters* (Chapel Hill, N. C., 1975), pp. 105–113.

16. "The Women of Cooper's Leatherstocking Tales," *American Quarterly*, XXIII (1971), 697.

Melville, "a Paradise for bachelors only."[17] Provocatively discussed by critics of different persuasions, the friendship of Natty and Chingachgook takes on a new vitality in the final two novels of the Leatherstocking series, not simply as a substitute for women but as a means of sustaining a negative conception to which Cooper is now committed. Cooper seems deliberately to pair his two characters in these novels. When Natty, in *The Pathfinder*, says that Chingachgook " 'has no children to delight with his trophies; no tribe to honor by his deeds,' " that he " 'is a lone man' " who " 'stands true to his training and his gifts,' " he could well be looking into a mirror (or a pond) and describing his red self (p. 82). As they come into *The Deerslayer*, neither Natty nor Chingachgook has yet slain a human being; and Glimmerglass is the first lake either has seen. Out of this pairing (as I have observed elsewhere) comes a developing strategy of doubling Natty's consciousness to include that of Chingachgook—so that innocence is at once protected and heightened by experience it does not, objectively, have.[18] The classic example can be seen in Natty's story of discovering six sleeping Mingos, told to Charles Cap in *The Pathfinder*. " 'What an opportunity that would have been for the Sarpent,' " muses Natty the storyteller, aware that Chingachgook would have claimed lives and scalps in an instant. So imminent was the Chingachgook-in-Natty at the time that the occasion was " 'a desperate trial' " (the " 'hardest' " temptation of his life) to one who could neither scalp nor kill sleeping enemies. Shortly after Natty's later ambush dispatched five of the six, Chingachgook appeared with the five Mingo scalps at his belt, " 'hanging where they ought to be.' " " 'So, you see,' " Natty concludes, " 'nothing was lost by doing right, either in the way of honor or in that of profit' " (pp. 479–480).

Not only does this intriguing little story illustrate the idea of racial *gifts*. It suggests a dependence on Chingachgook as an agent who allows Natty to practice a morality of abstention and then take an almost Franklinesque satisfaction that " 'nothing was lost' " by resisting temptation. By attributing to Natty Bumppo the consciousness, but not the act, of savage experience, Cooper makes the solitary Serpent serve the interests of the solitary Adam. And he leaves a legacy to future negative characters who would need a noncivilized friend to extend the asocial range of their experience.

Only once in Faulkner's *Go Down, Moses* does Isaac McCaslin succumb to the pressures that would have him accept his family inheritance. From the opening pages of the novel we learn that Ike "owned no property and

---

17. *The Romance in America: Studies in Cooper, Poe, Hawthorne, Melville, and James* (Middletown, Conn., 1969), p. 28.
18. "Surviving on the Frontier: The Doubled Consciousness of Natty Bumppo," *South Atlantic Quarterly*, LXXV (1976), 447–459.

never desired to." [19] He rejects the idea that he has repudiated the inheritance because, as he says (in beginning an argument that equates ownership with original sin), " 'It was never mine to repudiate' " (p. 256). But Ike does marry, and it is his wife, intent on possessing " 'The farm. Our farm Your farm' " (p. 312), who coerces a promise that the swirling conversations with McCaslin Edmonds could never extract. Faulkner's scene implicates the eternal Eve with the desire for property; what society cannot do for itself, she will. Ike hears "the bell ring for supper," locks the door and undresses at his wife's command, sees her nakedness as "the composite of all woman-flesh" since the creation of man, feels the pressure of her fingers on his wrist ("as though hand and arm were a piece of wire cable with one looped end") while he says " 'No, . . . I wont. I cant. Never,' " until he surrenders to passion with " 'Yes' " and the thought that *"We were all born lost"* (pp. 313–314). Following this encounter Ike becomes "unwidowered but without a wife" (p. 281).

With immense sweep, *Go Down, Moses* engages the turbulent issues of American history, alludes to the discovery of an "already tainted" promise in the new world, and appropriates the story of man's dispossession from Eden to its thematic purpose. Faulkner's aggressive negative language attains its greatest intensity in "The Bear." When Isaac McCaslin finds Fonsiba's cabin, for example, rain is reducing it "to a nameless and valueless rubble of dissolution in that roadless and even pathless waste of unfenced fallow and wilderness jungle—no barn, no stable, not so much as a hen-coop: just a log cabin built by hand and no clever hand either . . ." (p. 277). Predictably, there is no fire on the stove; predictably, too, out of a succession of negatives come Fonsiba's only words—" 'I'm free' " (p. 280). It is by means of this negating style that Faulkner evokes the "anachronism" (p. 193) of the bear and creates the wilderness which will be Ike's "mistress and his wife" (p. 326).[20] But the wilderness—threatened long before by " 'the axes of the choppers,' " as Natty Bumppo remembers (*Prairie*, p. 264)—is the doomed victim of accelerated progress in *Go Down, Moses*: Ike has seen it retreat "year by year before the onslaught of axe and saw and log-lines and then dynamite and tractor plows" (p. 354). Having outlived Old Ben and Sam Fathers, he incorporates their spirit into his feeling that he and the wilderness are coeval. He has no Glimmerglass to enrich a life after death. "Born old," however, he does become "steadily younger and younger until" (nearing eighty) "he had acquired something of a young boy's high and selfless innocence" (p. 106). And Faulkner grants him a corollary vision of himself and the wilderness "running out to-

---

19. *Go Down, Moses* (New York, 1955), p. 3. Subsequent page references to this edition of the novel will be noted parenthetically in the text.

20. Richard Poirier notes how Faulkner's style strips away expectations in *A World Elsewhere: The Place of Style in American Literature* (New York, 1966), pp. 78–80.

gether, not toward oblivion, nothingness, but into a dimension free of both time and space" in which all the hunters he has survived can move "again among the shades of tall unaxed trees and sightless brakes where the wild strong immortal game ran forever before the tireless belling immortal hounds, falling and rising phoenix-like to the soundless guns" (p. 354). It is a harmless hunting ground that Ike envisions, sport made eternal by the extravagant use of negative rhetoric. In such a paradise Ike would surely be entitled to echo Fonsiba's words, " 'I'm free.' "

What Ike does say, of course, is " 'Sam Fathers set me free' " (p. 300). For it is the half-Indian and half-Negro Sam Fathers who schools Isaac Mc-Caslin in the ways of the wilderness and makes his vision possible. The negative and hence asocial impulse in "The Bear" issues from the wilderness itself, emerges, shaped, in the colossal figure of Old Ben—"so long unwifed and childless as to have become its own ungendered progenitor" (p. 210), and passes mystically into the human form of Sam Fathers, who *"had no children, no people, none of his blood anywhere above earth that he would ever meet again"* (p. 215). It is from Sam, "his spirit's father" (p. 326), that Ike inherits the invincible purity of the wilderness which stands opposed to the rapacious legacy of Carothers McCaslin. Faulkner has conceived a character who struggles to be negative but who must witness the spectacle of a family history that remains in motion and inevitably breeds injustice out of the original injustice. By means of Ike's negative stance Faulkner projects in high relief the agony of "a whole land in miniature" (p. 293). But the lesson of "Delta Autumn" is that Ike is not only "outmoded" like the wilderness (p. 343); he is, finally, encumbered by the social attitudes of his time and place. If the cost of being negative remains high, the conception itself comes under the unremitting pressure of a history in which we are all involved.

As Isaac McCaslin seeks release from the past, Huckleberry Finn needs relief from the present. Transposed into Huck's idiom, metaphors of feeling cramped and smothered by society carry over from *Tom Sawyer* into *Huckleberry Finn* and prevail throughout the narrative. For if the fact of Huck being literally a boy removes him from the encumbering threat of marriage, it likewise leaves him defenseless against the aggressive demands of any social context. Between the regulations of Miss Watson and life with Pap one may not see much choice; initially, however, Huck prefers the latter because he can smoke and fish and because there are "no books nor study." [21] Only when Pap, already a threat with his hickory stick, locks him in the cabin for days at a time is Huck driven to stage his own death— the ultimate act of negating a vulnerable social self. At this point Mark

---

21. *The Writings of Mark Twain*, Author's National Edition (New York, 1907–1918), XIII, 33. Subsequent references to this edition of *Huckleberry Finn* will be noted parenthetically in the text.

Twain introduces a runaway Jim and thus incorporates the issue of property into the nonwhite character who will serve as the unconscious mentor of Huck's conscience on the trip down river. Since the moral tension of the narrative comes from Huck's developing awareness of Jim as a human being, his obvious triumph is that he decides to go to hell rather than see Jim become property again. The society that enslaved Jim can make him a freed man. But Huck has shared the raft with a *free* Jim whose natural goodness transforms the narrator's asocial instincts into antisocial behavior. In all his innocence, Huck stands self-defined as a social outcast.

In commenting on the passivity of Huckleberry Finn, William C. Spengemann points out that Huck's world "arises entirely out of his immediate experience." Thrust at him from the outside, bristling with "insoluble problems," experience for Huck is both "unwelcome" and "unavoidable."[22] On the raft, to be sure, he can enjoy the luxury of a presocial world which is the dream of the negative character: as they speculate that the stars may have been laid by the moon, Huck and Jim enact man's primary impulse to explain the creation of the universe, their naiveté a comic substitute for the genuinely primitive.[23] But if the river itself is often dangerous, society is never far away. In its most persistent form, as we know, it surfaces as the Tom Sawyer-in-Huck Finn. No matter the difficulties Mark Twain encountered in ending this novel, it is appropriate that Huck becomes Tom Sawyer when he reaches the Phelps farm. For that is precisely what he will be if he allows society to define him.

Perhaps more than any other negative character, however, Huckleberry Finn—as a boy—needs the society that constricts him. Only twice in the Leatherstocking Tales (once in *The Pioneers* and once in *The Pathfinder*) do we learn that Natty Bumppo is lonesome in his solitary life. But Huck is a frequent prey to lonesomeness. Although he claims to love the woods, his true habitat is on the fringes of the community with his hogsheads and barrels of "odds and ends" in which the food "gets mixed up, and the juice kind of swaps around, and things go better" (p. 2). Farthest from social dictates after he tears up his letter to Miss Watson (with the image of Jim victorious in his consciousness), he nonetheless is overjoyed to be taken for Tom Sawyer a short time later: "it was like being born again," he says, "I was so glad to find out who I was" (p. 310). In the opening chapter of the novel Huck "lit out" from the Widow Douglas' house because he "couldn't stand it no longer" (p. 2). Locked up by Pap, he flees because

---

22. *The Adventurous Muse: The Poetics of American Fiction, 1789–1900* (New Haven, 1977), p. 232.

23. Alan Henry Rose discusses this episode as a manifestation of Jim's "fecundity" in *Demonic Vision: Racial Fantasy and Southern Fiction* (Hamden, Conn., 1976), pp. 91–92. Rose also points out a provocative relationship between Huck Finn and Injun Joe in *Tom Sawyer* (pp. 84–85).

he "couldn't stand it" (p. 33). And in the famous last sentence of the novel Huck shrinks from the idea of being adopted by Aunt Sally and says "I can't stand it" one final time. Debate over the credibility of Huck's decision to "light out for the territory ahead of the rest" will doubtless continue. But in engaging the issue one should understand that Huck's statement is a gesture, the final negative gesture of a character who functions in a tradition adapted to the purpose of this particular novel. Again, the negative character has measured society. Again, as we see, the negative conception proves difficult to sustain—all the more so since Huck is our narrator and there is no alternative perspective into which his voice can be subsumed. But this chronically lonesome boy who seeks to evade experience does what he must at the end of *Huckleberry Finn* when he signals a desire *not* to join society because he has "been there before."

What is true of Huckleberry Finn is likewise true of the other characters I have discussed. The negative character must renounce society if we are to see it anew. Much of the plentiful criticism devoted to these characters, however, overlooks the fact of their negative conception—with curious results. Under the aegis of D. H. Lawrence, for example, Natty Bumppo's friendship with Chingachgook has been seen as the "nucleus of a new society";[24] alternatively, Natty has virtually been blamed for not making his virtues effective in a social context. Hailed as a hero by some early critics for repudiating his inheritance, Isaac McCaslin has more recently been deemed irresponsible by others. And McMurphy has become either the champion of everyone's struggle against the system or an offensive case of immaturity masquerading as manhood in a stereotyped world. Robert Penn Warren is characteristically more helpful when (forced to negatives himself) he describes *Huckleberry Finn* as "the American un-success story" and includes Leatherstocking and Isaac McCaslin in the recurring "drama of the innocent outside of society."[25] But a sense of the entire negative tradition in American writing, I believe, allows us to define these characters (and others) still more precisely, to understand their function in a significant context even as we distinguish among them—and thus to come to the critical act with a developing responsibility.

24. *Studies in Classic American Literature* (New York, 1923), p. 78.
25. "Mark Twain," *Southern Review*, VIII (1972), 471.

Notes on Photography and American Culture, 1839-1890

RUSSEL B. NYE

In one of those amazing outbreaks of invention, photography burst on the world in 1839. In that year Louis Daguerre, in France, perfected his silver plate images; Sir John Herschel, in England, reported to the Royal Society of London on "The Art of Photography," the first use of the term; W. H. Fox revealed his method of "photogenic drawing." [1] Men's attitudes toward what they saw, and their ways of seeing it, were never again the same. What followed was a virtual explosion of information, whose impact on society and culture is difficult to imagine, much less measure. "Bursting on the world as it did quite unexpectedly," wrote Gaspard F. T. Tournachon, "upsetting all previous ideas of what was even possible, this new discovery must surely have seemed—as it indeed was—the most extraordinary of the many inventions which have made our century, even before its close, the greatest age of science ever." [2]

Photography represented the most important invention affecting communications since the introduction of moveable type. It altered the visual conditions under which men lived, expanded the capacities of the visual media, and influenced the transfer of visual information in ways still relatively unexplored. [3] The reproducible photographic image permanently changed the way men perceived, ordered, and interpreted experience. The nineteenth century realized this and found the implications staggering to contemplate. It considered the camera, said one writer, "one of the great wonders of the phenomena of created matter," its discovery "one of those wonderful manifestations of the presence of Omniscient Intelligence." [4] Rapid technological progress in the medium multiplied both the era's

1. "Photography: Its History and Applications," *Living Age*, XCII (1867), 195–218, is a historical account from a nineteenth-century point of view, a review of thirteen books on photography.
2. Quoted by Michel Braive, *The Photograph: A Social History* (New York, 1960), p. 55. Tournachon, a journalist, was also one of the nineteenth century's most famous photographers under the name "Nadar."
3. See the introduction to Estelle Jussim, *Visual Communication and the Graphic Arts: Photographic Technologies in the Nineteenth Century* (New York, 1974), for a provocative, informative discussion of this point.
4. John Towler, *The Silver Sunbeam* (New York, 1864), p. 325.

enthusiasm and wonder.⁵ Photography became the new "craze"; lecturers (including Daguerre's assistant, François Gouraud) toured America; lyceum speakers demonstrated it; itinerant photographers penetrated the frontier and studios sprang up in hundreds of cities and towns; photographic "schools" proliferated; "handbooks" sold widely.⁶

The idea that the photograph was not merely the result of a mechanical process, but Nature replicating herself (as Daguerre noted) intrigued the century. The camera's sole tool was sunlight; all the camera did was allow Nature to speak directly to the viewer. Scientists, in fact, were the first to be awed by the miracle of it all—such as Samuel F. B. Morse, a painter and physicist; John William Draper, a chemistry professor; J. C. Frazer at the Franklin Institute; or A. S. Wolcott, who manufactured dental equipment. Emerson, Thoreau, Whitman and the whole contemporary range of literati, critics, philosophers—print- and paint-oriented all—paid little attention to the new phenomenon. Among them only Oliver Wendell Holmes seemed to understand what had happened when Daguerre exhibited his pictures in Paris.⁷

It is the purpose of this essay to consider only a few of the many speculations about and reactions to photography with which the nineteenth century received it. I deal with the years 1839 to 1890, since after 1880 a swift succession of technical innovations made everyone a photographer and everything photographable. After that, the "snapshot" introduced an-

---

5. The first actual photograph is usually attributed to Joseph Nicéphore Niepce in 1826. Daguerre's method used a silver-coated metal plate, Talbot's calotype used paper. The ambrotype, a wet glass plate process, appeared in the fifties, while the tintype used a sheet of emulsion-coated tin. Binocular lenses, leading to stereoscopic photos, were also perfected in the fifties. Dry plate photography, sixty times more sensitive than earlier processes, came in the eighties. Eastman's box Brownie went on the market in 1886 and roll film in 1889. Scores of other inventions, too many to list, appeared between, but the point is that from daguerreotype to snapshot took only fifty years.

6. By 1855 there seem to have been 10,000–15,000 photographers of one kind or another operating in the United States with perhaps as many more people employed in allied supply trades. Exact figures are hard to establish. The 1850 census listed about a thousand photographers who considered themselves professionals; part-time practitioners were no doubt many times that. *Living Age* in 1867 estimated those associated with the art in England at 20,000 or more; in the United States, 15,000. The number of photographs submitted to the London Exposition of 1862 was 1,860,000; the *New York Daily Tribune* in 1853 thought that over 3,000,000 daguerreotypes alone were made annually in the United States.

7. The *North American Review*, for example, mentioned photography only a few times prior to 1876. Emerson's and Thoreau's journals show few entries dealing with photography; Emerson sat for a daguerreotype in 1841 and was not pleased with the result. Holmes, who invented an improved stereoscope, wrote three essays which together comprise the most imaginative photographic criticism written in the United States in his time. He was well aware of the "immensity of its applications and suggestions," and predicted "a new epoch in human progress." See "The Stereoscope and the Stereograph," *Atlantic Monthly*, III (June, 1859), 738–748; "Sun Painting and Sun Sculpture," ibid., VIII (July, 1861), 13–29; and "Doings of the Sunbeam," ibid., XII (July, 1863), 1–15.

other significant change in how people saw, and once more reshaped their conceptions of "real" experience.[8]

The universal reaction of those who first saw photographs (the earliest were daguerreotypes) was amazement at the complexity, profusion, and perfection of their detail. Accounts of Daguerre's Paris exhibition emphasized that these were "exact pictures" down to the "smallest details," and observers looked with wonder at the "delicacy of the scenes," the "faultless facsimiles," "the exquisite finish" of the mirrorlike plates. "We distinguish the smallest details," exclaimed one reporter, "We count the paving stones; we see the dampness caused by the rain—all were reproduced as in Nature." Samuel F. B. Morse visited Daguerre's exhibition in Paris and wrote back to the *New York Observer* in ecstatic terms of the "exquisite minuteness of the delineation" and "the intricacy of detail, like Rembrandt perfected."[9] Visitors "counted again and again roof tiles and chimney bricks," and "marveled at the lacelike fretwork . . . and the very lichens clinging to the rugged surface" of Notre Dame.[10]

This quality of "exquisite minuteness" was a constant theme in comments on photography over the next thirty years. The camera's ability to capture all the "richness and delicacy" of nature rarely failed to captivate nineteenth-century viewers. As Lewis Gaylord Clark wrote in the *Knickerbocker*, a photograph's "perfection almost transcends the bounds of sober belief." "There is not an object, even the most minute," he continued, "which was not in the original and it is impossible that one should have been omitted. Think of that!" And it was utterly *complete*. John Robison reported to the Edinburgh Society in 1839, with some wonder, after he saw his first daguerreotypes, that "the perfection and fidelity of the pictures are such that on examining them with the microscopic power, details are discovered which are not perceivable to the eye in the original objects."[11] The lens saw "all that the all-beholding sun could see"; the human eye could study the result indefinitely and still not see it all.

Photographs not only reproduced scenes and objects in astonishing completeness, but did so with "absolute accuracy" and "perfect fidelity."

8. For further discussion, see the essays in Jonathan Green, ed., *The Snapshot: Aperture #19* (New York, 1974). Sensitized gelatin plates (which allowed the camera to stop action), anastigmat lenses, roll film, hand-held cameras, and mass production, all of which appeared between 1878 and 1890, were among such innovations.

9. Morse's letter and other reports of Daguerre's exhibition were reprinted in *United States Magazine and Democratic Review*, V (May, 1839), 517–520.

10. Quoted in Helmut Gernsheim, *Creative Photography* (New York, 1942), p. 25; Beaumont Newhall, *Photography 1839–1937* (New York, 1937), p. 23; and "The Pencil of the Sun," *Living Age*, XXVIII (Feb., 1851), 296.

11. These and other quotations appear in Robert Taft, *Photography and the American Scene* (New York, 1943), pp. 3, 11, 15; Beaumont Newhall, *The Latent Image* (Garden City, N.Y., 1967), pp. 84–85; and Helmut and Alison Gernsheim, *L. J. M. Daguerre* (Cleveland, 1956), p. 86.

Photographs were *real, true,* or as close to reality and truth as one could possibly get. Reporting on a photographic exhibition, a commentator in *Living Age* wrote, "This is no fiction . . . but *Nature* herself we behold"; *Niles' Register,* remarking on Daguerre's pictures, thought "the representation immaculate . . . nothing could be possibly more *true.*" A photograph was an analogue of reality, to be used as source of information, stimulus to memory, or aid to reflection.[12]

A photograph, in other words, represented to the nineteenth century a new version of visual truth. Seeing a thing and seeing a picture of it were readily accepted as substantially the same. The camera was direct visual perception; it provided objective, authentic experience: it gave form the same visibility and permanence that print gave thought. All the various kinds of images presented by the customary media—painting, engraving, lithography, and the like—were immediately superseded by this incredibly exact, detailed way of seeing. Here, in the photograph, was reality.

The popular conviction that the camera was a scientifically reliable machine which precisely replicated reality, had profound influence on nineteenth-century concepts of the true and the real. One could trust the photographic image as one could trust the original. The "truthful sunbeam" (as O. W. Holmes called it) "transformed shadows into substance," and almost magically turned light into reality. Holmes clearly articulated the intimate relationship between picture and reality. When one has a photograph of something, he wrote, the thing is no longer needed—the negative contains and preserves its reality: "Form is henceforth divorced from matter. In fact, matter as a visible object is of no great use any longer. . . . Give us a few negatives of a thing worth seeing, taken from various points of view, and that is all we want of it. Pull it down or burn it up, as you please."[13]

The swift progress of phototechnology, of course, made the photograph's presumed truthfulness even more convincing. To the contemporary mind, the camera's objectivity was one of its more thought-provoking qualities. It was the first medium to provide accurate, repeatable information directly to the user. Other methods of transmitting visual information involved human intervention, whereas the photograph (except for the developing process) apparently excluded the human element. Since people trusted technology, they trusted the camera.[14] "There is an instinct in every unwarped mind," wrote a reviewer in the *Westminster Review,* "which prefers truth to extravagance, and a photographic picture . . . is a pleasanter

---

12. "Pencil of the Sun," p. 297; *Niles' National Register,* May 9, 30, 1840.

13. "The Stereoscope and the Stereograph," p. 747.

14. The photograph's "mechanical exactness, beyond the power of eye or pencil," and the implications of its "great power of multiplication" particularly impressed the writer of "Progress of the Photograph," *Eclectic Magazine,* XXXI (Aug., 1854), 506.

subject in the eyes of most people (were they brave enough to admit it) than many a piece of mythology."[15]

The implications of this struck the mind of the age like a bomb. No longer was it the imagination that created reality; the camera did it, swiftly and accurately, in endless duplication. Romantic poets and painters and philosophers might argue that they alone could know truth, intuitively or otherwise, but here was a machine, based on invincible laws of chemistry and optics, that directly, objectively, and in devastating detail reproduced the exact, real world without the aid of the creative imagination at all. A photograph or a collection of them (a trip to Niagara Falls or a family picnic) produced an alternate world that was far more "true" and "real" than anything poet, painter, or novelist could ever fashion.[16]

From the beginning, then, the nineteenth century treated the photograph as authentic experience. The lens saw more than the human eye and saw it more truthfully. If a photograph showed that someone or something looked a certain way, then the viewer knew that that was how it "really" looked. If the sun and the lens and a sensitized plate agreed on something's appearance, no one could disagree. On the other hand, as familiarity with the medium spread and photographers proliferated, more sophisticated discussions of "truth" and "reality" began to appear in the journals. Was simple reproduction of what the lens saw the whole truth? No, said some; duplication alone, however accurate, "does not of itself insure a *perfect* transcript of reality." The photographer must select, choose, arrange—he must himself be deeply involved if the result is to be something truer and more real than mere replication.[17] Photographers themselves emphasized more and more the importance of individual choice in selecting a subject, choosing the right moment to photograph it, and manipulating angle, light, and development. They were not averse to calling this an art.[18]

Debates over the camera's "truth" set off an argument between painting and photography that continued, with considerable heat, through the century and into the next. No one in the nineteenth century (nor in the twentieth) was able to produce a satisfactory test for either the truth or reality of a photograph. But beginning with Daguerre, people learned to

15. "The Progress of Fiction as an Art," *Westminster Review*, LX (Oct., 1853), 187–188. The reviewer may have been George Eliot.

16. Alexander Black, in 1896, recommended creating novels by photographs alone, eliminating the text, and tried it. See "The Camera and the Comedy," *Scribner's*, XX (Dec., 1896), 604–610.

17. For example, see Marcus Root, *The Camera and the Pencil: or the Heliographic Art* (Philadelphia, 1864), p. 437. Root differentiated between photographic "artists" and "mere mechanics"; see also his discussion of the differences between photographers and painters, pp. 437–439.

18. Herman Vogel's chapter, "On the Correctness of Photography," in *The Chemistry of Light and Photography* (New York, 1875), is an interesting discussion of this point.

see the world as the lens saw it and generally to trust the photographic image. As one writer remarked in 1867, "The term has now become idiomatic in our language, that a truthful transcript of a thing is 'photographic' in its resemblance." One of the most potent qualities of the photograph, as the era perceived it, was its credibility, a conviction which influenced in a multitude of ways how man subsequently looked at himself and the world.[19]

The Self was one of the Romantics' great discoveries. In the late eighteenth century men's interest began to turn inward; self-consciousness, introspection, subjectivity pervaded all modes of thought. The final step in the development of self-awareness took place around 1800, when everyone seems to have stood aside, looked at and within himself, explored his connections with the outside world, and contemplated the quality and extent of his inner experience.[20] The nineteenth century was obsessed by self-study, and the photograph supplied a new and effective instrument with which to engage in it. Daguerre's invention came at exactly the right time to satisfy the Romantic need for self-contemplation.

The photograph—in its early stages the daguerreotype—provided an inexpensive, accurate, portable account of one's self. It was a much better and more convenient medium of self-delineation than the portrait paintings, miniatures, silhouettes, pantagraph copies, or physniocratic drawings then available. How one looked told what one was; nothing could have been more helpful than a photograph in the study of character, one's own or another's. As a writer remarked in 1846: "Daguerreotypes properly regarded, are the indices of human character. Lavater judged of men by their physiognomies and in a voluminous treatise has developed the principles by which he was guided. The photograph one considers to be the grand climacteric of that science . . . hence postures, attitudes, and expressions of countenance are so many exponential signs of dispositions, designs, character."[21]

Technical improvements came swiftly—calotypes, ambrotypes, tintypes, wet plates, dry plates—so that within a few years almost anyone could have his picture taken easily and cheaply. Improvements in chemicals, lenses, and development processes by the mid-forties reduced exposure

19. "Photography: Its History and Application," *Living Age*, XCII (1867), 210. See the history of these discussions in Aaron Scharf, *Creative Photography* (New York and London, 1965), pp. 14–15, 28–35, passim, and his extensive bibliography. See also I. H. Adams' amusing article, "Photography, the Munchausen of the Arts," *Outing*, XVI (1896), 476–478, in which he nominates the camera as "supreme Prince of Liars."

20. Relatively few autobiographies, for example, were published before 1800; a bibliography of nineteenth-century autobiographies would fill a large volume. A photograph was, in effect, a capsule autobiography.

21. "Daguerreotypy," *Living Age*, IX (June 20, 1846), 552.

times from 10 or 15 minutes to 2 or 3. The invention of the carte de visite method in 1854 made it possible to record a series of poses on a single plate and expanded the marketability of the portrait enormously.[22]

A major attraction of the photographic portrait was its truthfulness. It was "a facial map" of "accurate landmarks and expressions," by which to measure a person "in perfect certainty that the ground plan is founded on fact." It was the closest thing to the real person, possessed of what Elizabeth Barrett called "an association and sense of nearness." It was also a permanent image; as Miss Barrett added, a photographic portrait was "the *very shadow of the person,* lying there fixed forever." This sense of permanence and actuality added immeasurably to the portrait's impact on the viewer. Painters might adapt and idealize; a camera did not. It produced "not only likenesses, but faithful representations. . . . The observer cannot help feeling he is in the presence of a living, acting organism."[23]

By reason of its illusion of authenticity, photography individualized people. Even if idealized and retouched, a photograph contradicted any concept of human stereotypes. Shown by the camera, great statesmen did not always fit the image; laborers did not always look like laborers, generals like generals, criminals like criminals—or for that matter, royalty like royalty. The rumpled skirt, bulbous nose, ample bosom, or straggling mustache could quickly turn an abstraction into an individual. If one needed proof in an age of democratic revolution that society was not a mass but a collection of particularized individuals, each with his or her own singularity, the photograph supplied it. One could no longer generalize so easily about humanity, or establish "typical" categories. Thus an extremely high proportion of nineteenth-century photographs were

---

22. The carte de visite was a small, postcard-sized photograph given as a present, exchanged with friends, or kept as a memento. Its popularity was enormous; albums to hold it, manufactured by the millions, graced hall and parlor tables in most American homes. See "Cartes de visite," *Living Age* LXXII, (1862), 673–676, and Holmes' remarks on their popularity in *Atlantic Monthly,* XII (July, 1863), 1–15. There were a number of interesting experiments in portrait photography in the fifties and sixties. "Diamond Cameos" put together four small portraits, representing four different views of the face, which were then punched into convexity to resemble relief. There was also an attempt to imitate sculpture by a series of photographs taken all around the sitter, which were then copied by a pantagraph arm in modelling clay; the system never worked satisfactorily, but the series combined all the photos to give an illusion of three dimensions. The binocular stereograph portrait did work well. The large cabinet-size photograph was also tremendously popular by the fifties.

23. Quoted in Colin Ford and Ray Strong, *An Early Victorian Album* (London, 1974), p. 43. It soon became obvious, as generations of painters already knew, that sitters did not always want absolute accuracy. Photographers quickly began to arrange lighting and poses; by the fifties they were routinely retouching plates so that the results would conform more closely to subjects' tastes and to contemporary ideals of feminine and masculine attractiveness.

portraits, for a photograph was a nearly perfect way of discovering one's nature and of establishing one's identity.[24]

The photographic portrait, in addition to its value as a self-revelation, had yet another function, that of revealing one's self to another. You had your own picture taken to contemplate yourself, certainly, but you could also give it to another so that he or she might know and remember you, too. The picture itself was but one element in a complicated set of relationships that developed among photographer, subject, and viewer. Everyone involved was aware that the purpose of the picture was essentially analytical, intended to reveal the personality of the subject as well as reflect his appearance. Good photographers knew the value of lighting, dress, posture, props, and background in the process; they also recognized the importance of finding the precise instant at which the expression of the face and position of the body best revealed the sitter's character. The good photographer, remarked a critic in 1862, must have "a sense of beauty and instinctive art of catching the best momentary pose" to give the picture "a distinctive character of its own."[25] No less than the portrait painter, the photographer aimed to fix the image of the person, fully, realistically, perceptively. Quite genuinely, the nineteenth century was convinced that photography, better than any other medium, searched out and revealed a person's true nature. "A good photograph," according to a writer in *Living Age*, "often possesses a subtlety of resemblance which brings out characteristics . . . scarcely seen in the individual, but which undoubtedly exist."[26]

Poses chosen by the photographer were intended to illustrate the sitter's "inner nature." Certain poses came to symbolize certain personal qualities, and photographers developed long catalogues of poses from which they selected those which best represented the sitter's character.[27] Settings provided additional information—statuary, drapes, background drops, books, furniture, and the like. The paraphernalia of one's vocation or profession showed who and what the subject was. Blacksmiths, bakers,

24. One Worcester, Mass., portrait photographer in 1845 advertised that he had made 6,000 daguerreotypes the previous year, about 500 a month. Some of the larger photographic studios had twenty or more employees, and the plate went from polisher to sensitizer to cameraman to gilder to tinter in true assembly line fashion.

25. "Cartes de visite," p. 675. "The difference between a good photographic portrait and a bad one," the writer continues, "is *not* a mere mechanical trick," but the result of thoughtful skill.

26. "Photography: Its History and Applications," p. 209. Hawthorne's plot of *The House of The Seven Gables* of course pivots on this belief; Hawthorne thought the camera had "wonderful insight" which "actually brings out the secret character with a truth no painter would ever venture upon, even could he detect it."

27. Hands, for example, were considered to be particularly important symbols. See Braive, *The Photograph*, chap. 4. Donald D. Keyes, "The Daguerreotype's Popularity in America," *Art Journal*, XXVI (Winter 1976–1977), 116–122, is an excellent survey.

shoemakers, and others were often photographed in work clothes with the tools of their trade; lawyers might hold an open book, ship owners a compass, a merchant a ledger.

Naturally, given the opportunity, people could help the camera—if it could not lie—at least to exaggerate a bit. With the proper pose and props and the assistance of a resourceful photographer, one might appear to be something he was not, which itself could implicitly reveal something of what he was. Having one's picture taken was an ego-inflating act, based on the assumption that one was sufficiently important for himself and others to see. The pretentious scholar posed with hand to brow; the inept musician held a sheet of music he might not be able to play, the timid man could look fierce and the crook pious; rings, watches, baubles, and fine clothes showed pretentious affluence.[28]

Later in the century, as the art became more sophisticated and technology improved, one could even act out one's fantasies in the studio. A man might be photographed as explorer with pith helmet and pack, as hunter in the West with a buffalo robe and gun, as traveller in Russia with fur hat and sleigh. Women might be oriental beauties in Chinese robes, Roman matrons, English nobility, Greek princesses. Or one could be photographed at a dramatic moment, as if acting a part in a tableau vivant. Here the portrait took on a narrative cast, one's choice of role serving as another index to his character. The nineteenth-century portrait, then, carried a great deal of information; it told what one was, where he belonged in society, and what he dreamed of. Studied and properly interpreted, it personalized him, analyzed him, and placed him in human and social context.

Another discovery of the Romantic philosophers was Memory, handmaiden to the imagination and vital element in the creative process. To the Romantics, memory furnished the essential connection between then and now, what was and what is. It occurred immediately to some of the era's more astute observers that a photograph was quite literally memory. Oliver Wendell Holmes' imaginative name for Daguerre's invention, "mirror with a memory," and other names—"frozen memory," "second memory," and the like—testified how quickly the age recognized the camera's implications. If one drew art from "emotion recollected in tranquillity," the photograph was a substantive recall of the experience that evoked the emotion. Memory was a way of defeating time, and the photograph supplied a palpable, concrete piece of the past preserved in the present.

W. H. F. Talbot was first inspired to experiment with photography by the possibility of stopping time. Looking at natural scenes with a camera

---

28. This aspect of portrait photography is treated with delightful wit in "Daguerreotypy," pp. 551–552.

obscura, he pondered on these "creations of a moment, and destined as rapidly to fade away. . . . The idea occurred to me, how charming it would be if it were possible to cause these natural images to imprint themselves durably, and remain fixed upon the paper."[29] Another critic looked with wonder at a picture of the Seine, noting that a breeze had rippled the water for a single instant in 1840—yet there it was, made permanent. Significantly, Daguerre himself, on seeing his first successful picture, cried out, "I have seized the fleeting light and imprisoned it!" and the newspaper accounts of his 1839 exhibition marvelled at the fact that his plates caught "the fugitive and impalpable." In Holmes' words, the photograph "fixed the most fleeting of our illusions, that which the apostle and the philosopher and the poet alike have used as the type of instability and unreality."[30] Quite literally, then, the camera conquered chronology, a mind-shattering concept suddenly thrust into the framework of Romantic thought. The lens caught the instant "when all life and motion, for a time apparently suspended . . . the moment captured . . . nothing omitted or neglected."[31]

The fact that a photograph fixed a moment fascinated the age. By stopping time, one could obtain insight into the events too ephemeral to permit study and reflection. A photograph gave one a kind of control, hitherto impossible, over the transitory moments of experience; they could be trapped and studied, their meanings assessed, their contexts and relationships examined. Via the photograph, it was now possible as never before to explore the implications of past events. To a meditative, introspective age, few things could be more important.

In thus defeating time, the camera allowed man at least a partial victory over age and death, a fact the nineteenth century was quick to reflect upon. Holmes, for example, pointed out that photographs were "faithful memorials of those we love" and that even if they departed, as they must, their duplicate remained—"How these shadows last, and how their originals fade away!"[32] Photographing the dead became a fairly widespread custom (not to sell, but for members of the family and friends) and such mortuary mementos soon replaced the death mask.

The photograph, because of its association with past experience and emotion, was (and still is) associated with the souvenir, another mani-

29. W. H. Fox Talbot, *The Pencil of Nature* (London, 1844), p. 6. This was the first book to be illustrated with photographs. The camera obscura was a box fitted with a lens that threw an image on a small screen where it could be traced on paper.

30. "Photogenic Drawing," *United States Magazine and Democratic Review*, V (May, 1839), 516; Holmes, "The Stereoscope and the Stereograph," p. 738.

31. "The Pencil of the Sun," p. 301.

32. "Sun Painting and Sun Sculpture," p. 18. He suggested that photographic records be kept of persons from childhood to old age, not merely as keepsakes but as aids to "the physiologist and moralist," since they provided documentary evidence of the aging process and the reflection of character in the features. "Doings of a Sunbeam," pp. 8–10.

festation of the Romantic preoccupation with memory. A photograph, because of its documentary quality, was obviously the best kind of souvenir—derived from a particular, personal experience; capable of recalling all the emotions connected with that experience; repeating the experience itself. Like the souvenir, it retained experience—"I was there," the photograph says, "at this place at this time." The introduction of roll film and the snapshot camera, of course, swiftly made the photo-souvenir omnipresent in Western society.33 Photography was fundamentally a new way of seeing, completely fascinating to an age already deeply interested in theories of perception and cognition. The invention of the camera loosed a tremendous flood of images on the world, the opening of the final phase of a movement toward mass communication that began with printing in the fifteenth century.34 The printed page, for four centuries the primary vehicle for transferring information, was now challenged by the photograph, the first visual medium to give precise, repeatable information "not subject to the omissions, the distortions, and the subjective difficulties" inherent in other media.35 As a result, the knowledge supplied by a photograph (or so it seemed) could be trusted absolutely, ratifying the old adage that "seeing is believing." "Each photograph," affirmed a writer in the *Eclectic Magazine* in 1854, "tells a *true* tale concerning a particular spot at a particular time."

For this reason, photography introduced the public to a different set of expectations concerning the transfer of information. As William Ivins has said, "Up to that time very few people had been aware of the difference between pictorial expression and pictorial communication of statements of fact. The profound difference between creating something and making a statement about the quality and character of something had not been perceived." 36 This change in expectations was noted by a writer in *Harper's* in 1856, who remarked on how one looked differently at a painting and a

33. George Eastman in 1892 noted that for every person interested in serious photography there were probably a thousand who simply wanted "personal pictures or memoranda of their everyday life, objects, places or people that interest them in travel, etc." An excellent discussion of the souvenir is that of Dean McCannell, *The Tourist* (New York, 1976), pp. 119–120.

34. Moving pictures and television are merely extensions of the camera and phonograph, inventions which appeared less than fifty years apart in the nineteenth century.

35. William Ivins, *Prints and Visual Communication* (London, 1953), p. 122. Ivins' book and James J. Gibson's *Perception of the Visual World* (London, 1950) are the key studies of photography and information theory. Information transfer involves a channel (the physical medium), a code (the structure imposed on the message), and a codifier (which imposes the structure). Theoretically, photography eliminates the codifier and obtains the coded message directly. Precamera communication codes were line-and-dot, such as etching, lithography, engraving, mezzotint, printing, and the like.

36. *Visual Communication*, p. 305. Jussim's elaboration of Ivins' view, pp. 305–308, is important for a full understanding of this aspect of communications theory as it relates to photography.

photograph, and how one anticipated separate kinds of information from each.

> We look with a very different eye on the representation of some architectural subject, or even landscape, when it has been sketched by a painter or taken by the photographer. In the latter case we minutely examine every detail, which presents an indescribable charm to us because we know that mere imagination had nothing to do with its presence, but that it is there because it is a fac-simile—a *truth*.[37]

In other words, the distinction between creating and reporting—between an imitation and a replication of the thing—was clarified by the camera. An engraving or lithograph, for example, was a creation, subject to codifier distortions and other inadequacies; a photograph was a document. Both were technological means of transmitting information, but a photograph distorted the message least—or to its earliest partisans, not at all. The new impact of this new set of expectations in how people "saw," was undoubtedly tremendous, and is as yet comparatively uninvestigated.

Scientists enthusiastically endorsed the new medium. Archeologists, astronomers, architects, engineers, medical researchers, and others found immediate use for it and praised the camera's "accuracy, fidelity, and facility," certain it was "one of the greatest boons at the disposal of scientific man." As early as 1842 cameras were used to prepare sales catalogues and business inventories; salesmen later carried photographs instead of samples. The camera's usefulness in police work was self-evident; police departments soon built up criminal files and some courts predicted acceptance of photographic evidence.[38] As photographic technology improved—better lenses, dry-plates, smaller cameras, reduced exposure times—camera work became easier and more precise. Photographs provided unmatchable records of people, objects, scenes, events—a unique method of capturing and storing information about everything at which one could point a lens.

Journalists quickly recognized the camera's potential but the necessary technology for reproducing photographs did not arrive until the eighties. Newspaper artists had developed lithography and engraving to a high art,

---

37. "On the Application of Photography to Printing," *Harper's New Monthly Magazine*, XIII (Sept., 1856), 433. This is a review of John W. Draper's *Human Physiology*, the first book in an exact science to be illustrated by photographs.

38. Representative articles are "Photography as an Aid to Science," *Nature*, VI (May 23, 1872); J. Wells Champney, "Fifty Years of Photography," *Harper's New Monthly Magazine*, LXXIX (July, 1889), 357–362; "Recent Photographic Invention," *North American Review*, CLXII (July, 1896), 375–376. Champney reported that police files in the United States contained over 100,000 photographs of criminals. See also "Photography as Social Documentation," in *The Beginnings of Photography*, a catalog prepared for the Victoria and Albert Exhibition of 1972 (London, 1972). Curiously enough, *Blackwood's* (April, 1842) could see at that time "no practical use at all" for Daguerre's invention and recommended ignoring it.

and photomechanical processes available prior to the eighties were less satisfactory to readers than the reproductions to which they were accustomed.[39] After the perfection of the half-tone in the eighteen-eighties, using photographs in newspapers was comparatively easy, making it possible almost to catch the event as it happened.[40] The results were (and are) of great cultural and social importance; first, because the photograph transmitted current information (in television the transmission is instant); second, because it distributed increasingly greater amounts of information to the public; and third, because the picture possessed an inbuilt simultaneity that engravings or prints did not have. This last had powerful (if unconscious) influence on the quality of information furnished by a newspaper photograph. The engraver, for example, although working from sketches made on the spot, was removed from the event; the photographer was included in it by his presence. Thus a photograph involved the viewer, too, as an engraving could not. The artists and technicians who produced the engraving or lithograph always intervened between event and viewers; no matter how accurate the drawing, it lacked the photograph's immediacy. An engraving depended on the artist's memory; he could not record all the details of a moment, so he usually recorded the basic information in his sketch book and filled in the details later. The practice was, in fact, for the artist to add figures, objects, and landscape details to the original eyewitness sketch in order to give his viewers a sense of actuality he could not directly record.

The nineteenth-century viewer knew these things and had long before learned how to "read" an engraving, a drawing, or a painting. A photograph presented him with a new problem, for it could not be "read" in the same way. A Brady or Gardner photograph of a Civil War battlefield, compared to an Alfred Waud sketch of it, conveyed information of quite different quality and required a different way of seeing it. The public soon became accustomed to the new medium, but the implications of its new ways of transferring information have not been fully understood or explored. The arrival of modern photojournalism may be conveniently dated

39. The Crimean War was the first photographed war, but not for the newspapers. Several daguerreotypes exist of cavalrymen, taken during the Mexican War of 1846–1847. Brady, O'Sullivan, Gardner, and others brought the Civil War directly to the public, the first time a war was so covered by photographers, though newspapers still depended largely on artists and sketches. The first real on-the-spot journalistic photographs were probably those taken by Platt Babbitt in 1853, who took several views of a man trapped in the current above Niagara Falls, swept over to his death after eighteen hours.

40. The first newspaper half-tone to be printed in conjunction with a news story was apparently Henry Newton's of New York's shantytown in the *New York Daily Graphic*, March 4, 1880. *Harper's* in March, 1899, used thirty-five photographs and eight drawings; *Leslie's*, forty-four photos and three drawings. The first daily paper to be entirely illustrated by photographs was probably the *London Daily Mirror* in January, 1904. The half-tone of course created a whole new advertising industry.

from the work of Jacob Riis, Lewis Hine, and others in the eighties.

Meanwhile, the use of captions added another dimension to the photographic message. A caption related the photograph to the text and gave date, place, and context; it served the viewer as a guide to its content and helped to determine his attitude toward it.[41] No longer was a photograph presumed to speak for itself. Soon newspapers and magazines were printing photographs in sequence to "tell a story," leading eventually to the publication of the picture magazine whose purpose was solely that. There was much for the nineteenth century to record. Trains, bridges, buildings, streets, houses, machines, natural wonders—things and scenes, people working, playing, living, dying—and no other medium could record them so well and truthfully as the camera. Nineteenth-century photographers, who had no preconceived biases about what one should or should not take pictures of, simply photographed it all. Thus America documented itself.

41. See Braive, *The Photograph*, chap. 10, for a discussion of journalistic photography; Arthur Rothstein, "Photojournalism: Its First 100 Years," *New York Times*, May 2, 1976, is a good summary. The most sophisticated treatments of captions appear in the work of Jean Keim and Roland Barthes in France. See Keim's essay "La photographie et sa légende," in *Communications #2* (Paris, 1963), pp. 41–55; and Barthes' "Le message photographique," *Communications #1* (Paris, 1960–1961), pp. 127–138.

Contributors

GAY WILSON ALLEN, A.B., M.A., and Doctor of Literature (1975), Duke University, is Emeritus Professor of English at New York University. His principal publications include a study of American prosody and biographies of Walt Whitman and William James; he is coeditor of the *Collected Writings of Walt Whitman*.

GEORGE ARMS is Professor Emeritus of English at The University of New Mexico, where he joined the faculty in 1944. He is the author of many studies in American poetry, fiction, and criticism and has served on numerous editorial boards, including that of *A Selected Edition of W. D. Howells*.

SACVAN BERCOVITCH, Professor of English and Comparative Literature at Columbia University, has written extensively on American Puritanism and its legacy in American life and literature, most recently in *The Puritan Origins of the American Self* and *The American Jeremiad*.

WALTER BLAIR is Professor Emeritus of English at The University of Chicago, where he first began teaching in 1929. His publications in the field of American humor and of literary realism include important studies of the work of Mark Twain. He is, most recently, coauthor of *America's Humor from Poor Richard to Doonesbury* (1978).

RICHARD BEALE DAVIS is Alumni Distinguished Service Professor of American Literature, Emeritus, at The University of Tennessee, where he began teaching in 1947. He has written widely on the intellectual life of the colonial South and the literature of the early republic. He recently published, in three volumes, *Intellectual Life in the Colonial South, 1585–1763*, winner of the 1979 National Book Award in history.

L. S. DEMBO has written on a broad range of topics in twentieth-century American literature, including, most notably, studies of Hart Crane, Ezra Pound, and contemporary poetry and criticism. Since 1965 he has been Professor of English at the University of Wisconsin, Madison, where he is also editor of *Contemporary Literature*.

BERNARD DUFFEY, Professor of English at Duke University, has written on the Chicago renaissance and twentieth-century American poetry and criticism. In 1978 he published *Poetry in America: Expression and Its Values in the Times of Bryant, Whitman, and Pound.*

RICHARD HARTER FOGLE is University Distinguished Professor of English at The University of North Carolina in Chapel Hill. He has written chiefly on American and British romanticism, including studies of Keats, Shelley, Coleridge, Hawthorne, and Melville. In 1974 he published *The Permanent Pleasure: Essays on Classics of Romanticism.*

C. HUGH HOLMAN is Kenan Professor of English at The University of North Carolina in Chapel Hill, where he has also served as Dean of the Graduate School, Provost, and Special Assistant to the Chancellor. His publications include numerous studies of southern fiction, particularly the work of Simms, Wolfe, and Faulkner.

TERENCE MARTIN is the author of *The Instructed Vision, Nathaniel Hawthorne,* and other studies of American fiction of both the nineteenth and twentieth centuries. He is Professor of English at Indiana University, where he joined the faculty in 1954.

RUSSEL B. NYE is Distinguished Professor of English at Michigan State University. He has written extensively on American literature, history, and popular culture. His biography of George Bancroft was awarded a Pulitzer Prize in 1945. In 1974 he published *Society and Culture in America, 1830–1860.*

DONALD PIZER has written on Hamlin Garland, Frank Norris, and other authors of realistic fiction of the late nineteenth century in America. In 1976 he published *The Novels of Theodore Dreiser: A Critical Study.* He is Pierce Butler Professor of English in Newcomb College, Tulane University.

JOHN SEELYE, Alumni Distinguished Professor at The University of North Carolina in Chapel Hill, is the author of numerous studies of American fiction. In 1977 he published *Prophetic Waters: The River in Early American Life and Literature.*

LEWIS P. SIMPSON is William A. Read Professor of English Literature and coeditor of *The Southern Review* at Louisiana State University, Baton Rouge. His literary studies have focussed on southern literature, the literature of the early republic, and the vocation of literature in America.

ROBERT E. SPILLER, Felix E. Schelling Emeritus Professor of English Literature at the University of Pennsylvania, is well known for his studies of Cooper and Emerson. He is Past President of the American Studies Association and Chairman of the Editorial Board of *Literary History of the United States*.

WALTER SUTTON has written chiefly in the field of modern American poetry and criticism, including, in 1973, *American Free Verse: The Modern Revolution in Poetry*. He is Distinguished Professor of Humanities at Syracuse University.

DARWIN T. TURNER, Professor of English and Head of Afro-American Studies at The University of Iowa, is the editor of collections of Afro-American writing and the author, in 1971, of *In a Minor Chord: Three Afro-American Writers and Their Search for Identity*.

Arlin Turner: Vita

Born in Abilene, Texas, November 25, 1909

Military service
> U.S. Naval Reserve, 1942–1946, Lt.(j.g.) to Lt. Cdr.; Secretary of the Navy Citation

Education
> B.A., West Texas State University, 1927
> M.A., University of Texas, 1930
> Ph.D., University of Texas, 1934

Teaching
> University of Texas, 1934–36 (Instructor)
> Louisiana State University, 1936–53 (Instructor to Professor)
> Duke University, 1953–74 (Professor); 1974–79 (James B. Duke Professor); Chairman, Department of English, 1958–64
> State University of New York at Albany, Spring semester 1978 (Visiting Professor)

Foreign
> University of Montreal, 1951
> University of Western Australia, 1952 (Fulbright)
> University of Bombay, 1964
> University of Hull, 1966–67 (Fulbright)

Summer
> Duke University, 1947, 1948, 1949, 1953
> University of Colorado, 1951
> University of Texas, 1957
> University of Virginia, 1958
> University of Illinois, 1961
> University of Iowa, 1962
> New York University, 1963
> University of Pennsylvania, 1968

Awards
> Guggenheim Fellowships, 1947–48, 1959–60
> Huntington Library Research Award, 1969
> American Council of Learned Societies Grant-in-aid, 1972
> Senior Fellowship, National Endowment for the Humanities, 1973–74

Huntington Library—National Endowment for the Humanities Fellowship, 1977

Phi Beta Kappa (Honorary), 1965

Sydnor Award of the Southern Historical Association for the best book in Southern history for the years 1956 and 1957 (for *George W. Cable: A Biography*)

James B. Duke Professorship, Duke University, 1974

Doctor of Humane Letters (Berea College), 1976

Honorary Fellow, Poe Studies Association, 1977

Affiliations, Offices, and Assignments

American Literature, Managing Editor, 1954–63; Editor, 1969–79

The South Atlantic Quarterly: Member, Editorial Board, 1956–79

The Arlington Quarterly: Member, Advisory Editorial Board, 1967–

The Southern Literary Journal: Member, Advisory Editorial Board, 1968–

Resources for American Literary Study: Member, Advisory Editorial Board, 1970–

Studies in American Humor: Member, Advisory Editorial Board, 1974–

Georgia Review: Member, Advisory and Contributing Editorial Board, 1975–

Abstracts of Popular Culture (Past), Member, Advisory Board, 1976

Modern Language Association of America

American Literature Section: Secretary, 1949–53; Chairman, 1966–67

Twentieth-Century American Literature Division: Member, Executive Committee, 1977–

Chairmen of Departments of English: Member, Executive Committee, 1962–64

Scholar's Library: Member, Selection Committee, 1968–71

Center for Editions of American Authors

Organizing Committee: Member, 1962–63

Panel of Textual Consultants: Member, 1966–

Edition of the Works of George W. Cable: Member, Editorial Board, 1967–

American Studies Association:

Member, Advisory Council, 1955–57; 1967–72

Member, Executive Committee, 1958–59

Vice-President, 1969–70

Southeastern American Studies Association: Vice-President, 1955–56; 1968–70; President, 1956–57; 1970–72

South Atlantic Modern Language Association: Chairman, American Literature Section, 1956–57

National Endowment for the Humanities
    Chairman, Fellowship Selection Committee, 1968–72 (for younger scholars)
    Member, Advisory Panel on Media Programs, 1976

Phi Beta Kappa: Member, Selection Committee for the Ralph Waldo Emerson Prize, 1969–71

Society for the Study of Southern Literature: Member, Executive Committee, 1968–74, 1978; Vice-President, 1971–73; President, 1973–74

Conference Board of Associated Research Councils: Fulbright Selection Committee for American Studies: Member, 1956–60; 1962–63; 1967–68; Chairman, 1957–60

American Council of Learned Societies
    Regional Associate, 1956–67
    Fellowship Selection Committee, Member, 1962–63; 1965–66

Graduate Record Examination: Member, Committee for Literature, 1965–67

National Council of Teachers of English
    Director, 1961–64
    Director, Commission on Literature, 1964–66

Nathaniel Hawthorne Society: Advisory Board, Member, 1974–76; Vice-President, 1977–

North Carolina Literary and Historical Society: Vice-President, 1976–77

Dissertations directed at Louisiana State University
    1943 Richard M. Weaver. The Confederate South, 1865–1910: A Study in the Survival of a Mind and a Culture
    1952 Winfred S. Emmons, Jr. The Materials and Methods of American Horror Fiction in the Nineteenth Century
        Frank T. Meriwether. The Rogue in the Humor of the Old Southwest
    1953 Lee Miller. Ralph Waldo Emerson and the Bible
        Milton Rickels. Thomas Bangs Thorpe
        James Colvert. Stephen Crane: The Development of His Art

Dissertations directed at Duke University
    1960 Norman Eugene Hoyle. Melville as a Magazinist
    1961 Louise Young Gossett. Violence in Recent Southern Fiction

1962 Dewayne August Patterson. Poe's Grotesque Humor: A Study of
the Grotesque Effects in His Humorous Tales

Francis Edwin Skipp. Thomas Wolfe and His Scribner's Editors

1963 Walter Paschal Reeves, Jr. Race and Nationality in the Works
of Thomas Wolfe

1964 Michael Daniel True. The Social and Literary Criticism of
Randolph Bourne: A Study of His Development as a Writer

Mary Ann Wimsatt. The Comic Sense of William Gilmore
Simms: A Study of the Humor in His Fiction and Drama

1965 David Eugene Whisnant. James Boyd, 1888–1944: A Literary
Biography

1966 Frank Mark Davis. Herman Melville and the Nineteenth-
Century Church Community

Robert Dorset Graves. Polarity in the Shorter Fiction of Herman
Melville

Jerry Allen Herndon. Social Comment in the Writings of Joel
Chandler Harris

John Harmon McElroy. Images of the Seventeenth-Century
Puritan in American Novels, 1823–1860

James Engel Rocks. The Mind and Art of Caroline Gordon

Calvin Lee Skaggs. Narrative Point of View in Edgar Allan Poe's
Criticism and Fiction

Merrill Maguire Skaggs. The Plain-Folk Tradition in Southern
Local-Color Fiction

Margaret Sue Sullivan. Carson McCullers, 1917–1947: The Conversion of Experience

1968 Frank Gado. Kay Boyle: From the Aesthetics of Exile to the
Polemics of Return

Henry Dunham Herring. The Environment in Robert Penn
Warren's Fictional South

David William Mascitelli. Faulkner's Characters of Sensibility

1969 Robert Bruce Bickley. Literary Influences and Technique in
Melville's Short Fiction, 1853–1856

Larry Wayne Cook. Narrators in the Works of Nathaniel
Hawthorne

Sally Rigsbee Page. Woman in the Works of William Faulkner

Allen Frederick Stein. The Presentation and Criticism of the
American Scene in the Works of Cornelius Mathews

Charles Nelles Watson, Jr. Characters and Characterization in
the Works of Herman Melville

1970 James William Clark. The Tradition of Salem Witchcraft in
American Literature, 1820–1870

Samuel Scoville. The Domestic Motif in Hawthorne: A Study of the House, the Family, and the Home in His Fiction

Harry Carter West. The Atmospherical Medium of Hawthorne's Fiction

1971 William Priestley Black. The *Virginia Gazette*, 1766–1774: Beginnings of an Indigenous Literature

James Louis Gray. The Development of the Early American Short Story to Washington Irving

Walter Bertram Hitchcock. The Achievement of the Forlorn Hope: Pedagogical Portraits in American Literature, 1820–1871

1972 George Stephen Friedman. Reconstruction and Redemption in Selected American Novels, 1878–1915

Jack Charles Meathenia. A Study of the Functional Aspects of Humor in the Works of Nathaniel Hawthorne

Russell Paul Sparling. A Study of Nathaniel Hawthorne's Skeptical Meliorism

1973 Patricia Ann Carlson. Hawthorne's Functional Settings: A Study of Artistic Method

John Gerald Kennedy. The Test of Reason: Realistic Techniques in the Fiction of Edgar Allan Poe

Alton Taylor Loftis. A Study of *Russell's Magazine*: Ante-Bellum Charleston's Last Literary Periodical

Jerome McNeill Loving. Civil War Letters of George Washington Whitman

Arthur John Roche, III. A Literary Gentleman in New York: Evert A. Duyckinck's Relationship with Nathaniel Hawthorne, Herman Melville, Edgar Allan Poe, and William Gilmore Simms

1974 Roberta Brodie Langford. The Comic Sense of Flannery O'Connor

Becky Jon Hayward. Nature Imagery in the Poetry of Herman Melville

Larry John Reynolds. A Study of Herman Melville's Views of Man

Betty Jean Steele. Quaker Characters in Selected American Novels, 1823–1899

1976 John Edwin Holsberry, Jr. Hawthorne and the English Romantic Poets

Bruce Thomas Harper. The Narrative Techniques of Simms's Revolutionary War Romances

Arlin Turner: Bibliography

BOOKS

George W. Cable: A Biography. Durham: Duke University Press, 1956.
xi, 391 pp.; Baton Rouge: Louisiana State University Press, 1966.

Nathaniel Hawthorne: An Introduction and Interpretation. New York:
Barnes & Noble, 1961. x, 149 pp.; New York: Holt, Rinehart & Winston, 1967.

George W. Cable. Southern Writers Series, No. 1. Austin: Steck-Vaughan
Company, 1969. ii, 44 pp.

EDITIONS

*Hawthorne as Editor: Selections from His Writings in The American
Magazine of Useful and Entertaining Knowledge.* Baton Rouge: Louisiana State University Press, 1941. vii, 290 pp.; Folcroft, Pa.: Folcroft
Library Editions, 1969; Port Washington, N. Y.: Kennikat Press, 1972;
Folkestone, Kent: Bailey Brothers and Swinfen, 1972.

Mark Twain and George W. Cable: The Record of a Literary Friendship.
Lansing: Michigan State University Press, 1960. xi, 141 pp.

The Silent South together with The Freedman's Case in Equity, The Convict Lease System, The Appendix to the 1889 Edition, and Eight Uncollected Essays on Prison and Asylum Reform. By George W. Cable.
Patterson Smith Reprint Series in Criminology, Law Enforcement,
and Social Problems, Publication No. 57. Montclair, N. J.: Patterson
Smith, 1969. xxxii, 271 pp.

INTRODUCTIONS, CHAPTERS, OR SECTIONS OF BOOKS

"Hawthorne's Methods of Using His Source Materials," in *Studies for
William A. Read,* ed. Nathaniel M. Caffee and Thomas A. Kirby.
Baton Rouge: Louisiana State University Press, 1940. Pp. 301–312.

Introduction to *The Negro Question: A Selection of Writings on Civil
Rights in the South* by George W. Cable. Garden City, N. Y.: Doubleday & Company, 1958. xx, 257 pp. (paperback), xix, 286 pp. (hardback); New York: W. W. Norton, 1968. xx, 257 pp.

Introduction to *The Blithedale Romance.* By Nathaniel Hawthorne. New
York: W. W. Norton, 1958. 251 pp.

Introduction to *Creoles and Cajuns: Stories of Old Louisiana*. By George W. Cable. Garden City, N. Y.: Doubleday & Company, 1959. 432 pp.

Introduction to *Southern Stories*. New York: Rinehart & Company, 1960. xl, 336 pp.

"The Literature of Reform in America," in *American Studies Conference (Literature and History)*. Chandigarh, India: Panjab University, 1964. Pp. 24–35.

"Recent Scholarship on Hawthorne and Melville," in *The Teacher and American Literature*, ed. Lewis Leary. Champaign, Illinois: National Council of Teachers of English, 1965. Pp. 95–109.

"Teaching Literature in the Space Age," in *New Trends in English Education: Selected Addresses . . .* , ed. David Stryker. Champaign, Illinois: National Council of Teachers of English, 1966. Pp. 83–90.

Introduction to *Chita: A Memory of Last Island*. By Lafcadio Hearn. Southern Literary Classics Series. Chapel Hill: University of North Carolina Press, 1969. xxxiv, 224 pp.

Introduction to *Miss Ravenel's Conversion from Secession to Loyalty*. By John William DeForest. Columbus, Ohio: Charles E. Merrill Publishing Company, 1969. xix, iv, 521 pp.

Introduction to *The Merrill Studies in* The Scarlet Letter. Columbus, Ohio: Charles E. Merrill Publishing Company, 1970. vi, 153 pp.

Introduction to *The Works of George W. Cable*. New York: Garrett Press, 1970 (distributed by MSS Information Corporation, 1972), in each volume: *Old Creole Days*, xxx, 229 pp.; *Bonaventure*, xxix, vii, 314 pp.; *The Creoles of Louisiana*, xxix, ix, 320 pp.; *Strong Hearts*, xxix, 214 pp.; *Dr. Sevier*, xxix, 473 pp.; *John March Southerner*, xxix, viii, 513 pp.

"Poe and Simms: Friendly Critics, Sometime Friends," in *Papers on Poe in Honor of John Ward Ostrom*, ed. Richard P. Veler. Springfield, Ohio: Chantry Music Press, Inc. at Wittenberg University, 1972. Pp. 140–160.

"The Uncertainties of Authorship in the South after the Civil War," in *Popular Literature in America: A Symposium in Honor of Lyon N. Richardson*, ed. James C. Austin and Donald A. Koch. Bowling Green, Ohio: Bowling Green University Popular Press, 1972. Pp. 184–198.

"Consistency in the Mind and Work of Hawthorne," in *The Chief Glory of Every People: Essays on Classic American Writers*, ed. Matthew J. Bruccoli. Carbondale, Illinois: Southern Illinois University Press, 1973. Pp. 97–116.

"Comedy and Reality in Local Color Fiction, 1865–1900," in *The Comic Imagination in American Literature*, ed. Louis D. Rubin, Jr. New Brunswick, N. J.: Rutgers University Press, 1973. Pp. 157–164.

"Dim Pages in Literary History: The South since the Civil War," in *Southern Literary Study: Problems and Possibilities*, ed. Louis D. Rubin, Jr., and C. Hugh Holman. Chapel Hill: University of North Carolina Press, 1975. Pp. 36–47.

"Writing in the New South." Casette #901. Deland, Florida: Everett / Edwards, Inc., 1976.

"Nathaniel Hawthorne," in *The American Renaissance in New England*, ed. Joel Myerson. Vol. 1 of *Dictionary of Literary Biography*, ed. Matthew J. Bruccoli et al. Detroit: Gale Research Co., 1978. Pp. 80–101.

ARTICLES

"A Note on Poe's 'Julius Rodman,' " (Texas) *Studies in English*, X (1930), 147–151.

"Autobiographical Elements in Hawthorne's *The Blithedale Romance*," (Texas) *Studies in English*, XV (1935), 39–62.

"Another Source of Poe's 'Julius Rodman,' " *American Literature*, VIII (March, 1936), 69–70.

"Hawthorne's Literary Borrowings," *PMLA*, LI (June, 1936), 543–562. Reprinted in *American Literature: A Critical Survey*, ed. Thomas D. Young and Ronald E. Fine. New York: American Book Company, 1968. Vol. I, pp. 224–247.

"A Note on Hawthorne's Revisions," *Modern Language Notes*, LI (November, 1936), 426–429.

"Hawthorne as Self-Critic," *The South Atlantic Quarterly*, XXXVII (April, 1938), 132–138.

"Joaquin Miller in New Orleans," *The Louisiana Historical Quarterly*, XXII (January, 1939), 216–222.

"The Southern Novel," *Southwest Review*, XXV (January, 1940), 205–212.

"George Washington Cable's Literary Apprenticeship," *The Louisiana Historical Quarterly*, XXIV (January, 1941), 168–186.

"Writing of Poe's 'The Bells,' " *American Notes & Queries*, II, No. 5 (August, 1942), 73.

"Hawthorne and Reform," *The New England Quarterly*, XV (December, 1942), 700–714.

(With T. O. Mabbott) "Two Poe Hoaxes by the Same Hand?" *American Notes & Queries*, II, No. 10 (January, 1943), 147–148.

"James K. Paulding and Timothy Flint," *The Mississippi Valley Historical Review*, XXXIV (June, 1947), 105–111.

"Sources of Poe's 'A Descent into the Maelstrom,' " *Journal of English and Germanic Philology*, XLVI (July, 1947), 298–301.

(With Lewis Leary) "John Howard Payne in New Orleans," *The Louisiana Historical Quarterly*, XXXI (January, 1948), 110–122.

"Whittier Calls on George W. Cable," *The New England Quarterly*, XXII (March, 1949), 92–96.

"George W. Cable, Novelist and Reformer," *The South Atlantic Quarterly*, XLVIII (October, 1949), 539–545.

"George W. Cable's Beginnings as a Reformer," *Journal of Southern History*, XVII (May, 1951), 135–161.

"Notes on Mark Twain in New Orleans," *The McNeese Review*, VI (1954), 10–22.

"George W. Cable's Revolt against Literary Sectionalism," *Tulane Studies in English*, V (1955), 5–27.

"Mark Twain, Cable, and 'A Professional Newspaper Liar,'" *The New England Quarterly*, XXVIII (March, 1955), 18–33.

"James Lampton, Mark Twain's Model for Colonel Sellers," *Modern Language Notes*, LXX (December, 1955), 592–594.

"Seeds of Literary Revolt in the Humor of the Old Southwest," *The Louisiana Historical Quarterly*, XXXIX (April, 1956), 143–151.

"The Undergraduate Meets Emerson," *Emerson Society Quarterly*, No. 10 (First Quarter, 1958), 11–12.

"Realism and Fantasy in Southern Humor," *The Georgia Review*, XII (Winter, 1958), 451–457.

"The Many Sides of Southern Humor," *The Mississippi Quarterly*, XIII (Fall, 1960), 155–156.

"William Faulkner, Southern Novelist," *The Mississippi Quarterly*, XIV (Summer, 1961), 117–130.

"Trends in American Literary Scholarship: Across an Editor's Desk," *The South Central Bulletin* (of the South Central Modern Language Association), XXXIII, No. 1 (March, 1963), 5, 16–20.

"Nathaniel Hawthorne in American Studies," *College English*, XXVI (November, 1964), 133–139.

"Scholars Discover the Commonwealth Literatures," *Australian Literary Studies*, I (June, 1964), 203–205.

"Literature and the Student in the Space Age," *College English*, XXVII (April, 1966), 519–522.

"William Faulkner and the Literary Flowering in the American South," *The Durham* (England) *University Journal*, LX, No. 2 (n.s. XXIX, No. 2) (March, 1968), 109–118.

"Mark Twain and the South: An Affair of Love and Anger," *The Southern Review*, n.s. IV (Spring, 1968), 493–519. Reprinted in part as "Mark Twain and the South: Pudd'nhead Wilson," in *Mark Twain: A Collection of Criticism*, ed. Dean Morgan Schmitter. New York: McGraw-Hill, 1974. Pp. 123–132.

"Hawthorne and Longfellow: Abortive Plans for Collaboration," *The*

Nathaniel Hawthorne Journal 1971. Washington, D.C.: NCR Microcard Editions, 1971. Pp. 3–11.

"Needs in Hawthorne Biography," *The Nathaniel Hawthorne Journal 1972.* Washington, D.C.: NCR Microcard Editions, 1973. Pp. 43–45.

"Park Benjamin on the Author and the Illustrator of 'The Gentle Boy,'" *The Nathaniel Hawthorne Journal 1974.* Englewood, Colorado: Microcard Editions Books, 1975. Pp. 85–91.

"George W. Cable's Use of the Past," *The Mississippi Quarterly*, XXX (Fall, 1977), 512–516.

"The Scholarly Journal: An Extension of the Graduate School," *Editors' News*, Spring, 1978, pp. 14–18.

DOCUMENTS

"Hawthorne at Martha's Vineyard," *The New England Quarterly*, XI (June, 1938), 394–400.

"A Novelist Discovers a Novelist: The Correspondence of H. H. Boyesen and George W. Cable," *The Western Humanities Review*, V (Autumn, 1951), 343–372.

"George W. Cable's Recollections of General Forrest," *Journal of Southern History*, XXI (May, 1955), 224–228.

"George W. Cable on Prison Reform," *Huntington Library Quarterly*, XXXVI (November, 1972), 69–75.

"Hawthorne's Final Illness and Death: Additional Reports," *ESQ*, XIX, No. 2 (Second Quarter, 1973), 124–127.

"Elizabeth Peabody Visits Lincoln, February, 1865," *The New England Quarterly*, XLVIII (March, 1975), 116–124.

"Elizabeth Peabody Reviews *Twice-Told Tales*," *The Nathaniel Hawthorne Journal 1974.* Englewood, Colorado: Microcard Editions Books, 1975. Pp. 75–84.

REFERENCE ARTICLES

"Cable, George W(ashington)," "Green, Julian," "Goodrich, Samuel Griswold," "Hale, Edward Everett," in *Collier's Encyclopedia*, 1958 and later editions.

"Cable, George W(ashington)," in *Encyclopedia Britannica*, 1961 edition; revised, 1967 and later editions.

"Local Color," "Charles Gayarré," "Grace Elizabeth King," in *A Bibliographical Guide to the Study of Southern Literature*, ed. Louis D. Rubin, Jr. Baton Rouge: Louisiana State University Press, 1969. Pp. 79–81, 202–203, 234–235.

"Joel Chandler Harris (1848–1908)," *American Literary Realism, 1870–1910*, I, No. 3 (Summer, 1968), 18–23.

"Interpreting Nineteenth-Century American Literature," *American Studies: An International Newsletter*, XI, No. 3 (Spring, 1973), 3–15. Reprinted in *American Studies: Topics and Sources*, ed. Robert H. Walker. Contributions in American Studies, No. 24. Westport, Conn.: Greenwood Press, 1976. Pp. 38–49.

REVIEW ESSAYS

"Fiction of the Bayou Country," *The Saturday Review of Literature*, XVIII, No. 1 (April 30, 1938), 3–4, 16.

"William Gilmore Simms in His Letters," *The South Atlantic Quarterly*, LIII (July, 1954), 404–415.

"Emily Dickinson Complete," *The South Atlantic Quarterly*, LV (October, 1956), 501–504.

"Review of North Carolina Fiction, 1962–63," *The North Carolina Historical Review*, XLI (Spring, 1964), 226–230.

"Nathaniel Hawthorne in Our Time," *The Southern Review*, n.s. I (Autumn, 1965), 961–967.

"Stephen Crane's Lifelong Experiment in Misery," *The Virginia Quarterly Review*, XLIV (Autumn, 1968), 678–682.

"Joel Chandler Harris in the Currents of Change," *The Southern Literary Journal*, I, No. 1 (Autumn, 1968), 105–111.

"Literary History and National Identity: The Example of Canada," *The Southern Review*, n.s. VI (Spring, 1970), 520–528.

"Two Ways to Approach Southern Literature," *The Southern Literary Journal*, VI, No. 1 (Fall, 1973), 111–116.

"William Faulkner: The Growth and Survival of a Legend—A Review Essay," *Southern Humanities Review*, IX (Winter, 1975), 91–97.

Reviews in *American Literature, The South Atlantic Quarterly, Journal of Southern History, Modern Language Quarterly, The Sewanee Review, Journal of American Folklore, Modern Philology, The Southwest Historical Quarterly, Southwest Review, Panhandle-Plains Historical Review, South Atlantic Bulletin, The Georgia Review, The Mississippi Quarterly, Nineteenth-Century Fiction, The North Carolina Historical Review, American Literary Realism, College English, Early American Literature, Clio, English Language Notes, South Central Modern Language Association Bulletin, The Nathaniel Hawthorne Journal, Resources for American Literary Study, The Southern Humanities Review, Journal of Popular Culture.*

Index